MAIL HANDLER

MAIL PROCESSOR

U.S. POSTAL SERVICE

ARCO

MAIL HANDLER

MAIL PROCESSOR
U.S. POSTAL SERVICE

E.P. Steinberg

PRENTICE HALL

New York   London   Toronto   Sydney   Tokyo   Singapore

Eleventh Edition

Prentice Hall General Reference
15 Columbus Circle
New York, NY 10023

An Arco Book

Arco, Prentice Hall, and colophons are
registered trademarks of Simon & Schuster, Inc.

Library of Congress Cataloging-in-Publication Data

Steinberg, Eve P.
  Mail handler : mail processor / Eve P. Steinberg—11th ed.
    p. cm.
  At head of title: Arco.
  "An Arco book"—T.p. verso
  ISBN 0-671-84642-6
  1. Postal service—United States—Examinations, questions, etc.
I. Arco Publishing. II. Title.
HE6499.S7497 1993
383'.145'076—dc20   92-12872
                                               CIP

Manufactured in the United States of America

1 2 3 4 5 6 7 8 9 10

CONTENTS

INTRODUCTION: WORKING FOR THE POST OFFICE

The United States Postal Service is an independent agency of the Federal Government. As such, employees of the Postal Service are federal employees who enjoy the very generous benefits offered by the government. These benefits include an automatic raise at least once a year, regular cost of living adjustments, liberal paid vacation and sick leave, life insurance, hospitalization, and the opportunity to join a credit union. At the same time, the operation of the Postal Service is businesslike and independent of politics. A postal worker's job is secure even though administrations may change. An examination system is used to fill vacancies. The examination system provides opportunities for those who are able and motivated to enter the Postal Service and to move within it.

The Postal Service handles billions of pieces of mail a year, including letters, magazines, and parcels. Close to a million workers are required to process and deliver this mail. The vast majority of Postal Service jobs are open to workers with 4 years of high school or less. The work is steady. Some of the jobs, such as mail carrier, offer a good deal of personal freedom. Other jobs, however, are more closely supervised and more routine.

NATURE AND LOCATION OF THE INDUSTRY

Most people are familiar with the duties of the mail carrier and the post office window clerk. Yet few are aware of the many different tasks required in processing mail and of the variety of occupations in the Postal Service.

At all hours of the day and night, a steady stream of letters, packages, magazines, and papers moves through the typical large post office. Mail carriers have collected some of the mail from neighborhood mailboxes; some has been trucked in from surrounding towns or from the airport. When a truck arrives at the post office, mail handlers unload the mail. Postal clerks then sort it according to destination. After being sorted, outgoing mail is loaded into trucks for delivery to the airport or nearby towns. Local mail is left for carriers to deliver the next morning.

To keep buildings and equipment clean and in good working order, the Postal Service employs a variety of service and maintenance workers, including janitors, laborers, truck mechanics, electricians, carpenters, and painters. Some workers specialize in repairing machines that process mail.

Postal inspectors audit the operations of post offices to see that they are run efficiently, that funds are spent properly, and that postal laws and regulations are observed. They also prevent and detect crimes such as theft, forgery, and fraud involving use of the mail.

Postmasters and supervisors are responsible for the day-to-day operation of the post office, for hiring and promoting employees, and for setting up work schedules.

The Postal Service also contracts with private businesses to transport mail. There are more than 12,500 of these "Star" route contracts. Most "Star" route carriers use trucks to haul mail, but in some remote areas horses or boats are used instead.

Almost 85 percent of all postal workers are in jobs directly related to processing and delivering mail. This group includes postal clerks, mail carriers, mail handlers, and truck drivers. Postmasters and supervisors make up nearly 10 percent of total employment, and maintenance workers about 4 percent. The remainder includes such workers as postal inspectors, guards, personnel workers, and secretaries.

The Postal Service operates more than 41,000 installations. Most are post offices, but some serve special purposes such as handling payroll records or supplying equipment.

Although every community receives mail service, employment is concentrated in large metropolitan areas. Post offices in cities such as New York, Chicago, and Los Angeles employ a great number of workers because they not only process huge amounts of mail for their own populations but also serve as mail processing points for the smaller communities that surround them. These large city post offices have sophisticated machines for sorting the mail. In these post offices, distribution clerks who have qualified as machine operators quickly scan addresses and send letters on their way automatically by pushing the proper button. These clerks must be able to read addresses quickly and accurately, must be able to memorize codes and sorting schemes and must demonstrate machine aptitude by their performance on the Number Series part of the exam.

TRAINING, OTHER QUALIFICATIONS, AND ADVANCEMENT

An applicant for a Postal Service job must pass an examination and meet minimum age requirements. Generally, the minimum age is 18 years, but a high school graduate may begin work at 16 years if the job is not hazardous and does not require use of a motor vehicle. Many Postal Service jobs do not require formal education or special training. Applicants for these jobs are hired on the basis of their examination scores.

Applicants should apply at the post office where they wish to work and take the entrance examination for the job they want. Examinations for most jobs include a written test. A physical examination is required as well. Applicants for jobs that require strength and stamina are sometimes given a special test. For example, mail handlers must be able to lift mail sacks weighing up to 70 pounds. The names of applicants who pass the examinations are placed on a list in the order of their scores. Separate eligibility lists are maintained for each post office. Five extra points are added to the score of an honorably discharged veteran and 10 extra points to the score of a veteran wounded in combat or disabled. Disabled veterans who have a compensable, service-connected disability of 10 percent or more are placed at the top of the eligibility list. When a job opens, the appointing officer chooses one of the top three applicants. Others are left on the list so that they can be considered for openings which may occur until the next time the exam is offered.

New employees are trained either on the job by supervisors and other experienced employees or in local training centers. Training ranges from a few days to several months, depending on the job. For example, mail handlers and mechanics' helpers can learn their jobs in a relatively short time. Postal inspectors, on the other hand, need months of training.

Advancement opportunities are available for most postal workers because there is a management commitment to provide career development. Also, employees can get preferred assignments, such as the day shift or a more desirable delivery route, as their seniority increases. When an opening occurs, employees may submit written requests, called "bids," for assignment to the vacancy. The bidder who meets the qualifications and has the most seniority gets the job.

In addition, postal workers can advance to better paying positions by learning new skills. Training programs are available for low-skilled workers who wish to become technicians or mechanics.

Applicants for supervisory jobs must pass an examination. Additional requirements for promotion may include training or education, a satisfactory work record, and appropriate personal characteristics such as leadership ability. If the leading candidates are equally qualified, length of service also is considered.

Although opportunities for promotion to supervisory positions in smaller post offices are limited, workers may apply for vacancies in a larger post office and thus increase their chances.

Since postal employment is so popular, entry is very competitive. In many areas the Mail Handler Exam is administered only once every three years. The resulting list is used to fill vacancies as they occur in the next three years. An individual who has been employed by the Postal Service for at least a year may ask to take the exam for any position and, if properly qualified, may fill a vacancy ahead of a person whose name is on the regular list. (The supervisor may or may not grant the request to take a special exam to fill a vacancy, but most supervisors readily grant such permission to employees with good performance records who have served an adequate period in their current positions.)

With increased automation, some of the best employment opportunities are for the title of Distribution Clerk, Machine (also called Letter Sorting Machine Operator). It would be wise to prepare yourself for this exam as well and to watch for the announcement when the exam opens in your area.

EMPLOYMENT OUTLOOK

Employment in the Postal Service is expected to grow more slowly than the average for all industries into the twenty-first century. Mechanization of mail processing and more efficient delivery should allow the Postal Service to handle increasing amounts of mail without corresponding increases in employment. Nevertheless, thousands of job openings will result as workers retire, die, or transfer to other fields.

EARNINGS AND WORKING CONDITIONS

Postal Service employees are paid under several separate pay schedules depending upon the duties of the job and the knowledge, experience, or skill required. For example, there are separate schedules for production workers such as clerks and mail handlers, for rural carriers, for postal managers, and for postal executives. In all pay schedules, except that of executives, employees receive periodic "step" increases up to a specified maximum if their job performance is satisfactory.

The conditions that follow are subject to collective bargaining and may well be different by the time you are employed by the Postal Service. At the time of your employment, you should make your own inquiry as to salary, hours, and other conditions as they apply to you.

Full-time employees work an 8-hour day, 5 days a week. Both full-time and part-time employees who work more than 8 hours a day or 40 hours a week receive overtime pay of one and one-half times their hourly rates. In addition, pay is higher for those on the night shift.

Postal employees earn 13 days of annual leave (vacation) during each of their first 3 years of service, including prior Federal civilian and military service; 20 days each year for 3 to 15 years of service; and 26 days after 15 years. In addition, they earn 13 days of paid sick leave a year regardless of length of service.

Other benefits include retirement and survivorship annuities, free group life insurance, and optional participation in health insurance programs supported in part by the Postal Service.

Most post office buildings are clean and well-lighted, but some of the older ones are not. The Postal Service is in the process of replacing and remodeling its outmoded buildings, and conditions are expected to improve.

The postal workers have a very effective union that bargains for them and gains increasingly better conditions. Most Mail Handlers are members of the American Postal Workers Union and are covered by a national agreement between the Postal Service and the union.

HOW TO USE THIS BOOK

This book is logically arranged for you to work through from beginning to end in order, though most certainly not all at once. Your preparation should begin many weeks in advance of your examination so that you do not feel rushed because your study is crowded into too short a time. You will learn more efficiently if you leave time between work sessions to allow new instructions to "sink in" and new skills to become part of your test-taking behavior.

Begin by choosing a well-lighted spot, a cleared-off desk or table, with as few surrounding distractions as possible. Turn off the radio or television. If practical, set aside a specific period of time each day for study and do your best to stick to your study schedule.

If you have not already read the introduction, read it now. Find out what it is that you are studying for. Get yourself "psyched" towards a postal career and all that it offers.

When you have finished the introduction and this chapter, read on to find out how to apply for the job. In the third chapter you will learn about what a mail handler does and what physical abilities are required. You will also have a chance to practice filling out all the application forms that you will need to file. Having these actual forms ahead of time allows you a chance to gather whatever information you may need without time pressure. The forms call for the dates and places you went to school; dates and places of previous employment along with description of duties, names of supervisors and beginning and ending salaries; and service history, as well as other information. You may have to do some searching before you can fill all the blanks. This chapter will also give you an overview of the exam you must take. The sample questions are the official sample questions released by the Postal Service before a recent exam.

The next chapter tells you how to take the Mail Handler Exam. You will find instructions on filling out the answer sheet and hints for when and how to guess.

When you finish the first four chapters, you will come to the "meat" of the book. Try the Preliminary Model Exam. Follow instructions exactly. Stick to the time limits. Do not peek at the answers while taking the exam. Score yourself accurately and look at all the explanations. By taking the Preliminary Model Exam before any real instruction, you will know just where you are starting. Fill in your scores on the Progress Charts at the end of the book. As you fill in your scores after each model exam, you will be able to follow your improvement. The model exams are not actual exams. The Postal Service does not release actual exams. However, the models are closely patterned on the real thing. They are accurate as to number of questions, style of questions, timing and difficulty.

After the Preliminary Model Exam come three chapters that will show you how to answer each type of question on the Mail Handler Exam. Allow many days for these three chapters. They can make the difference between passing and failing the exam.

The remainder of the book consists of five more full-length model exams. Do not attempt more than one a day. As with the Preliminary Model Exam, time yourself accurately, do not cheat, score your exam and study the explanations provided. Then calculate your scores and chart your progress.

The more you practice, the better your chances of success. By exam day you should be confident of your ability to take the Mail Handler Exam and score high.

The last chapter offers you a chance to try your hand at the Distribution Clerk, Machine, exam. Prepare yourself for this exam and compete for this high-paying job with the Postal Service.

APPLYING FOR A POSITION AS MAIL HANDLER OR MAIL PROCESSOR

The job title "Mail Processor" is one of the newest titles in the Postal Service. The person applying for a job as mail processor takes exactly the same exam as the applicant for mail handler. Since the mail handler job title is so much older and is so well known, the exam itself is known as the "Mail Handler Exam."

The Mail Handler Exam is not a regularly scheduled exam given on the same date all over the country. Rather, the Mail Handler Exam is separately scheduled in each postal geographic area as needed. An area may comprise a number of states or, in densely populated regions, may consist of only a portion of one county. The frequency of administration also varies, although generally the exam is offered every two or three years.

When the Mail Handler Exam is about to open in a postal area, the postal examiner for the area sends notices to all the post offices serviced by that area. The examiner also places ads in local newspapers and commercials with local radio stations. State employment offices receive and post copies of the announcement, and Civil Service newspapers carry the information as well. The announcement that you can pick up at your post office will look something like this:

THE OPPORTUNITY

Applications are now being accepted, and examinations will be given to establish a register of eligibles or to expand the current register of eligibles from which future mail handler vacancies in this Post Office will be filled. All interested persons who meet the requirements described in this announcement are urged to apply.

Qualification Requirements

No experience is required. All applicants will be required to take a written examination designed to test (1) Address Checking, (2) Following Oral Directions, and (3) Understanding of Meaning of Words. The test and completion of the forms will require approximately 2 hours. Competitors will be rated on a scale of 100. They must score at least 70 on the examination as a whole.

Duties

Mail Handler:
Loads, unloads, and moves bulk mail, and performs duties incidental to the movement and processing of mail. Duties may include separation of mail sacks, facing letter mail, canceling stamps on parcel post; operating canceling machines, addressograph, mimeograph; operating fork-lift truck; rewrapping parcels, etc.

Mail Processor:
Operates mail-processing equipment, including bar code sorters and optical bar code readers; acts as minor trouble-shooter for the equipment; collates and bundles processed mail and transfers it from one work area to another; hand-processes mail that cannot be handled by the machines; loads mail into bins and onto trucks; and performs other related tasks.

Physical Requirements

Applicants must be physically able to perform the duties described elsewhere in this announcement. Any physical condition which would cause the applicant to be a hazard to himself or to others will be disqualifying for appointment.

Persons with amputation of arm, leg or foot should not apply.

A physical examination will be required before appointment.

Strength and Stamina Test

Mail Handler:
When eligibles are within reach for appointment, they will be required to pass a test of strength and stamina. In this test they will be required to lift, shoulder, and carry two 70-pound sacks—one at a time—15 feet and load them on a hand truck. They will be required to push that truck to where there are some 40-, 50-, and 60-pound sacks. They will be required to load those sacks onto the truck. They will then have to unload the truck and return the truck to its original location. Eligibles will be notified when and where to report for the test of strength and stamina.

Persons with certain physical conditions will not be permitted to take the test of strength and stamina without prior approval of a physician. These physical conditions are (a) hernia or rupture, (b) back trouble, (c) heart trouble, (d) pregnancy, (e) or any other condition which makes it dangerous to the eligible to lift and carry 70-pound weights. Persons with these physical conditions will be given special instructions at the time they are notified to report for the strength and stamina test.

An eligible being considered for an appointment who fails to qualify on the strength and stamina test will not be tested again in the same group of hires. If he fails the test a second time, his eligibility for the position of mail handler will be cancelled.

Mail Processor:
Physical requirements for mail processors are not as stringent as those for mail handlers because the work is not as strenuous.

Age Requirement

The general age requirement is 18 years or 16 years for high school graduates, except for those for whom age limits are waived. In general, there is no maximum age limit.

Citizenship

All applicants must be citizens of or owe allegiance to the United States of America or have been granted permanent resident alien status in the United States.

Salary

Results from collective bargaining.

Consideration

Consideration to fill these positions will be made of the highest eligibles on the register who are available.

How to Apply

Submit application Form 2479-AB to the postmaster of this office or place designated by him.

Opening date for application _____

                                        Month   Day   Year

Closing Date For Application

_____

       Month   Day   Year

Written Examination

Applicants will be notified of date, time, and place of examination and will be sent sample questions.

Ask for an application card at your local post office. The card is bright-yellow. It is in two sections, joined at a perforation. Do NOT separate the two sections. The section on the left is called the Application Card, the one on the right the Admission Card. Instructions for filling out both sections are printed right on the back of the card. Follow these directions precisely, and carefully fill out both sections of the card. Hand in or mail the completed application as instructed.

The application and admission card looks like this: (We have had to separate the sections to fit the book page. You must not separate the sections.)

(Front)

APPLICATION CARD

Name *(Last, First, Middle Initials)*

Address *(House/Apt. No. & Street)*

City, State, ZIP Code

Birthdate *(Month, Date, Year)*

Do Not Write In This Space

Telephone Number | Today's Date

Title of Examination

Post Office Applied For

PS Form **2479-A**, April 1983

(Back)

Instructions to Applicants

Furnish all the information requested on these cards. The attached card will be returned to you with sample questions and necessary instructions, including the time and place of the written test.

TYPEWRITE OR PRINT IN INK. DO NOT SEPARATE THESE CARDS. FOLD ONLY AT PERFORATION.

Mail or Take This Form—Both Parts—to The Postmaster of the Post Office Where You Wish to Be Employed.

PS Form 2479-A, April 1983 *(Reverse)*

✿ U.S. G.P.O. 1983-655-793

(Front)

ADMISSION CARD

Title of Examination	Social Security No.	Do Not Write In This Space

Date of Birth	Today's Date	Post Office Applied For	

If you have performed active duty in the Armed Forces of the United States and were separated under honorable conditions indicate periods of service

From *(Mo., Day, Yr.)* _____ to *(Mo., Day, Yr.)* _____

DO YOU CLAIM VETERAN PREFERENCE?   NO   YES   IF YES, BASED ON
(1) Active duty in the Armed Forces of the U.S. during World War I or the period December 7, 1941, through July 1, 1955, (2) More than 180 consecutive days of active duty (other than for training) in the Armed Forces of the U.S. any part of which occurred between Jan. 31, 1955 and Oct. 14, 1976, or (3) Award of a campaign badge or service medal Your status as (1) a disabled veteran or a veteran who was awarded the purple heart for wounds or injuries received in action, (2) a veteran's widow who has not remarried, (3) the wife of an ex serviceman who has a service connected disability which disqualifies him for civil service appointment, or (4) the widowed, divorced or separated mother of an ex-service son or daughter who died in action or who is totally and permanently disabled

Print or Type Your Name and Address ⟶	Name *(First, Middle, Last)*
	Address *(House, Apt. No. & Street)*
	City, State, ZIP Code *(ZIP Code must be included!)*

This card will be returned to you. Bring it, along with personal identification bearing your picture or description, with you when you report for the test. ID's will be checked, and a fingerprint or signature specimen may be required.

PS Form **2479-B**, April 1983

(Back)

Final Eligibility in This Examination is Subject to Suitability Determination

The collection of information on this form is authorized by 39 U.S.C. 401.1001; completion of this form is voluntary. This information will be used to determine qualification, suitability, and availability of applicants for USPS employment, and may be disclosed to relevant Federal Agencies regarding eligibility and suitability for employment, law enforcement activities when there is an indication of a potential violation of law, in connection with private relief legislation (to Office of Management and Budget); to a congressional office at your request, to a labor organization as required by the NLRA, and where pertinent, in a legal proceeding to which the Postal Service is a party. If this information is not provided, you may not receive full consideration for a position.

Disclosure by you of your Social Security Number (SSN) is mandatory to obtain the services, benefits, or processes that you are seeking. Solicitation of the SSN by the United States Postal Service is authorized under provisions of Executive Order 9397, dated November 22, 1943. The information gathered through the use of the number will be used only as necessary in authorized personnel administration processes.

PS Form 2479-B, April 1983 *(Reverse)*

Applicant	Fingerprint
Make no marks on this side of the card unless so instructed by examiner.	
Signature of Applicant	

Political Recommendations Prohibited

The law (39 U.S. Code 1002) prohibits political and certain other recommendations for appointments, promotions, assignments, transfers, or designations of persons in the Postal Service. Statements relating solely to character and residence are permitted, but every other kind of statement or recommendation is prohibited unless it either is requested by the Postal Service and consists solely of an evaluation of the work performance, ability, aptitude, and general qualifications of an individual or is requested by a Government representative investigating the individual's loyalty, suitability, and character. Anyone who requests or solicits a prohibited statement or recommendation is subject to disqualification from the Postal Service and anyone in the Postal Service who accepts such a statement may be suspended or removed from office.

Have You Answered All Questions on the Reverse of This Form?

When the examination date, time and place have been set, your post office will return to you by mail the Admission Card portion of the application form 2479-B that you filled out (see above). In the area which says "Do Not Write In This Space," the post office will have filled in "Report to Room _____ , at *(address)* at *(time)* on *(date)*." In addition, you will receive a set of sample questions for your examination.

These are the Official Sample Questions sent to applicants for a recent administration of the Mail Handler Exam.

UNITED STATES POSTAL SERVICE

Sample Questions

The following samples show the types of questions you will see in the written tests. They also show how the questions are to be answered. Read the directions. Then answer the sample questions. Mark your answers on the Sample Answer Sheet. Then compare your answers with those given in the Correct Answers to Sample Questions.

In the *Address Checking* test, you will have to decide whether two addresses are alike or different. If the two addresses are exactly *Alike* in every way, darken space A for the question. If the two addresses are *Different* in any way, darken space D for the question. Questions 1 to 5 are samples of this test.

Mark your answers to these sample questions on the Sample Answer Sheet on the next page.

1. Acme La   Acme La
   Since the two addresses are exactly alike, mark A for questions 1 on the Sample Answer Sheet.
2. Orleans Mass   Orleans Mich
3. Saxe Va   Saxis Va
4. Chappaqua NY 10514   Chappaqua NY 10514
5. Los Angeles Calif 90013   Los Angeles Calif 90018

The *Meaning of Words* test asks you what a word or phrase means. In each question a word or phrase is in italics. Five other words or phrases—lettered A, B, C, D, and E—are given as possible meanings. Only one is *right*. You are to pick out the one that is right. Then on the answer sheet, find the answer space numbered the same as the question, and darken the space with the letter of the right answer. Questions 6 and 7 are samples of this test.

Mark your answers to questions 6 and 7 on the Sample Answer Sheet on this page.

6. The letter was *short*. *Short* means most nearly
   (A) tall
   (B) wide
   (C) brief
   (D) heavy
   (E) dark

For this question, you should darken space C because *brief* is the suggested answer that means most nearly the same as *short*, the word in italics.

7. A small crane was used to *raise* the heavy part. *Raise* means most nearly
   (A) lift
   (B) drag
   (C) drop
   (D) deliver
   (E) guide

<table>
<tr><td>
SAMPLE ANSWER SHEET

1. Ⓐ Ⓓ   5. Ⓐ Ⓓ
2. Ⓐ Ⓓ   6. Ⓐ Ⓑ Ⓒ Ⓓ Ⓔ
3. Ⓐ Ⓓ   7. Ⓐ Ⓑ Ⓒ Ⓓ Ⓔ
4. Ⓐ Ⓓ
</td><td>
CORRECT ANSWERS

1. ● Ⓓ   5. Ⓐ ●
2. Ⓐ ●   6. Ⓐ Ⓑ ● Ⓓ Ⓔ
3. Ⓐ ●   7. ● Ⓑ Ⓒ Ⓓ Ⓔ
4. ● Ⓓ
</td></tr>
</table>

In the test of *Following Oral Directions*, you will be told to follow directions by writing in a test booklet and then on an answer sheet. The test booklet will have lines of material like the following five samples:

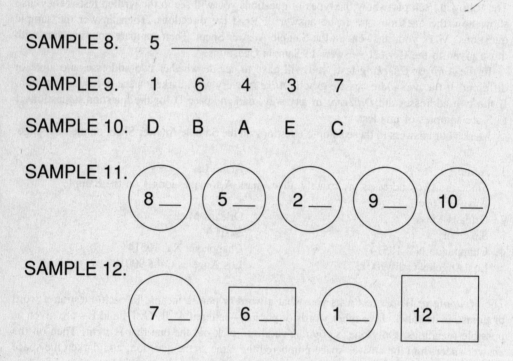

SAMPLE 8.   5 _____

SAMPLE 9.   1   6   4   3   7

SAMPLE 10.   D   B   A   E   C

SAMPLE 11.   8 __   5 __   2 __   9 __   10 __

SAMPLE 12.   7 __   6 __   1 __   12 __

To practice this test, tear out this page. Then have somebody read the instructions to you and you follow the instructions.

When he tells you to darken the space on the Sample Answer Sheet, use the one on this page.

SAMPLE ANSWER SHEET

1. Ⓐ Ⓑ Ⓒ Ⓓ Ⓔ   7. Ⓐ Ⓑ Ⓒ Ⓓ Ⓔ
2. Ⓐ Ⓑ Ⓒ Ⓓ Ⓔ   8. Ⓐ Ⓑ Ⓒ Ⓓ Ⓔ
3. Ⓐ Ⓑ Ⓒ Ⓓ Ⓔ   9. Ⓐ Ⓑ Ⓒ Ⓓ Ⓔ
4. Ⓐ Ⓑ Ⓒ Ⓓ Ⓔ   10. Ⓐ Ⓑ Ⓒ Ⓓ Ⓔ
5. Ⓐ Ⓑ Ⓒ Ⓓ Ⓔ   11. Ⓐ Ⓑ Ⓒ Ⓓ Ⓔ
6. Ⓐ Ⓑ Ⓒ Ⓓ Ⓔ   12. Ⓐ Ⓑ Ⓒ Ⓓ Ⓔ

Instructions to be read aloud by someone else (the words in parentheses should not be read aloud). *The person taking the test must NOT read these instructions.*

You are to follow the instructions that I shall read to you. I cannot repeat them.

Look at the samples. Sample 8 has a number and a line beside it. On the line write an A. (Pause 2 seconds.) Now on the Sample Answer Sheet, find number 5 (pause 2 seconds) and darken the space for the letter you just wrote on the line (Pause 2 seconds.)

Look at Sample 9. (Pause slightly.) Draw a line under the third number. (Pause 2 seconds.) Now look on the Sample Answer Sheet, find the number under which you just drew a line and darken space B as in baker for that number. (Pause 5 seconds.)

Look at the letters in Sample 10. (Pause slightly.) Draw a line under the third letter in the line. (Pause 2 seconds.) Now on your answer sheet, find number 9 (pause 2 seconds) and darken the space for the letter under which you drew a line. (Pause 5 seconds.)

Look at the five circles in Sample 11. (Pause slightly.) Each circle has a number and a line in it. Write D as in dog on the blank in the last circle. (Pause 2 seconds.) Now on the Sample Answer Sheet, darken the space for the number-letter combination that is in the circle you just wrote in (Pause 5 seconds.)

Look at Sample 12. (Pause slightly.) There are two circles and two boxes of different sizes with numbers in them. (Pause slightly.) If 4 is more than 2 and if 5 is less than 3, write A in the smaller circle. (Pause slightly.) Otherwise write C in the larger box. (Pause 2 seconds.) Now on the Sample Answer Sheet, darken the space for the number-letter combination in the box or circle in which you just wrote. (Pause 5 seconds.)

Now look at the Sample Answer Sheet. (Pause slightly.) You should have darkened spaces 4B, 5A, 9A, 10D, and 12C on the Sample Answer Sheet. (If the person preparing to take the examination made any mistakes, try to help him see why he made wrong marks.)

TEST-TAKING TECHNIQUES

Many factors enter into a test score. The most important factor should be true ability to answer the questions, which should provide a measure of ability to learn and perform the duties of the job. Assuming, however, that you have this ability, knowing what to expect on the exam and being familiar with the techniques of effective test-taking should go a long way toward reducing test-anxiety and raising test scores.

On examination day make sure the test itself is the main attraction of the day. Do not squeeze it in between other activities. Arrive rested, relaxed, and on time. In fact, plan to arrive a little bit early. Leave plenty of time for traffic tie-ups or other complications which might upset you and interfere with your test performance.

In the test room the examiner will hand out forms for you to fill out. He or she will give you the instructions that you must follow in taking the examination. The examiner will distribute the pencils to be used for marking the answer sheet and will tell you how to fill in the grids on the forms. Time limits and timing signals will be explained. If you do not understand any of the examiner's instructions, ASK QUESTIONS. There is no penalty for asking questions before the exam begins, so go ahead and satisfy yourself that you know what to do. It would be foolish to lose points because of poor communication.

During the testing session you will answer both sample questions and actual test questions. You will see the answers to the sample questions. You will not be given the answers to the actual test questions, even after the test is over.

At the examination, you must follow instructions exactly. Use only the Postal Service pencils which are issued to you. Fill in the grids on the forms carefully and accurately. Misgridding may lead to loss of veterans' credits to which you may be entitled or to errors in the addressing of your test results. Do not begin until you are told to begin. Stop as soon as the examiner tells you to stop. Do not turn pages until you are told to. Do not go back to parts you have already completed. Any infraction of the rules is considered cheating. If you cheat, your test paper will not be scored, and you will not be eligible for appointment.

Using the Answer Sheet

The answer sheet for your postal exam is machine scored. You cannot give any explanations to the machine, so you must fill out the answer sheet clearly and correctly.

1. Blacken your answer space firmly and completely. ● is the only correct way to mark the answer sheet. ◑, ⊗, ⊘, and ∅ are all unacceptable. The machine might not read them at all.
2. Mark only one answer for each question. If you mark one than one answer you will be considered wrong even if one of the answers is correct.
3. If you change your mind, you must erase your mark. Attempting to cross out an incorrect answer like this ✖ will not work. You must erase any incorrect answer completely. An incomplete erasure might be read as a second answer.
4. All of your answering should be in the form of blackened spaces. The machine cannot read English. Do not write any notes in the margins.
5. MOST IMPORTANT: Answer each question in the right place. Question 1 must be answered in space 1; question 52 in space 52. If you should skip an answer space and mark a series of answers in the wrong places, you must erase all those answers and do the questions over, marking your answers in the proper places. You cannot afford to use the limited time in this way. Therefore, as you answer *each* question, look at its number and check that you are marking your answer in the space with the same number.

6. You may be wondering whether or not it is wise to guess when you are not sure of an answer, or whether it is better to skip a question when you are not certain of the answer.

The wisdom of guessing depends on the scoring method for the particular examination part.

The Meaning of Words Test is scored "rights only." You are granted one point for each correct answer and no points for wrong answers or blank answer spaces. Therefore, it is worthwhile, on this type of test, to guess. Read the question and all of the answer choices carefully. Eliminate those answer choices which you know are wrong. Guess from among the remaining choices. Remember that only those questions you answer correctly will be counted, so do not leave any spaces blank. If it appears that you are about to run out of time before completing this part of the test, mark all the remaining blanks with the same letter. According to the law of averages, you should get some portion of the answers right.

If the scoring method is "rights minus wrongs," such as on the Address Checking Test, DO NOT GUESS. A wrong answer counts heavily against you. On this part of the test, work as quickly and as accurately as possible until time is called. Then stop and leave the remaining answer spaces blank.

The format of the Following Oral Directions Test does not lend itself to guessing even though only correct answers are counted in calculating your score.

HOW THE EXAM IS SCORED

When the exam is over, the examiner will collect test booklets and answer sheets. The answer sheets will be sent to the test center in Virginia where a machine will scan your answers and mark them right or wrong. Then your raw score will be calculated. Your raw score is the score you get according to the scoring formulae previously discussed: number right minus number wrong on Address Checking, total number of correct answers on Meaning of Words and Following Oral Directions.

As far as the Postal Service is concerned, your raw score is not your final score. The Postal Service takes the raw scores on all parts of your exam, combines them according to a formula of its own, and converts them to a scaled score, on a scale of 1 to 100. The entire process of conversion from raw to scaled score is confidential information. The score you receive is not your number right, is not your raw score, and is not a percent. The score you receive is a *scaled score*. Before reporting any scaled scores, the Postal Service adds any veterans' service points or any other advantages to which the applicant might be entitled. Veterans' service points are added only to passing scaled scores of 70 or more. A failing score cannot be brought to passing level by veterans' points. The score earned *plus* veterans' service points results in the final scaled score.

A total scaled score of 70 is a passing score. The names of all persons with scaled scores of 70 or more are placed on the list sent to the local post office. Those names are placed on the list in order, with the highest scorer at the top of the list. Hiring then takes place from the top of the list as vacancies occur.

The scoring process may take six or ten weeks or even longer. Be patient. If you pass the exam, you will receive notice of your scaled score. Applicants who fail the exam are not told their scores. They are simply notified that they will not be considered for the position.

TIPS FOR SCORING HIGH

Here is a summary of the most important suggestions for test takers.

1. *Read.* Read every word of the instructions. Read every word of every question. On the Meaning of Words Test, read all the answer choices before you mark your answer. It is

statistically true that most errors are made when the correct answer is the last choice. Too many people mark the first answer that seems correct without reading through all the choices to find out which answer is BEST.

2. Mark your answers by completely filling in the answer space of your choice.

3. Mark only *one* answer for each question, even if you think that more than one answer is correct. You must choose only one. If you mark more than one answer space, the scoring machine will count your answer as incorrect.

4. If you change your mind, erase completely.

5. If your exam permits use of scratch paper or the margins of the test booklet for figuring, don't forget to mark the answer on the answer sheet. Only the answer sheet is scored.

6. Check often to be sure that the question number matches the answer space and that you have not skipped a space by mistake.

7. Guess according to the rules we have given you for guessing.

8. Stay alert. Be careful not to mark a wrong answer just because you were not concentrating.

9. Do not panic. If you cannot finish any part before time is up, do not worry. If you are accurate, you will probably do well even without finishing. At any rate, do not let your performance on one part of the exam affect your performance on any other part.

10. Check and recheck, time permitting. If you finish any part before time is up, do not daydream. Check to be sure that each question is answered in the right space and that there is only one answer for each question. Return to the difficult questions and rethink them.

Good luck!

PRELIMINARY MODEL EXAM
ANSWER SHEET

ADDRESS CHECKING TEST

1. Ⓐ Ⓓ	17. Ⓐ Ⓓ	33. Ⓐ Ⓓ	49. Ⓐ Ⓓ	65. Ⓐ Ⓓ	81. Ⓐ Ⓓ
2. Ⓐ Ⓓ	18. Ⓐ Ⓓ	34. Ⓐ Ⓓ	50. Ⓐ Ⓓ	66. Ⓐ Ⓓ	82. Ⓐ Ⓓ
3. Ⓐ Ⓓ	19. Ⓐ Ⓓ	35. Ⓐ Ⓓ	51. Ⓐ Ⓓ	67. Ⓐ Ⓓ	83. Ⓐ Ⓓ
4. Ⓐ Ⓓ	20. Ⓐ Ⓓ	36. Ⓐ Ⓓ	52. Ⓐ Ⓓ	68. Ⓐ Ⓓ	84. Ⓐ Ⓓ
5. Ⓐ Ⓓ	21. Ⓐ Ⓓ	37. Ⓐ Ⓓ	53. Ⓐ Ⓓ	69. Ⓐ Ⓓ	85. Ⓐ Ⓓ
6. Ⓐ Ⓓ	22. Ⓐ Ⓓ	38. Ⓐ Ⓓ	54. Ⓐ Ⓓ	70. Ⓐ Ⓓ	86. Ⓐ Ⓓ
7. Ⓐ Ⓓ	23. Ⓐ Ⓓ	39. Ⓐ Ⓓ	55. Ⓐ Ⓓ	71. Ⓐ Ⓓ	87. Ⓐ Ⓓ
8. Ⓐ Ⓓ	24. Ⓐ Ⓓ	40. Ⓐ Ⓓ	56. Ⓐ Ⓓ	72. Ⓐ Ⓓ	88. Ⓐ Ⓓ
9. Ⓐ Ⓓ	25. Ⓐ Ⓓ	41. Ⓐ Ⓓ	57. Ⓐ Ⓓ	73. Ⓐ Ⓓ	89. Ⓐ Ⓓ
10. Ⓐ Ⓓ	26. Ⓐ Ⓓ	42. Ⓐ Ⓓ	58. Ⓐ Ⓓ	74. Ⓐ Ⓓ	90. Ⓐ Ⓓ
11. Ⓐ Ⓓ	27. Ⓐ Ⓓ	43. Ⓐ Ⓓ	59. Ⓐ Ⓓ	75. Ⓐ Ⓓ	91. Ⓐ Ⓓ
12. Ⓐ Ⓓ	28. Ⓐ Ⓓ	44. Ⓐ Ⓓ	60. Ⓐ Ⓓ	76. Ⓐ Ⓓ	92. Ⓐ Ⓓ
13. Ⓐ Ⓓ	29. Ⓐ Ⓓ	45. Ⓐ Ⓓ	61. Ⓐ Ⓓ	77. Ⓐ Ⓓ	93. Ⓐ Ⓓ
14. Ⓐ Ⓓ	30. Ⓐ Ⓓ	46. Ⓐ Ⓓ	62. Ⓐ Ⓓ	78. Ⓐ Ⓓ	94. Ⓐ Ⓓ
15. Ⓐ Ⓓ	31. Ⓐ Ⓓ	47. Ⓐ Ⓓ	63. Ⓐ Ⓓ	79. Ⓐ Ⓓ	95. Ⓐ Ⓓ
16. Ⓐ Ⓓ	32. Ⓐ Ⓓ	48. Ⓐ Ⓓ	64. Ⓐ Ⓓ	80. Ⓐ Ⓓ	

MEANING OF WORDS TEST

1. Ⓐ Ⓑ Ⓒ Ⓓ Ⓔ	8. Ⓐ Ⓑ Ⓒ Ⓓ Ⓔ	15. Ⓐ Ⓑ Ⓒ Ⓓ Ⓔ	22. Ⓐ Ⓑ Ⓒ Ⓓ Ⓔ	29. Ⓐ Ⓑ Ⓒ Ⓓ Ⓔ
2. Ⓐ Ⓑ Ⓒ Ⓓ Ⓔ	9. Ⓐ Ⓑ Ⓒ Ⓓ Ⓔ	16. Ⓐ Ⓑ Ⓒ Ⓓ Ⓔ	23. Ⓐ Ⓑ Ⓒ Ⓓ Ⓔ	30. Ⓐ Ⓑ Ⓒ Ⓓ Ⓔ
3. Ⓐ Ⓑ Ⓒ Ⓓ Ⓔ	10. Ⓐ Ⓑ Ⓒ Ⓓ Ⓔ	17. Ⓐ Ⓑ Ⓒ Ⓓ Ⓔ	24. Ⓐ Ⓑ Ⓒ Ⓓ Ⓔ	31. Ⓐ Ⓑ Ⓒ Ⓓ Ⓔ
4. Ⓐ Ⓑ Ⓒ Ⓓ Ⓔ	11. Ⓐ Ⓑ Ⓒ Ⓓ Ⓔ	18. Ⓐ Ⓑ Ⓒ Ⓓ Ⓔ	25. Ⓐ Ⓑ Ⓒ Ⓓ Ⓔ	32. Ⓐ Ⓑ Ⓒ Ⓓ Ⓔ
5. Ⓐ Ⓑ Ⓒ Ⓓ Ⓔ	12. Ⓐ Ⓑ Ⓒ Ⓓ Ⓔ	19. Ⓐ Ⓑ Ⓒ Ⓓ Ⓔ	26. Ⓐ Ⓑ Ⓒ Ⓓ Ⓔ	
6. Ⓐ Ⓑ Ⓒ Ⓓ Ⓔ	13. Ⓐ Ⓑ Ⓒ Ⓓ Ⓔ	20. Ⓐ Ⓑ Ⓒ Ⓓ Ⓔ	27. Ⓐ Ⓑ Ⓒ Ⓓ Ⓔ	
7. Ⓐ Ⓑ Ⓒ Ⓓ Ⓔ	14. Ⓐ Ⓑ Ⓒ Ⓓ Ⓔ	21. Ⓐ Ⓑ Ⓒ Ⓓ Ⓔ	28. Ⓐ Ⓑ Ⓒ Ⓓ Ⓔ	

FOLLOWING ORAL DIRECTIONS TEST

1. Ⓐ Ⓑ Ⓒ Ⓓ Ⓔ	19. Ⓐ Ⓑ Ⓒ Ⓓ Ⓔ	37. Ⓐ Ⓑ Ⓒ Ⓓ Ⓔ	55. Ⓐ Ⓑ Ⓒ Ⓓ Ⓔ	73. Ⓐ Ⓑ Ⓒ Ⓓ Ⓔ
2. Ⓐ Ⓑ Ⓒ Ⓓ Ⓔ	20. Ⓐ Ⓑ Ⓒ Ⓓ Ⓔ	38. Ⓐ Ⓑ Ⓒ Ⓓ Ⓔ	56. Ⓐ Ⓑ Ⓒ Ⓓ Ⓔ	74. Ⓐ Ⓑ Ⓒ Ⓓ Ⓔ
3. Ⓐ Ⓑ Ⓒ Ⓓ Ⓔ	21. Ⓐ Ⓑ Ⓒ Ⓓ Ⓔ	39. Ⓐ Ⓑ Ⓒ Ⓓ Ⓔ	57. Ⓐ Ⓑ Ⓒ Ⓓ Ⓔ	75. Ⓐ Ⓑ Ⓒ Ⓓ Ⓔ
4. Ⓐ Ⓑ Ⓒ Ⓓ Ⓔ	22. Ⓐ Ⓑ Ⓒ Ⓓ Ⓔ	40. Ⓐ Ⓑ Ⓒ Ⓓ Ⓔ	58. Ⓐ Ⓑ Ⓒ Ⓓ Ⓔ	76. Ⓐ Ⓑ Ⓒ Ⓓ Ⓔ
5. Ⓐ Ⓑ Ⓒ Ⓓ Ⓔ	23. Ⓐ Ⓑ Ⓒ Ⓓ Ⓔ	41. Ⓐ Ⓑ Ⓒ Ⓓ Ⓔ	59. Ⓐ Ⓑ Ⓒ Ⓓ Ⓔ	77. Ⓐ Ⓑ Ⓒ Ⓓ Ⓔ
6. Ⓐ Ⓑ Ⓒ Ⓓ Ⓔ	24. Ⓐ Ⓑ Ⓒ Ⓓ Ⓔ	42. Ⓐ Ⓑ Ⓒ Ⓓ Ⓔ	60. Ⓐ Ⓑ Ⓒ Ⓓ Ⓔ	78. Ⓐ Ⓑ Ⓒ Ⓓ Ⓔ
7. Ⓐ Ⓑ Ⓒ Ⓓ Ⓔ	25. Ⓐ Ⓑ Ⓒ Ⓓ Ⓔ	43. Ⓐ Ⓑ Ⓒ Ⓓ Ⓔ	61. Ⓐ Ⓑ Ⓒ Ⓓ Ⓔ	79. Ⓐ Ⓑ Ⓒ Ⓓ Ⓔ
8. Ⓐ Ⓑ Ⓒ Ⓓ Ⓔ	26. Ⓐ Ⓑ Ⓒ Ⓓ Ⓔ	44. Ⓐ Ⓑ Ⓒ Ⓓ Ⓔ	62. Ⓐ Ⓑ Ⓒ Ⓓ Ⓔ	80. Ⓐ Ⓑ Ⓒ Ⓓ Ⓔ
9. Ⓐ Ⓑ Ⓒ Ⓓ Ⓔ	27. Ⓐ Ⓑ Ⓒ Ⓓ Ⓔ	45. Ⓐ Ⓑ Ⓒ Ⓓ Ⓔ	63. Ⓐ Ⓑ Ⓒ Ⓓ Ⓔ	81. Ⓐ Ⓑ Ⓒ Ⓓ Ⓔ
10. Ⓐ Ⓑ Ⓒ Ⓓ Ⓔ	28. Ⓐ Ⓑ Ⓒ Ⓓ Ⓔ	46. Ⓐ Ⓑ Ⓒ Ⓓ Ⓔ	64. Ⓐ Ⓑ Ⓒ Ⓓ Ⓔ	82. Ⓐ Ⓑ Ⓒ Ⓓ Ⓔ
11. Ⓐ Ⓑ Ⓒ Ⓓ Ⓔ	29. Ⓐ Ⓑ Ⓒ Ⓓ Ⓔ	47. Ⓐ Ⓑ Ⓒ Ⓓ Ⓔ	65. Ⓐ Ⓑ Ⓒ Ⓓ Ⓔ	83. Ⓐ Ⓑ Ⓒ Ⓓ Ⓔ
12. Ⓐ Ⓑ Ⓒ Ⓓ Ⓔ	30. Ⓐ Ⓑ Ⓒ Ⓓ Ⓔ	48. Ⓐ Ⓑ Ⓒ Ⓓ Ⓔ	66. Ⓐ Ⓑ Ⓒ Ⓓ Ⓔ	84. Ⓐ Ⓑ Ⓒ Ⓓ Ⓔ
13. Ⓐ Ⓑ Ⓒ Ⓓ Ⓔ	31. Ⓐ Ⓑ Ⓒ Ⓓ Ⓔ	49. Ⓐ Ⓑ Ⓒ Ⓓ Ⓔ	67. Ⓐ Ⓑ Ⓒ Ⓓ Ⓔ	85. Ⓐ Ⓑ Ⓒ Ⓓ Ⓔ
14. Ⓐ Ⓑ Ⓒ Ⓓ Ⓔ	32. Ⓐ Ⓑ Ⓒ Ⓓ Ⓔ	50. Ⓐ Ⓑ Ⓒ Ⓓ Ⓔ	68. Ⓐ Ⓑ Ⓒ Ⓓ Ⓔ	86. Ⓐ Ⓑ Ⓒ Ⓓ Ⓔ
15. Ⓐ Ⓑ Ⓒ Ⓓ Ⓔ	33. Ⓐ Ⓑ Ⓒ Ⓓ Ⓔ	51. Ⓐ Ⓑ Ⓒ Ⓓ Ⓔ	69. Ⓐ Ⓑ Ⓒ Ⓓ Ⓔ	87. Ⓐ Ⓑ Ⓒ Ⓓ Ⓔ
16. Ⓐ Ⓑ Ⓒ Ⓓ Ⓔ	34. Ⓐ Ⓑ Ⓒ Ⓓ Ⓔ	52. Ⓐ Ⓑ Ⓒ Ⓓ Ⓔ	70. Ⓐ Ⓑ Ⓒ Ⓓ Ⓔ	88. Ⓐ Ⓑ Ⓒ Ⓓ Ⓔ
17. Ⓐ Ⓑ Ⓒ Ⓓ Ⓔ	35. Ⓐ Ⓑ Ⓒ Ⓓ Ⓔ	53. Ⓐ Ⓑ Ⓒ Ⓓ Ⓔ	71. Ⓐ Ⓑ Ⓒ Ⓓ Ⓔ	89. Ⓐ Ⓑ Ⓒ Ⓓ Ⓔ
18. Ⓐ Ⓑ Ⓒ Ⓓ Ⓔ	36. Ⓐ Ⓑ Ⓒ Ⓓ Ⓔ	54. Ⓐ Ⓑ Ⓒ Ⓓ Ⓔ	72. Ⓐ Ⓑ Ⓒ Ⓓ Ⓔ	90. Ⓐ Ⓑ Ⓒ Ⓓ Ⓔ

PRELIMINARY MODEL EXAM

SCORE SHEET

ADDRESS CHECKING TEST: Your score on the Address Checking Test is based upon the number of questions you answered correctly minus the number of questions you answered incorrectly. To determine your score, subtract the number of wrong answers from the number of correct answers.

Number Right   −   Number Wrong   =   Raw Score

_____   −   _____   =   _____

MEANING OF WORDS TEST: Your score on the Meaning of Words Test is based only upon the number of questions you answered correctly.

Number Right   =   Raw Score

_____   =   _____

FOLLOWING ORAL DIRECTIONS TEST: Your score on the Following Oral Directions Test is based only upon the number of questions you marked correctly on the answer sheet. The Worksheet is not scored, and wrong answers on the answer sheet do not count against you.

Number Right   =   Raw Score

_____   =   _____

TOTAL SCORE: To find your total raw score, add together the raw scores for each section of the exam.

Address Checking Score   _____
+
Meaning of Words Score   _____
+
Following Oral Directions Score   _____
=
Total Raw Score   _____

ADDRESS CHECKING TEST

DIRECTIONS AND SAMPLE QUESTIONS

In the Address Checking Test you will have to decide whether two addresses are alike or different. Any difference at all makes the two addresses different. Look carefully at the address at the left and the address at the right. If the two addresses are *exactly alike in every way*, darken space Ⓐ for the question. If the two addresses are *different in any way*, darken space Ⓓ for the question. Mark your answers to these sample questions on the sample answer sheet on this page.

1. New London CT 06320   New London CT 06230
2. Tulsa OK   Tulsa OK
3. Williamstown MA 01267   Williamstown ME 01267
4. Albany NY 12222   Albany NY 1222
5. Dayton OH 45469   Dayton OH 45469
5. Claremont CA   Clairmont CA

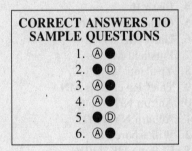

SAMPLE ANSWER SHEET	CORRECT ANSWERS TO SAMPLE QUESTIONS
1. Ⓐ Ⓓ	1. Ⓐ ●
2. Ⓐ Ⓓ	2. ● Ⓓ
3. Ⓐ Ⓓ	3. Ⓐ ●
4. Ⓐ Ⓓ	4. Ⓐ ●
5. Ⓐ Ⓓ	5. ● Ⓓ
6. Ⓐ Ⓓ	6. Ⓐ ●

Explanations

Question 1 is marked Ⓓ because two numbers are reversed in the zip code.
Question 3 is marked Ⓓ because the states are different.
Question 4 is marked Ⓓ because the second zip code is incomplete.
Question 6 is marked Ⓓ because the city is spelled differently.

ADDRESS CHECKING TEST

95 questions—6 minutes

DIRECTIONS: This is a test of your speed and accuracy in comparing addresses. For each question in the test, blacken the correspondingly numbered answer space as follows:

- Blacken Ⓐ if the two addresses are exactly ALIKE.
- Blacken Ⓓ if the two addresses are DIFFERENT in **any** way.

Correct answers are on page 43.

1.	Vallejo CA 94590	Vallejo CA 94590
2.	Lamar CO 80236	Lamar CO 82036
3.	East Point GA	West Point GA
4.	Elsah IL	Elsah IL
5.	Ottumwa IA 52501	Ottunwa IA 52501
6.	Unity ME 04988	Unity ME 04998
7.	Pittsfield MA	Pittsfield MA
8.	Ypsilanti MI 48197	Ypsilanti MI 48197
9.	Thief River Falls MN	Thief River Falls MN
10.	Antrim NH 03440	Antrim NM 03440
11.	Auburn NY 13021	Auburn NY 10321
12.	Wilkesboro NC	Willkesboro NC
13.	El Reno OK 73036	Reno OK 73036
14.	Beaver Falls PA	Beaver Falls PA
15.	Aberdeen SD 57401	Aberdeen SC 57401
16.	San Antonio TX 78203	San Antonio TX 78303
17.	Castleton VT	Castelton VT
18.	Midway WA 98031	Midway WA 98031
19.	Glenville WV 26351	Glenville WVa 26351
20.	Sheboygan WI	Sheboygan WI
21.	Cleveland WI 53015	Cleveland OH 53015
22.	Nashville TN 37203	Nashville, TN 37203
23.	Yankton SD 57078	Yankton SD 57078
24.	Bayamon PR	Bayamon PR
25.	Allentown PA	Allenstown PA
26.	Celina OH 45822	Celina OH 45822
27.	Roxboro NC 27573	Roxboro NC 25753
28.	South Fallsburg NY	South Fallsburgh NY
29.	Randolph NJ 07801	Randolph NJ 07801
30.	Cape Girardeau MO	Cape Girardeau MO
31.	Morris MN 56267	Morris MN 56267
32.	Roscommon MI 48653	Roscommon MI 48653
33.	Northampton MA 01063	Northhampton MA 01063
34.	McHenry MD	McHenry MD
35.	Houlton ME 04730	Houlton ME 04730
36.	Elizabethtown KY 42701	Elizabethtown KY 42701

37. Liberal KS 67901	Liberal KS 67801
38. Waverly IA 50677	Waverly LA 50677
39. Valparaiso IN	Valparaiso IN
40. Decatur IL 62522	Decatur IL 62522
41. Macon GA 31207	Macon GA 31207
42. Ocala FL 32670	Ocala FL 36270
43. West Haven CT	West Haven CT
44. Grand Junction CO	Grand Junction CO
45. Redlands CA 92373	Redwoods CA 92373
46. Fort Smith AK 72901	Fort Smith AR 72901
47. Douglas AZ 85607	Douglas AZ 85607
48. University AL 35486	University AL 35486
49. Dover DE 19901	Dover DE 19910
50. Lafayette LA 70504	Lafayette LA 70504
51. Jasper AL 35501	Jasper AK 35501
52. Anchorage AK 99504	Anchorage AK 99504
53. Ganado AZ 86505	Granado AZ 86505
54. Batesville AR	Batesville AR
55. Santa Maria CA	Santa Maria CA
56. Rangely CO 81648	Rangely ME 81648
57. Willimantic CT	Wilimantic CT
58. Washington DC 20052	Washington DC 20052
59. Key West FL 33040	Key West FL 33040
60. Cuthbert GA	Cathbert GA
61. Boise ID 83725	Boise ID 87325
62. Glen Ellyn IL 60137	Glen Ellyn IN 60137
63. Notre Dame IN	Notra Dame IN
64. Ankeny IA 50021	Ankeny IA 50021
65. Iola KS 66749	Iola KS 66749
66. Georgetown KY	Georgetown KY
67. Shreveport LA 71104	Shreveport LA 71004
68. Frostburg MD 21532	Frostburg MO 21532
69. Milton MA 02186	Milton MA 02186
70. Bloomfield Hills MI	Bloomfield Hills MI
71. Bemidji MN 56601	Bemidji MN 56601
72. Ellisville MS	Ellisville MS
73. Lexington MO 64067	Lexington MO 60467
74. Scottsbluff NB	Scottsbluff NB
75. Rutherford NU 07070	Rutherford NY 07070
76. Gallup NM 87301	Gallup NM 87301
77. Brooklyn NY 11204	Brooklyn NY 12104
78. Buies Creek NC	Buies Creek NC
79. Minot ND 58701	Minot ND 58701
80. Piqua OH 45356	Piqua OR 45356
81. Tonkawa OK	Tonkawa OK
82. Mount Angel OR 97362	Mount Angle OR 97362
83. Clarks Summit PA	Clarks Summit PA
84. Spartanburg SC	Spartansburg SC
85. Vermillion SD 57069	Vermillion SD 57069
86. Memphis TN 38152	Memphis TN 38852
87. Sherman TX 75090	Sherman TX 75090
88. Price UT 84602	Price UT 84602
89. Poultney VT	Poultney VT

90.	Bluefield VA 24605	Bluefield VA 24605
91.	Spokane WA 99204	Spokane WA 99204
92.	Bradley WV 24712	Bradley WV 24712
93.	Janesville WI	Janesville WI
94.	Torrington WY	Torrington WY
95.	Honolulu HI 96816	Honolulu HI 98616

END OF ADDRESS CHECKING TEST

Do not go on to the next page until the signal is given.

MEANING OF WORDS TEST

DIRECTIONS AND SAMPLE QUESTIONS

The Meaning of Words Test asks you what a word or phrase means. In each question, a word or phrase is in *italics*. Five other words or phrases—lettered A, B, C, D, and E—are given as possible meanings. Choose the lettered word or phrase that means most nearly the same as the word in italics and darken the space with the letter of the right answer. Mark your answers to these sample questions on the sample answer sheet below.

1. The knight rescued the *damsel* in distress. *Damsel* means most nearly
   - (A) small dog
   - (B) dragon
   - (C) young girl
   - (D) baby
   - (E) old woman

2. Instead of a jacket, the letter carrier wore a *cardigan*. *Cardigan* means most nearly
   - (A) storm coat
   - (B) sleeveless sweater
   - (C) turtleneck
   - (D) long-sleeved shirt
   - (E) buttoned sweater

3. The spectator gave a *graphic* description of the accident. *Graphic* means most nearly
   - (A) vivid
   - (B) unclear
   - (C) false
   - (D) repetitious
   - (E) sickening

4. Federal employees must *refrain* from political activity. *Refrain* means most nearly
   - (A) join in
   - (B) repeat
   - (C) sing
   - (D) abstain
   - (E) retire

SAMPLE ANSWER SHEET	CORRECT ANSWERS TO SAMPLE QUESTIONS
1. Ⓐ Ⓑ Ⓒ Ⓓ Ⓔ	1. Ⓐ Ⓑ ● Ⓓ Ⓔ
2. Ⓐ Ⓑ Ⓒ Ⓓ Ⓔ	2. Ⓐ Ⓑ Ⓒ Ⓓ ●
3. Ⓐ Ⓑ Ⓒ Ⓓ Ⓔ	3. ● Ⓑ Ⓒ Ⓓ Ⓔ
4. Ⓐ Ⓑ Ⓒ Ⓓ Ⓔ	4. Ⓐ Ⓑ Ⓒ ● Ⓔ

EXPLANATIONS

1. **(C)** A DAMSEL is a *young woman*, generally unmarried.
2. **(E)** A CARDIGAN is a collarless sweater that opens the full length of the center front and, ordinarily, is closed with buttons.
3. **(A)** GRAPHIC means *vivid* or *picturesque*. A graphic description may well be false or sickening, but what makes it graphic is its vividness.
4. **(D)** To REFRAIN from an act is to *keep oneself from doing it* or to *abstain*.

MEANING OF WORDS TEST

32 Questions—25 Minutes

DIRECTIONS: In each of the sentences below, one word is in *italics*. Following each sentence are five lettered words or phrases. You are to choose the word or phrase with the same meaning as the *italicized* word and mark its letter on the answer sheet. Correct answers are on page 45.

1. Improper office lighting may cause *fatigue*. *Fatigue* means most nearly
   (A) uniform
   (B) eyestrain
   (C) tiredness
   (D) overweight
   (E) mistakes

2. No matter what happens, you must never *abandon* the mail sacks. *Abandon* means most nearly
   (A) open up
   (B) store
   (C) lift
   (D) tie together
   (E) leave unattended

3. Please consult your office *manual* to learn the proper operation of our copying machine. *Manual* means most nearly
   (A) labor
   (B) handbook
   (C) typewriter
   (D) handle
   (E) cleaner

4. There is a specified punishment for each *infraction* of the rules. *Infraction* means most nearly
   (A) violation
   (B) use
   (C) interpretation
   (D) part
   (E) edition

5. After the accident, the vehicle was left *intact*. *Intact* means most nearly
   (A) a total loss
   (B) unattended
   (C) where it could be noticed
   (D) undamaged
   (E) for the tow truck

6. The negotiators reported that they had reached an *impasse*. *Impasse* means most nearly
   (A) agreement
   (B) compromise
   (C) signed contract
   (D) recess
   (E) deadlock ✓

7. He was surprised at the *temerity* of the new employee. *Temerity* means most nearly
   (A) shyness
   (B) enthusiasm
   (C) rashness ✓
   (D) self-control
   (E) lack of interest

8. The order was *rescinded* within the week. *Rescinded* means most nearly
   (A) revised
   (B) canceled ✓
   (C) misinterpreted
   (D) confirmed
   (E) implemented

9. The child's *candor* was most refreshing. *Candor* means most nearly
   (A) cleanliness
   (B) good looks
   (C) smile
   (D) clear voice
   (E) forthrightness ✓

10. He is an unpleasantly *vindictive* person. *Vindictive* means most nearly
    (A) prejudiced
    (B) unpopular
    (C) petty
    (D) revengeful ✓
    (E) cruel

11. If you have a question, please raise your hand to *summon* the test proctor. *Summon* means most nearly
    (A) ticket
    (B) fine
    (C) give
    (D) call
    (E) dismiss

12. The guitarist had *calluses* on his fingers. *Calluses* means most nearly
    (A) plastic picks
    (B) rubber tips
    (C) false fingernails
    (D) bleeding sores
    (E) thickened, tough skin ✓

13. The press secretary made an *innocuous* statement. *Innocuous* means most nearly
    (A) forceful
    (B) harmless
    (C) offensive
    (D) brief
    (E) important

14. *Stringent* requirements for advanced physics courses often result in small class sizes. *Stringent* means most nearly
    (A) lengthy
    (B) remarkable
    (C) rigid
    (D) vague
    (E) ridiculous

15. Once in a while you may find a *catchy* question on an exam. *Catchy* means most nearly
    (A) unfair
    (B) difficult
    (C) easy
    (D) impossible
    (E) tricky

16. A passing grade on the special exam may *exempt* the applicant from the experience requirements for that job. *Exempt* means most nearly
    (A) excuse
    (B) prohibit
    (C) subject
    (D) specify
    (E) recommend

17. The clergyman was considered to be *orthodox* in his practices. *Orthodox* means most nearly
    (A) pious
    (B) devout
    (C) godly
    (D) traditional
    (E) heretic

18. During the questioning of the witness, some unexpected information was *elicited*. *Elicited* means most nearly
    (A) eliminated
    (B) entertained
    (C) drawn out
    (D) deemed irrelevant
    (E) confirmed

19. We dared not prosecute the terrorist for fear of *reprisal*. *Reprisal* means most nearly
    (A) retaliation
    (B) advantage
    (C) warning
    (D) denial
    (E) losing

20. The increased use of dictation machines has severely *reduced* the need for office stenographers. *Reduced* means most nearly
    (A) enlarged
    (B) cut out
    (C) lessened
    (D) expanded
    (E) affected

21. At the end of the school year, the students took *divergent* paths. *Divergent* means most nearly
    (A) simultaneous
    (B) differing
    (C) approaching
    (D) parallel
    (E) worthwhile

22. Frequent use of marijuana may *impair* your judgment. *Impair* means most nearly
    (A) weaken
    (B) conceal
    (C) improve
    (D) expose
    (E) inflate

23. Students who are failing often need instruction in *judicious* use of their time. *Judicious* means most nearly
    (A) wise
    (B) biased
    (C) final
    (D) limited
    (E) organized

24. I *abhor* people who are prejudiced against minorities. *Abhor* means most nearly
    (A) tolerate
    (B) know many
    (C) try to change
    (D) avoid
    (E) hate

25. Rock salt has a *caustic* action on the front steps. *Caustic* means most nearly
    (A) melting
    (B) slippery
    (C) safety
    (D) corrosive
    (E) vital

26. It is altogether *fitting* that the parent discipline the child. *Fitting* means most nearly
    (A) illegal
    (B) bad practice
    (C) appropriate
    (D) required
    (E) unexpected

27. His seatmate's *inane* chatter induced the young man to leave the bus. *Inane* means most nearly
   (A) incessant
   (B) argumentative
   (C) prejudiced
   (D) obscene
   (E) foolish ✓

28. The decorative mirror had *bevelled* edges. *Bevelled* means most nearly
   (A) carved
   (B) painted
   (C) polished
   (D) antiqued
   (E) slanted

29. Compost is created by the *decay* of leaves and grass. *Decay* means most nearly
   (A) planting
   (B) burning
   (C) rotting
   (D) disposal
   (E) piling

30. One day, we *tramped* ten miles along the highway. *Tramped* means most nearly
   (A) begged
   (B) hitchhiked
   (C) bicycled
   (D) raced
   (E) hiked

31. He gave a *measly* $2.00 donation to the solicitor. *Measly* means most nearly
   (A) crumpled
   (B) contemptibly small ✓
   (C) grudging
   (D) ineffective
   (E) torn

32. The *proximity* of the famous rock star made the teenager shake with delight. *Proximity* means most nearly
   (A) nearness
   (B) hug
   (C) worldliness
   (D) adherence
   (E) warm smile

END OF MEANING OF WORDS TEST

If you finish your work on this test before time is up, check over your work on this test only. Do not go back to the Address Checking Test. Do not go on to the next page until you are told to do so.

FOLLOWING ORAL DIRECTIONS TEST

DIRECTIONS AND SAMPLE QUESTIONS

LISTENING TO INSTRUCTIONS: When you are ready to try these sample questions, give the following instructions to a friend and have the friend read them aloud to you at 80 words per minute. Do not read them to yourself. Your friend will need a watch with a second hand. Listen carefully and do exactly what your friend tells you to do with the worksheet and answer sheet. Your friend will tell you some things to do with each item on the worksheet. After each set of instructions, your friend will give you time to mark your answer by darkening a circle on the sample answer sheet. Since B and D sound very much alike, your friend will say "B as in baker" when he or she means B and "D as in dog" when he or she means D.

Before proceeding further, tear out the worksheet on page 35. Then hand this book to your friend.

TO THE PERSON WHO IS TO READ THE DIRECTIONS: The directions are to be read at the rate of 80 words per minute. Do not read aloud the material which is in parentheses. Do not repeat any directions.

READ ALOUD TO THE CANDIDATE

Look at line 1 on the worksheet. (Pause slightly.) Write a D as in dog in the fourth box. (Pause 2 seconds.) Now, on your answer sheet, find the number in that box and darken space D as in dog for that number. (Pause 5 seconds.)

Look at line 2. The number in each circle is the number of employees in a post office. In the circle holding the largest number of employees, write a B as in baker. (Pause 2 seconds.) Now, on your answer sheet, darken the space for the number-letter combination that is in the circle you just wrote in. (Pause 5 seconds.)

Look at line 3 on the worksheet. (Pause slightly.) Write the letter C on the blank next to the right-hand number. (Pause 2 seconds.) Now, on your answer sheet, find the number beside which you just wrote and darken space C. (Pause 5 seconds.)

Look at line 3 again. (Pause slightly.) Write the letter B as in baker on the blank next to the left-hand number. (Pause 2 seconds.) Now, on your answer sheet, find the number beside which you just wrote and darken space B as in baker. (Pause 5 seconds.)

Look at line 4 on your worksheet. (Pause slightly.) Draw a line under every "X" in the line. (Pause 5 seconds.) Count the number of lines that you have drawn, divide by 2, and write that number at the end of the line. (Pause 5 seconds.) Now, on your answer sheet, find that number and darken space C for that number. (Pause 5 seconds.)

SAMPLE WORKSHEET

DIRECTIONS: Listening carefully to each set of instructions, mark each item on this worksheet as directed. Then complete each question by marking the sample answer sheet below as directed. For each answer you will darken the answer for a number-letter combination. Should you fall behind and miss an instruction, don't become excited. Let that one go and listen for the next one. If, when you start to darken a space for a number, you find that you have already darkened another space for that number, either erase the first mark and darken the space for the new combination or let the first mark stay and do not darken a space for the new combination. Write with a pencil that has a clean eraser. When you finish, you should have no more than one space darkened for each number.

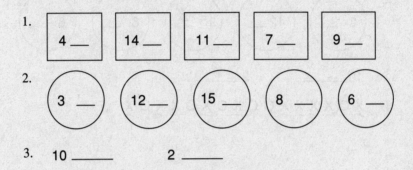

1.   4 __   14 __   11 __   7 __   9 __

2.   3 __   12 __   15 __   8 __   6 __

3.   10 _____   2 _____

4.   X O X X X X O O X O X O X X O X

SAMPLE ANSWER SHEET

1. Ⓐ Ⓑ Ⓒ Ⓓ Ⓔ	6. Ⓐ Ⓑ Ⓒ Ⓓ Ⓔ	11. Ⓐ Ⓑ Ⓒ Ⓓ Ⓔ
2. Ⓐ Ⓑ Ⓒ Ⓓ Ⓔ	7. Ⓐ Ⓑ Ⓒ Ⓓ Ⓔ	12. Ⓐ Ⓑ Ⓒ Ⓓ Ⓔ
3. Ⓐ Ⓑ Ⓒ Ⓓ Ⓔ	8. Ⓐ Ⓑ Ⓒ Ⓓ Ⓔ	13. Ⓐ Ⓑ Ⓒ Ⓓ Ⓔ
4. Ⓐ Ⓑ Ⓒ Ⓓ Ⓔ	9. Ⓐ Ⓑ Ⓒ Ⓓ Ⓔ	14. Ⓐ Ⓑ Ⓒ Ⓓ Ⓔ
5. Ⓐ Ⓑ Ⓒ Ⓓ Ⓔ	10. Ⓐ Ⓑ Ⓒ Ⓓ Ⓔ	15. Ⓐ Ⓑ Ⓒ Ⓓ Ⓔ

TEAR HERE

CORRECT ANSWERS TO SAMPLE QUESTIONS

1. Ⓐ Ⓑ Ⓒ Ⓓ Ⓔ   6. Ⓐ Ⓑ Ⓒ Ⓓ Ⓔ   11. Ⓐ Ⓑ Ⓒ Ⓓ Ⓔ
2. Ⓐ Ⓑ ● Ⓓ Ⓔ   7. Ⓐ Ⓑ Ⓒ ● Ⓔ   12. Ⓐ Ⓑ Ⓒ Ⓓ Ⓔ
3. Ⓐ Ⓑ Ⓒ Ⓓ Ⓔ   8. Ⓐ Ⓑ Ⓒ Ⓓ Ⓔ   13. Ⓐ Ⓑ Ⓒ Ⓓ Ⓔ
4. Ⓐ Ⓑ Ⓒ Ⓓ Ⓔ   9. Ⓐ Ⓑ Ⓒ Ⓓ Ⓔ   14. Ⓐ Ⓑ Ⓒ Ⓓ Ⓔ
5. Ⓐ Ⓑ ● Ⓓ Ⓔ   10. Ⓐ ● Ⓒ Ⓓ Ⓔ   15. Ⓐ ● Ⓒ Ⓓ Ⓔ

Correctly Filled Worksheet

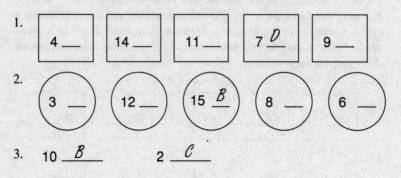

1. | 4 __ | 14 __ | 11 __ | 7 _D_ | 9 __ |

2. (3 __)   (12 __)   (15 _B_)   (8 __)   (6 __)

3. 10 _B_   2 _C_

4. X̲ O X̲ X̲ X̲ X̲ O O X̲ O X̲ O X̲ X̲ O X̲ *5*

FOLLOWING ORAL DIRECTIONS TEST

Total Time—25 Minutes

LISTENING TO DIRECTIONS

DIRECTIONS: When you are ready to try this test of the Model Exam, give the following instructions to a friend and have the friend read them aloud to you at 80 words per minute. Do NOT read them to yourself. Your friend will need a watch with a second hand. Listen carefully and do exactly what your friend tells you to do with the worksheet and with the answer sheet. Your friend will tell you some things to do with each item on the worksheet. After each set of instructions, your friend will give you time to mark your answer by darkening a circle on the answer sheet. Since B and D sound very much alike, your friend will say "B as in baker" when he or she means B and "D as in dog" when he or she means D.

Before proceeding further, tear out the worksheet on page 41. Then hand this book to your friend.

TO THE PERSON WHO IS TO READ THE DIRECTIONS: The directions are to be read at the rate of 80 words per minute. Do not read aloud the material which is in parentheses. Once you have begun the test itself, do not repeat any directions. The next three paragraphs consist of approximately 120 words. Read these three paragraphs aloud to the candidate in about one and one-half minutes. You may reread these paragraphs as often as necessary to establish an 80 words per minute reading speed.

READ ALOUD TO THE CANDIDATE

On the job you will have to listen to directions and then do what you have been told to do. In this test, I will read instructions to you. Try to understand them as I read them; I cannot repeat them. Once we begin, you may not ask any questions until the end of the test.

On the job you won't have to deal with pictures, numbers and letters like those in the test, but you will have to listen to instructions and follow them. We are using this test to see how well you can follow instructions.

You are to mark your test booklet according to the instructions that I'll read to you. After each set of instructions, I'll give you time to record your answers on the separate answer sheet.

The actual test begins now.

Look at line 1 on the worksheet. (Pause slightly.) Draw a line under the fourth number in the line. (Pause 2 seconds.) Now, on your answer sheet, find the number under which you just drew the line and darken space A for that number. (Pause 5 seconds.)

Look at the letters in line 2 on the worksheet. (Pause slightly.) Draw a line under the fifth letter in the line. Now on your answer sheet, find number 59 (pause 2 seconds) and darken the space for the letter under which you drew a line. (Pause 5 seconds.)

Look at the letters in line 2 on the worksheet again. (Pause slightly.) Now draw two lines under the third letter in the line. (Pause 2 seconds.) Now, on your answer sheet, find number 65 (pause 2 seconds) and darken the space for the letter under which you drew two lines. (Pause 5 seconds.)

Look at line 3 on the worksheet. (Pause slightly.) Write an E in the last box. (Pause 2 seconds.) Now, on your answer sheet, find the number in that box and darken space E for that number. (Pause 5 seconds.)

Now look at line 3 again. (Pause slightly.) Write an A in the first box. (Pause 2 seconds.) Now, on your answer sheet, find the number in that box and darken space A for that number. (Pause 5 seconds.)

Look at line 4. The number in each circle is the number of packages in a mail sack. In the circle for the sack holding the largest number of packages, write a B as in baker. (Pause 2 seconds.) Now, on your answer sheet, darken the space for the number-letter combination that is in the circle you just wrote in. (Pause 5 seconds.)

Look at line 4 again. In the circle for the sack holding the smallest number of packages, write an E. (Pause 2 seconds.) Now, on your answer sheet, darken the space for the number-letter combination that is in the circle you just wrote in. (Pause 5 seconds.)

Look at the drawings on line 5 on the worksheet. The four boxes are trucks for carrying mail. (Pause slightly.) The truck with the highest number is to be loaded first. Write B as in baker on the line beside the highest number. (Pause 2 seconds.) Now, on your answer sheet, darken the space for the number-letter combination that is in the box you just wrote in. (Pause 5 seconds.)

Look at line 6 on the worksheet. (Pause slightly.) Next to the middle number write the letter D as in dog. (Pause 2 seconds.) Now, on your answer sheet, find the space for the number beside which you wrote and darken space D as in dog. (Pause 5 seconds.)

Look at the five circles in line 7 on the worksheet. Write B as in baker on the blank in the second circle. (Pause 2 seconds.) Now, on your answer sheet, darken the space for the number-letter combination that is in the circle you just wrote in. (Pause 5 seconds.)

Now take the worksheet again and write C on the blank in the third circle on line 7. (Pause 2 seconds.) Now, on your answer sheet darken the space for the number-letter combination that is in the circle you just wrote in. (Pause 5 seconds.)

Now look at line 8 on the worksheet. (Pause slightly.) Write an A on the line next to the right-hand number. (Pause 2 seconds.) Now on your answer sheet, find the space for the number beside which you wrote and darken box A. (Pause 5 seconds.)

Look at line 9 on the worksheet. (Pause slightly.) Draw a line under every number that is more than 60 but less than 70. (Pause 12 seconds.) Now, on your answer sheet, for each number that you drew a line under, darken space C. (Pause 25 seconds.)

Look at line 10 on the worksheet. (Pause slightly.) Draw a line under every number that is more than 5 and less than 15. (Pause 10 seconds.) Now, on your answer sheet, for each number that you drew a line under, darken space D as in dog. (Pause 25 seconds.)

Look at line 11 on the worksheet. (Pause slightly.) In each circle there is a time when the mail must leave. In the circle for the latest time, write on the line the last two figures of the time. (Pause 5 seconds.) Now, on your answer sheet, darken the space for the number-letter combination that is in the circle you just wrote in. (Pause 5 seconds.)

Look at the five boxes in line 12 on your worksheet. (Pause slightly.) If 6 is less than 3, put an E in the fourth box. (Pause slightly.) If 6 is not less than 3, put a B as in baker in the first box. (Pause 10 seconds.) Now, on your answer sheet, darken the space for the number-letter combination that is in the box you just wrote in. (Pause 5 seconds.)

Now look at line 13 on the worksheet. (Pause slightly.) There are five circles. Each circle has a letter. (Pause slightly.) In the second circle, write the answer to this question: Which of the following numbers is smallest: 72, 51, 88, 71, 58? (Pause 10 seconds.) Now, on your answer sheet, darken the space for the number-letter combination that is in the circle you just wrote in. (Pause 5 seconds.) In the third circle on the same line, write 28. (Pause 2 seconds.) Now, on your answer sheet, darken the space for the number-letter combination that is in the circle you just wrote in. (Pause 5 seconds.) In the fourth circle do nothing. In the fifth circle write the answer to this question: How many months are there in a year? (Pause 5 seconds.) Now, on your answer sheet, darken the space for the number-letter combination that is in the circle you just wrote in. (Pause 5 seconds.)

Look at line 14 on your worksheet. (Pause slightly.) There are two circles and two boxes of different sizes with numbers in them. (Pause slightly.) If 2 is smaller than 4 and if 7 is less than 3, write A in the larger circle. (Pause slightly.) Otherwise write B as in baker in the smaller box. (Pause 10 seconds.) Now, on your answer sheet, darken the space for the number-letter combination in the box or circle in which you just wrote. (Pause 5 seconds.)

Look at the boxes and words in line 15 on the worksheet. (Pause slightly.) Write the second letter of the first word in the third box. (Pause 5 seconds.) Write the first letter of the second word in the first box. (Pause 5 seconds.) Write the first letter of the third word in the second box. (Pause 5 seconds.) Now, on your answer sheet, darken the spaces for the number-letter combinations that are in the three boxes you just wrote in. (Pause 15 seconds.)

Look at line 16 on the worksheet. (Pause slightly.) Draw a line under every "O" in the line. (Pause 5 seconds.) Count the number of lines that you have drawn, subtract 2, and write that number at the end of the line. (Pause 5 seconds.) Now, on your answer sheet, find that number and darken space D as in dog for that number. (Pause 5 seconds.)

Look at line 17 on the worksheet. (Pause slightly.) If the number in the left-hand circle is smaller than the number in the right-hand circle, add 2 to the number in the left-hand circle, and change the number in that circle to this number. (Pause 8 seconds.) Then write B as in baker next to the new number. (Pause slightly.) Next write E beside the number in the smaller box. (Pause 3 seconds.) Then, on your answer sheet, darken the spaces for the number-letter combinations that are in the box and circle you just wrote in. (Pause 5 seconds.)

Look at line 18 on the worksheet. (Pause slightly.) If in a year October comes before September, write A in the box with the smallest number. (Pause slightly.) If it does not, write C in the box with the largest number. (Pause 10 seconds.) Now, on your answer sheet, darken the space for the number-letter combination that is in the box you just wrote in. (Pause 5 seconds.)

FOLLOWING ORAL DIRECTIONS TEST

Total Time—25 Minutes

WORKSHEET

DIRECTIONS: Listening carefully to each set of instructions, mark each item on this worksheet as directed. Then complete each question by marking the answer sheet as directed. For each answer you will darken the answer for a number-letter combination. Should you fall behind and miss an instruction, don't get excited. Let that one go and listen for the next one. If, when you go to darken a box for a number, you find that you have already darkened another box for that number, either erase the first mark and darken the box for the new combination or let the first mark stay and do not darken a box for the new combination. Write with a pencil that has a clean eraser. When you finish, you should have no more than one box darkened for each number.

Correct answers are on page 47.

TEAR HERE

1. 13   23   2   19   6

2. E   B   D   E   C   A   B

3. | 30 __ | 18 __ | 5 __ | 14 __ | 7 __ |

4. 26 __   16 __   23 __   22 __   27 __

5. | 63 __ | 14 __ | 78 __ | 48 __ |

6. 12 ____   5 ____   22 ____

7. 14 __   1 __   36 __   7 __   19 __

8. 26 ____   89 ____

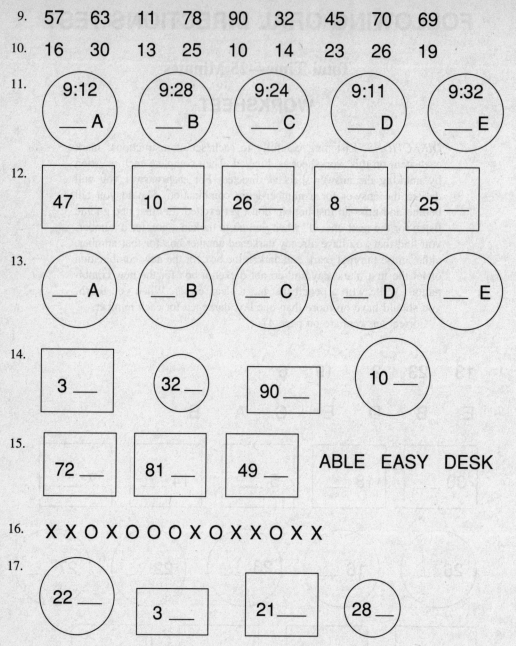

9.   57   63   11   78   90   32   45   70   69

10.   16   30   13   25   10   14   23   26   19

11.   9:12 ___A   9:28 ___B   9:24 ___C   9:11 ___D   9:32 ___E

12.   47 ___   10 ___   26 ___   8 ___   25 ___

13.   ___ A   ___ B   ___ C   ___ D   ___ E

14.   3 ___   32 ___   90 ___   10 ___

15.   72 ___   81 ___   49 ___   ABLE   EASY   DESK

16.   X X O X O O O X O X X O X X

17.   22 ___   3 ___   21 ___   28 ___

18.   21 ___   38 ___   29 ___   31 ___

END OF EXAMINATION

PRELIMINARY MODEL EXAM
ANSWER KEY

ADDRESS CHECKING TEST

1. A	17. D	33. D	49. D	65. A	81. A
2. D	18. A	34. A	50. A	66. A	82. D
3. D	19. D	35. A	51. D	67. D	83. A
4. A	20. A	36. A	52. A	68. D	84. D
5. D	21. D	37. D	53. D	69. A	85. A
6. D	22. A	38. D	54. A	70. A	86. D
7. A	23. A	39. A	55. A	71. A	87. A
8. A	24. A	40. A	56. D	72. A	88. A
9. A	25. D	41. A	57. D	73. D	89. A
10. D	26. A	42. D	58. A	74. A	90. A
11. D	27. D	43. A	59. A	75. D	91. A
12. D	28. D	44. A	60. D	76. A	92. A
13. D	29. A	45. D	61. D	77. D	93. A
14. A	30. A	46. D	62. D	78. D	94. A
15. D	31. D	47. A	63. D	79. A	95. D
16. D	32. A	48. A	64. A	80. D	

ADDRESS CHECKING TEST

Explanations of Differences

2. number reversal
3. city difference
5. spelling of city
6. number difference
10. different state
11. number reversal
12. spelling of city
13. city difference
15. different state
16. number difference
17. spelling of city
19. state difference
21. different state
25. city difference
27. number reversal
28. spelling of city
33. spelling of city
37. number difference
38. different state
42. number reversal
45. city difference
46. different state
49. number reversal
51. different state
53. city difference
56. different state
57. spelling of city
60. spelling of city
61. number reversal

62. different state
63. spelling of city
67. number difference
68. different state
73. number reversal
75. different state
77. number difference
80. different state
82. spelling of city
84. city difference
86. number difference
95. number reversal

Analysis of Differences

Fill in the column on the right with the total number of questions you answered incorrectly.

City difference	15	
Number difference	14	
State difference	12	
Total addresses with differences	41	
Total addresses with no differences	54	

MEANING OF WORDS TEST

1. C	7. C	12. E	17. D	22. A	27. E
2. E	8. B	13. B	18. C	23. A	28. E
3. B	9. E	14. C	19. A	24. E	29. C
4. A	10. D	15. E	20. C	25. D	30. E
5. D	11. D	16. A	21. B	26. C	31. B
6. E					32. A

MEANING OF WORDS TEST

Explanatory Answers

1. **(C)** While the everyday uniform of the army recruit is known as *fatigues,* choice A makes absolutely no sense in the context of the sentence. Choice D is ridiculous. B, C, and E all make sense, so you must know that FATIGUE is *tiredness* or *weariness* or else you must guess.

2. **(E)** To ABANDON is to *walk away from,* to *desert* or to *forsake.* You might also note the prefix *ab* meaning *away from.*

3. **(B)** Even if you do not recognize the root *manu* meaning *by hand* and relating directly to *handbook,* you should have no trouble getting this question right. If you substitute each of the choices in the sentence, you will readily see that only one makes sense.

4. **(A)** Within the context of the sentence, the thought of a specified punishment for use, interpretation, or an edition of the rules does not make too much sense. *Fraction* gives a hint of *part,* but you must also contend with the negative prefix *in.* Since it is reasonable to expect punishment for negative behavior with relation to the rules, *violation* which is the meaning of INFRACTION is the proper answer.

5. **(D)** Try etymology here. *In* means *not; tact* refers to *touch* (remember from science classes that the *tactile* sense is the *sense of touch*). *Not touched* is *undamaged.*

6. **(F)** An IMPASSE is a predicament offering no obvious escape, hence a *deadlock.* The etymology here is quite simple. The negative *im* appears before *pass.* If you can't pass, you are stuck.

7. **(C)** If you do not know the word *temerity,* you are likely to get this wrong. TEMERITY is not the same as *timidity;* in fact, they are opposites. *Enthusiasm* might be a reasonable synonym, but *rashness* or *boldness* are better.

8. **(B)** The prefix should help you narrow your choices. The prefix *re* meaning *back* or *again* narrows the choices to A or B. To RESCIND is to *take back* or to *cancel.*

9. **(E)** CANDOR means *honesty* or *forthrightness.* Since all the choices make sense in the sentence, and there are no etymological clues, this is one of the many cases in which a well-developed vocabulary will see you through.

10. **(D)** VINDICTIVE means *spiteful* or *seeking revenge.* Neither the context of the sentence nor the etymology, unless you know Latin, can help you here.

11. **(D)** First eliminate C and E since neither one makes sense in the sentence. Your experience with the word *summons* may be with relation to *tickets* and *fines,* but tickets and fines have nothing to do with asking questions while taking a test. Even if you are unfamiliar with the word SUMMON, you should be able to choose *call* as the best synonym in this context.

12. **(E)** CALLUSES are *hard, thickened areas on the skin.* Musicians who play string instruments are happy to develop calluses which ease the pain of constant contact with vibrating strings.

13. **(B)** The prefix *in,* meaning *not,* is your chief clue. INNOCUOUS means *inoffensive* or *harmless.*

14. **(C)** What kind of requirements would keep students out of advanced classes? *Tight, strict, rigid* or STRINGENT requirements weed out all but the most highly qualified.

15. **(E)** CATCHY means *tending to catch the interest or attention* or *tricky.*

16. **(A)** Read the sentence carefully. Obviously a passing grade on the exam will get the student out of meeting the experience requirements, hence *excuse* is the correct answer.

17. **(D)** One who is ORTHODOX *conforms to established doctrine* and is therefore *traditional.*

18. **(C)** To ELICIT means to *draw out.* Information was drawn out of the witness. Information could not be eliminated during questioning of a witness, though theories might be eliminated on the basis of the information.

19. **(A)** REPRISAL means injury done for injury received or *retaliation.*

20. **(C)** To REDUCE is to *make smaller* or to *lessen.*
21. **(B)** The prefix *di* means *away* or *apart.* With this knowledge, you should be able to choose *differing* as your answer even if you do not know the meaning of DIVERGENT. None of the other choices connotes pulling away or apart.
22. **(A)** To IMPAIR is to *make worse,* to *injure* or to *weaken.*
23. **(A)** The suffix *ious* means *having the quality of;* the stem *jud* means *right.* To *have the quality of right* means to *have sound judgment,* to be JUDICIOUS or to be *wise.*
24. **(E)** To ABHOR is to *loathe,* to *reject* or to *hate.*
25. **(D)** Rock salt does melt the ice but not the steps. CAUSTIC means *capable of destroying or eating away by chemical action* or *corrosive.*
26. **(C)** FITTING in this context means *suitable* or *appropriate.*
27. **(E)** INANE means *empty, insubstantial, silly* or *foolish.*
28. **(E)** A BEVEL is the angle that one surface or line makes with another when they are not at right angles, hence BEVELLED means *inclined* or *slanted.*
29. **(C)** While leaves and grass are piled up for purposes of creating compost, the actual formation of compost is the result of *decomposition, rotting* or DECAY.
30. **(E)** To TRAMP means to *travel on foot,* to *trudge* or to *hike.*
31. **(B)** Choices B, C, and D all seem quite reasonable. If you did not know the meaning of MEASLY you might not have guessed that it means *contemptibly small.*
32. **(A)** Even without knowing Latin or etymology, you should see the similarity to the word *approximate* and choose *nearness* as the meaning of PROXIMITY.

FOLLOWING ORAL DIRECTIONS TEST

Correctly Filled Worksheet

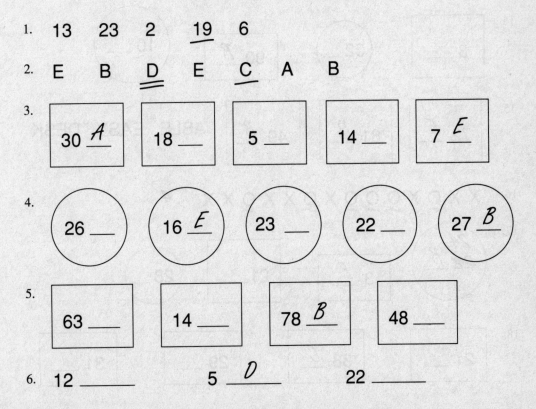

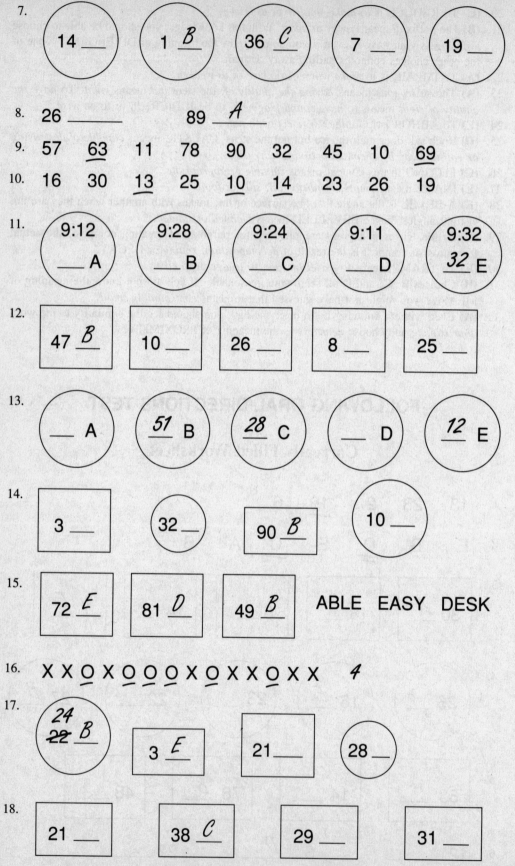

7. 14 ___   1 _B_   36 _C_   7 ___   19 ___

8. 26 _____   89 _A_

9. 57 _63_ 11 78 90 32 45 10 _69_

10. 16 30 _13_ 25 _10_ _14_ 23 26 19

11. 9:12 ___ A   9:28 ___ B   9:24 ___ C   9:11 ___ D   9:32 _32_ E

12. 47 _B_   10 ___   26 ___   8 ___   25 ___

13. ___ A   _51_ B   _28_ C   ___ D   _12_ E

14. 3 ___   32 ___   90 _B_   10 ___

15. 72 _E_   81 _D_   49 _B_   ABLE EASY DESK

16. X X O X O O O X O X X O X X   _4_

17. 24 22 _B_   3 _E_   21 ___   28 ___

18. 21 ___   38 _C_   29 ___   31 ___

FOLLOWING ORAL DIRECTIONS TEST

Correctly Filled Answer Grid

1. Ⓐ ● Ⓒ Ⓓ Ⓔ	24. Ⓐ ● Ⓒ Ⓓ Ⓔ	47. Ⓐ ● Ⓒ Ⓓ Ⓔ	70. Ⓐ Ⓑ Ⓒ Ⓓ Ⓔ
2. Ⓐ Ⓑ Ⓒ Ⓓ Ⓔ	25. Ⓐ Ⓑ Ⓒ Ⓓ Ⓔ	48. Ⓐ Ⓑ Ⓒ Ⓓ Ⓔ	71. Ⓐ Ⓑ Ⓒ Ⓓ Ⓔ
3. Ⓐ Ⓑ Ⓒ Ⓓ ●	26. Ⓐ Ⓑ Ⓒ Ⓓ Ⓔ	49. Ⓐ ● Ⓒ Ⓓ Ⓔ	72. Ⓐ Ⓑ Ⓒ Ⓓ ●
4. Ⓐ Ⓑ Ⓒ ● Ⓔ	27. Ⓐ ● Ⓒ Ⓓ Ⓔ	50. Ⓐ Ⓑ Ⓒ Ⓓ Ⓔ	73. Ⓐ Ⓑ Ⓒ Ⓓ Ⓔ
5. Ⓐ Ⓑ Ⓒ ● Ⓔ	28. Ⓐ Ⓑ ● Ⓓ Ⓔ	51. Ⓐ ● Ⓒ Ⓓ Ⓔ	74. Ⓐ Ⓑ Ⓒ Ⓓ Ⓔ
6. Ⓐ Ⓑ Ⓒ Ⓓ Ⓔ	29. Ⓐ Ⓑ Ⓒ Ⓓ Ⓔ	52. Ⓐ Ⓑ Ⓒ Ⓓ Ⓔ	75. Ⓐ Ⓑ Ⓒ Ⓓ Ⓔ
7. Ⓐ Ⓑ Ⓒ Ⓓ ●	30. ● Ⓑ Ⓒ Ⓓ Ⓔ	53. Ⓐ Ⓑ Ⓒ Ⓓ Ⓔ	76. Ⓐ Ⓑ Ⓒ Ⓓ Ⓔ
8. Ⓐ Ⓑ Ⓒ Ⓓ Ⓔ	31. Ⓐ Ⓑ Ⓒ Ⓓ Ⓔ	54. Ⓐ Ⓑ Ⓒ Ⓓ Ⓔ	77. Ⓐ Ⓑ Ⓒ Ⓓ Ⓔ
9. Ⓐ Ⓑ Ⓒ Ⓓ Ⓔ	32. Ⓐ Ⓑ Ⓒ Ⓓ ●	55. Ⓐ Ⓑ Ⓒ Ⓓ Ⓔ	78. Ⓐ ● Ⓒ Ⓓ Ⓔ
10. Ⓐ Ⓑ Ⓒ ● Ⓔ	33. Ⓐ Ⓑ Ⓒ Ⓓ Ⓔ	56. Ⓐ Ⓑ Ⓒ Ⓓ Ⓔ	79. Ⓐ Ⓑ Ⓒ Ⓓ Ⓔ
11. Ⓐ Ⓑ Ⓒ Ⓓ Ⓔ	34. Ⓐ Ⓑ Ⓒ Ⓓ Ⓔ	57. Ⓐ Ⓑ Ⓒ Ⓓ Ⓔ	80. Ⓐ Ⓑ Ⓒ Ⓓ Ⓔ
12. Ⓐ Ⓑ Ⓒ Ⓓ ●	35. Ⓐ Ⓑ Ⓒ Ⓓ Ⓔ	58. Ⓐ Ⓑ Ⓒ Ⓓ Ⓔ	81. Ⓐ Ⓑ Ⓒ ● Ⓔ
13. Ⓐ Ⓑ Ⓒ ● Ⓔ	36. Ⓐ Ⓑ ● Ⓓ Ⓔ	59. Ⓐ Ⓑ ● Ⓓ Ⓔ	82. Ⓐ Ⓑ Ⓒ Ⓓ Ⓔ
14. Ⓐ Ⓑ Ⓒ ● Ⓔ	37. Ⓐ Ⓑ Ⓒ Ⓓ Ⓔ	60. Ⓐ Ⓑ Ⓒ Ⓓ Ⓔ	83. Ⓐ Ⓑ Ⓒ Ⓓ Ⓔ
15. Ⓐ Ⓑ Ⓒ Ⓓ Ⓔ	38. Ⓐ Ⓑ ● Ⓓ Ⓔ	61. Ⓐ Ⓑ Ⓒ Ⓓ Ⓔ	84. Ⓐ Ⓑ Ⓒ Ⓓ Ⓔ
16. Ⓐ Ⓑ Ⓒ Ⓓ ●	39. Ⓐ Ⓑ Ⓒ Ⓓ Ⓔ	62. Ⓐ Ⓑ Ⓒ Ⓓ Ⓔ	85. Ⓐ Ⓑ Ⓒ Ⓓ Ⓔ
17. Ⓐ Ⓑ Ⓒ Ⓓ Ⓔ	40. Ⓐ Ⓑ Ⓒ Ⓓ Ⓔ	63. Ⓐ Ⓑ ● Ⓓ Ⓔ	86. Ⓐ Ⓑ Ⓒ Ⓓ Ⓔ
18. Ⓐ Ⓑ Ⓒ Ⓓ Ⓔ	41. Ⓐ Ⓑ Ⓒ Ⓓ Ⓔ	64. Ⓐ Ⓑ Ⓒ Ⓓ Ⓔ	87. Ⓐ Ⓑ Ⓒ Ⓓ Ⓔ
19. ● Ⓑ Ⓒ Ⓓ Ⓔ	42. Ⓐ Ⓑ Ⓒ Ⓓ Ⓔ	65. Ⓐ Ⓑ Ⓒ ● Ⓔ	88. Ⓐ Ⓑ Ⓒ Ⓓ Ⓔ
20. Ⓐ Ⓑ Ⓒ Ⓓ Ⓔ	43. Ⓐ Ⓑ Ⓒ Ⓓ Ⓔ	66. Ⓐ Ⓑ Ⓒ Ⓓ Ⓔ	89. ● Ⓑ Ⓒ Ⓓ Ⓔ
21. Ⓐ Ⓑ Ⓒ Ⓓ Ⓔ	44. Ⓐ Ⓑ Ⓒ Ⓓ Ⓔ	67. Ⓐ Ⓑ Ⓒ Ⓓ Ⓔ	90. Ⓐ ● Ⓒ Ⓓ Ⓔ
22. Ⓐ Ⓑ Ⓒ Ⓓ Ⓔ	45. Ⓐ Ⓑ Ⓒ Ⓓ Ⓔ	68. Ⓐ Ⓑ Ⓒ Ⓓ Ⓔ	
23. Ⓐ Ⓑ Ⓒ Ⓓ Ⓔ	46. Ⓐ Ⓑ Ⓒ Ⓓ Ⓔ	69. Ⓐ Ⓑ ● Ⓓ Ⓔ	

HOW TO ANSWER ADDRESS CHECKING QUESTIONS

The Address Checking Test is not difficult, but it requires great speed and it carries a heavy penalty for inaccuracy. You must learn to spot differences very quickly and to make firm, fast decisions about addresses that are exactly alike. This chapter will help you to develop a system for comparing addresses. Once you have a system, practice with that system will help you to build up speed.

The directions make it very clear that if there is *any difference at all* between the two addresses they are to be marked as different. This means that once you spot a difference, mark the answer as Ⓓ and go immediately to the next question. There is no point in looking at the remainder of an address once you have found a difference. You will be amazed at how much time you can save by not reading the whole of every address.

READ EXACTLY WHAT YOU SEE

The best way to read addresses being compared is to read exactly what you see and to sound out words by syllables. For example:

- If you see "St," read "es tee" not "street."
- If you see "NH," read "en aitch" not "New Hampshire."
- If you see "1035," read "one oh three five" not "one thousand thirty-five."
- Read "sassafrass" as "sas-sa-frass."

Psychologists have discovered that the human mind always tries to complete a figure. If you read "Pky" as "Parkway," you will probably read "Pkwy" as "Parkway," and will never notice the difference. Your mind will complete the word without allowing you to focus on the letters. If, however, you read the abbreviation as an abbreviation, you will notice that the two abbreviations are different. If you read "Kansas City MO" as "Kansas City Missouri," you are unlikely to catch the difference with "Kansas City MD." But if you read "Kansas City em oh," you will readily pick up on "Kansas City em dee."

USE YOUR HANDS

Since speed is so important in answering Address Checking questions and since it is so easy to lose your place, you must use both hands during your work on this part. In the hand with which you write, hold your pencil poised at the number on your answer sheet. Run the index finger of your other hand under the addresses being compared. The finger will help you to focus on one line at a time, will help keep your eyes from jumping up or down a line. By holding your place on both question and answer sheet, you are less likely to skip a question or an answer space.

One effective way to tackle address checking questions quickly and accurately is to look for differences in only one area at a time. Most addresses consist of both numbers and words.

If you narrow your focus to compare only the numbers or only the words, you are more likely to notice differences and less apt to see what you expect to see rather than what is actually printed on the page.

LOOK FOR DIFFERENCES IN NUMBERS

Look first at the numbers. Read the number in the left column, then skip immediately to the number in the right column. Do the two numbers contain the same number of digits?

A difference of this type should be easy to see. In the questions that follow, blacken Ⓐ if the two numbers are exactly alike and Ⓓ if the numbers are different in any way.

Is the Number of Digits the Same?

1. 2003	2003	1. Ⓐ Ⓓ
2. 75864	75864	2. Ⓐ Ⓓ
3. 7300	730	3. Ⓐ Ⓓ
4. 50106	5016	4. Ⓐ Ⓓ
5. 2184	2184	5. Ⓐ Ⓓ

Answers: 1. A 2. A 3. D 4. D 5. A

Did you spot the differences? Train your eye to count digits rapidly.

Is the Order of Digits the Same?

1. 7516	7561	1. Ⓐ Ⓓ
2. 80302	80302	2. Ⓐ Ⓓ
3. 19832	18932	3. Ⓐ Ⓓ
4. 6186	6186	4. Ⓐ Ⓓ
5. 54601	54610	5. Ⓐ Ⓓ

Answers: 1. D 2. A 3. D 4. A 5. D

Did you get these all correct? If not, look again right now. See where you made your mistakes.

Is There a Substitution of One Digit for Another?

1. 16830	16830	1. Ⓐ Ⓓ
2. 94936	94636	2. Ⓐ Ⓓ
3. 3287	3285	3. Ⓐ Ⓓ
4. 54216	54216	4. Ⓐ Ⓓ
5. 32341	33341	5. Ⓐ Ⓓ

Answers: 1. A 2. D 3. D 4. A 5. D

Did you catch all the differences? Were you able to mark Ⓐ with confidence when there was no difference?

Practice Finding Differences in Numbers

In the following set of practice questions, all differences are in the numbers. Work quickly, focusing only on the numbers. You may find any of the three varieties of differences just described.

1. Ware MA 08215	Ware MA 08215	1. Ⓐ Ⓓ
2. Scarsdale NY 10583	Scarsdale NY 10583	2. Ⓐ Ⓓ
3. Milwaukee Wisc 53202	Milwaukee Wisc 52302	3. Ⓐ Ⓓ
4. Portland OR 97208	Portland OR 99208	4. Ⓐ Ⓓ
5. Omaha NB 68127	Omaha NB 6827	5. Ⓐ Ⓓ
6. San Francisco CA 94108	San Francisco CA 94108	6. Ⓐ Ⓓ
7. Dallas TX 75234	Dallas TX 75324	7. Ⓐ Ⓓ
8. Westport Conn 06880	Westport Conn 06680	8. Ⓐ Ⓓ
9. Newark DE 19711	Newark DE 19771	9. Ⓐ Ⓓ
10. Granville OH 43023	Granville OH 43023	10. Ⓐ Ⓓ
11. Denver CO 80208	Denver CO 802008	11. Ⓐ Ⓓ
12. Greencastle IN 46135	Greencastle IN 46135	12. Ⓐ Ⓓ
13. Detroit Mich 48221	Detroit Mich 48321	13. Ⓐ Ⓓ
14. Carlisle PA 17013	Carlisle PA 17103	14. Ⓐ Ⓓ
15. Madison NJ 07940	Madison NJ 09740	15. Ⓐ Ⓓ
16. Durham NC 27706	Durham NC 27706	16. Ⓐ Ⓓ
17. Richmond Ind 47374	Richmond Ind 47374	17. Ⓐ Ⓓ
18. Pittsburgh Penna 15219	Pittsburgh Penna 15219	18. Ⓐ Ⓓ
19. Atlanta GA 30322	Atlanta GA 30323	19. Ⓐ Ⓓ
20. Hanover NH 03755	Hanover NH 03577	20. Ⓐ Ⓓ
21. Tallahassee FL 32306	Tallahassee FL 32360	21. Ⓐ Ⓓ
22. Bronx NY 10458	Bronx NY 1458	22. Ⓐ Ⓓ
23. Ithaca NY 14853	Ithaca NY 14583	23. Ⓐ Ⓓ
24. Davidson NC 28036	Davidson NC 28036	24. Ⓐ Ⓓ
25. New London CT 06320	New London CT 06320	25. Ⓐ Ⓓ

Answers

1. A	6. A	11. D	16. A	21. D
2. A	7. D	12. A	17. A	22. D
3. D	8. D	13. D	18. A	23. D
4. D	9. D	14. D	19. D	24. A
5. D	10. A	15. D	20. D	25. A

Were you able to focus on the numbers? Were you able to spot the differences quickly? Could you make a rapid decision when there was no difference? If you got any of these questions wrong, look now to see why.

If you find a difference between the two numbers, mark Ⓓ and go on to the next question. Do not bother to look at the words in any pair of addresses in which you find a difference between the numbers.

If, while concentrating on numbers, you happen to catch a difference in spelling or abbreviations, by all means mark Ⓓ and go on to the next question. In other words, if you spot *any* difference, mark Ⓓ at once. A system may be useful, but do not stick to it slavishly when an answer is obvious.

LOOK FOR DIFFERENCES IN ABBREVIATIONS

When you are satisfied that the numbers are alike, and if no other difference has "struck you between the eyes," turn your attention to the abbreviations. Keep alert for differences such as:

NH	NM
Mass	Miss
CO	CA

Try these practice questions, sounding out or spelling the abbreviations exactly as you see them.

1.	New Orleans LA 70153	New Orleans LA 70153	1. Ⓐ Ⓓ
2.	Boiceville NY	Boiceville NY	2. Ⓐ Ⓓ
3.	Freeport ME 04033	Freeport NE 04033	3. Ⓐ Ⓓ
4.	Jacksonville FL	Jacksonville Fla	4. Ⓐ Ⓓ
5.	Baltimore MD 21218	Baltimore MO 21218	5. Ⓐ Ⓓ
6.	Kalamazoo MI 49007	Kalamazoo MI 49007	6. Ⓐ Ⓓ
7.	Lexington KY 40506	Lexington WY 40506	7. Ⓐ Ⓓ
8.	Gambier Ohio 43002	Gambier Ohio 43002	8. Ⓐ Ⓓ
9.	Lawrence KS	Lawrence KS	9. Ⓐ Ⓓ
10.	Galesburg IL 61401	Galesburg IN 61401	10. Ⓐ Ⓓ
11.	Appleton WI	Appleton Wisc	11. Ⓐ Ⓓ
12.	Cambridge Mass 02139	Cambridge Miss 02139	12. Ⓐ Ⓓ
13.	Bethlehem PA 18015	Bethlehem PN 18015	13. Ⓐ Ⓓ
14.	Minneapolis MN	Minneapolis MN	14. Ⓐ Ⓓ
15.	East Lansing MI	East Lansing MI	15. Ⓐ Ⓓ
16.	Boulder CO 80302	Boulder CA 80302	16. Ⓐ Ⓓ
17.	Coral Gables FL	Coral Gables FL	17. Ⓐ Ⓓ
18.	Missoula MT 59812	Missoula MO 59812	18. Ⓐ Ⓓ
19.	Lincoln Neb 68508	Lincoln Nebr 68508	19. Ⓐ Ⓓ
20.	Chapel Hill NC 27518	Chapel Hill ND 27518	20. Ⓐ Ⓓ
21.	Stony Brook NY	Stony Brook N York	21. Ⓐ Ⓓ
22.	Baltimore MD 21239	Baltimore MD 21239	22. Ⓐ Ⓓ
23.	Albuquerque NM 87131	Albuquerque NJ 87131	23. Ⓐ Ⓓ
24.	Sarasota FL 33580	Sarasota FL 33580	24. Ⓐ Ⓓ
25.	Notre Dame IN 46556	Notre Dame IA 46556	25. Ⓐ Ⓓ

Answers

1. A	6. A	11. D	16. D	21. D
2. A	7. D	12. D	17. A	22. A
3. D	8. A	13. D	18. D	23. D
4. D	9. A	14. A	19. D	24. A
5. D	10. D	15. A	20. D	25. D

If you made any mistakes, take another look. By now you should be getting the knack of seeking the simplest differences before looking for the harder-to-find spelling differences.

LOOK FOR DIFFERENCES IN CITY NAMES

If, after you have compared the numbers and the abbreviations, you have still not spotted any differences, you must look at the city names. First of all, are the cities in the two addresses really the same?

1. Brookfield	Brookville	1. Ⓐ Ⓓ
2. Wayland	Wayland	2. Ⓐ Ⓓ
3. Ferncliff	Farmcliff	3. Ⓐ Ⓓ
4. Spring	Springs	4. Ⓐ Ⓓ
5. New City	New City	5. Ⓐ Ⓓ

Answers: 1. D 2. A 3. D 4. D 5. A

Sound out the words by syllables or spell them out. Is the spelling exactly the same? Are the same letters doubled? Are two letters reversed?

1. Beech	Beach	1. Ⓐ Ⓓ
2. Torrington	Torington	2. Ⓐ Ⓓ
3. Brayton	Brayton	3. Ⓐ Ⓓ
4. Collegiate	Collegaite	4. Ⓐ Ⓓ
5. Weston	Wetson	5. Ⓐ Ⓓ

Answers: 1. D 2. D 3. A 4. D 5. D

Practice Finding Differences in Names

Now try some practice questions in which differences may be found between the city names.

1. Natick MA 01760	Natick MA 01760	1. Ⓐ Ⓓ
2. Gt Barrington MA	Gt Barnington MA	2. Ⓐ Ⓓ
3. Irvington NY 10533	Rivington NY 10533	3. Ⓐ Ⓓ
4. Westminster MI	Westminster MI	4. Ⓐ Ⓓ
5. Providence RI 02903	Providence RI 02903	5. Ⓐ Ⓓ
6. Arundel ME 04046	Anurdel ME 04046	6. Ⓐ Ⓓ
7. Oakland CA 94604	Oakland CA 94604	7. Ⓐ Ⓓ
8. Middlebury VT	Middleberry VT	8. Ⓐ Ⓓ
9. Columbia MO 65201	Columbus MO 65201	9. Ⓐ Ⓓ
10. University MS 39677	University MS 39677	10. Ⓐ Ⓓ
11. Lancaster Penna	Lancaster Penna	11. Ⓐ Ⓓ
12. Ft Collins CO 80523	Ft Collins CO 80523	12. Ⓐ Ⓓ
13. Washington DC 20057	Washington DC 20057	13. Ⓐ Ⓓ
14. Atlanta GA 30303	Athens GA 30303	14. Ⓐ Ⓓ
15. Grinnel IA 50112	Grinnel IA 50112	15. Ⓐ Ⓓ
16. Towson MD 21204	Towsen MD 21204	16. Ⓐ Ⓓ
17. West Hartford Conn	East Hartford Conn	17. Ⓐ Ⓓ
18. Hempstead NY 11550	Hemstead NY 11550	18. Ⓐ Ⓓ
19. Houston Texas	Houston Texas	19. Ⓐ Ⓓ
20. Pocatello ID 83209	Poccatello ID 83209	20. Ⓐ Ⓓ
21. Bloomington IN	Broomingtown IN	21. Ⓐ Ⓓ
22. Iowa City Iowa 52242	Iona City Iowa 52242	22. Ⓐ Ⓓ
23. Haverford PA 19041	Haverford PA 19041	23. Ⓐ Ⓓ
24. Amherst Mass 01002	Amherst Mass 01002	24. Ⓐ Ⓓ
25. Geneva NY 14456	N Geneva NY 14456	25. Ⓐ Ⓓ

Answers

1. A	6. D	11. A	16. D	21. D
2. D	7. A	12. A	17. D	22. D
3. D	8. D	13. A	18. D	23. A
4. A	9. D	14. D	19. A	24. A
5. A	10. A	15. A	20. D	25. D

Check your answers. Then look at the questions to see where you made your mistakes. If your mistakes fall into any sort of pattern, guard especially against those errors in the future. If your mistakes seem to be random, then practice and care should help you to improve.

Comparing first the numbers, then abbreviations, and finally the cities must, of course, be done in a flash. If you have gone through this process and have spotted no errors, do not dwell on the question. Do not look again to see if you might have missed something. Trust yourself. Mark Ⓐ and go on to the next question.

Keeping these suggestions in mind, try the practice questions that follow. In these questions, you may find differences between numbers, abbreviations or cities, or you may find no difference at all.

ADDRESS CHECKING PRACTICE TEST

1.	Chestnut Hill Mass	Chestnut Hills Mass	1. Ⓐ Ⓓ
2.	Point Lookout MO 65726	Point Lookout MO 65726	2. Ⓐ Ⓓ
3.	Silver City NM 88061	Silver City NM 88601	3. Ⓐ Ⓓ
4.	Fayetteville NC 28301	Fayetteville ND 28301	4. Ⓐ Ⓓ
5.	Bryn Mawr Penn	Bryn Mawr Penna	5. Ⓐ Ⓓ
6.	Greenville SC 29606	Greenwood SC 29606	6. Ⓐ Ⓓ
7.	Cisco Texas 76437	Cisco Texas 76347	7. Ⓐ Ⓓ
8.	Melfa VA 23410	Melfa VA 23410	8. Ⓐ Ⓓ
9.	Bremerton WA 98310	Bremerton WY 98310	9. Ⓐ Ⓓ
10.	Janesville WI 53545	Janeville WI 53545	10. Ⓐ Ⓓ
11.	Portland OR 97220	Portland OR 97720	11. Ⓐ Ⓓ
12.	New York New York	New York New York	12. Ⓐ Ⓓ
13.	Canton MO 63435	Canton MO 63485	13. Ⓐ Ⓓ
14.	Holyoke Mass	Hollyoak Mass	14. Ⓐ Ⓓ
15.	Marion IN 46962	Marian IN 46962	15. Ⓐ Ⓓ
16.	Palatka Fla	Palatka Fla	16. Ⓐ Ⓓ
17.	Ukiah CA 95482	Ukiah CA 95482	17. Ⓐ Ⓓ
18.	Blytheville AR 72315	Blytheville AZ 72315	18. Ⓐ Ⓓ
19.	Marydel DE	Marydel MD	19. Ⓐ Ⓓ
20.	Ketchikan AK 99901	Ketchikan AK 99901	20. Ⓐ Ⓓ
21.	Rainsville Ala 35986	Rainsville AL 35986	21. Ⓐ Ⓓ
22.	San Pablo Calif	San Pueblo Calif	22. Ⓐ Ⓓ
23.	Macon Georgia	Macon Georgia	23. Ⓐ Ⓓ
24.	Decatur IL 62522	W Decatur IL 62522	24. Ⓐ Ⓓ
25.	Decorah IA 52001	Decorah IA 52001	25. Ⓐ Ⓓ
26.	Lexington KY	Lexington KY	26. Ⓐ Ⓓ
27.	Honolulu HI 96822	Honolululu HI 96822	27. Ⓐ Ⓓ
28.	Coeur D'Alene ID	Coeur D'Alene ID	28. Ⓐ Ⓓ
29.	Kokomo IN 46901	Kokomo IN 46910	29. Ⓐ Ⓓ
30.	Dodge City KS	Dodge City KS	30. Ⓐ Ⓓ
31.	W Lafayette IN	N Lafayette IN	31. Ⓐ Ⓓ
32.	Waterville ME 04901	Waterville ME 04901	32. Ⓐ Ⓓ
33.	Buzzards Bay MA	Buzzards Bay MA	33. Ⓐ Ⓓ
34.	Marquette MI 49855	Marquette MI 48955	34. Ⓐ Ⓓ
35.	West Point MS 39773	West Pointe MS 39773	35. Ⓐ Ⓓ
36.	Hackensack NJ 07601	Hackensack NJ 07601	36. Ⓐ Ⓓ
37.	Sparkill NY 10968	Sparkill NY 10968	37. Ⓐ Ⓓ
38.	Misenheimer NC	Misenheimer NC	38. Ⓐ Ⓓ
39.	Chillicothe OH 45601	Chillicothe OH 45501	39. Ⓐ Ⓓ
40.	LaGrande OR 97850	LeGrande OR 97850	40. Ⓐ Ⓓ
41.	Villanova Penna	Villanova Penna	41. Ⓐ Ⓓ
42.	Newberry SC 29108	Newberry SC 29108	42. Ⓐ Ⓓ
43.	Harrowgate TN 37752	Harrogate TN 37752	43. Ⓐ Ⓓ
44.	Clarendon TX 79226	Clarendon TX 7926	44. Ⓐ Ⓓ
45.	Bennington VT	Burlington VT	45. Ⓐ Ⓓ
46.	Lynchburg VA	Lynchburg VA	46. Ⓐ Ⓓ
47.	Lynnwood WA 98036	Lynwood WA 98036	47. Ⓐ Ⓓ
48.	Bethany WV 26032	Bethany WV 26032	48. Ⓐ Ⓓ
49.	Waukesha Wisc 53186	Waukesha Wisc 53136	49. Ⓐ Ⓓ
50.	Torrington WY 82240	Torrington Wyo 82240	50. Ⓐ Ⓓ
51.	Salt Lake City UT	Salt Lake City UT	51. Ⓐ Ⓓ
52.	Odessa TX 79760	Oddesa TX 79760	52. Ⓐ Ⓓ

53. Sewanee TN 37375	Swanee TN 37375	53. Ⓐ Ⓓ
54. Gaffney SC 29340	Gaffney SC 29340	54. Ⓐ Ⓓ
55. Smithfield RI	Smithfield RI	55. Ⓐ Ⓓ
56. Schuylkill Haven PA	Schuylkill Haven PA	56. Ⓐ Ⓓ
57. Tishomingo OK	Tishomingo Okla	57. Ⓐ Ⓓ
58. Steubenville OH 43952	Steubenville OH 43952	58. Ⓐ Ⓓ
59. Haw River NC 27258	Haw Rivers NC 27258	59. Ⓐ Ⓓ
60. Geneseo NY 14454	Genesco NY 14454	60. Ⓐ Ⓓ
61. New Brunswick NJ	New Brunswick NJ	61. Ⓐ Ⓓ
62. Henniker NH 03242	Henniker NH 03242	62. Ⓐ Ⓓ
63. Sedalia MO 65301	Sedalia MS 65301	63. Ⓐ Ⓓ
64. St. Paul MN 55104	St. Peter MN 55104	64. Ⓐ Ⓓ
65. Owosso Mich	Owosso Mich	65. Ⓐ Ⓓ
66. West Barnstable MA	West Barnstable MA	66. Ⓐ Ⓓ
67. Thibodaux LA 70301	Thibodauz LA 70301	67. Ⓐ Ⓓ
68. Overland Parks KS 66210	Overland Park KS 62201	68. Ⓐ Ⓓ
69. Muscatine Iowa 52761	Muscatine IA 52761	69. Ⓐ Ⓓ
70. St Meinrad IN 47577	Sta Meinrad IN 47577	70. Ⓐ Ⓓ
71. East St Louis IL	East St Louis IL	71. Ⓐ Ⓓ
72. Pearl City HI 96782	Pearl City HI 96782	72. Ⓐ Ⓓ
73. Milledgeville GA 31061	Milledgeville GA 31061	73. Ⓐ Ⓓ
74. Boynton Beach FL 33435	Boynton Bch FL 33435	74. Ⓐ Ⓓ
75. Storrs Conn 06268	Storrs Conn 06268	75. Ⓐ Ⓓ
76. La Junta CO 81050	La Junta CO 81050	76. Ⓐ Ⓓ
77. La Jolla CA 92093	LaJolla CA 92093	77. Ⓐ Ⓓ
78. Monticello AR 71655	Monticello AK 71655	78. Ⓐ Ⓓ
79. Thatcher AZ 85552	Thatcher AZ 855552	79. Ⓐ Ⓓ
80. Chattahoochee AL	Chattahoochee AL	80. Ⓐ Ⓓ
81. Leadville CO 80461	Leadville CO 80461	81. Ⓐ Ⓓ
82. Rising Sun DE	Rising Sun DE	82. Ⓐ Ⓓ
83. Niceville FL 33401	Niceville FL 33401	83. Ⓐ Ⓓ
84. Mount Berry GA 30149	Mount Berry GE 30149	84. Ⓐ Ⓓ
85. Rexburg ID 83440	Rexburg ID 83340	85. Ⓐ Ⓓ
86. Cahokia Ill	Cahokia Ill	86. Ⓐ Ⓓ
87. Terre Haute IN 47809	Terre Haute IN 47809	87. Ⓐ Ⓓ
88. Olathe KS 66061	Olathe KS 66061	88. Ⓐ Ⓓ
89. Natchitoches LA	Natchitoches LA	89. Ⓐ Ⓓ
90. St Marys City MD	St Marys City MD	90. Ⓐ Ⓓ
91. Ann Arbor MI 48105	Ann Harbor MI 48105	91. Ⓐ Ⓓ
92. Hattiesburg MS 39401	Harriesburg Miss 39401	92. Ⓐ Ⓓ
93. Poplar Bluff MO	Popular Bluff MO	93. Ⓐ Ⓓ
94. Scottsbluff NB 69361	Scottsbluff NB 69361	94. Ⓐ Ⓓ
95. Canandaigua NY 14424	Canandaigua NY 14424	95. Ⓐ Ⓓ

Answers

1. D	17. A	33. A	49. D	65. A	81. A
2. A	18. D	34. D	50. D	66. A	82. A
3. D	19. D	35. D	51. A	67. D	83. A
4. D	20. A	36. A	52. D	68. D	84. D
5. D	21. D	37. A	53. D	69. D	85. D
6. D	22. D	38. A	54. A	70. D	86. A
7. D	23. A	39. D	55. A	71. A	87. A
8. A	24. D	40. D	56. A	72. A	88. A
9. D	25. A	41. A	57. D	73. A	89. A
10. D	26. A	42. A	58. A	74. D	90. A
11. D	27. D	43. D	59. D	75. A	91. D
12. A	28. A	44. D	60. D	76. A	92. D
13. D	29. D	45. D	61. A	77. D	93. D
14. D	30. A	46. A	62. A	78. D	94. A
15. D	31. D	47. D	63. D	79. D	95. A
16. A	32. A	48. A	64. D	80. A	

Explanations of Differences

1. spelling of city
3. number reversal
4. different states
5. state abbreviation
6. different cities
7. number reversal
9. different states
10. different cities
11. different numbers
13. different numbers
14. spelling of city
15. spelling of city
18. different states
19. different states
21. state abbreviation
22. different cities
24. different cities
27. spelling of city
29. number reversal
31. different cities
34. number reversal
35. spelling of city
39. different numbers
40. spelling of city
43. spelling of city

44. missing number
45. different cities
47. spelling of city
49. different numbers
50. state abbreviation
52. spelling of city
53. spelling of city
57. state abbreviation
59. spelling of city
60. spelling of city
63. different states
64. different cities
67. spelling of city
68. different numbers
69. state abbreviation
70. different cities
74. spelling of city
77. spacing of city name
78. different states
79. extra number
84. state abbreviation
85. different numbers
91. different cities
92. state abbreviation
93. different cities

Analysis of Differences

The chart below breaks down the address differences into the three major categories—city differences, number differences and state differences. It also lumps together all the addresses in which there are differences and all the addresses in which there are no differences. After you check your answers against the correct answers on this practice set, check your mistakes against the list of explanations of differences. In the right hand column on the chart, write the number of questions that you got wrong in each category. It is also important to note how many questions in which there was no difference you marked "D". If you are aware of the types of errors you make most often, you should be able to concentrate your attention and avoid making these errors.

Analysis Chart		
City difference	25	
Number difference	12	
State difference	13	
Total addresses with differences	50	
Total addresses with no differences	45	

The Model Exams that follow will offer you plenty of practice with Address Checking questions. The error analysis which follows the explanation of differences will help you to pinpoint just where you slip up most often in comparing addresses. Fill out the chart with each Model Exam so that you can direct your concentration on the next exam. Practice should improve both your speed and your accuracy in Address Checking. If you feel the need, you may flip back to this chapter between Model Exams as you work through the book. Reread the chapter the day before your exam for a quick refresher.

REMEMBER: Look first for differences between numbers.
Next, look at the abbreviations.
Read what is written, as it is written.
Finally, sound out or spell out the cities.
When you find any difference, mark Ⓓ and go immediately to the next question.
If you find no difference, do not linger. Mark Ⓐ and move right on to the next question.
Do NOT read the whole address as a unit.

HOW TO ANSWER MEANING
OF WORDS QUESTIONS

The second part of the Mail Handler test is a test of vocabulary called Meaning of Words. This test indicates the ability of the individual to understand oral instructions from supervisors, to understand fellow workers and to make himself or herself understood by others. Ordinarily, mail handlers work in groups, and communication between members of the group is essential to performance of the job. The best preparation for the Meaning of Words test is a good basic vocabulary.

BUILDING A BETTER VOCABULARY

One way to build your vocabulary is to make a conscious effort to add those words you encounter in your daily life. To do this, develop the habit of reading with a notebook and pencil at hand. As you read, jot down every unfamiliar word you come across. Start with this book. Write down unfamiliar words from the text, from the practice exercises and from the explanations. When you reach the end of an exam, the end of a chapter, or any convenient stopping place, look up the new words in a dictionary. Write the definition of each new word in your notebook. You are much more likely to remember the meaning of words you look up for yourself than words someone else defines for you. When you look up a word, do not simply read the meaning, read the "small print" as well. Often the explanation of the derivation of the word, the foreign words from which is was formed, will help you to understand similar words when you meet them in your reading or conversation. The study of word formation is called etymology. Many English words are built from basic word parts. One of the most efficient ways of increasing your vocabulary is to learn some of these parts. Once you know some of the basic building blocks, you will find it easier to remember words you have learned and to puzzle out unfamiliar ones. The basic building blocks of words are these:

- A **root** or **stem** is the word part that provides the basic meaning of a word. Many word stems come from other languages—Greek, Latin, Anglo-Saxon, and French to name a few.
- A **prefix** is a word part that is added to the beginning of a word stem and alters the meaning of that stem.
- A **suffix** is a word part that is added to the end of a word or stem and alters the meaning of that word or stem. Suffixes often indicate whether a word is a noun, a verb, an adjective, or an adverb.

Word analysis is a kind of arithmetic. Instead of adding numbers, you add the meanings contained in each part of an unfamiliar word. The sum of these parts is the definition of the whole word.

EXAMPLE: PROCESSION
        pro- is a prefix that means "forward."
        cess is a stem that means "go" or "move."
        -ion is a noun suffix that means "the act of."
pro + cess + ion = *the act of going before*

The meaning you find through word analysis is basic and may not be exactly the same as one of the answer choices on your test. However, word analysis *will* give you a good clue to the right answer in many cases.

EXAMPLE: The man has a *receding* hairline. He
(A) has an irregular hairline
(B) is becoming bald
(C) has very long hair
(D) combs his hair onto his forehead

The stem *cede* means "go." The prefix *re-* means "back," and *-ing* is an active verb suffix. The word *receding* means "going back," so the correct answer to this question would be (B), *is becoming bald*.

EXAMPLE: The attorney *dissected* the testimony of the first witness. *Dissected* means most nearly
(A) questioned
(B) directed
(C) put together
(D) took apart

The root *sect* means "to cut." The prefix *dis-* means "apart," and *-ed* is a verb suffix showing past action. *Dissected* means "cut apart," so the answer is (D).

Here are some of the most useful prefixes, suffixes and stems. Look them over carefully and try to learn as many as you can. A good way to learn is to try to add some examples of your own after the examples given. If you are not certain of the correctness of your own examples, look them up in a dictionary.

PREFIX	MEANING	EXAMPLES
a	not	amoral, _____, _____
ab	away from	absent, _____, _____
ad, ac, ag, at	to, against	aggressive, attract, _____, _____
an	without	anarchy, _____, _____
ante	before	antedate, _____, _____
anti, ant	against	antipathy, antonym, _____, _____
bene	well	benefactor, _____, _____
bi	two	biannual, _____, _____
circum	around	circumvent, _____, _____
com, con, col	together	commit, collate, _____, _____
contra	against	contraband, _____, _____
de	from, down	descend, _____, _____
dis, di	apart, away	distract, divert, _____, _____
dom	home, rule	domicile, dominate, _____, _____
ex, e	out, from	exit, emit, _____, _____
extra	beyond, outside	extracurricular, _____, _____
homo	same	homogenize, _____, _____
in, im, ir, il, un	not	inept, illegal, _____, _____

in, im	in, into	interest, imbibe, _____, _____
inter	between	interscholastic, _____, _____
intra, intro	within	intramural, _____, _____
mal	bad	malcontent, _____, _____
mis	wrong	misspell, _____, _____
non	not	nonentity, _____, _____
ob	against	obstacle, _____, _____
omni	all	omnivorous, _____, _____
per	through	permeate, _____, _____
peri	around, about	periscope, _____, _____
poly	many	polytheism, _____, _____
post	after	post-mortem, _____, _____
pre	before	premonition, _____, _____
pro	forward, for	propose, _____, _____
re	again, back	review, redeem, _____, _____
se	apart, away	seclude, _____, _____
semi	half	semicircle, _____, _____
sub	under	submarine, _____, _____
super	above	superimpose, _____, _____
sur	on, upon	surmount, _____, _____
syn, sym	together, with	sympathy, _____, _____
trans	across, beyond	transpose, _____, _____
un	not	unwelcome, _____, _____

SUFFIX	**MEANING**	**EXAMPLES**
able, ible	capable of, able	reversible (*adj.*), _____, _____
age	place, thing, idea	storage (*n.*), _____, _____
al	pertaining to	instructional (*adj.*), _____, _____
ance	relating to	reliance (*n.*), _____, _____
ary	relating to	dictionary (*n.*), _____, _____
ate	an action of	confiscate (*v.*), _____, _____
cy	the quality of	democracy (*n.*), _____, _____
ed	past action	subsided (*v.*), _____, _____
ence	relating to	confidence (*n.*), _____, _____
er, or	one who	adviser, actor (*n.*), _____, _____
ic	pertaining to	democratic (*adj.*), _____, _____
ing	present action	surmising (*v.*), _____, _____
ion	the act or state of	radiation (*n.*), _____, _____
ious	full of	rebellious (*adj.*), _____, _____
ive	having the quality of	creative (*adj.*), _____, _____
ize	to make	harmonize (*v.*), _____, _____
ly	to do with the quality of	carefully (*adv.*), _____, _____
ment	the result of	amusement (*n.*), _____, _____
ness	the quality of being	selfishness (*n.*), _____, _____
ty	condition of being	sanity (*n.*), _____, _____

STEM	MEANING	EXAMPLES
ag, ac	do	agenda, action, _____, _____
agri	farm	agriculture, _____, _____
aqua	water	aquatic, _____, _____
auto	self	automatic, _____, _____
biblio	book	bibliography, _____, _____
bio	life	biography, _____, _____
cad, cas	fall	cadence, casual, _____, _____
cap, cep, cept	take	captive, accept, _____, _____
capit	head	capital, _____, _____
ced, cede, ceed, cess	go	intercede, _____, _____
celer	speed	accelerate, _____, _____
chrom	color	monochromatic, _____, _____
chron	time	chronological, _____, _____
cide, cis	cut	incision, _____, _____
clude, clud, clus	close, close in	include, cluster, _____, _____
cog, cogn	knowledge of	recognize, _____, _____
cur, curs	run	incur, recur, _____, _____
ded	give	dedicate, _____, _____
dent, dont	tooth	dental, _____, _____
duce, duct	lead	induce, deduct, _____, _____
fact, fect, fict	make, do	perfect, fiction, _____, _____
fer, late	carry	refer, dilate, _____, _____
flect, flex	bend, turn	reflect, _____, _____
fring, fract	break	infringe, refract, _____, _____
graph, gram	picture, writing	graphic, telegram, _____, _____
greg	group, gather	gregarious, _____, _____
gress, grad	move	progress, degrade, _____, _____
hydr	water	hydrate, _____, _____
ject	throw	inject, _____, _____
jud	right	judicial, _____, _____
junct	join	conjunction, _____, _____
juris	law, justice	jurist, _____, _____
lect, leg	read, choose	collect, _____, _____
logue	speech, speaking	dialogue, _____, _____
logy	study of	psychology, _____, _____
log, loc	speak	elocution, _____, _____
lude, lus	play, perform	delude, _____, _____
manu	by hand	manuscript, _____, _____
mand	order	remand, _____, _____
mar	sea	maritime, _____, _____
med	middle	intermediate, _____, _____
ment, mem	mind, memory	mention, _____, _____
meter	measure	thermometer, _____, _____
micro	small	microscope, _____, _____

min	lessen	miniature, _____, _____
mis, miss, mit	send	remit, dismiss, _____, _____
mot, mov	move	remote, remove, _____, _____
mute	change	commute, _____, _____
naut	sailor, sail	nautical, _____, _____
nounce, nunci	declare, state	announce, enunciate, _____, _____
ped, pod	foot	pedal, _____, _____
pel, pulse	drive, push	dispel, impulse, _____, _____
pend, pense	hang, way	depend, dispense, _____, _____
plac	please	placate, _____, _____
plic	fold	implicate, _____, _____
port	carry	portable, _____, _____
pose, pone	put, place	depose, component, _____, _____
reg, rect	rule	regulate, direct, _____, _____
rupt	break	disruption, _____, _____
sec, sect	cut	bisect, _____, _____
sed	remain	sedentary, _____, _____
sert	state, place	insert, _____, _____
serve	keep, save	preserve, _____, _____
scend, scent	move	ascent, _____, _____
scribe, script	write	describe, _____, _____
sist	stand, set	insist, _____, _____
spect	look	inspect, _____, _____
spire, spirat	breath, breathe	perspire, _____, _____
strict	tighten	restrict, _____, _____
tain	hold	detain, _____, _____
term	end	terminate, _____, _____
tract	draw, drag	detract, _____, _____
tort	twist	distort, _____, _____
vene, vent	come	intervene, invent, _____, _____
vict, vince	overcome, conquer	victor, invincible, _____, _____
volve, volu	roll, turn	evolve, revolution, _____, _____

The word list on the following pages includes many words which have appeared on previous exams. You already know some of these words; you cannot possibly learn them all. Do try to learn some, the more the better. A rich vocabulary will stand you in good stead for your exam, for your career, and for your life.

WORD LIST

This list contains hundreds of words of the sort that may appear on the test you are planning to take. Many of them will be familiar to you, although you may not be sure precisely what they mean or how they are used. Many of them are words you will encounter in the Model Exams in this book or on your Mail Handler Exam.

Each word is briefly defined and then used in a sentence. For the roots of words and more extended definitions, check your dictionary.

The physical act of writing a word and its definition helps to reinforce this information so that you will remember new vocabulary words and their meanings. You may not have time to learn all the words listed here before your exam, but you can certainly learn many of them. Start by choosing 15 or 20 words whose meanings you don't know. Write them down, leaving enough space on your paper to write the correct definitions beside each word. Then copy the definition from the word list onto your paper. You now have a smaller word list that you can carry with you and review whenever you have some spare time. When you have mastered this list, prepare another in the same way.

Another useful study technique is to make flash cards. Write a word on one side of an index card or piece of paper and its meaning on the other side. Prepare 15 to 25 cards in this way. Study the words and definitions carefully, then test yourself. Arrange the cards in a deck so that the sides of the cards with the new vocabulary words are face up. Then, on a separate sheet of paper, write the meaning of the word shown on the top card. Turn this card over and write the meaning of the second word. Do this until you have gone through the entire deck. Check yourself by comparing your answers with the definitions on the backs of your flash cards. You can reverse the cards and, looking at the definitions, write the correct words. You can also have a friend hold the cards up for you as you tell her or him the correct meaning of each word.

abate—to lessen in intensity or number: After an hour the storm *abated*, and the sky began to clear.

abdicate—to give up a power or function: The father *abdicated* his responsibility by not setting a good example for the boy.

abet—to encourage or countenance the commission of an offense: Aiding and *abetting* a criminal makes one a party to crime.

abhor—to regard with horror and loathing: The pacifist *abhors* war.

abject—miserable, wretched: Many people in underdeveloped and overpopulated countries live in *abject* poverty.

abide by—to live up to, submit to: We will *abide* by the decision of the court.

abolish—to do away with, as an institution: Slavery was *abolished* in Massachusetts shortly after the American Revolution.

abort—to come to nothing, cut short: The mission was *aborted* when several of the helicopters broke down.

abrasive—scraping or rubbing, annoyingly harsh or jarring: The high-pitched whine of the machinery was *abrasive* to my nerves.

abridge—to shorten: The paperback book was an *abridged* edition.

absenteeism—condition of being habitually absent, as from work: *Absenteeism* at the plant becomes more of a problem around holidays.

abstain—to refrain voluntarily from some act: Alcoholics must *abstain* from any indulgence in alcoholic drinks.

absurd—clearly untrue, nonsensical: The parents dismissed the child's story of meeting men from outer space as *absurd*.

abundant—plentiful, more than enough: Rich soil and *abundant* rainfall make the region lush and fruitful.

accelerate—to increase in speed: Going downhill, a vehicle will naturally *accelerate*.

access—means of approach: Public libraries insure that the people have *access* to vast stores of information.

acclaim—to applaud, approve loudly: The crowd in the square *acclaimed* their hero as the new president.

accommodate—to make room for, adjust: The room can *accommodate* two more desks. We will *accommodate* ourselves to the special needs of those clients.

accumulate—to gather, pile up: Over the years she has *accumulated* a large collection of antique bric-a-brac.

accustom—to get or be used to: The supervisor was not *accustomed* to having her instructions ignored.

acknowledge—to admit, recognize as true or legitimate: We do not *acknowledge* the state's authority to legislate people's beliefs.

acquit—to set free from an accusation: The jury *acquitted* the defendant.

adamant—inflexible, hard: She was *adamant* in her determination to succeed.

adaptable—able to adjust to new circumstances: Thanks to the intelligence that has made technology possible, humans are more *adaptable* to a variety of climates than any other species.

adept—skilled, well-versed: A journalist is *adept* at writing quickly.

adequate—sufficient, enough: Without *adequate* sunlight, many tropical plants will not bloom.

adhere—to hold, stick to, cling: Many persons *adhere* to their beliefs despite all arguments.

adjourn—to suspend proceedings, usually for the day: Since it is now five o'clock, I move that we *adjourn* until tomorrow morning.

advantageous—useful, favorable: Our opponent's blunders have been *advantageous* to our campaign.

adverse—opposing, contrary: *Adverse* winds slowed the progress of the ship.

advocate—to plead for or urge: Socialists *advocate* public ownership of utilities.

affable—amiable, pleasant, easy to talk to: The smiling face and *affable* manner of the agent put the child at ease.

affect—to influence: The judge did not allow his personal feelings to *affect* his judgment of the case's legal merits.

affiliation—connection, as with an organization: His *affiliation* with the club has been of long standing; he has been a member for ten years at least.

affix—to attach, fasten: A price tag was *affixed* to each item.

affluence—wealth: The new *affluence* of the family made them the object of curiosity and envy to their poorer neighbors.

agenda—list of things to be done: The *agenda* of the conference included the problem of tariffs.

agitate—to stir up or disturb: Rumors of change in the government *agitated* the population.

aggression—unprovoked attack: The invasion of Afghanistan was denounced in the Western press as *aggression*.

alarm—disturb, excite: The parents were *alarmed* when their child's temperature rose suddenly.

alien—(*adj*) strange, foreign: Their customs are *alien* to us. (*n*) foreigner who has not become a citizen of the country where he lives: There are, it is estimated, over a million illegal *aliens* living in New York City.

allege—to declare without proof: The *alleged* attacker has yet to stand trial.

alleviate—to lessen, make easier: The aspirin helped to *alleviate* the pain.

aloof—distant, reserved or cold in manner: Her elegant appearance and formal politeness made her seem *aloof,* though in reality she was only shy.

altercation—angry dispute: The *altercation* stopped just short of physical violence.

altitude—height, especially above sea level or the earth's surface: The plane had reached an *altitude* of four miles.

amass—to collect, pile up: Through careful investment he had *amassed* a sizable fortune.

ambiguous—having more than one possible meaning: The *ambiguous* wording of some legislative acts requires clarification by the courts.

ambivalent—having conflicting feelings: I am *ambivalent* about the job; although the atmosphere is pleasant, the work itself is boring.

amenable—agreeable, open to suggestion: He was *amenable* to the proposed schedule change.

amicable—friendly: Courts often seek to settle civil suits in an *amicable* manner.

amnesty—pardon for a large group: The president granted *amnesty* to those who had resisted the draft.

amplify—to enlarge, expand: Congressmen may *amplify* their remarks for appearance in the Record.

anemia—deficiency of red blood corpuscles or hemoglobin in the blood: Before it was treated, her *anemia* caused her to tire easily.

annual—yearly, once a year: The company holds an *annual* picnic on the Fourth of July.

annul—to wipe out, make void: The Supreme Court can *annul* a law that it deems unconstitutional.

anonymous—bearing no name, unsigned: Little credence should be given to an *anonymous* accusation.

anticipate—to foresee, give thought to in advance;

expect: We *anticipate* that this movie will be a box office hit.

apathy—lack of interest or emotion: Voter *apathy* allows minorities of politically concerned people to influence elections out of proportion to their numbers.

apex—summit, peak: Some people reach the *apex* of their careers before forty.

appearance—outward aspect; act of coming in sight: The celebrity put in an *appearance* at the fund-raising activities.

append—to attach as a supplement: Exhibits should be *appended* to the report.

appendix—extra material added at the end of a book: A chronology of the events described may be found in the *appendix*.

applicable—able to be applied, appropriate: Since you are single, the items on the form concerning your spouse are not *applicable;* leave those spaces blank.

appraise—to set a value on: The price at which authorities *appraise* a building determines its taxes.

apprehend—to arrest: The police moved to *apprehend* the suspect.

apprehensive—fearing some coming event: The students were *apprehensive* about the examination.

arbitration—settling a dispute by referring it to an outsider for decision: Under the agreement, disputes were to be settled by *arbitration*.

archaic—no longer in use: Some words like "thou," once a common form of address, are now *archaic*.

ardent—passionately enthusiastic: His *ardent* patriotism led him to risk his life in the underground resistance movement.

aroma—fragrance: The *aroma* of good coffee stimulates the salivary glands.

ascertain—to find out with certainty: Because the woman's story was so confused, we have been unable to *ascertain* whether a crime was committed or not.

assailant—attacker: Faced with a line-up, the victim picked out his alleged *assailant*.

assemblage—a group or collection of things or persons: Out of the *assemblage* of spare parts in the garage, we found the pieces to repair the bicycle.

assent—to concur, comply, consent: All parties involved *assented* to the statement.

assert—to claim or state positively: She *asserted* her title to the property.

assess—to set a value on: The house has been *assessed* for taxes at far below its market value.

assign—to appoint, prescribe: The new reporters were *assigned* to cover local sports events.

assist—to give aid, help: The laboratory aide *assists* the chemist in researching the properties of chemical substances.

assumption—something taken for granted or supposed to be fact: I prepared dinner on the *assumption* that they would be home by seven.

assure—to make something certain, guarantee; to promise with confidence: The fact that they left their tickets *assures* that they will return. I *assured* her that someone would be there to meet her.

attain—to get through effort, to achieve or reach: Thanks to their generous contribution, the campaign has *attained* its goal.

auction—to sell to the highest bidder: Bidding started at five dollars, but the chair eventually was *auctioned* for thirty.

authorize—to give official permission: The guard is *authorized* to demand identification from anyone entering the building.

automatically—involuntarily, spontaneously, mechanically: The computer *automatically* records the amount of sales for each month.

averse—having a dislike or reluctance: The local population disliked tourists and were *averse* to having their pictures taken.

avert—to turn aside or ward off: By acting quickly we *averted* disaster.

avow—to declare openly: She *avowed* her belief in the political system.

baffle—to perplex, frustrate: The intricacies of the game *baffle* description.

banter—light, good-natured teasing: The comments were mere *banter,* not intended to wound.

barren—unfruitful, unproductive: Only a few scrubby trees clung to the rocky soil of that *barren* landscape.

barter—to trade by direct exchange of one commodity for another: At the Indian market I *bartered* my sleeping bag for a handwoven poncho.

basic—fundamental: The teacher explained the *basic* concepts of democracy.

beneficiary—one who benefits, especially one who receives a payment or inheritance: The man named his wife as the *beneficiary* of the insurance policy.

benign—kindly: Her *benign* influence helped to alleviate their depression.

berate—to scold vehemently: The teacher who *berates* his class is rationalizing his own faults.

bestow—to grant or confer: The republic *bestowed* great honors upon its heroes.

bibliography—list of sources of information on a particular subject: She assembled a *bibliography* of major works on early American history published since 1960.

bigot—narrow-minded, intolerant person: A *bigot* is not swayed from his beliefs by rational argument.

bolster—to prop up, support: The announcement that refreshments were being served *bolstered* the flagging spirits of the company.

boycott—to refuse to do business with or use: Consumers *boycotted* the company's products to show support for the striking workers.

brazen—brassy, shameless: The delinquents demonstrated a *brazen* contempt for the law.

breach—opening or gap, failure to keep the terms, as of a promise or law: When they failed to deliver the goods, they were guilty of a *breach* of contract.

brevity—conciseness, terseness: *Brevity* is the essence of journalistic writing.

brochure—pamphlet: *Brochures* on many topics are available free of charge.

budget—plan for the spending of income during a certain period: The present *budget* allocates one fourth of our joint income for rent and utilities.

candid—honest, open: She was always *candid* about her feelings; if she liked you, you knew it.

capacious—roomy, spacious: The travelers had all their possessions in one *capacious* suitcase.

capitulate—surrender: The city *capitulated* to the victors.

capricious—changing suddenly, willfully erratic: He is so *capricious* in his moods that no one can predict how he will take the news.

carcinogenic—producing cancer: In tests on laboratory animals, the drug was shown to be *carcinogenic*.

category—class or division in a system of classification: Patients are listed according to *categories* which designate the seriousness of their condition.

caustic—biting, burning, stinging: The surface of the wood had been marred by some *caustic* substance.

censure—to disapprove, blame, condemn as wrong: The unprofessional conduct of several of its members has been officially *censured* by the organization.

chaos—complete confusion or disorder: By the time the children had finished playing with all the toys, the room was in *chaos*.

characteristic—typical trait, identifying feature: The curved yellow bill is a *characteristic* of this species.

chide—to rebuke, scold: The parents *chided* the disobedient child.

chronic—long-lasting, recurring: His *chronic* asthma flares up at certain times of the year.

chronology—arrangement by time, list of events by date: The book included a *chronology* of the poet's life against the background of the major political events of his age.

circumvent—to go around, frustrate: A technicality allowed people to *circumvent* the intention of the law.

clemency—leniency: The governor granted *clemency* to the prisoners.

cliché—trite, overworked expression: "White as snow" is a *cliché*.

coalition—temporary union of groups for a specific purpose: Various environmentalist groups formed a *coalition* to work for the candidate most sympathetic to their cause.

coherent—logically connected or organized: They were too distraught to give a *coherent* account of the crash.

coincide—to be alike, to occur at the same time: This year Thanksgiving *coincides* with her birthday.

collaborate—to work together on a project: The friends decided to *collaborate* on a novel.

collate—to put the pages of a text in order: The photocopies have been *collated* and are ready to be stapled.

colleague—fellow worker in a profession: The biologist enjoyed shoptalk with her *colleagues* at the conference.

commend—to praise: The supervisor *commended* them for their excellent work.

commiserate—to express sympathy for: It is natural to *commiserate* with the innocent victim of an accident.

commission—to authorize, especially to have someone perform a task or to act in one's place: I have *commissioned* a neighbor to collect the mail while I'm away.

common—ordinary, widespread: Financial difficulty is a *common* problem for young married couples today.

commute—to travel regularly between home and work: *Commuting* is a daily routine for most working people.

comparable—equivalent, able or worthy to be compared: His degree from a foreign university is *comparable* to our master's degree.

compatible—harmonious, in agreement: Since they

have similar attitudes, interests, and habits, they are a *compatible* couple.

compel—to force: He was *compelled* by law to make restitution.

compensate—to be equal to, make up for: Money could not *compensate* him for his sufferings.

competent—fit, capable, qualified: I am not *competent* to judge the authenticity of this document; you should take it to an expert.

competition—rivalry for the same object. The theory of free enterprise assumes an unrestricted *competition* for customers among rival businesses.

complete—to finish, bring an end to: The project was *completed* in time for the fall science fair.

complex—a whole made up of interconnected or related parts: The school grew from a few classrooms to a whole *complex* of buildings organized around the computer center.

comply—to go along with, obey: The crowd *complied* with the order to disperse.

compose—to put together, create: I spent an hour *composing* a formal letter of protest.

comprehensible—able to be understood: The episode was only *comprehensible* to those who knew the story thus far.

comprise—to include, be made up of, consist of: The test will *comprise* the subject matter of the previous lessons.

compromise—a settlement of a difference in which both sides give up something: We are willing to make some concessions in order to reach a *compromise*.

compulsory—required, forced: Attendance is *compulsory* unless one has a medical excuse.

compute—to figure, calculate: He *computed* the total on his pocket calculator.

concede—to yield, as to what is just or true: When the candidate realized she could not win, she *conceded* gracefully.

concept—idea, general notion: The *concept* that all individuals have inherent and inalienable rights is basic to our political philosophy.

condole—to express sympathy: His friends gathered to *condole* with him over his loss.

condone—to pardon, overlook an offense: The law will not *condone* an act on the plea that the culprit was intoxicated.

conducive—leading to, helping: Mother found the waterbed *conducive* to a restful sleep.

conduct—behavior: Her cool *conduct* in the emergency inspired confidence in those around her.

confidential—private, secret: Respondents were assured that the census was *confidential* and would be used for statistical purposes only.

confiscate—to seize, appropriate: The government has no right to *confiscate* private property without just compensation.

conflagration—large fire: New York City was almost destroyed in the 1835 *conflagration*.

conformity—harmony, agreement: In *conformity* with the rule, the meeting was adjourned.

conscientious—honest, faithful to duty or to what is right: He is *conscientious* in his work, and so has won the trust of his employers.

conservative—tending to preserve what is, cautious: At the annual conference, they presented their *conservative* views on the future of education.

considerable—important, large, much: The director has *considerable* clout among the members of the board; they value her recommendations highly.

constant—unchanging, fixed, continual: It is difficult to listen to his *constant* complaining.

construe—to interpret, analyze: His attitude was *construed* as one of opposition to the proposal.

contagious—transmittable by direct or indirect contact: Hepatitis is a *contagious* disease.

contaminate—to pollute, make unclean or unfit: The pesticide seeped into the water table, *contaminating* the wells.

contingent—depending upon something's happening: Our plans were *contingent* on the check's arriving on time.

contract—a formal agreement, usually written: The company signed a *contract* to operate a bookstore on campus.

controversy—highly charged debate, conflict of opinion: A *controversy* arose over whether to use the funds for highway improvement or for mass transit.

convene—to gather together, as an assembly: The graduates will *convene* on the campus.

converge—to move nearer together, head for one point: The flock *converged* on the seeded field.

cooperate—to work together for a common goal: If everyone *cooperates* on decorations, entertainment and refreshments, the party is sure to be a success.

coordinate—to bring different elements into order or harmony: In a well-run office, schedules are *coordinated* so that business is uninterrupted.

correlate—to bring into or show relation between two things: Studies have *correlated* smoking and heart disease.

correspondence—letters, communication by letter: A copy of the book order will be found in the *correspondence* file under the name of the publisher.

courteous—polite, considerate: A *courteous* manner—friendly but not personal—is essential for anyone who deals with the public.

credible—worthy or able to be believed: The tale, though unusual, was entirely *credible,* considering the physical evidence.

criterion—standard of judging: Logical organization was a *criterion* for grading the essays. *Plural:* **criteria.**

crucial—of utmost importance: The discovery of the letter was *crucial* to the unraveling of the whole mystery.

curative—concerning or causing the cure of disease: The grandmother had faith in the *curative* powers of certain herbs.

curtail—to reduce, shorten: Classes were shortened in the winter to *curtail* heating costs.

customary—usual, according to habit or custom: Today, because of the traffic jam, he did not take his *customary* route.

debate—to argue formally for and against: The candidate challenged the incumbent to *debate* the issues on television.

deceive—to trick, be false to: They *deceived* us by telling us that our donations would be used to provide food to the needy; in reality, the money was used to supply guns to the rebels.

deduct—to subtract, take away: Because the package was damaged, the seller *deducted* two dollars from the price.

deem—to judge, think: The newspaper did not *deem* the event worthy of coverage.

default—failure to do what is required: In *default* of the payment, the property was seized by the creditor.

deficient—not up to standard, inadequate: The child is *deficient* in reading but excels in arithmetic.

defoliate—to strip of leaves: All the trees in the yard had been *defoliated* by an infestation of moths.

defray—to pay (costs): The company *defrayed* the costs of the vacation trip for the winner of the essay contest.

delegate—to authorize or assign to act in one's place: Since I will be unable to attend the conference, I have *delegated* my assistant to represent me.

delegation—group of persons officially authorized to act for others: Our *delegation* to the United Nations is headed by the ambassador.

delete—to strike out, erase: Names of those who fail to pay their dues for over a year are *deleted* from the membership rolls.

deliberate—intended, meant: It was no accident but a *deliberate* act.

delinquent—delaying or failing to do what rules or law require: Since she was *delinquent* in paying her taxes, she had to pay a fine.

demolish—to destroy, especially a building: The wrecking crew arrived and within a few hours the structure was *demolished*.

demonstrable—able to be shown: The tests showed that the consumers' preference was justified by that brand's *demonstrable* superiority.

demote—to lower in rank: He was stripped of his rank and *demoted* to private.

deny—to declare untrue, refuse to recognize: I categorically *deny* the accusation.

deplete—to empty, use up: At the present rates of consumption, the known reserves will be *depleted* before the end of the century.

deplore—to lament, disapprove strongly: Pacifists *deplore* violence even on behalf of a just cause.

depreciate—to lessen in value: Property will *depreciate* rapidly unless kept in good repair.

deprive—to take away, often by force: No person may be *deprived* of his liberty without due process of law.

designate—to name, appoint: We will meet at the time and place *designated* on the sheet.

despicable—contemptible: The villain in melodramas is always a *despicable* character.

destitute—in extreme want: Three successive years of crop failures had left the peasants *destitute*.

deteriorate—to get worse: Storing it in a cedar chest will keep the antique fabric from *deteriorating* further.

determine—to find out; to be the cause of, decide: The doctor interviewed the mother to *determine* whether there was a family history of diabetes. The result of this test will *determine* our next step.

deterrent—a thing that discourages: The absolute certainty of punishment is a powerful *deterrent* to some types of crime.

detonate—to explode: An electrical charge can be used to *detonate* certain explosives.

detract—to take away a part, lessen: The old-fashioned engraving *detracted* from the value of the piece of jewelry.

detrimental—causing damage or harm: The support of fringe groups can be *detrimental* to the campaign of an office-seeker.

deviate—to stray, turn aside from: The honest man never *deviated* from telling the truth as he saw it.

devise—to contrive, invent: I will *devise* a plan of escape.

dexterity—quickness, skill and ease in some act: The

art of juggling is one that calls for the highest degree of *dexterity*.

disability—loss of ability: The accident resulted in a temporary *disability;* the employee was out for two weeks.

discard—to throw away: Dead files more than ten years old may be *discarded*.

discern—to perceive, identify: The fog was so thick we could barely *discern* the other cars.

disclose—to reveal: The caller did not *disclose* the source of her information.

disconcert—to throw into confusion: A noisy audience may *disconcert* even the most experienced performer.

dismantle—to take apart: The machine must be *dismantled,* cleaned, repaired and reassembled.

dispatch—to send on an errand: The bank *dispatched* a courier to deliver the documents by hand.

dispel—to drive away, make disappear: The good-humored joke *dispelled* the tension in the room.

dispense with—to get rid of, do without: Let's *dispense with* the formalities and get right down to business.

dissemble—to conceal or misrepresent the true nature of something: He *dissembled* his real motives under a pretence of unselfish concern.

disseminate—to spread, broadcast: With missionary zeal, they *disseminated* the literature about the new religion.

dissension—lack of harmony or agreement: There was *dissension* among the delegates about which candidate to support.

dissipate—to scatter aimlessly, spend foolishly: He soon *dissipated* his inheritance.

distinct—clear, notable: There is a *distinct* difference between these two musical compositions.

distortion—a twisting out of shape, misstatement of facts: The *distortions* of the historians left little of the man's true character for posterity.

distract—to divert, turn aside: The loud crash *distracted* the attention of the students.

diverge—to extend in different directions from a common point: The map showed a main lode with thin veins *diverging* in all directions.

diverse—varied, unlike: A realistic cross-section must include citizens of *diverse* backgrounds and opinions.

divisive—tending to divide, causing disagreement: The issue of abortion, on which people hold deep and morally-based convictions, was *divisive* to the movement.

divulge—to reveal, make public: Newspaper reporters have long fought the courts for the right not to *divulge* their sources of information.

docile—easily led: The child was *docile* until he discovered his mother was gone.

dogmatic—arbitrary, believing or believed without proof: The politician, *dogmatic* in his opposition, refused to consider alternative solutions.

durable—long-lasting, tough: Canvas, unlike lighter materials, is a *durable* fabric.

dynamic—in motion, forceful, energetic: A *dynamic* leader can inspire followers with enthusiasm and confidence.

ecology—science of the relation of life to its environment: Persons concerned about *ecology* are worried about the effects of pollution on the environment.

ecstasy—extreme happiness: The lovers were in *ecstasy,* oblivious to their surroundings.

effect—(*v*) to bring about: New regulations have *effected* a shift in policy on applications. (*n*) a result: The headache was an *effect* of sinus congestion.

egress—a going out, exit: The building code requires that the apartment have at least two means of *egress*.

elate—to make joyful, elevate in spirit: A grade of 100 will *elate* any student.

elicit—to draw out, evoke: Her direct questions only *elicited* further evasions.

eligible—fit to be chosen, qualified: Veterans are *eligible* for many government benefits, including low-cost loans.

eliminate—to remove, do away with: By consolidating forms, the new procedures have *eliminated* some needless paperwork.

elusive—hard to find or grasp: Because the problem is so complex, a definitive solution seems *elusive*.

emaciated—very thin, wasted away: He had a tall, bony figure, as *emaciated* as a skeleton.

embargo—governmental restriction or prohibition of trade: In retaliation for the invasion, the government imposed an *embargo* on grain shipments to the Soviet Union.

embellish—to decorate, adorn: She would *embellish* her narratives with fanciful events.

emigrate—to leave a country permanently to settle in another: Many people applied for visas, wishing to *emigrate* and escape persecution at home.

employ—to use: The artist *employed* charcoal in many of her sketches.

enable—to make able or possible: A summer job will *enable* you to pay for the course you need to take.

enact—to put into law, do or act out: A bill was

enacted lowering the voting age to eighteen.

endeavor—to attempt by effort, try hard: I *endeavored* to contact them several times but they never returned my calls.

endorse—to declare support or approval for: Community leaders were quick to *endorse* a project that would bring new jobs to the neighborhood.

enforce—to make forceful, to impose by force: Because of the holiday, parking restrictions are not being *enforced* today.

enhance—to improve, augment, add to: The neat cover *enhanced* the report.

enigma—riddle, anything that defies explanation: The origin of the statues on Easter Island is an *enigma*.

enlightened—free from prejudice or ignorance, socially or intellectually advanced: No *enlightened* society could condone the exploitation of children as it was once practiced in American industry.

ensue—to follow immediately or as a result: One person raised an objection and a long argument *ensued*.

entail—to involve or make necessary: Getting the report out on time will *entail* working all weekend.

entitle—to give a right or claim to: This pass *entitles* the bearer to two free admissions.

entrenched—firmly established: Protestant fundamentalism is deeply *entrenched* in the lives of those people.

environs—surroundings, suburbs: We searched the campus and its *environs*.

eradicate—to pluck up by the roots, wipe out: They tried to *eradicate* the hordes of rabbits by introducing a deadly epidemic.

erode—to eat into, wear away: The glaciers *eroded* the land, leaving deep valleys.

escapade—an adventurous prank, reckless adventure for amusement: Relieved from duty at last, the soldiers went on a three-day *escapade*.

essential—necessary, basic: A person must eat a variety of foods to obtain all the *essential* vitamins and minerals.

estimate—rough calculation: The contractor submitted a written *estimate* of the cost of a new roof.

estranged—alienated, separated: Her *estranged* husband had moved out six months previously.

etymology—origin and history of a word, study of the changes in words: The *etymology* of ''bedlam'' has been traced back to ''Bethlehem,'' the name of a London hospital for the mentally ill.

evacuate—to empty, clear out: The authorities ordered the town *evacuated* when the waters rose.

evaluate—to determine the value of: The purpose of the survey is to *evaluate* the effect of the new teaching methods on the students' progress.

evasive—avoiding direct confrontation: She admitted that she had been there but was *evasive* about her reasons.

evolution—gradual change: Through the discovery of ancient bones and artifacts, anthropologists hope to chart the *evolution* of the human species.

exacting—severe in making demands: She was an *exacting* tutor, never content with less than perfection from her pupils.

examine—to investigate, to test: The doctor *examined* the patient for symptoms of pneumonia.

exceed—to go beyond, surpass: The business's profits for this year *exceeded* last year's profits by $16,000.

excess—amount beyond what is necessary or desired: When the pieces are in place, wipe away the *excess* glue.

exclude—to shut out, not permit to enter or participate: The children made a pact that all adults were to be *excluded* from the clubhouse.

execute—to put into effect, perform: He *executed* the duties of his office conscientiously.

exemplary—serving as a pattern, deserving imitation: The leader's *exemplary* behavior in both her private and public life made her a model for all to follow.

exempt—excused: Having broken his leg, the child was *exempt* from gym for the rest of the term.

exhibit—to show, display: The paintings were *exhibited* in the municipal museum.

expansion—enlargement in scope or size: The company's *expansion* into foreign markets has increased its profits.

expedite—to speed, facilitate: In order to *expedite* delivery of the letter, he sent it special delivery.

expel—to push or force out: When a balloon bursts, the air is *expelled* in a rush.

expenditure—a spending: The finished mural more than justified the *expenditure* of time and money necessary for its completion.

experiment—test undertaken to demonstrate or discover something: *Experiments* were devised to test how motor skills were affected by emotional states.

expertise—skill or technical knowledge of an expert: The *expertise* with which she handled the animal delighted the spectators.

explicitly—openly, without disguise: When the annoying visitor refused to take a hint, the host told him *explicitly* that it was time he left.

exploit—to use, especially unfairly or selfishly:

Some employers *exploit* the labor of illegal immigrants, who are afraid to complain about long hours and substandard wages.

exquisite—perfect, especially in a lovely, finely tuned or delicate way: The handmade lace was *exquisite* in every detail.

extensive—broad, of wide scope, thorough: Several hundred persons were interviewed as part of an *extensive* survey.

facade—front of a building: People come from miles around to admire the *facade* of St. Marks' Church.

facilitate—to make easy or less difficult, free from impediment, lessen the labor of: This piece of machinery will *facilitate* production.

facility—ease: Her *facility* in reading several languages made her ideal for the cataloguing job.

fallible—capable of erring or being deceived in judgment: It is a shock for children to discover that their parents are *fallible*.

falter—to hesitate, stammer, flinch: He speaks with a *faltering* tongue.

fanatic—person with an unreasoning enthusiasm: The *fanatics* were eager to die for the glory of their religion.

fantastic—fanciful, produced or existing only in the imagination: Her story was so *fantastic* that no one could believe it.

fatigue—mental or physical weariness: After a full day's work, their *fatigue* was understandable.

favoritism—unfair favoring of one person over others: *Favoritism* in the office based on personal friendship is resented.

feasible—able to be performed or executed by human means or agency, practicable: It is *feasible* to plan to complete the project by July.

fiscal—financial, having to do with funds: The administration's *fiscal* policy entailed tighter controls on credit.

flammable—capable of being kindled into flame: They were careful to keep the material away from sparks because it was *flammable*.

fluctuate—to change continually from one direction to another: Stock market prices *fluctuate* unpredictably when the economy is unstable.

foresight—a looking ahead: She had the *foresight* to realize that the restaurant would be busy, so she called ahead for reservations.

forfeit—to lose because of a fault: The team made a couple of decisive errors and so *forfeited* their lead.

formality—fixed or conventional procedure, act or custom; quality of being formal: Skipping the *formality* of a greeting, she got straight to the point. The *formality* of his attire was entirely appropriate to the ceremonious occasion.

forum—place for public business or discussion: A television interview would be the best *forum* for bringing our views to the attention of the public.

forward—to promote, send, especially to a new address: The secretary promised to *forward* the request to the person in charge.

fracture—a break, split: He sustained a compound *fracture* of the left leg.

fraud—intentional deceit for the purpose of cheating: The land development scheme was a *fraud* in which gullible investors lost tens of thousands of dollars.

fraudulent—false, deceiving for gain: His claim to be the true heir was exposed as *fraudulent*.

fundamental—basic: Education is *fundamental* to your future security.

furious—full of madness, raging, transported with passion: The animal was so *furious* that it had to be confined.

futile—trifling, useless, pointless: The entire matter was dropped because the arguments were *futile*.

genial—pleasant, friendly: The president's rotund and *genial* face made him the perfect Santa Claus.

geriatrics—science of care for the aged: Our longer life span has made the study of *geriatrics* increasingly important.

germane—pertinent, on the subject at hand: The point, though true, was not *germane* to the argument.

glutton—person habitually greedy for food and drink: The man was too much of a *glutton* to stick to any diet.

gracious—socially graceful, courteous, kind: A *gracious* host puts his guests at ease and is concerned only that they enjoy themselves.

grandeur—splendor, magnificence, stateliness: The *grandeur* of the lofty mountains was admired by all.

gratuity—tip: He left a *gratuity* for the chambermaid.

gregarious—fond of company: They are a *gregarious* couple who cultivate many friendships among diverse people.

gruff—rough: His manner was so *gruff* that most of the children feared him.

gullible—easily deceived: Naive people are often *gullible*.

habitable—capable of being inhabited or lived in, capable of sustaining human beings: The climate of the North Pole makes it scarcely *habitable*.

haggard—gaunt, careworn, wasted by hardship or terror: After three days of being lost on the mountain, the *haggard* campers staggered into the village.

hallucination—apparent perceiving of things not present: In her *hallucinations* she saw bizarre faces and heard voices calling to her.

haphazard—random, without order: He studied in such a *haphazard* manner that he learned nothing.

harass—to annoy with repeated attacks: The students perpetually *harassed* the teacher with unnecessary questions.

hazardous—dangerous: Trucks carrying *hazardous* materials such as explosives are not permitted on the bridge.

hectic—fevered, hurried and confused: The tour turned out to be somewhat *hectic*, covering three cities in as many days.

heterogeneous—composed of unlike elements: Since the school favored *heterogeneous* groupings, there was a wide range of ability and achievement in every class.

hinder—to retard, slow down, prevent from moving forward: Cold weather has *hindered* the growth of the plants.

hindsight—a looking backward: With *hindsight* I realize that everything she said to me was true, though I couldn't accept it at the time.

homicide—killing of one person by another: Killing in self-defense is considered justifiable *homicide*.

homogeneous—same, uniform throughout: The entering class was fairly *homogeneous;* nearly all the students were the same age and from similar middle-class homes.

horizontal—flat, parallel to the horizon: *Horizontal* stripes are frequently unflattering because they make the figure appear wider.

hospitable—welcoming, generous to guests: It was a *hospitable* room, with a soothing color scheme and deep, comfortable chairs.

hostile—conflicting, antagonistic, expressing enmity: Many tribes were *hostile* to the white settlers, just as the settlers viewed the Indians as enemies and rivals for the land.

huddle—to crowd together, press together without order or regularity: The crowd *huddled* under the shelter to get out of the rain.

hypertension—high blood pressure: *Hypertension* is often linked with serious diseases.

illicit—not licensed: *Illicit* love is the root of many divorce actions.

illuminate—to throw light on, explain: The editor's notes *illuminated* the more obscure passages in the text.

illusion—false appearance, vision that is misleading: The optical *illusion* made the lines of equal length appear to be unequal.

immune—not susceptible, protected, as from disease: An inoculation for smallpox makes one *immune* to the disease.

impartial—not favoring one side or another: The squabbling children appealed to the babysitter for an *impartial* judgment.

impassioned—animated, excited, expressive of passion or ardor: The *impassioned* performance of the actor was moving and convincing.

impediment—hindrance, something that delays or stops progress: Lack of training may be an *impediment* to advancement.

impel—to drive forward, push, incite: Although she was not personally involved, her sense of justice *impelled* her to speak out.

imperative—of greatest necessity or importance: This is an emergency; it is *imperative* that I reach them at once.

imperil—to put in danger: The incompetence of the pilot *imperiled* the safety of all on board.

impervious—not to be penetrated or passed through: Heavy cardboard is *impervious* to light.

impetuous—impulsive, acting suddenly and without forethought: The *impetuous* boy leaped before he looked.

imply—to suggest, say without stating directly: Although they said nothing about it, their cool manner *implied* strong disapproval of the scheme.

imprecise—not precise, vague, inaccurate: The description was *imprecise* because the witness had had only a fleeting glimpse of the man.

impressive—having the power of affecting or of exciting attention and feeling: The view was so *impressive* that we'll never forget it.

impunity—exemption from punishment, penalty, injury or loss: No person should be permitted to violate the laws with *impunity*.

inadequate—not equal to the purpose, insufficient to effect the object: He could not maintain his car because of *inadequate* funds.

inarticulate—not able to speak or speak clearly, not distinct as words: The *inarticulate* noises of the infant soon give way to recognizable words.

incarcerate—to imprison: The sheriff ordered the prisoner *incarcerated*.

inception—beginning: The scheme was harebrained from its *inception;* it was no surprise when it was abandoned.

incessant—unceasing, uninterrupted, continual: The *incessant* rain kept the children indoors all day.

incompatibility—inconsistency, lack of agreement, inability to get along: The *incompatibility* of their tastes made for endless disagreement.

inconsiderable—not worthy of consideration or notice, unimportant, small, trivial: The distance between Minneapolis and St. Paul is *inconsiderable.*

incontestable—not able to be disputed or denied: With the development of the atomic bomb, U.S. military superiority became *incontestable.*

increase—to enlarge, become greater, multiply: Class attendance *increased* by 30 percent after the flu epidemic ended.

incriminate—to accuse or implicate in a crime or fault: Picked up by the police, the boy *incriminated* his companions by naming them as accomplices in the theft.

indelible—not able to be erased, blotted out or washed away: The form must be signed in *indelible* ink; pencil is not acceptable.

indict—to accuse formally: The grand jury *indicted* two of the company's executives.

indigent—poor, penniless: The home is for the *indigent* aged who depend on the state for support.

indiscriminate—not selective: The police made *indiscriminate* arrests, taking into custody scores of people who had broken no law.

indolent—lazy: An *indolent* student never learns much.

inept—incompetent, clumsy, inefficient: The basketball team's center is tall and powerful but so physically *inept* that he frequently loses the ball.

infer—to conclude from reasoning or implication: From hints that the student dropped, the instructor *inferred* that she was having problems at home.

inflammatory—tending to arouse to anger or violence: An *inflammatory* speech incited the crowd to riot.

inflate—to blow up or swell, to increase beyond what is right or reasonable: The store is able to get away with charging *inflated* prices because of its convenient location and long hours.

infraction—violation, breaking of a law or regulation: The building inspector noted several *infractions* of the health and safety codes.

initiate—to begin, introduce: The fraternity *initiates* new members every semester.

innocuous—harmless: His words were *innocuous,* but his look could have killed.

innovation—something new, a change, as in custom or method: The celebration of the Mass in languages other than Latin is a major twentieth-century *innovation* in the Roman Catholic Church.

inquisitive—curious, asking questions: Private eyes in detective fiction often get into trouble for being too *inquisitive.*

insatiable—never satisfied, always greedy: His appetite for wealth was *insatiable;* no matter how rich he became, he always craved more.

insert—to put into something else: The nurse *inserted* the needle into the patient's arm.

insignificant—not important, too small to matter: The difference in scores between the two groups was statistically *insignificant.*

inspect—to examine, view closely: She *inspected* the cloth for rips or tears.

instruct—to teach, direct: The employees were *instructed* in the use of the computers during the training session.

insufficient—inadequate to a need, use or purpose: The provisions are *insufficient* in quantity.

insure—to make certain, guarantee: Bail is set to *insure* the defendant's appearance in court. *Also:* **ensure.**

intangible—not able to be touched or easily defined: The company's goodwill among its customers is a genuine but *intangible* asset.

integrate—to absorb into an organization or group: Company orientation programs help to *integrate* new employees into an existing organization.

intend—to mean, signify, plan: They *intend* to make repairs on their old car.

intensive—concentrated, intense: *Intensive* private tutoring is needed to take care of this student's reading problem.

intercept—to cut off, meet something before it reaches its destination: The missile was *intercepted* and destroyed before it reached its target.

intractable—stubborn, unruly: An *intractable* person is slow to learn a new way of life.

intrepid—brave, fearless: The *intrepid* explorers stepped out onto the lunar surface.

inventory—the stock or goods of a business, list of stock or property: The annual *inventory* check showed that several cartons of paper had been damaged by water.

investigation—close examination and observation, inquiry: The *investigation* showed that arson was the cause of the blaze.

invoice—a bill, itemized list of goods sent to a buyer: The book was packed with the *invoice* charging $24.00, including shipping.

irreplaceable—not able to be replaced: The painting is priceless in the sense that it is *irreplaceable;* it is the only one of its kind.

irritate—to annoy, inflame: The harsh cleansers used in the job can *irritate* the skin.

jeopardy—risk, danger, especially the legal situation of a person on trial: Do not put your health in *jeopardy* by exposing yourself to infection needlessly. A person shall not be put in *jeopardy* twice for the same offense.

judicial—having to do with courts or judges: Chief Justice of the Supreme Court is the highest *judicial* position in the United States.

judicious—prudent: His policy was *judicious,* he got results without taking great risks.

justify—to prove by evidence, verify, absolve: The defendant was able to *justify* her statement with evidence.

lament—to bewail, mourn for: The boy *lamented* the death of his father.

lapse—slip, minor or temporary fault or error: I was embarrassed by a momentary *lapse* of memory when I couldn't recall her name.

larceny—legal term for theft: The shoplifter was apprehended and charged with petty *larceny.*

legacy—something inherited: He acquired the house as a *legacy* from his grandmother.

legible—written clearly, able to be read: Please print or type if your handwriting is not easily *legible.*

legislature—lawmaking body: The federal *legislature* of the United States, the Congress, has two houses.

legitimate—lawful, genuine: The government is a *legitimate* one, duly elected by the people in free elections.

leniency—mercy, gentleness, lack of strictness: The *leniency* of the court in suspending the sentence was well repaid by the convicted man's later contribution to the community.

liability—debt, something disadvantageous: An older person returning to the job market may find his or her age a *liability.*

liable—legally responsible; likely, in a negative sense: If you trip and hurt yourself on the stairs because the light is out, the landlord is *liable.* He is *liable* to lose his temper when he hears the news.

limitation—restriction: There is a *limitation* on time in which you can redeem the ticket.

logical—according to reason or logic: Using the data from the experiment, he made a *logical* conclusion about the eating habits of white mice.

longevity—life span, long life: The Bible credits the first generations of men with a *longevity* unheard of today.

lucid—clear, transparent: The directions were written in a style so *lucid* that a child could follow them.

lurid—shocking, sensational, tastelessly violent or passionate: The cheap novel told a *lurid* tale of murder and lust.

magnitude—size: The apparent *magnitude* of the moon is greater near the horizon than at the zenith.

mar—to damage: The floor has been *marred* by scratches and scuff marks.

margin—edge, border: Cattails grow in the swampy area at the *margin* of the pond.

marquee—roof projecting from a building over the sidewalk: The theater's *marquee* protects patrons from the rain.

matriarch—mother who rules a family or clan: All important decisions were referred to the *matriarch* of the tribe.

maximum—most: In this course the *maximum* number of cuts allowed is six.

median—middle, middle item in a series: In a series of seven items the fourth is the *median.*

medicinal—having the property of healing: The plants had a high *medicinal* value.

mediocre—of average or middle quality: A *mediocre* student in high school will rank low among candidates for college.

memorandum—written reminder, informal written interoffice communication. The office manager circulated a *memorandum* outlining the procedures to be followed in the fire drill. *Plural:* **memoranda.**

menace—to threaten, express an intention to inflict injury: The periodic floods *menaced* the city with destruction.

merchant—shopkeeper, one who buys and sells goods for a profit: The *merchants* who operate businesses in the mall have formed an association.

meticulous—showing careful attention to detail, very precise: The sewing in the jacket was so *meticulous* that one could hardly see the stitches.

militant—defiant, ready to fight, especially for a cause: *Militant* in their political beliefs, they considered any compromise a sellout.

mingle—to mix, join a group: The mayor *mingled* with the crowd at the reception, shaking hands and thanking her supporters.

miniature—very small, done on a scale smaller than usual: The *miniature* microphone could be concealed in a piece of jewelry.

minute—tiny; very precise: The device records the presence of even *minute* amounts of radiation. The writer's *minute* attention to the refinements of style resulted in an elegantly worded essay. Pronounced: "my-noot."

miscalculate—to calculate erroneously: *Miscalculating* the distance, he fell short.

miscellany—collection of various or unlike things: The old steamer trunk contained a *miscellany* of papers, clothes and assorted junk.

misdemeanor—a misbehaving, a minor legal offense: The *misdemeanor* resulted in a $50 fine.

molest—to disturb, annoy, bother: The children were warned not to *molest* the bulldog.

monetary—pertaining to money, consisting of money, financial: A penny is the smallest *monetary* unit in this country.

monitor—to watch over, check on: An office was set up to *monitor* all radio broadcasts originating within the country.

morale—level of spirits, mental or emotional condition: After a landslide victory at the polls, *morale* in the party was at a peak.

mortgage—to pledge property as security for a loan: Few people can afford to buy a house without taking a *mortgage* on it.

motivation—reason for doing something: The *motivation* for her questions was not mere curiosity but a genuine desire to help.

mutilate—to cut up, damage severely: The computer cannot read a *mutilated* card.

necessitate—to render unavoidable, compel: Sickness *necessitated* a long hospital stay.

negate—to make nothing, undo or make ineffective: The witness's full confession *negated* the need for further questions.

neglectful—careless, heedless: Because he was *neglectful* of his duties as principal, he was asked to resign by the board of education.

negligible—too small or insignificant to be worthy of consideration: The difference in their ages is *negligible*.

negotiate—to bargain, confer with the intent of reaching an agreement: As long as both sides are willing to *negotiate* in good faith, a strike can be avoided.

noncompliance—failure to comply: His *non-compliance* with the terms of the contract forced them to sue.

nonsensical—meaningless, characterized by nonsense: Until analyzed and interpreted, dreams often seem *nonsensical*.

normal—regular, average, usual: The doctor found that her blood pressure and temperature were *normal*.

notify—to let know, inform: Applicants will be *notified* of the results by mail.

notorious—famous in an unfavorable way: The official was *notorious* among his associates for failing to keep appointments.

novice—person new to a job or activity, someone inexperienced: A *novice* in the job, she needed more time than an experienced worker to complete the same tasks.

noxious—harmful, injurious, unwholesome: The *noxious* fumes from the refinery poisoned the air.

null and void—legal expression for not valid, without legal force: If it is not properly signed, the will may be declared *null and void*.

nullify—to make void or without effect: The new contract *nullifies* their previous agreement.

obesity—excessive fatness: Her *obesity* was due to her love of rich foods.

obituary—account of the decease of a person: Newspapers keep files on famous people in case they have to run an *obituary*.

objective—(*adj*) unbiased, not influenced by personal involvement, detached: It is extremely difficult to be *objective* about one's own weaknesses. (*n*) aim, goal: Our *objective* is greater efficiency; we must study the possible means to that goal.

obligatory—required, morally or legally binding: He feels nothing in common with his family, yet he makes an *obligatory* visit to them once or twice a year.

obliterate—to demolish, destroy all trace of: The building had been *obliterated;* we could not even be sure exactly where it had stood.

oblivious—so preoccupied as not to notice: The patron, absorbed in her reading, was *oblivious* to the librarian's question.

obnoxious—odious, hateful, offensive, repugnant: They left because of the *obnoxious* odors.

obscure—dim, murky, not easily seen or understood: Despite attempts at interpretation, the meaning of the passage remains *obscure*.

observable—able to be seen, noticeable: There has been no *observable* change in the patient's condition.

obsess—to beset, haunt the mind: He was *obsessed* with the idea that he was being followed.

obsolete—outmoded, no longer in use or appropriate: Since several offices have been relocated, the old directory is *obsolete*.

obstacle—hindrance, something that bars a path or prevents progress: She refused to think of her handicap as an *obstacle* to a fulfilling career.

obvious—self-evident: The truth was *obvious* to the well-informed.

occasionally—sometimes, from time to time: We go to the theater *occasionally*.

omit—to leave out, pass by, neglect: He *omitted* an important passage when he read his speech.

onus—burden, responsibility: The *onus* of proof is on the accuser; the defendant is presumed innocent until proved guilty.

operational—in working order, able to be operated: The elevator will not be *operational* until tomorrow; it is being repaired.

optimum—best for a purpose, most favorable: Under *optimum* conditions of light and moisture, the plant will grow to over three feet.

optional—not required, open to choice: Air conditioning is *optional;* its cost is not included in the sticker price.

origin—beginning, source: The *origin* of the irrational fear was in a childhood catastrophe.

outcome—result, end: The *outcome* of the race was never in doubt.

pacific—calm, tranquil, placid: The explorer who named the ocean *pacific* found it free from storms and tempests.

painstaking—very careful or diligent: The search for the lost ring was long and *painstaking*.

pamphlet—very brief, paperbound book or treatise: The planes dropped *pamphlets* urging the population to surrender and promising fair treatment.

panic—sudden and overwhelming terror, exaggerated alarm: When the children heard the noise, they fled the old house in *panic*.

paralyze—to unnerve or render ineffective: The catastrophe *paralyzed* the community.

parole—conditional release, release from prison before full sentence is served: Freed on *parole,* the convict was required to report periodically to an officer assigned to his case.

partially—in part: Bald tires were *partially* responsible for the skid; however, slick road conditions also contributed.

participate—to take part in: At the meet all contestants will *participate* in the opening festivities.

partition—division into parts: The present *partition* of Germany followed from the occupation of the country by the Allied forces in World War II.

peculiar—odd, special, unique, not ordinary: The fragrance is *peculiar* to violets; no other flower smells the same.

penal—concerning legal punishment: The *penal* code defines crimes and their legal penalties.

pending—waiting to be decided: Our petition is still *pending;* we don't know what will be decided.

pension—regular payments to someone who has fulfilled certain requirements: After twenty years of service she retired on a full *pension*.

per capita—for each person: The country has a *per capita* income of under $800.

perceive—to feel, comprehend, note, understand: I *perceived* that the beast was harmless.

perforate—to make holes in: The top of the box had been *perforated* to allow the air to circulate.

peripheral—of an edge or boundary: The person who notices people almost behind him has excellent *peripheral* vision.

perpendicular—in an up-and-down direction, vertical, upright, at a right angle: The lamp post, having been grazed by the truck, was no longer *perpendicular*.

perpetrate—to do something evil, to commit, as a crime: The committee *perpetrated* the hoax in an attempt to defame the rival candidate.

persist—to continue, especially against opposition: Despite the rebuffs, he *persisted* in his efforts to befriend the disturbed youngster.

pertinent—relevant, concerning the matter at hand: Since those circumstances were vastly different, that example is not *pertinent* to this case.

petty—small, trivial, unimportant, small-minded: Don't bother the supervisor with *petty* problems but try to handle them yourself.

placate—to soothe the anger of, pacify: A quick temper is often easily *placated*.

placid—peaceful, undisturbed: The drug had relieved her anxiety, leaving her in a *placid* and jovial mood.

plausible—seeming credible, likely, trustworthy: Since his clothes were soaked, his story of falling into the creek seemed *plausible*.

pliable—flexible, able to bend, readily influenced, yielding: Having no preconceived opinion on the matter, we were *pliable*, ready to be swayed by a forceful speech.

portable—able to be carried easily: The *portable* typewriter was equipped with a carrying case.

posterity—succeeding generations: Many things we build today are for *posterity*.

postmark—official mark on a piece of mail showing the post office from which it was delivered and the date: Although the letter had been written in Tulsa, the *postmark* showed that it had been mailed from Omaha.

potential—possible, not yet realized: If she qualifies for the promotion, her *potential* earnings for the next year might be close to $20,000.

precarious—insecure: The animal had found a *precarious* perch on the window ledge.

precedent—similar earlier event, especially one used as a model or justification for present action: The lawyer's brief argued that the legal *precedents* cited by the opposition were not relevant because of subsequent changes in the law.

precipitous—steep like a precipice: The road had a *precipitous* drop on the south side.

precise—exact: The coroner determined the *precise* time of murder by examining the victim.

preclude—to make impossible: Obeying the speed limit would *preclude* my getting home in five minutes.

predatory—plundering, hunting: The hawk is a *predatory* bird.

predecessor—one who has preceded or gone before another in a position or office: In his inaugural address the new president of the association praised the work done by his *predecessor*.

predicament—troublesome or perplexing situation from which escape seems difficult: Having promised to balance the budget, to cut taxes and to increase defense spending, the newly-elected president found himself in a hopeless *predicament*.

predominantly—for the most part: Although there are a few older students, the class is *predominantly* made up of eighteen-year-olds.

preempt—to exclude others by taking first: Regularly scheduled programs were *preempted* by convention coverage.

prejudiced—biased, judging in advance without adequate evidence: Since I have never liked Westerns, I was *prejudiced* against the film before I ever saw it.

preliminary—going before the main event or business, introductory: A few easy *preliminary* questions put the applicant at ease.

premature—not yet mature or ripe, happening too soon: As she got to know him better, she decided that her initial judgment of him had been *premature*.

prescribe—to recommend, especially in a professional capacity: For the headache the physician *prescribed* aspirin.

presume—to accept as true without proof; to anticipate or take for granted, overstep bounds: An accused person is *presumed* innocent until proved guilty. I was furious that she had *presumed* to take the car without permission.

prevalent—current, widely found, common: Feelings of anger and helplessness are *prevalent* among the voters in that district.

preventive—aiming to prevent or keep from happening: *Preventive* measures must be taken to guard against malaria.

primary—first, most important: Our *primary* goal is to train people for jobs that are actually available; other aspects of the program are secondary.

prior—earlier, and therefore usually taking precedence: The director will not be able to meet with you today due to a *prior* engagement.

privileged—exempt from usual conditions, receiving special benefit; not to be made known, confidential: Only a few *privileged* outsiders have been permitted to observe the ceremony. Since communications between spouses are *privileged*, a man cannot be compelled to testify against his wife.

probability—likelihood: The *probability* that your plane will crash is practically nil.

probation—period of testing or evaluation: After a week's *probation* the employee was hired permanently.

proceed—to go forward, continue: Because of numerous interruptions, the work *proceeded* slowly.

proclaim—to announce loudly, publicly and with conviction: When the victory was announced, a holiday was *proclaimed* and all work ground to a halt.

procrastinate—to delay doing something, put off without reason: Since you'll have to get it done eventually, you might as well stop *procrastinating* and get started.

procure—to get, obtain, cause to occur: At the last

minute the convict's attorney *procured* a stay of execution.

prolong—to draw out to greater length: The treatment *prolongs* life but cannot cure the disease, which is terminal.

prompt—quick, following immediately: Correspondents appreciate *prompt* replies to their inquiries.

proper—suitable, appropriate: It is *proper* to write a letter of thanks to someone who has given you a present.

prosper—to thrive, do well, grow richer: An expensive suit and a new car suggested that the man's business was *prospering*.

protagonist—leading character: Mike Hammer is the *protagonist* of a whole series of detective stories.

provisional—temporary, for the time being only: The *provisional* government stepped down after the general elections.

provocation—a provoking, a cause for resentment or attack: The attack, coming without *provocation*, took them by surprise.

proximity—nearness: The *proximity* of the shopping mall is a great advantage to those residents who don't drive.

punctuality—being on time: The train had an excellent record for *punctuality;* it almost always arrived precisely at 8:15.

purchase—to buy: We need to *purchase* or borrow a tent before we can go camping.

qualification—that which makes one qualified or eligible: The applicant's *qualifications* for the position are a degree in library science and two years' experience in a small branch library.

quantity—amount: Speeding up the process would result in an increased *quantity* but a poorer quality.

quench—to extinguish, put out: She *quenched* the flames with water.

query—to question: He *queried* the witness about his alibi.

quote—to cite word for word, as a passage from some author, to name or repeat: He *quoted* the words of Woodrow Wilson in his acceptance speech.

rabid—furious, raging; suffering from rabies: The *rabid* animal was destroyed before it could bite anyone.

radiation—divergence in all directions from a point, especially of energy: Solar *radiation* is the *radiation* of the sun as estimated from the amount of energy that reaches the earth.

randomly—in an unplanned or haphazard way, without order or pattern: The papers had been strewn *randomly* about the room.

rapidity—speed: The *rapidity* with which her hands flew over the piano keys was too great to follow with the eye.

ratify—to give formal approval to: The proposed amendment must be *ratified* by the states before it can become law.

ratio—proportion, fixed relation of number or amount between two things: The *ratio* of women to men in middle-level positions in the firm is only one to seven.

rebuff—a snub, repulse, blunt or impolite refusal: When overtures of friendship are met with *rebuff*, they are not likely to be renewed.

rebuke—to reprimand, criticize sharply: He *rebuked* the puppy in stern tones for chewing up the chair.

rebuttal—contradiction, reply to a charge or argument. Each side was allowed five minutes for *rebuttal* of the other side's arguments.

recapitulate—to mention or relate in brief, summarize: The abstract *recapitulated* the main points of the argument.

recede—to go back or away: The waters *receded* and left the beach covered with seaweed.

receptive—able and tending to receive and accept, open to influence: The manager, unsatisfied with the store's appearance, was *receptive* to the idea of a major remodeling.

recipient—one who receives: The *recipient* of the award had been chosen from among 200 candidates.

reciprocal—done in return, affecting both sides, mutual: The United States has *reciprocal* trade agreements with many nations.

reckless—not thinking of consequences, heedless, causing danger: People who feel they have nothing to lose often become *reckless*.

reconsider—to think over again: When he refused the appointment, the committee asked whether he would *reconsider* his decision if more money were offered.

recreation—relaxation, play: Physical *recreation* often relieves tension and improves the emotional outlook.

rectitude—honesty, integrity, strict observance of what is right: Her unfailing *rectitude* in business dealings made her well trusted among her associates.

recuperate—to become well, get better: It is best to stay home from work until you have *recuperated* completely.

recur—to happen again: Unless social conditions are improved, the riots are bound to *recur*.

redundant—wordy, repeating unnecessarily: The expressions "more preferably" and "continue to remain" are *redundant*.

refrain—to keep from doing something, to not do: Considerate parents *refrain* from criticizing their children in front of others.

rehabilitate—to restore to a former state or capacity: The stated object of the program is to *rehabilitate* ex-offenders.

reimburse—to refund, pay back: The company found it difficult to *reimburse* the salesman for all his expenses.

reiterate—to repeat: The instructions were *reiterated* before each new section of the test.

relevant—concerning the matter at hand, to the point, related: Her experience in government is *relevant* to her candidacy; her devotion to her family is not.

relinquish—to give up, hand over: The aunt *relinquished* custody of the child to its mother.

reminisce—to remember, talk about the past: When old friends get together, they love to *reminisce*.

remit—to pay, to send payment: The invoice was *remitted* by check; you should be receiving it shortly.

remuneration—reward, payment, as for work done: Health benefits are part of the *remuneration* that goes with the position.

renounce—to give up or disown, usually by formal statement: The nation was urged to *renounce* its dependence on imports and to buy more American cars.

replenish—to supply again, to make full or complete again something that has been depleted: Some natural resources, such as lumber, can be *replenished*.

repress—to subdue, hold back, keep down, keep from expression or consciousness: We could not *repress* a certain nervousness as the plane bumped along the runway.

reprimand—severe criticism, especially a formal rebuke by someone in authority: Since it was a first offense, the judge let the teenager off with a *reprimand*.

reprisal—injury in return for injury: The Israelis launched a raid in *reprisal* for the night attack.

request—to ask for: The students *requested* a meeting with the college president to discuss the new policy.

requisition—formal written order or request: The office manager sent in a *requisition* for another desk and chair.

rescind—to cancel formally or take back: They *rescinded* their offer of aid when they became disillusioned with the project.

reserve—to keep back or save for use at a later time; to set aside for the use of a particular person: The runner had *reserved* energy for a burst of speed in the final lap. Call the restaurant to *reserve* a table for four.

residence—place where a person lives, fact of living in a place: According to the phone company, that number is a *residence*, not a business.

resilient—able to spring back: The spring was still *resilient* after years of use.

respondent—person who responds or answers: Several *respondents* refused to answer most of the questions in the survey.

restrict—to confine, keep within limits: Use of the computer room is *restricted* to authorized personnel.

resume—to begin again after an interruption: The courtroom proceedings *resumed* after an hour's recess for lunch.

resuscitate—to bring back to life: Artificial respiration was used to *resuscitate* the swimmer.

retain—to keep: Throughout the grueling day she had managed somehow to *retain* her sense of humor.

retaliate—to give injury for injury: The boxer *retaliated* for the punch with a stunning blow to the head.

retard—to slow: Drugs were successfully used to *retard* the progress of the disease.

retroactive—applying to what is past: A law cannot be made *retroactive;* it can only apply to future actions.

reveal—to make known, display: His dishonesty was *revealed* during the trial.

reverence—feeling of deep respect or awe, as for something sacred: The great novelist was disconcerted by the *reverence* with which her students greeted her most casual remark.

revive—to come or bring back to life: A cool drink and a bath *revived* her spirits.

robust—hardy, strong, healthy: Her *robust* health was apparent in her springy walk and glowing skin.

rue—to be sorry for, regret: He *rued* the day he made that mistake.

rupture—a breaking off, breach: The bungling of the rescue operation, which resulted in the death of the ambassador, led to a *rupture* of diplomatic relations between the two nations.

salvage—to save or recover from disaster, such as shipwreck or fire: Divers *salvaged* gold coins and precious artifacts from the sunken Spanish galleon.

salvation—act of preserving from danger, destruction or great calamity: The governor's strategy of delay proved to be the *salvation* of the province.

saturate—to fill fully, soak, cause to become completely penetrated: The cloth was thoroughly *saturated* with the soapy water.

scrupulous—having scruples, conscientiously honest and upright: That attorney is too *scrupulous* to get involved in racketeering.

secular—not religious, not concerned with religion: The *secular* authorities often have differences with the church in Italy.

secure—(*adj*) safe, reliable, free from fear or danger: Her *secure* job assured her of a steady income for as long as she chose to work. (*v*) to make safe, to obtain: I have *secured* two tickets for tonight's performance.

severe—harsh, extreme, serious: The tough drug laws required *severe* penalties for repeat offenders.

simultaneous—happening or existing at the same time: There were *simultaneous* broadcasts of the game on local television and radio stations.

site—piece of land considered as a location for something, such as a city: The archeologists began excavations at the *site* of the ancient city.

skepticism—doubt, partial disbelief: He listened to the fantastic story with obvious *skepticism*. *Also:* **scepticism.**

slander—spoken false statement damaging to a person's reputation: The witness was guilty of *slander* when he falsely testified that his partner had connived in the tax fraud scheme.

slate—to put on a list, to schedule: The meeting is *slated* for next Tuesday.

smirk—annoyingly smug or conceited smile: His arrogant behavior and *smirk* of satisfaction whenever he won made him unpopular with the fans.

soporific—causing sleep: Because of the drug's *soporific* effect, you should not try to drive after taking it.

specialize—to adapt to a special condition, concentrate on only one part of a field or endeavor: The assembly line caused labor to become more *specialized* as each worker performed only a small part of the whole manufacturing process.

specific—precise, well-defined, not general: The patron was not looking for any *specific* book but had just come in to browse.

spontaneous—coming from natural impulse, having no external cause, unplanned: Oily rags improperly disposed of may cause a fire by *spontaneous* combustion.

sporadic—occasional, happening at random intervals: He made *sporadic* attempts to see his estranged wife.

squalid—wretched, filthy, miserable: The *squalid* shantytown was infested with vermin and rife with disease.

stalemate—deadlock, situation in which neither side in a game or contest can make a move: Talks have reached a *stalemate;* neither side is authorized to make the necessary concessions.

stamina—power of endurance, physical resistance to fatigue or stress: While younger swimmers tend to be faster over short distances, older swimmers often have more *stamina.*

stature—height, elevation (often used figuratively): His work in physics was widely admired in the profession and his *stature* as an expert in his field unquestioned.

status—position, rank, present condition: Her *status* as vice president allows her to take such action without prior approval by the board of directors.

stealthy—furtive, secret: While their grandfather was distracted by the phone, the children made a *stealthy* raid on the refrigerator.

sterile—free from germs, barren, infertile, unproductive, lacking in liveliness or interest: The room was depressingly *sterile* with its drab colors, bare walls, and institutional furniture.

strenuous—rugged, vigorous, marked by great energy or effort: Climbing the volcano was *strenuous* exercise even for the physically fit.

strident—harsh-sounding: She had a *strident* voice that sent shivers down my back.

stringent—severe, strict, compelling: The speaker presented *stringent* arguments for the unwelcome cutbacks.

suave—smoothly polite: His *suave* manners reflected great confidence and poise.

subdue—to overcome, calm, render less harsh or less intense: The understanding actions of the nurse helped to *subdue* the stubborn and unruly child.

submit—to give in, surrender, yield; to give, hand in: Although the doctors were dubious of his full recovery, the patient refused to *submit* to despair. The couple *submitted* their application to the loan officer.

subsidy—financial aid granted by the government: Ship operators and airlines receive federal *subsidies* in the form of mail delivery contracts.

substitute—person or thing put in place of something else: A temporary worker filled in as a *substitute* for personnel on vacation.

subversive—tending to undermine or destroy secretly: The editor was accused of disseminating propaganda *subversive* to the national security.

successive—following one after another without interruption: Last week it rained on four *successive* days.

successor—one who follows another, as in an office or job: Retiring from office, the mayor left a budget crisis and a transit strike to his *successor*.

succinct—to the point, terse: A *succinct* report summed up the situation in four words.

succor—aid, help in distress: Despite the threat of harsh reprisals, many townspeople gave *succor* to the refugees.

sufficient—ample, adequate, enough: Our supplies are *sufficient* to feed an army for a week.

summarize—to cover the main points: The newscaster *summarized* the content of the president's speech.

superficial—on or concerned with the surface only, shallow: The *superficial* review merely gave a synopsis of the movie's plot.

superfluous—extra, beyond what is necessary: It was clear from the scene what had happened; his lengthy explanations were *superfluous*.

supersede—to take the place of: The administration appointed new department heads to *supersede* the old.

supervise—to oversee, direct work, superintend: A new employee must be carefully *supervised* to insure that he learns the routine correctly and thoroughly.

supplement—to add to, especially in order to make up for a lack: The dietician recommended that she *supplement* her regular meals with iron pills.

support—to uphold, assist: I *support* our country's policy of aid to underdeveloped nations.

surpass—to excel, go beyond: The success of our program *surpassed* even our high expectations.

surrogate—acting in place of another, substituting: The housekeeper acted as *surrogate* mother for the children after their own mother died.

surveillance—a watching: The suspect was kept under *surveillance*.

susceptible—easily affected, liable: She is *susceptible* to colds because of her recent illness.

suspend—to stop or cause to be inactive temporarily; to hang: Service on the line was *suspended* while the tracks were being repaired. The light fixture was *suspended* from the beam by a chain.

systematic—orderly, following a system: A *systematic* review of hiring in the past two years revealed discrepancies between official policy and actual practice.

tangible—capable of being touched, having objective reality and value: The new position offered an opportunity for creativity as well as the more *tangible* reward of a higher salary.

tardiness—lateness: His *tardiness* was habitual; he was late getting to class most mornings.

tedious—boring, long and tiresome: The film was so *tedious* that we walked out in disgust before it was half over.

tenacity—persistence, quality of holding firmly: His *tenacity* as an investigator earned him the nickname "Bulldog."

tentative—done as a test, experiment, or trial: The negotiators have reached a *tentative* agreement, the details of which have yet to be worked out.

terminate—to end: She *terminated* the interview by standing up and thanking us for coming.

terse—to the point, using few words: The official's *terse* replies to our questions indicated that he did not welcome being interrupted.

textile—cloth, woven material: New England in the nineteenth century was dotted with *textile* mills operated by water power.

theory—speculative truth, proposition to be proved by evidence or chain of reasoning: The professor emphasized that the explanation was only a *theory* subject to verification, not an established fact.

tirade—vehement speech: He shouted a long *tirade* at the driver who had hit his car from behind.

tolerate—to permit, put up with: We *tolerate* ignorance in ourselves because we are too lazy to study.

total—complete, entire, whole: The *total* cost of our European vacation will be more than $4,000.

tractable—easily led: A *tractable* worker is a boon to a supervisor but is not always a good leader.

tranquil—quiet, calm, peaceful: The *tranquil* morning was disturbed by the appearance on the lake of a motorboat.

transcribe—to make a written copy of: These almost illegible notes must be *transcribed* before anyone else will be able to use them.

transcript—written copy: The court reporter read from the *transcript* of the witness's testimony.

transgression—a breaking of a law or commandment: We ask God to forgive our *transgressions*.

transition—change, passage from one place or state to another: The weather made a quick *transition* from sweltering to freezing.

translate—to change from one medium to another, especially from one language or code to another: The flight attendant *translated* the announcement into Spanish for the benefit of two of the passengers.

treaty—formal agreement between nations: An economic alliance between the governments was established by *treaty*.

truss—to support, tie up in a bundle: The chicken should be *trussed* with string before roasting.

turbulent—violent, in wild motion, agitated: The *turbulent* stream claimed many lives.

ubiquitous—existing everywhere: Papaya trees, *ubiquitous* in the region, bear large yellow fruits.

ultimate—final, last: After hours of soul-searching, her *ultimate* decision was no different from her original one.

unaccountable—mysterious, not able to be explained: The *unaccountable* disappearance of the family led to wild stories of flying saucers.

unavoidable—not preventable: Because he is a republican and she is a democrat, their disagreement about economic policy was *unavoidable*.

uncanny—weird, so acute as to appear mysterious: After a lifetime of fishing those waters, the old man was able to predict weather changes with *uncanny* precision.

uncouth—unrefined, awkward: The girl was so *uncouth* she could hardly handle a knife and fork and had no notion of table manners.

unethical—without or not according to moral principles: Although he did not break any law, the man's conduct in taking advantage of innocent clients was certainly *unethical*.

unilateral—one-sided, coming from or affecting one side only: The decision to separate was *unilateral;* one spouse moved out against the other's wishes.

uniformity—sameness, lack of variation: Although the temperature is pleasant, the *uniformity* in weather from season to season can become boring.

unique—without a like or equal, unmatched, single in its kind: The statue was valuable because of its *unique* beauty.

unkempt—uncombed, not cared for, disorderly: He was recognized by his *unkempt* beard.

unprecedented—never before done, without precedent: Our space program accomplished *unprecedented* feats.

unreliable—not dependable: Because of his *unreliable* attendance at conferences, the professor was not asked to prepare a speech.

unwieldy—ponderous, too bulky and clumsy to be moved easily: I need help moving this *unwieldy* mattress.

urgent—pressing, having the nature of an emergency: We received an *urgent* message to call the hospital.

utensil—implement, tool: Forks and other *utensils* are in the silverware drawer.

utilize—to use, put to use: We will *utilize* all the resources of the department in the search for the missing child.

vacant—empty, unoccupied: The *vacant* lot was overgrown with weeds.

vacate—to leave empty: The court ordered the demonstrators to *vacate* the premises.

vain—unsuccessful, useless: A *vain* rescue attempt only made the situation worse.

validity—strength, force, being supported by fact, proof or law: The bill was never paid because its *validity* could not be substantiated.

valor—worthiness, courage, strength of mind in regard to danger: His *valor* enabled him to encounter the enemy bravely.

vandal—one who deliberately disfigures or destroys property: *Vandals* broke all the windows in the vacant building.

variable—changing, fluctuating: The weather report stated that winds would be *variable*.

venerate—to respect: She was a great philanthropist whose memory deserves to be *venerated*.

verbatim—word for word, in the same words: The lawyer requested the defendant to repeat the speech *verbatim*.

verbose—using more words than are necessary, tedious because of wordiness: The paper is well-organized but *verbose;* it should be cut to half its present length.

verdant—green, fresh: The *verdant* lawn made the old house look beautiful.

verdict—decision, especially a legal judgment of guilt or innocence: In our legal system, the *ver-*

dict of a jury in convicting a defendant must be unanimous.

verge—to be on the border or edge: Their behavior *verged* on hysteria.

verify—to prove to be true, establish the proof of: You should *verify* the rumor before acting on it; it may not be true at all.

vertical—upright, in an up-and-down position: A graph is constructed around a *vertical* and a horizontal axis.

veterinary—concerning the medical treatment of animals: Reliable *veterinary* services are indispensable in areas where people raise animals for their livelihood.

vex—to irritate, distress, cause disquiet: She was periodically *vexed* by anonymous phone calls.

vigilant—watchful, on guard: As a Supreme Court justice he has always been *vigilant* against any attempt to encroach on the freedoms guaranteed by the Bill of Rights.

vindictive—unforgiving, showing a desire for revenge: Stung by the negative reviews of his film, in the interview the director made *vindictive* personal remarks about critics.

vitality—life, energy, liveliness, power to survive: She had been physically active all her life and at the age of eighty still possessed great *vitality*.

volition—deliberate will: He performed the act of his own *volition*.

voracious—ravenous, very hungry, eager to devour: The *voracious* appetite of the man startled the other guests.

waive—to forego, give up voluntarily something to which one is entitled: In cases of unusual hardship, the normal fee may be *waived*.

warp—to bend slightly throughout: The board had *warped* in the sun.

warrant—to deserve, justify: The infraction was too minor to *warrant* a formal reprimand.

weaken—to lose strength or effectiveness: His argument was *weakened* by the evidence.

weld—to join pieces of metal by compression and great heat: Steel bars were *welded* to make a frame.

wield—to use with full command or power: The soldier was skilled at *wielding* his sword.

wily—artful, cunning: He was *wily* enough to avoid detection.

wince—to shrink, as from a blow or from pain, flinch: She *winced* when the dentist touched the tooth.

worthless—having no value or use: His suggestions are *worthless* because he has not studied the problems thoroughly.

wrest—to take by violence: It was impossible for the child to *wrest* the toy from the hands of the bigger boy.

yearn—to feel longing or desire: The parents *yearned* for their recently deceased child.

zeal—ardor, fervor, enthusiasm, earnestness: She left a record for *zeal* that cannot fail to be an inspiration.

SYNONYM STRATEGIES

Knowing the meaning of the words themselves is clearly the most important factor in choosing the correct answers to Meaning of Words questions. However, a systematic approach to each synonym question can help you to choose the correct answer more quickly, to figure out the answer more intelligently when you are in doubt and to guess with greater success when you do not know the meaning at all.

The basic task in synonym questions is always the same. You must choose a word that has the same or nearly the same meaning as a given word. The Mail Handler Exam presents each word as part of a sentence. You must choose a synonym for the italicized word in the sentence. In some instances, the sentence itself gives contextual clues which make it easier for you to figure out the synonym. You should always try substituting each answer choice in place of the indicated word. This procedure may help you to find the answer. Consider the following question:

The surface of the *placid* lake was as smooth as glass. *Placid* means most nearly
(A) cold
(B) muddy
(C) deep
(D) calm

Any one of the choices might be substituted for the word *placid,* and the sentence would still make sense. However, if the surface of the lake was as smooth as glass, the water would have had to be very *calm.* Thus, while a cold, muddy, or deep lake could have a smooth surface, it is most reasonable to assume, on the basis of the sentence, that *placid* means *calm.*

Or, consider the following question:

The camel is sometimes called the ship of the *desert. Desert* means most nearly
(A) abandon
(B) ice cream
(C) sandy wasteland
(D) leave

Here the sentence is absolutely necessary to the definition of the word. Without the sentence, you would not know whether the word *desert* is to be pronounced *de·sert',* which means *to leave* or *to abandon,* or *de'sert,* which means a *sandy wasteland.* If you are not sure of your spelling, the sentence can also spare you the confusion of *desert* with *dessert,* which is the last course of a meal.

On the other hand, the sentence may be of little or no use at all in helping you to choose the synonym. The sentence may help you to determine the part of speech of the indicated word, but not its meaning, as in:

The robbery suspect has a *sallow* complexion. *Sallow* means most nearly
(A) ruddy
(B) pale
(C) pock-marked
(D) freckled

The sentence shows you a use of the word *sallow,* that it is used to describe a complexion, but it gives no clue that *sallow* means *pale.* You either know the meaning of the word or you must guess.

If the sentence is of no use in defining the word, you must rely on other clues. Perhaps you have seen the word used but were never sure what it meant. Look carefully. Can you see any part of a word of which you do know the meaning? An example:

The child who had been ill was given *remedial* classes when he returned to school. *Remedial* means most nearly
(A) reading
(B) slow
(C) corrective
(D) special

Your association is probably "remedial reading." Be careful. *Remedial* does not mean *reading*. *Remedial* is an adjective, *reading* the noun it modifies. Slow readers may receive remedial reading instruction in special classes. The *remedial* reading classes are intended to *correct* bad reading practices. Do you see the word *remedy* in *remedial*? You know that a *remedy* is a *cure* or a *correction* for an ailment. If you combine all the information you now have, you can choose *corrective* as the word which most nearly means *remedial*.

Sometimes you can figure out the meaning of a word by combining your knowledge of etymology and your general knowledge with the elimination of wrong answers. For instance:

On the poster was a picture of our town's most *infamous* citizen. *Infamous* means most nearly
(A) well-known
(B) poor
(C) disgraceful
(D) young

The first word you see when you look at *infamous* is *famous*. *Famous*, of course, means *well-known*. Since the prefix *in* often means *not*, you will eliminate A as the answer. A person who is not well-known might be poor, but not necessarily. *Poor* should not be eliminated as a possible answer, but you should carefully consider the other choices before choosing *poor*. Since *in*, meaning *not*, is a negative prefix, you should be looking for a negative word as the meaning of *infamous*. There is no choice meaning *not famous*, so you must look for negative fame. *Disgrace* is a negative kind of *fame*. A person who behaves *disgracefully* is well-known for his bad behavior; he is *infamous*. If you had chosen *young* as your answer, you would have mistakenly seen *infant* in *infamous*. You must be careful and thorough when figuring out the meanings of words.

In the past few paragraphs we have given you suggestions for figuring out the meanings of words when there is any possibility of doing so. Many synonym questions give you no such possibility. Often, you simply must know the meaning of the word.

DEVELOP YOUR VOCABULARY!

HOW TO ANSWER FOLLOWING ORAL DIRECTIONS QUESTIONS

The key to success with Following Oral Directions questions is total concentration. You must not let your attention wander for even a second. And you must be prepared to follow through instantly on whatever it is you are told to do. Many of the instructions consist of just one step on the worksheet followed by one step on the answer sheet. Such an instruction might read: "Find the smallest number on line 3 and draw one line under that number. Now, on your answer sheet find the number under which you just drew one line and blacken space C." This is a relatively simple instruction on which to follow through. The moment you hear the word "smallest" you should rivet your attention on line 3 and search out the lowest number. However, you cannot stop listening. You must know what to do with that number. "Draw one line" is uncomplicated. The two second pause which your reader will take after reading this instruction should be adequate time for you to find the smallest number and to draw one line under it. The second part of the instruction is also uncomplicated, however you must not let your attention wander while your reader is reading it. You must concentrate on which lettered space you are to blacken. You then have five seconds in which to find the number and blacken the space.

When the directions get a bit more complicated, you are given more time to follow them. If the directions tell you to circle each even number between 12 and 25, you will be allowed at least ten seconds, maybe more, to decide which numbers to circle and to circle them. Then, after the instructions which tell you what letters to darken, you will be allowed five seconds for each combination. (Please note that when the directions speak of the numbers *between 12 and 25* they mean only the numbers that fall between these two numbers, not the numbers themselves.)

The most difficult directions to carry out are ones like these: "If January comes before June and Monday comes after Wednesday, write the letter E in the left hand box: if not, write the letter A in the right hand circle." Take this one step at a time. January comes before June. Part one of the statement is true. Monday does not come after Wednesday. Part two is false. Since the directions say "and," they require both parts of the statement to be true. In this statement, one part is false, so you know you must ignore the directive to write the letter E in the left hand box. Listen hard for the direction which tells you how to proceed if the entire statement is not true. In this case, that direction is to write the letter A in the right hand circle. Whenever a direction begins with "IF" be wary and redouble your concentration. Fortunately, only a small number of the questions will be this difficult.

It is very important that you not get flustered or frantic while taking this part of your exam. You must remain calm. If you miss a portion of an instruction try to follow through without it or just let that instruction pass and be ready for the next one. Your reader is not permitted to repeat. Since the Following Oral Directions Test is marked on the basis of right answers only, one wrong answer here or there or a couple of missed questions will not be likely to rule out your candidacy for a position as Mail Handler. Just take a missed instruction in stride and listen hard for the next one. Likewise, if you go to mark a lettered space for a particular number and find that you have already darkened a space for that number, your best bet is probably to leave the mark that is there and wait for the next instruction. You may darken only one space for each number, and the time you spend erasing and changing an answer may cause you to miss the beginning of the next direction.

The paragraph in the box below should take exactly one minute to read. You may want to offer it to your reader for practice. Since this paragraph is not related to any part of the exam, your reader can read it over and over to perfect his or her reading speed. You will not see the directions on the actual exam, and you should not read the directions that go with the Model

Exams that follow. However, you certainly may read the one-minute practice paragraph below. This will help you to get a feel for how fast the instructions will come at you.

> *DIRECTIONS:* (The words in parentheses should *not* be read aloud. They tell you how long you should pause at the various spots. You should time the pauses with a watch with a second hand. The instruction "Pause slightly" means that you should stop long enough to take a breath.) You should not repeat any directions.

ONE-MINUTE PRACTICE PARAGRAPH

Look at line 20 on your worksheet. (Pause slightly.) There are two circles and two boxes of different sizes with numbers in them. If 7 is less than 3 and if 2 is smaller than 4, write a C in the larger circle. Otherwise write B as in baker in the smaller box. (Pause 10 seconds.) Now on your answer sheet darken the space for the number-letter combination in the box or circle. (Pause 5 seconds.)

SECOND MODEL EXAM ANSWER SHEET

ADDRESS CHECKING TEST

1. Ⓐ Ⓓ	17. Ⓐ Ⓓ	33. Ⓐ Ⓓ	49. Ⓐ Ⓓ	65. Ⓐ Ⓓ	81. Ⓐ Ⓓ
2. Ⓐ Ⓓ	18. Ⓐ Ⓓ	34. Ⓐ Ⓓ	50. Ⓐ Ⓓ	66. Ⓐ Ⓓ	82. Ⓐ Ⓓ
3. Ⓐ Ⓓ	19. Ⓐ Ⓓ	35. Ⓐ Ⓓ	51. Ⓐ Ⓓ	67. Ⓐ Ⓓ	83. Ⓐ Ⓓ
4. Ⓐ Ⓓ	20. Ⓐ Ⓓ	36. Ⓐ Ⓓ	52. Ⓐ Ⓓ	68. Ⓐ Ⓓ	84. Ⓐ Ⓓ
5. Ⓐ Ⓓ	21. Ⓐ Ⓓ	37. Ⓐ Ⓓ	53. Ⓐ Ⓓ	69. Ⓐ Ⓓ	85. Ⓐ Ⓓ
6. Ⓐ Ⓓ	22. Ⓐ Ⓓ	38. Ⓐ Ⓓ	54. Ⓐ Ⓓ	70. Ⓐ Ⓓ	86. Ⓐ Ⓓ
7. Ⓐ Ⓓ	23. Ⓐ Ⓓ	39. Ⓐ Ⓓ	55. Ⓐ Ⓓ	71. Ⓐ Ⓓ	87. Ⓐ Ⓓ
8. Ⓐ Ⓓ	24. Ⓐ Ⓓ	40. Ⓐ Ⓓ	56. Ⓐ Ⓓ	72. Ⓐ Ⓓ	88. Ⓐ Ⓓ
9. Ⓐ Ⓓ	25. Ⓐ Ⓓ	41. Ⓐ Ⓓ	57. Ⓐ Ⓓ	73. Ⓐ Ⓓ	89. Ⓐ Ⓓ
10. Ⓐ Ⓓ	26. Ⓐ Ⓓ	42. Ⓐ Ⓓ	58. Ⓐ Ⓓ	74. Ⓐ Ⓓ	90. Ⓐ Ⓓ
11. Ⓐ Ⓓ	27. Ⓐ Ⓓ	43. Ⓐ Ⓓ	59. Ⓐ Ⓓ	75. Ⓐ Ⓓ	91. Ⓐ Ⓓ
12. Ⓐ Ⓓ	28. Ⓐ Ⓓ	44. Ⓐ Ⓓ	60. Ⓐ Ⓓ	76. Ⓐ Ⓓ	92. Ⓐ Ⓓ
13. Ⓐ Ⓓ	29. Ⓐ Ⓓ	45. Ⓐ Ⓓ	61. Ⓐ Ⓓ	77. Ⓐ Ⓓ	93. Ⓐ Ⓓ
14. Ⓐ Ⓓ	30. Ⓐ Ⓓ	46. Ⓐ Ⓓ	62. Ⓐ Ⓓ	78. Ⓐ Ⓓ	94. Ⓐ Ⓓ
15. Ⓐ Ⓓ	31. Ⓐ Ⓓ	47. Ⓐ Ⓓ	63. Ⓐ Ⓓ	79. Ⓐ Ⓓ	95. Ⓐ Ⓓ
16. Ⓐ Ⓓ	32. Ⓐ Ⓓ	48. Ⓐ Ⓓ	64. Ⓐ Ⓓ	80. Ⓐ Ⓓ	

MEANING OF WORDS TEST

1. Ⓐ Ⓑ Ⓒ Ⓓ Ⓔ	8. Ⓐ Ⓑ Ⓒ Ⓓ Ⓔ	15. Ⓐ Ⓑ Ⓒ Ⓓ Ⓔ	22. Ⓐ Ⓑ Ⓒ Ⓓ Ⓔ	29. Ⓐ Ⓑ Ⓒ Ⓓ Ⓔ
2. Ⓐ Ⓑ Ⓒ Ⓓ Ⓔ	9. Ⓐ Ⓑ Ⓒ Ⓓ Ⓔ	16. Ⓐ Ⓑ Ⓒ Ⓓ Ⓔ	23. Ⓐ Ⓑ Ⓒ Ⓓ Ⓔ	30. Ⓐ Ⓑ Ⓒ Ⓓ Ⓔ
3. Ⓐ Ⓑ Ⓒ Ⓓ Ⓔ	10. Ⓐ Ⓑ Ⓒ Ⓓ Ⓔ	17. Ⓐ Ⓑ Ⓒ Ⓓ Ⓔ	24. Ⓐ Ⓑ Ⓒ Ⓓ Ⓔ	31. Ⓐ Ⓑ Ⓒ Ⓓ Ⓔ
4. Ⓐ Ⓑ Ⓒ Ⓓ Ⓔ	11. Ⓐ Ⓑ Ⓒ Ⓓ Ⓔ	18. Ⓐ Ⓑ Ⓒ Ⓓ Ⓔ	25. Ⓐ Ⓑ Ⓒ Ⓓ Ⓔ	32. Ⓐ Ⓑ Ⓒ Ⓓ Ⓔ
5. Ⓐ Ⓑ Ⓒ Ⓓ Ⓔ	12. Ⓐ Ⓑ Ⓒ Ⓓ Ⓔ	19. Ⓐ Ⓑ Ⓒ Ⓓ Ⓔ	26. Ⓐ Ⓑ Ⓒ Ⓓ Ⓔ	
6. Ⓐ Ⓑ Ⓒ Ⓓ Ⓔ	13. Ⓐ Ⓑ Ⓒ Ⓓ Ⓔ	20. Ⓐ Ⓑ Ⓒ Ⓓ Ⓔ	27. Ⓐ Ⓑ Ⓒ Ⓓ Ⓔ	
7. Ⓐ Ⓑ Ⓒ Ⓓ Ⓔ	14. Ⓐ Ⓑ Ⓒ Ⓓ Ⓔ	21. Ⓐ Ⓑ Ⓒ Ⓓ Ⓔ	28. Ⓐ Ⓑ Ⓒ Ⓓ Ⓔ	

FOLLOWING ORAL DIRECTIONS TEST

1. Ⓐ Ⓑ Ⓒ Ⓓ Ⓔ	19. Ⓐ Ⓑ Ⓒ Ⓓ Ⓔ	37. Ⓐ Ⓑ Ⓒ Ⓓ Ⓔ	55. Ⓐ Ⓑ Ⓒ Ⓓ Ⓔ	73. Ⓐ Ⓑ Ⓒ Ⓓ Ⓔ
2. Ⓐ Ⓑ Ⓒ Ⓓ Ⓔ	20. Ⓐ Ⓑ Ⓒ Ⓓ Ⓔ	38. Ⓐ Ⓑ Ⓒ Ⓓ Ⓔ	56. Ⓐ Ⓑ Ⓒ Ⓓ Ⓔ	74. Ⓐ Ⓑ Ⓒ Ⓓ Ⓔ
3. Ⓐ Ⓑ Ⓒ Ⓓ Ⓔ	21. Ⓐ Ⓑ Ⓒ Ⓓ Ⓔ	39. Ⓐ Ⓑ Ⓒ Ⓓ Ⓔ	57. Ⓐ Ⓑ Ⓒ Ⓓ Ⓔ	75. Ⓐ Ⓑ Ⓒ Ⓓ Ⓔ
4. Ⓐ Ⓑ Ⓒ Ⓓ Ⓔ	22. Ⓐ Ⓑ Ⓒ Ⓓ Ⓔ	40. Ⓐ Ⓑ Ⓒ Ⓓ Ⓔ	58. Ⓐ Ⓑ Ⓒ Ⓓ Ⓔ	76. Ⓐ Ⓑ Ⓒ Ⓓ Ⓔ
5. Ⓐ Ⓑ Ⓒ Ⓓ Ⓔ	23. Ⓐ Ⓑ Ⓒ Ⓓ Ⓔ	41. Ⓐ Ⓑ Ⓒ Ⓓ Ⓔ	59. Ⓐ Ⓑ Ⓒ Ⓓ Ⓔ	77. Ⓐ Ⓑ Ⓒ Ⓓ Ⓔ
6. Ⓐ Ⓑ Ⓒ Ⓓ Ⓔ	24. Ⓐ Ⓑ Ⓒ Ⓓ Ⓔ	42. Ⓐ Ⓑ Ⓒ Ⓓ Ⓔ	60. Ⓐ Ⓑ Ⓒ Ⓓ Ⓔ	78. Ⓐ Ⓑ Ⓒ Ⓓ Ⓔ
7. Ⓐ Ⓑ Ⓒ Ⓓ Ⓔ	25. Ⓐ Ⓑ Ⓒ Ⓓ Ⓔ	43. Ⓐ Ⓑ Ⓒ Ⓓ Ⓔ	61. Ⓐ Ⓑ Ⓒ Ⓓ Ⓔ	79. Ⓐ Ⓑ Ⓒ Ⓓ Ⓔ
8. Ⓐ Ⓑ Ⓒ Ⓓ Ⓔ	26. Ⓐ Ⓑ Ⓒ Ⓓ Ⓔ	44. Ⓐ Ⓑ Ⓒ Ⓓ Ⓔ	62. Ⓐ Ⓑ Ⓒ Ⓓ Ⓔ	80. Ⓐ Ⓑ Ⓒ Ⓓ Ⓔ
9. Ⓐ Ⓑ Ⓒ Ⓓ Ⓔ	27. Ⓐ Ⓑ Ⓒ Ⓓ Ⓔ	45. Ⓐ Ⓑ Ⓒ Ⓓ Ⓔ	63. Ⓐ Ⓑ Ⓒ Ⓓ Ⓔ	81. Ⓐ Ⓑ Ⓒ Ⓓ Ⓔ
10. Ⓐ Ⓑ Ⓒ Ⓓ Ⓔ	28. Ⓐ Ⓑ Ⓒ Ⓓ Ⓔ	46. Ⓐ Ⓑ Ⓒ Ⓓ Ⓔ	64. Ⓐ Ⓑ Ⓒ Ⓓ Ⓔ	82. Ⓐ Ⓑ Ⓒ Ⓓ Ⓔ
11. Ⓐ Ⓑ Ⓒ Ⓓ Ⓔ	29. Ⓐ Ⓑ Ⓒ Ⓓ Ⓔ	47. Ⓐ Ⓑ Ⓒ Ⓓ Ⓔ	65. Ⓐ Ⓑ Ⓒ Ⓓ Ⓔ	83. Ⓐ Ⓑ Ⓒ Ⓓ Ⓔ
12. Ⓐ Ⓑ Ⓒ Ⓓ Ⓔ	30. Ⓐ Ⓑ Ⓒ Ⓓ Ⓔ	48. Ⓐ Ⓑ Ⓒ Ⓓ Ⓔ	66. Ⓐ Ⓑ Ⓒ Ⓓ Ⓔ	84. Ⓐ Ⓑ Ⓒ Ⓓ Ⓔ
13. Ⓐ Ⓑ Ⓒ Ⓓ Ⓔ	31. Ⓐ Ⓑ Ⓒ Ⓓ Ⓔ	49. Ⓐ Ⓑ Ⓒ Ⓓ Ⓔ	67. Ⓐ Ⓑ Ⓒ Ⓓ Ⓔ	85. Ⓐ Ⓑ Ⓒ Ⓓ Ⓔ
14. Ⓐ Ⓑ Ⓒ Ⓓ Ⓔ	32. Ⓐ Ⓑ Ⓒ Ⓓ Ⓔ	50. Ⓐ Ⓑ Ⓒ Ⓓ Ⓔ	68. Ⓐ Ⓑ Ⓒ Ⓓ Ⓔ	86. Ⓐ Ⓑ Ⓒ Ⓓ Ⓔ
15. Ⓐ Ⓑ Ⓒ Ⓓ Ⓔ	33. Ⓐ Ⓑ Ⓒ Ⓓ Ⓔ	51. Ⓐ Ⓑ Ⓒ Ⓓ Ⓔ	69. Ⓐ Ⓑ Ⓒ Ⓓ Ⓔ	87. Ⓐ Ⓑ Ⓒ Ⓓ Ⓔ
16. Ⓐ Ⓑ Ⓒ Ⓓ Ⓔ	34. Ⓐ Ⓑ Ⓒ Ⓓ Ⓔ	52. Ⓐ Ⓑ Ⓒ Ⓓ Ⓔ	70. Ⓐ Ⓑ Ⓒ Ⓓ Ⓔ	88. Ⓐ Ⓑ Ⓒ Ⓓ Ⓔ
17. Ⓐ Ⓑ Ⓒ Ⓓ Ⓔ	35. Ⓐ Ⓑ Ⓒ Ⓓ Ⓔ	53. Ⓐ Ⓑ Ⓒ Ⓓ Ⓔ	71. Ⓐ Ⓑ Ⓒ Ⓓ Ⓔ	89. Ⓐ Ⓑ Ⓒ Ⓓ Ⓔ
18. Ⓐ Ⓑ Ⓒ Ⓓ Ⓔ	36. Ⓐ Ⓑ Ⓒ Ⓓ Ⓔ	54. Ⓐ Ⓑ Ⓒ Ⓓ Ⓔ	72. Ⓐ Ⓑ Ⓒ Ⓓ Ⓔ	90. Ⓐ Ⓑ Ⓒ Ⓓ Ⓔ

SECOND MODEL EXAM

SCORE SHEET

ADDRESS CHECKING TEST: Your score on the Address Checking Test is based upon the number of questions you answered correctly minus the number of questions you answered incorrectly. To determine your score, subtract the number of wrong answers from the number of correct answers.

Number Right   −   Number Wrong   =   Raw Score

_____   −   _____   =   _____

MEANING OF WORDS TEST: Your score on the Meaning of Words Test is based only upon the number of questions you answered correctly.

Number Right   =   Raw Score

_____   =   _____

FOLLOWING ORAL DIRECTIONS TEST: Your score on the Following Oral Directions Test is based only upon the number of questions you marked correctly on the answer sheet. The Worksheet is not scored, and wrong answers on the answer sheet do not count against you.

Number Right   =   Raw Score

_____   =   _____

TOTAL SCORE: To find your total raw score, add together the raw scores for each section of the exam.

Address Checking Score   _____
+
Meaning of Words Score   _____
+
Following Oral Directions Score   _____
=
Total Raw Score   _____

ADDRESS CHECKING TEST

DIRECTIONS AND SAMPLE QUESTIONS

In the Address Checking Test, you will have to decide whether two addresses are alike or different. Any difference at all makes the two addresses different. Look carefully at the address at the left and the address at the right. If the two addresses are *exactly alike in every way*, darken space Ⓐ for the question. If the two addresses are *different in any way*, darken space Ⓓ for the question. Mark your answers to these sample questions on the sample answer sheet on this page.

1. Provo UT 84601   Prova UT 84601
2. Baylor TX 76706   Baylor TX 76760
3. Annandale-on-Hudson NY Annandale-on-Hudson NY
4. Tempe AZ 85281   Tempe AZ 85281
5. Lynchburg VA   Lynchburgh VA
6. Medford MA 02155   Medford MA 02155

SAMPLE ANSWER SHEET
1. Ⓐ Ⓓ
2. Ⓐ Ⓓ
3. Ⓐ Ⓓ
4. Ⓐ Ⓓ
5. Ⓐ Ⓓ
6. Ⓐ Ⓓ

CORRECT ANSWERS TO SAMPLE QUESTIONS

1. Ⓐ ●
2. Ⓐ ●
3. ● Ⓓ
4. ● Ⓓ
5. Ⓐ ●
6. ● Ⓓ

Explanations

Question 1 is marked Ⓓ because the city name is different.
Question 2 is marked Ⓓ because of number reversal in the zip code.
Question 5 is marked Ⓓ because the city name is different.

ADDRESS CHECKING TEST

95 Questions—6 Minutes

DIRECTIONS: This is a test of your speed and accuracy in comparing addresses. For each question in the test, blacken the correspondingly numbered answer space as follows:

- Blacken Ⓐ if the two addresses are exactly ALIKE.
- Blacken Ⓓ if the two addresses are DIFFERENT in **any** way.

Correct answers are on page 115.

1.	Hannibal MO 63401	Hannible MO 63401
2.	Grantsboro NC	Grantsboro NC
3.	Bryn Athyn PA 19009	Bryn Athyn PA 19009
4.	Santurce PR	Santurce PR
5.	Collegedale TN 37315	Collegedale TN 37135
6.	Odessa TX 79762	Odessa TX 97962
7.	Port Angeles WA	Port Angeles WA
8.	Fond du Lac WI	Fond Du Lac WI
9.	Cullowhee NC 28723	Cullowhee NC 28732
10.	Cazenovia NY 13035	Cazenovia NY 13035
11.	New Brunswick NJ	New Brunswick NM
12.	Mankato MN 56001	Mankato MN 56001
13.	Ketchikan AK	Ketchikan AK
14.	Yuma AZ 85552	Yuma AZ 85552
15.	Talladega AL	Talladega AL
16.	Paragould AR 72450	Paragould AZ 72450
17.	Pasadena CA 91123	Pasadena CO 91123
18.	Norwich CT 06430	Norwich CT 06430
19.	Fort Collins CO	Fort Collings CO
20.	Georgetown DE 19947	Georgetown DE 19947
21.	Washington DC 20064	Washington DC 20064
22.	St. Augustine FL	St. Augustine FL
23.	Franklin Springs GA 30638	Franklin Springs GA 30639
24.	Kahului HI 96732	Kahulului HI 96732
25.	Rock Island IL	Rook Island IL
26.	Winona Lake IN 46590	Winona Lake IN 45690
27.	Epworth IA 52045	Epworth IA 52045
28.	McPherson KS 67460	McPherson KA 67460
29.	Madisonville KY	Madisonville KY
30.	Bossier City LA	Bossier City VA
31.	Castine ME 04421	Castine ME 04421
32.	Frostburg MD 21532	Frostburg MD 21532
33.	Quincy MA 02169	Quincy MA 02169
34.	Albion MI	Albion MI
35.	Brainerd MN 56401	Brainard MN 56401
36.	Lorman MS 39096	Lorman MS 39096
37.	Concordia MO 64020	Concordia MD 64020
38.	Kearney NB 68847	Kaerney NB 68847

39. Incline Village NV	Incline Village NV
40. Rindge NH 03461	Rindge NH 03641
41. Zarephath NJ	Zarephath NJ
42. Las Cruces NM 88003	Las Cruces NM 88003
43. Syracuse NY 13203	Syracuse NJ 13203
44. Charlotte NC 28202	Charlotte NC 28202
45. Wahpeton ND	Wahpeton ND
46. Wickliffe OH 44092	Wickliffe OH 44092
47. Poteau OK 74953	Poteau OR 74953
48. Pendleton OR	Pendleton OR
49. California PA 15419	California PA 15419
50. Barranquitas PR	Barranquitas PR
51. Barrington RI 02806	Barrington RI 02806
52. Cheraw SC 29502	Cheraw SC 29502
53. Aberdeen SC	Aberdeen SC
54. Dyersburg TN 38024	Dyersburg TN 38204
55. Beeville TX 78102	Beesville TX 78102
56. Salt Lake City UT	Salt Lake City UT
57. Bennington VT 05201	Bennington VT 05201
58. Melfa VA 23401	Melfa VA 23401
59. Bremerton WA 98310	Brementon WA 98310
60. Bluefield WV	Bluefield WV
61. Sheboygan WI	Sheboygan WI
62. Casper WY 82601	Caspar WY 82601
63. Demarest NJ 07627	Demarest NJ 07627
64. St. Thomas VI 00801	St. Thomas VI 00810
65. Balboa CZ	Balboa CZ
66. Beaumont TX 77710	Beaumont TN 77710
67. Jenkintown PA	Jenkintown PA
68. Winston-Salem NC	Winton-Salem NC
69. Schenectady NY	Schenectady NY
70. Jackson MS 39210	Jackson MS 29310
71. Hathorne MA 01937	Hawthorne MA 01937
72. Oskaloosa IA 52577	Oskaloosa IL 52577
73. Evansville IN 47712	Evansville IN 47712
74. New Britain CT	New Britain CT
75. La Mirada CA 90639	La Mirada CA 90639
76. Barrow AK 99723	Barrow AK 99723
77. Unity ME 04988	Unity ME 14988
78. Fort Wayne IN 46805	Ft. Wayne IN 46805
79. Moorhead MN 56560	Moosehead MN 56560
80. Convent Station NJ	Convent Station NJ
81. New York NY 10021	New York NY 10021
82. Morganton NC 28655	Morganton NC 28655
83. Elyria OH 44035	Elyria OH 44035
84. Loretto PA	Loretto PA
85. Allendale SC	Allendale SC
86. Seguin TX 78155	Sequin TX 78155
87. Roanoke VA 24011	Roanoke VA 24011
88. Mount Vernon WA	Mount Vernon WA
89. Salina KS 67401	Salina KS 67501
90. Caldwell ID 83605	Caldwell ID 86305
91. Danielson CT	Danielson CT
92. Ukiah CA 95482	Ukiah CA 94582

93.	Arkadelphia AK	Arkadelphia AK
94.	Dothan AL 36301	Dothan AL 63601
95.	Lake Worth FL 33461	Lake Worth FL 33461

END OF ADDRESS CHECKING TEST

> **Do not turn to the next page until the signal is given.**

MEANING OF WORDS TEST

DIRECTIONS AND SAMPLE QUESTIONS

The Meaning of Words Test asks you what a word or phrase means. In each question, a word or phrase is in *italics*. Five other words or phrases—lettered A, B, C, D, and E—are given as possible meanings. Choose the lettered word or phrase that means most nearly the same as the word in italics and darken the space with the letter of the right answer. Mark your answers to these sample questions on the sample answer sheet below.

1. Lions and tigers are *carnivores*. *Carnivores* means most nearly
   (A) meat eaters
   (B) members of the cat family
   (C) natives of Asia
   (D) trainable as circus performers
   (E) unsafe as house pets

2. The *calligraphy* on the envelope was difficult to read. *Calligraphy* means most nearly
   (A) address
   (B) scrawl
   (C) label
   (D) penmanship
   (E) numbers

3. The letter carrier's route was the *perimeter* of the housing development. *Perimeter* means most nearly
   (A) length
   (B) width
   (C) area
   (D) north end
   (E) outer edge

4. The only course of action was to wait for the flood waters to *abate*. *Abate* means most nearly
   (A) finish rising
   (B) subside
   (C) overflow the banks
   (D) disappear
   (E) freeze

```
SAMPLE ANSWER
     SHEET
  1. Ⓐ Ⓑ Ⓒ Ⓓ Ⓔ
  2. Ⓐ Ⓑ Ⓒ Ⓓ Ⓔ
  3. Ⓐ Ⓑ Ⓒ Ⓓ Ⓔ
  4. Ⓐ Ⓑ Ⓒ Ⓓ Ⓔ
```

Explanations

1. **(A)** A CARNIVORE is a *flesh-eating animal*. All five choices make correct statements about lions and tigers, but you must choose the phrase which correctly defines the italicized word.

2. **(D)** CALLIGRAPHY is *beautiful handwriting* or *penmanship*. You might have recognized the Greek root *graph* which means *writing*.

3. **(E)** The PERIMETER is the *outer boundary* of an enclosed area. The prefix *peri* means around; the root *meter* means *measure*.

4. **(B)** To ABATE is to *decrease*, to *wane*, or to *subside*.

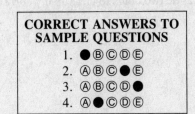

MEANING OF WORDS TEST

32 Questions—25 Minutes

DIRECTIONS: In each of the sentences below, one word is in *italics*. Following each sentence are five lettered words or phrases. You are to choose the word or phrase with the same meaning as the *italicized* word and mark its letter on the answer sheet. Correct answers are on page 117.

1. This afternoon I shall set aside two hours to clear up my *correspondence. Correspondence* means most nearly
   (A) letters
   (B) agreement
   (C) files
   (D) testimony
   (E) response

2. I cannot *endorse* my congressman's behavior. *Endorse* means most nearly
   (A) sign up for
   (B) lobby for
   (C) announce support for
   (D) renounce
   (E) publicize

3. The payment card read, "Do not fold, spindle or *mutilate." Mutilate* means most nearly
   (A) paint
   (B) damage
   (C) alter
   (D) write on
   (E) tear

4. The modern painting consisted only of one *horizontal* line. *Horizontal* means most nearly
   (A) marginal
   (B) in a circle
   (C) zig-zag
   (D) up and down
   (E) right to left

5. Some people say that students in the 80s display a great deal of *apathy. Apathy* means most nearly
   (A) sorrow
   (B) compassion
   (C) ability
   (D) indifference
   (E) sickness

6. The President's action served to stir up *controversy. Controversy* means most nearly
   (A) publicity
   (B) debate
   (C) revolution
   (D) revocation
   (E) denial

7. Even after hiring a lawyer, some people still *inspect* legal documents themselves. *Inspect* means most nearly
   (A) disregard
   (B) annoy
   (C) look at ✓
   (D) criticize
   (E) rewrite

8. When the treasurer resigned, the secretary was burdened with *fiscal* responsibility. *Fiscal* means most nearly
   (A) critical
   (B) basic
   (C) personal
   (D) financial ✓
   (E) extra

9. The union leader emerged from the meeting with a *tentative* agreement. *Tentative* means most nearly
   (A) persistent
   (B) permanent
   (C) thoughtful
   (D) favorable
   (E) provisional ✓

10. The IRS requires that you *retain* records for four years. *Retain* means most nearly
    (A) pay out
    (B) play
    (C) keep ✓
    (D) inquire
    (E) file

11. The retarded child was dull and *intractable*. *Intractable* means most nearly
    (A) confused
    (B) misleading
    (C) instinctive
    (D) unruly ✓
    (E) unattractive

12. With time, certain memories may be *obliterated*. *Obliterated* means most nearly
    (A) praised
    (B) doubted
    (C) erased ✓
    (D) improved
    (E) changed

13. In some states, Bingo games are a *legitimate* enterprise. *Legitimate* means most nearly
    (A) democratic
    (B) legal ✓
    (C) genealogical
    (D) underworld
    (E) illicit

14. A space launch *preempted* the time slot of the soap opera. *Preempted* means most nearly
    (A) changed
    (B) emptied
    (C) previewed
    (D) paid for
    (E) appropriated

15. The supervisor looked over the report and declared it to be *deficient*. *Deficient* means most nearly
    (A) sufficient
    (B) outstanding
    (C) inadequate
    (D) bizarre
    (E) sloppy

16. Do not forget to *deduct* the cost of the goods when calculating profits. *Deduct* means most nearly
    (A) conceal
    (B) consider
    (C) terminate
    (D) add
    (E) subtract

17. The state reported a *per capita* income of $12,000 per year. *Per capita* means most nearly
    (A) for each person
    (B) for each adult
    (C) for every family
    (D) for every household
    (E) for each business

18. He is in a *category* all by himself. *Category* means most nearly
    (A) class
    (B) sailboat
    (C) jail cell
    (D) cave
    (E) dilemma

19. *Presumably*, the people aboard the sunken ship have all drowned. *Presumably* means most nearly
    (A) positively
    (B) helplessly
    (C) recklessly
    (D) supposedly
    (E) in addition

20. Last week I received a *brochure* in the mail. *Brochure* means most nearly
    (A) ornament
    (B) flowery statement
    (C) broken object
    (D) pamphlet
    (E) free sample

21. The young accountant was most *scrupulous* about his work. *Scrupulous* means most nearly
    (A) conscientious
    (B) unprincipled
    (C) intricate
    (D) neurotic
    (E) uncommunicative

22. There is no *limit* to the amount of money the group will spend. *Limit* means most nearly
    (A) budget
    (B) sky
    (C) point
    (D) source
    (E) boundary

23. After the coup, the dictator was *supplanted* by a military governor. *Supplanted* means most nearly
    (A) conquered
    (B) exiled
    (C) replaced
    (D) assisted
    (E) beheaded

24. The Red Cross gives *succor* to flood victims. *Succor* means most nearly
    (A) assistance
    (B) Mayday
    (C) vitality
    (D) distress
    (E) food

25. The boys who play street hockey at the end of our block constitute a *haphazard* team. *Haphazard* means most nearly
    (A) devious
    (B) without order
    (C) precise
    (D) talented
    (E) dangerous

26. The determined young woman reached her goal despite every *obstacle*. *Obstacle* means most nearly
    (A) imprisonment
    (B) retaining wall
    (C) leap
    (D) setback
    (E) hindrance

27. The most *competent* people should be put in charge of the refugees. *Competent* means most nearly
    (A) capable
    (B) caring
    (C) inept
    (D) informed
    (E) confident

28. At one time, the *textile* industry was the backbone of our economy. *Textile* means most nearly
    (A) linen
    (B) cloth
    (C) printing
    (D) garment
    (E) farming

29. The newspaper reporter *implied* that he knew the source of the rumor. *Implied* means most nearly
    (A) acknowledged
    (B) stated
    (C) predicted
    (D) hinted
    (E) denied

30. The doctor told Mrs. Brown to *restrict* her sugar consumption. *Restrict* means most nearly
    (A) limit
    (B) replace
    (C) watch
    (D) record
    (E) measure

31. The postal patron *purchased* six sheets of first class stamps. *Purchased* means most nearly
    (A) charged
    (B) ordered
    (C) produced
    (D) licked
    (E) bought

32. Sometimes road conditions make it difficult not to *accelerate*. *Accelerate* means most nearly
    (A) speed up
    (B) reroute
    (C) drive fast
    (D) decline rapidly
    (E) weave back and forth

END OF MEANING OF WORDS TEST

> **If you finish your work on this test before time is up, check over your work on this test only. Do not go back to the Address Checking Test. Do not go on to the next page until you are told to do so.**

FOLLOWING ORAL DIRECTIONS TEST

DIRECTIONS AND SAMPLE QUESTIONS

LISTENING TO INSTRUCTIONS: When you are ready to try these sample questions, give the following instructions to a friend and have the friend read them aloud to you at 80 words per minute. Do not read them to yourself. Your friend will need a watch with a second hand. Listen carefully and do exactly what your friend tells you to do with the worksheet and answer sheet. Your friend will tell you some things to do with each item on the worksheet. After each set of instructions, your friend will give you time to mark your answer by darkening a circle on the sample answer sheet. Since B and D sound very much alike, your friend will say "B as in baker" when he or she means B and "D as in dog" when he or she means D.

Before proceeding further, tear out the worksheet on page 107. Then hand this book to your friend.

TO THE PERSON WHO IS TO READ THE DIRECTIONS: The directions are to be read at the rate of 80 words per minute. Do not read aloud the material which is in parentheses. Do not repeat any directions.

READ ALOUD TO THE CANDIDATE

Look at line 1 on the worksheet. (Pause slightly.) Draw a line under the second number in the line. (Pause 2 seconds.) Now, on your answer sheet, find the number under which you just drew the line and darken space B as in baker for that number. (Pause 5 seconds.)

Look at the letters in line 2 on the worksheet. (Pause slightly.) Draw a line under the second letter in the line. Now, on your answer sheet, find number 6 (Pause 2 seconds) and darken the space for the letter under which you drew a line. (Pause 5 seconds.)

Look at the letters in line 2 again. (Pause slightly.) Now draw two lines under the first letter in the line. (Pause 2 seconds.) Now, on your answer sheet, find number 12 (Pause 2 seconds) and darken the space for the letter under which you drew two lines. (Pause 5 seconds.)

Look at line 3. (Pause slightly.) Draw a circle around the number which is the smallest in the line. (Pause 2 seconds.) Now, on your answer sheet, find the number which you just drew a circle around and darken the space A for that number. (Pause 5 seconds.)

Now look at line 4 on your worksheet. There are 3 boxes with words and letters in them. (Pause slightly.) Each box represents a station in a large city. Station A delivers mail in the Regent Street area, Station B delivers mail in Broadway Plaza, and Station C delivers mail in Sunset Park. Ms. Kelly lives in Sunset Park. Write the number 2 on the line inside the box which represents the station that delivers Ms. Kelly's mail. (Pause 2 seconds.) Now, on your answer sheet, find the number 2 and darken the space for the letter that is in the box you just wrote in. (Pause 5 seconds.)

WORKSHEET

DIRECTIONS: Listening carefully to each set of instructions, mark each item on this worksheet as directed. Then complete each question by marking the sample answer sheet below as directed. For each answer you will darken the answer for a number-letter combination. Should you fall behind and miss an instruction, don't become excited. Let that one go and listen for the next one. If when you start to darken a space for a number, you find that you have already darkened another space for that number, either erase the first mark and darken the space for the new combination or let the first mark stay and do not darken a space for the new combination. Write with a pencil that has a clean eraser. When you finish, you should have no more than one space darkened for each number.

1. 31   14   7   26   5

2. B   A   E   A   C   D   C

3. 31   15   19   1   32

4.

A REGENT STREET	B BROADWAY PLAZA	C SUNSET PARK
_____	_____	_____

SAMPLE ANSWER SHEET

1. Ⓐ Ⓑ Ⓒ Ⓓ Ⓔ	6. Ⓐ Ⓑ Ⓒ Ⓓ Ⓔ	11. Ⓐ Ⓑ Ⓒ Ⓓ Ⓔ
2. Ⓐ Ⓑ Ⓒ Ⓓ Ⓔ	7. Ⓐ Ⓑ Ⓒ Ⓓ Ⓔ	12. Ⓐ Ⓑ Ⓒ Ⓓ Ⓔ
3. Ⓐ Ⓑ Ⓒ Ⓓ Ⓔ	8. Ⓐ Ⓑ Ⓒ Ⓓ Ⓔ	13. Ⓐ Ⓑ Ⓒ Ⓓ Ⓔ
4. Ⓐ Ⓑ Ⓒ Ⓓ Ⓔ	9. Ⓐ Ⓑ Ⓒ Ⓓ Ⓔ	14. Ⓐ Ⓑ Ⓒ Ⓓ Ⓔ
5. Ⓐ Ⓑ Ⓒ Ⓓ Ⓔ	10. Ⓐ Ⓑ Ⓒ Ⓓ Ⓔ	15. Ⓐ Ⓑ Ⓒ Ⓓ Ⓔ

TEAR HERE

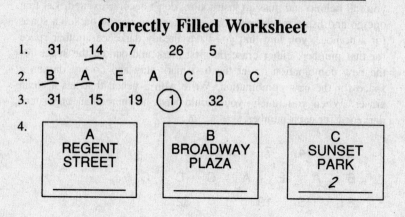

CORRECT ANSWERS TO SAMPLE QUESTIONS

1. ●ⒷⒸⒹⒺ	6. ●ⒷⒸⒹⒺ	11. ⒶⒷⒸⒹⒺ
2. ⒶⒷ●ⒹⒺ	7. ⒶⒷⒸⒹⒺ	12. Ⓐ●ⒸⒹⒺ
3. ⒶⒷⒸⒹⒺ	8. ⒶⒷⒸⒹⒺ	13. ⒶⒷⒸⒹⒺ
4. ⒶⒷⒸⒹⒺ	9. ⒶⒷⒸⒹⒺ	14. Ⓐ●ⒸⒹⒺ
5. ⒶⒷⒸⒹⒺ	10. ⒶⒷⒸⒹⒺ	15. ⒶⒷⒸⒹⒺ

Correctly Filled Worksheet

1. 31   <u>14</u>   7   26   5

2. <u>B</u>   <u>A</u>   E   A   C   D   C

3. 31   15   19   ①   32

4.

A REGENT STREET	B BROADWAY PLAZA	C SUNSET PARK
_____	_____	*2*

FOLLOWING ORAL DIRECTIONS TEST

Total Time—25 Minutes

LISTENING TO DIRECTIONS

DIRECTIONS: When you are ready to try this test of the Model Exam, give the following instructions to a friend and have the friend read them aloud to you at 80 words per minute. Do NOT read them to yourself. Your friend will need a watch with a second hand. Listen carefully and do exactly what your friend tells you to do with the worksheet and with the answer sheet. Your friend will tell you some things to do with each item on the worksheet. After each set of instructions, your friend will give you time to mark your answer by darkening a circle on the answer sheet. Since B and D sound very much alike, your friend will say "B as in baker" when he or she means B and "D as in dog" when he or she means D.

Before proceeding further, tear out the worksheet on page 113 of this test. Then hand this book to your friend.

TO THE PERSON WHO IS TO READ THE DIRECTIONS: The directions are to be read at the rate of 80 words per minute. Do not read aloud the material which is in parentheses. Once you have begun the test itself, do not repeat any directions. The next three paragraphs consist of approximately 120 words. Read these three paragraphs aloud to the candidate in about one and one-half minutes. You may reread these paragraphs as often as necessary to establish an 80 words per minute reading speed.

READ ALOUD TO THE CANDIDATE

On the job you will have to listen to directions and then do what you have been told to do. In this test, I will read instructions to you. Try to understand them as I read them; I cannot repeat them. Once we begin, you may not ask any questions until the end of the test.

On the job you won't have to deal with pictures, numbers and letters like those in the test, but you will have to listen to instructions and follow them. We are using this test to see how well you can follow instructions.

You are to mark your test booklet according to the instructions that I'll read to you. After each set of instructions, I'll give you time to record your answers on the separate answer sheet.

The actual test begins now.

Look at line 1 on your worksheet. (Pause slightly.) Next to the left-hand number write the letter E. (Pause 2 seconds.) Now, on your answer sheet, find the space for the number beside which you wrote and darken space E. (Pause 5 seconds.)

Now look at line 2 on your worksheet. (Pause slightly.) There are 5 boxes. Each box has a letter. (Pause slightly.) In the fifth box write the answer to this question: Which of the following numbers is largest: 18, 9, 15, 19, 13? (Pause 5 seconds.) Now, on your answer sheet, darken the space for the number-letter combination that is in the box you just wrote in. (Pause 5 seconds.) In the fourth box on the same line do nothing. In the third box write 5. (Pause 2 seconds.) Now, on your answer sheet, darken the space for the number-letter combination that is in the box you just wrote in. (Pause 5 seconds.) In the second box, write the answer to this question: How many hours are there in a day? (Pause 2 seconds.) Now, on your answer sheet, darken the space for the number-letter combination that is in the box you just wrote in. (Pause 5 seconds.)

Look at line 3 on your worksheet. (Pause slightly.) Draw a line under every number that is more than 50 but less than 85. (Pause 12 seconds.) Now, on your answer sheet, for each number that you drew a line under, darken space D as in dog. (Pause 25 seconds.)

Look at line 4 on your worksheet. (Pause slightly.) Write a B as in baker in the third circle. (Pause 2 seconds.) Now, on your answer sheet, find the number in that circle and darken space B for that number. (Pause 5 seconds.)

Look at line 4 again. (Pause slightly.) Write C in the first circle. (Pause 2 seconds.) Now, on your answer sheet, find the number in that circle and darken space C for that number. (Pause 5 seconds.)

Look at line 5 on your worksheet. (Pause slightly.) There are two circles and two boxes of different sizes with numbers in them. (Pause slightly.) If 4 is more than 6 and if 9 is less than 7, write D as in dog in the smaller box. (Pause slightly.) Otherwise write A in the larger circle. (Pause 2 seconds.) Now, on your answer sheet, darken the space for the number-letter combination for the box or circle you just wrote in. (Pause 5 seconds.)

Now look at line 6 on your worksheet. (Pause slightly.) Write an E in the second circle. (Pause 2 seconds.) Now, on your answer sheet, find the number in that circle and darken space E for that number. (Pause 5 seconds.)

Now look at line 6 again. (Pause slightly.) Write a B as in baker in the middle circle. (Pause 2 seconds.) Now, on your answer sheet, find the number in that circle and darken space B as in baker for that number. (Pause 5 seconds.)

Look at the numbers on line 7 on your worksheet. (Pause slightly.) Draw a line under the largest number in the line. (Pause 2 seconds.) Now, on your answer sheet, find the number and darken space C for that number. (Pause 5 seconds.)

Now look at line 7 again. (Pause slightly.) Draw a circle around the smallest number in the line. (Pause 2 seconds.) Now, on your answer sheet, find the number which you just drew a circle around and darken space A for that number. (Pause 5 seconds.)

Now look at line 8 on your worksheet. There are 3 boxes with words and letters in them. (Pause slightly.) Each box represents a station in a large city. Station A delivers mail in the Chestnut Street area, Station B delivers mail in Hyde Park, and Station C delivers mail in the Prudential Plaza. Mr. Adams lives in Hyde Park. Write the number 30 on the line inside the box which represents the station that delivers Mr. Adams' mail. (Pause 2 seconds.) Now, on your answer sheet, find number 30 and darken the space for the letter that is in the box you just wrote in. (Pause 5 seconds.)

Now look at line 9 on your worksheet. (Pause slightly.) Write a D as in dog in the third box. (Pause 2 seconds.) Now, on your answer sheet, find the number that is in the box you just wrote in and darken space D as in dog for that number. (Pause 5 seconds.)

Now look at line 10 on your worksheet. (Pause slightly.) Draw a line under all the even numbers in line 10. (Pause 5 seconds.) Find the second number with a line drawn under it. (Pause 2 seconds.) On your answer sheet blacken space C for that number. (Pause 5 seconds.)

Now look at line 11 on your worksheet. (Pause slightly.) Count the number of C's in line 11 and write the number at the end of the line. (Pause 3 seconds.) On your answer sheet blacken the letter E for that number. (Pause 5 seconds.)

Now look at line 12 on your worksheet. (Pause slightly.) The time written in each circle represents the last pickup of the day from a particular street box. Write the last two numbers of the earliest pickup time on the line next to the letter in that circle. (Pause 2 seconds.) Now, on your answer sheet, blacken the space for the number-letter combination in the circle in which you just wrote. (Pause 5 seconds.)

Look at line 12 on the worksheet again. (Pause slightly.) Find the second earliest pickup time and write the last two numbers of the second earliest pickup time on the line next to the letter in that circle. (Pause 2 seconds.) Now, on your answer sheet, blacken the space for the number-letter combination in the circle in which you just wrote. (Pause 5 seconds.)

Look at line 13 on the worksheet. (Pause slightly.) If there are 365 days in a leap year, write the letter B as in baker in the small circle. (Pause 2 seconds.) If not, write the letter A in the triangle. (Pause 2 seconds.) Now, on your answer sheet, blacken the space for the letter-number combination in the figure in which you just wrote. (Pause 5 seconds.)

Look at line 13 again. (Pause slightly.) Write the letter D as in dog in the box with the lower number. (Pause 2 seconds.) Now, on your answer sheet, blacken the space for the number-letter combination in the box in which you just wrote. (Pause 5 seconds.)

Look at line 14 on the worksheet. (Pause slightly.) Draw two lines under all the numbers that are greater than 12 but less than 41. (Pause 8 seconds.) Count the number of numbers under which you drew two lines and blacken the letter B as in baker for that number on your answer sheet. (Pause 10 seconds.) Still on *line 14* on the worksheet, (pause slightly) circle all the even numbers. (Pause 2 seconds.) Count all the numbers that you marked in any way and blacken the letter E for that number on your answer sheet. (Pause 10 seconds.)

Look at line 15 on the worksheet. (Pause slightly.) Circle the fourth letter in the line. (Pause 2 seconds.) Add together the number of hours in a day, the number of months in a year and the number of days in a week. (Pause 10 seconds.) Now on your answer sheet blacken the circled letter for that number. (Pause 5 seconds.)

Look at line 16 on the worksheet. (Pause slightly.) Write the first letter of the third word in the second box. (Pause 5 seconds.) On your answer sheet, mark the number-letter combination in the box in which you just wrote. (Pause 5 seconds.) Look again at line 16. (Pause slightly.) Write the third letter of the second word in the first box. (Pause 5 seconds.) On your answer sheet, mark the number-letter combination in the box in which you just wrote. (Pause 5 seconds.) Look once more at line 16. (Pause slightly.) Write the second letter of the second word in the third box. (Pause 5 seconds.) Now, on your answer sheet, mark the number-letter combination in the box in which you just wrote. (Pause 5 seconds.)

Look at line 17 on the worksheet. (Pause slightly.) Draw a wavy line under the middle letter in the line. (Pause 2 seconds.) On your answer sheet, blacken that letter for answer space 36. (Pause 5 seconds.)

Look at line 18 on the worksheet. (Pause slightly.) Count the number of Y's in the line and write the number at the end of the line. (Pause 2 seconds.) Add 27 to that number (pause 2 seconds) and blacken B as in baker for the space which represents the total of 27 plus the number of Y's. (Pause 5 seconds.)

FOLLOWING ORAL DIRECTIONS TEST

Total Time—25 Minutes

WORKSHEET

DIRECTIONS: Listening carefully to each set of instructions, mark each item on this worksheet as directed. Then complete each question by marking the answer sheet as directed. For each answer you will darken the answer for a number-letter combination. Should you fall behind and miss an instruction, don't become excited. Let that one go and listen for the next one. If when you start to darken a space for a number, you find that you have already darkened another space for that number, either erase the first mark and darken the space for the new combination or let the first mark stay and do not darken a space for the new combination. Write with a pencil that has a clean eraser. When you finish, you should have no more than one space darkened for each number. Correct answers are on page 119.

TEAR HERE

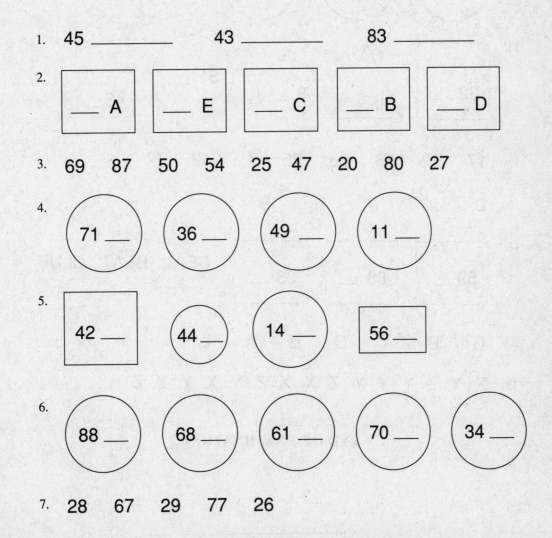

1. 45 _____   43 _____   83 _____

2. [___ A]   [___ E]   [___ C]   [___ B]   [___ D]

3. 69   87   50   54   25   47   20   80   27

4. (71 ___)   (36 ___)   (49 ___)   (11 ___)

5. [42 ___]   (44 ___)   (14 ___)   [56 ___]

6. (88 ___)   (68 ___)   (61 ___)   (70 ___)   (34 ___)

7. 28   67   29   77   26

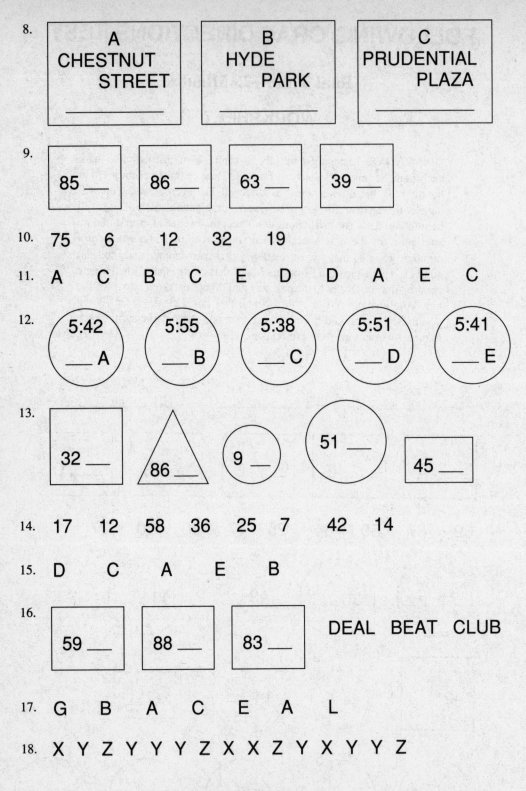

8.

| A
CHESTNUT
STREET
_____ | B
HYDE
PARK
_____ | C
PRUDENTIAL
PLAZA
_____ |

9. 85 ___   86 ___   63 ___   39 ___

10. 75   6   12   32   19

11. A   C   B   C   E   D   D   A   E   C

12. 5:42 ___ A   5:55 ___ B   5:38 ___ C   5:51 ___ D   5:41 ___ E

13. 32 ___   86 ___   9 ___   51 ___   45 ___

14. 17   12   58   36   25   7   42   14

15. D   C   A   E   B

16. 59 ___   88 ___   83 ___   DEAL   BEAT   CLUB

17. G   B   A   C   E   A   L

18. X   Y   Z   Y   Y   Y   Z   X   X   Z   Y   X   Y   Y   Z

END OF EXAMINATION

SECOND MODEL EXAM ANSWER KEY

ADDRESS CHECKING TEST

1. D	17. D	33. A	49. A	65. A	81. A
2. A	18. A	34. A	50. A	66. D	82. A
3. A	19. D	35. D	51. A	67. A	83. A
4. A	20. A	36. A	52. A	68. D	84. A
5. D	21. A	37. D	53. A	69. A	85. A
6. D	22. A	38. D	54. D	70. D	86. D
7. A	23. D	39. A	55. D	71. D	87. A
8. D	24. D	40. D	56. A	72. D	88. A
9. D	25. D	41. A	57. A	73. A	89. D
10. A	26. D	42. D	58. A	74. D	90. D
11. D	27. A	43. D	59. D	75. A	91. A
12. A	28. D	44. A	60. A	76. A	92. D
13. A	29. A	45. A	61. A	77. D	93. A
14. A	30. D	46. A	62. D	78. D	94. D
15. A	31. A	47. D	63. A	79. D	95. A
16. D	32. A	48. A	64. D	80. A	

ADDRESS CHECKING TEST

Explanations of Differences

1. spelling of city
5. number reversal
6. number difference
8. capitalization of city
9. number reversal
11. state difference
16. different states
17. different states
19. city difference
23. number difference
24. city difference
25. city difference
26. number reversal
28. different states
30. different states
35. spelling of city
37. different states
38. spelling of city
40. number reversal
42. spacing of city name
43. different states
47. different states
54. number reversal
55. city difference
59. city difference
62. spelling of city
64. number reversal
66. different states

68. spelling of city
70. number difference
71. spelling of city
72. different states
74. spelling of city
77. number difference
78. spelling of city
79. city difference
86. city difference
89. number difference
90. number reversal
92. number reversal
94. number difference

Analysis of Differences

Fill in the column on the right with the total number of questions you answered incorrectly.

City difference	17	
Number difference	14	
State difference	10	
Total addresses with differences	41	
Total addresses with no differences	54	

MEANING OF WORDS TEST

1. A	7. C	12. C	17. A	22. E	27. A
2. C	8. D	13. B	18. A	23. C	28. B
3. B	9. E	14. E	19. D	24. A	29. D
4. E	10. C	15. C	20. D	25. B	30. A
5. D	11. D	16. E	21. A	26. E	31. E
6. B					32. A

MEANING OF WORDS TEST

Explanatory Answers

1. **(A)** CORRESPONDENCE refers to *communication by letters*. The prefix *co* meaning *together* along with the root *respond* implies to give and take of letters. *Agreement* is indeed a dictionary definition of the word *correspondence*, but it does not make sense in the context of this sentence.

2. **(C)** To ENDORSE is to *approve* or *support*. The other meaning of *endorse*, *to sign on the back of*, does not make sense in this sentence.

3. **(B)** To MUTILATE is to *cripple*, to *maim* or to *damage*. Of course, mutilation of the card alters it, but you must choose as your answer the synonym of the italicized word, not its effect upon the subject of the sentence.

4. **(E)** HORIZONTAL means *parallel to the horizon*, obviously *right to left*. You probably figured this out without resorting to the formal etymological basis of the suffix *al* meaning *pertaining to* following the word *horizon*.

5. **(D)** APATHY is *lack of interest* and *lack of emotion*, hence, *indifference*. The prefix *a* means *not* or *without*; the Greek stem *pathos* means *feeling*. This is the same stem one finds in *sympathy* which means *feeling together*.

6. **(B)** CONTROVERSY is *discussion marked by the expression of opposing views*, *quarrel* or *dispute*.

7. **(C)** To INSPECT is to *scrutinize* or *to look at carefully*.

8. **(D)** FISCAL means relating to *financial* matters.

9. **(E)** TENTATIVE means *hesitant*, *uncertain*, *temporary* or *provisional*. If you knew the meaning of *tentative* but not the meaning of *provisional*, you could still have chosen the correct answer by eliminating the other four choices as absolutely not meaning *tentative*.

10. **(C)** RETAIN means *keep*. The only other choice which makes any sense in this sentence is *file*. You might very well *file* the records in order to keep them, but *retain* means *keep*.

11. **(D)** INTRACTABLE means *obstinate*, *not easily managed*, or *unruly*. The etymology of *intractable* is *in* meaning *not*, *able* meaning *capable of*, and *tract* meaning *being led*.

12. **(C)** To OBLITERATE is to *remove*, to *cancel* or to *erase*. All the choices except *praised* make perfect sense in this context. This is one of those instances in which you must simply know the word.

13. **(B)** LEGITIMATE means *lawful* or *legal*. It stems directly from the Latin word for *law*. Among the choices offered, *illicit* is an antonym (opposite); *underworld* makes perfect sense and may even be true, but it is not a synonym for *legitimate*.

14. **(E)** TO PREEMPT is to *take over for oneself* or to *appropriate*. The financial arrangements involved when a program is *preempted* have nothing to do with the meaning of the word, nor do the rearrangements of scheduling.

15. **(C)** DEFICIENT means *lacking a necessary element*, *defective*, or *inadequate*. The prefix *de* meaning *down* gives a clue to the negative connotation of the word. If there were no better synonym, *sloppy* might do, but, since it is offered, *inadequate* is much better.

16. **(E)** To DEDUCT is to *take away from a total* or to *subtract*. The same prefix *de* is at work here. If you read the sentence carefully, it should not be difficult to choose the correct synonym.

17. **(A)** PER CAPITA means *for each person. Capita* is the Latin word for *head. Per capita,* then, literally means *for each head.*

18. **(A)** A CATEGORY is a *class* in which something belongs.

19. **(D)** To PRESUME is to *assume,* to *take for granted* or to *suppose.* PRESUMABLY means *supposedly.*

20. **(D)** A BROCHURE is a small *booklet* or a *pamphlet.*

21. **(A)** SCRUPULOUS means *exact, painstaking, careful, upright* and *conscientious. Unprincipled* is, of course, just the opposite.

22. **(E)** LIMIT means *prescribed maximum or minimum, restriction* or *boundary.*

23. **(C)** To SUPPLANT is to *supercede* or to *replace.*

24. **(A)** SUCCOR is *aid, assistance, relief* or *help. Food* is only one aspect of *succor.*

25. **(B)** HAPHAZARD means *random, aimless,* or *marked by lack of plan or order.* A group of boys playing street hockey is a real pick-up group—no written rules, no assigned positions, no strategies. "Team" is almost a misnomer; *haphazard* is an apt description.

26. **(E)** An OBSTACLE is *something that stands in the way,* an *obstruction* or a *hindrance.* A *setback* is even more extreme a problem than an obstacle in that it implies reverses as well as temporary halts.

27. **(A)** COMPETENT means *fit, qualified* and *capable.*

28. **(B)** TEXTILE means *cloth,* usually knit or woven. The *garment* industry is heavily dependent upon the *textile* industry to produce the *cloth* from which clothing is made.

29. **(D)** To IMPLY is to *express indirectly,* to *suggest* or to *hint.* The context of the sentence allows for nearly any one of the choices and the etymology is not very useful in this case. Add this word to your vocabulary list if you did not already know it.

30. **(A)** To RESTRICT is to *restrain* or to *limit.*

31. **(E)** To PURCHASE is to *buy.* Any preordering or manner of payment are irrelevant to the meaning of *purchased.*

32. **(A)** To ACCELERATE is to *speed up.* This word is made up of the prefix *ad* meaning *toward,* the suffix *ate* meaning *an action of,* and the stem *celer* meaning *swift.*

FOLLOWING ORAL DIRECTIONS TEST

Correctly Filled Worksheet

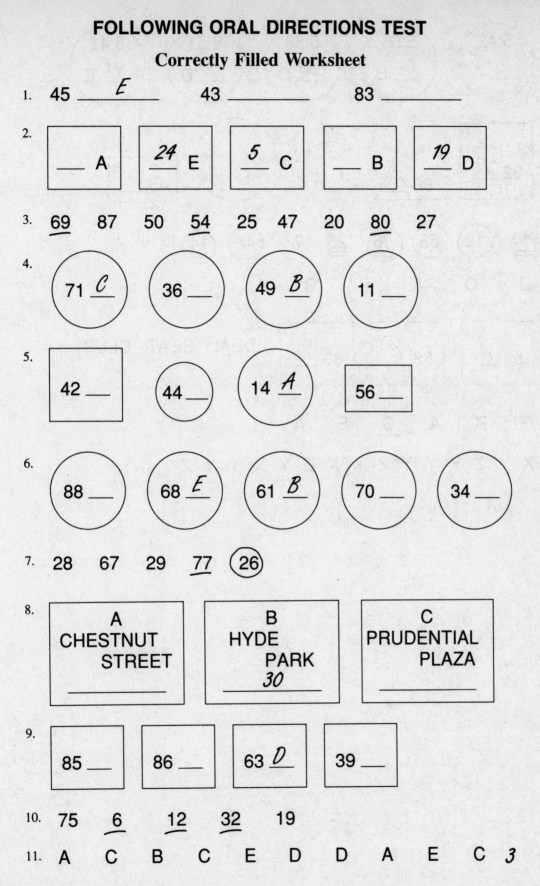

1. 45 ___*E*___   43 _____   83 _____

2. ___ A   _*24*_ E   _*5*_ C   ___ B   _*19*_ D

3. <u>69</u> 87 50 <u>54</u> 25 47 20 <u>80</u> 27

4. (71 _*C*_)   (36 __)   (49 _*B*_)   (11 __)

5. [42 __]   (44 __)   (14 _*A*_)   [56 __]

6. (88 __)   (68 _*E*_)   (61 _*B*_)   (70 __)   (34 __)

7. 28   67   29   <u>77</u>   (26)

8.
A CHESTNUT STREET	B HYDE PARK *30*	C PRUDENTIAL PLAZA
_____	_____	_____

9. [85 __]   [86 __]   [63 _*D*_]   [39 __]

10. 75   <u>6</u>   <u>12</u>   <u>32</u>   19

11. A   C   B   C   E   D   D   A   E   C   *3*

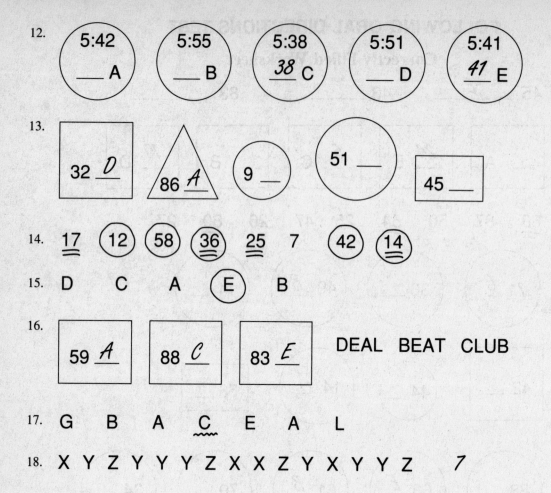

12.
5:42 ___ A 5:55 ___ B 5:38 *38* C 5:51 ___ D 5:41 *41* E

13.
32 *D* 86 *A* 9 ___ 51 ___ 45 ___

14.
17 12 58 36 25 7 42 14

15.
D C A E B

16.
59 *A* 88 *C* 83 *E*   DEAL BEAT CLUB

17.
G B A C E A L

18.
X Y Z Y Y Y Z X X Z Y X Y Y Z   *7*

FOLLOWING ORAL DIRECTIONS TEST

Correctly Filled Answer Grid

1. Ⓐ Ⓑ Ⓒ Ⓓ Ⓔ	31. Ⓐ Ⓑ Ⓒ Ⓓ Ⓔ	61. Ⓐ ● Ⓒ Ⓓ Ⓔ
2. Ⓐ Ⓑ Ⓒ Ⓓ Ⓔ	32. Ⓐ Ⓑ Ⓒ ● Ⓔ	62. Ⓐ Ⓑ Ⓒ Ⓓ Ⓔ
3. Ⓐ Ⓑ Ⓒ Ⓓ ●	33. Ⓐ Ⓑ Ⓒ Ⓓ Ⓔ	63. Ⓐ Ⓑ Ⓒ ● Ⓔ
4. Ⓐ ● Ⓒ Ⓓ Ⓔ	34. Ⓐ ● Ⓒ Ⓓ Ⓔ	64. Ⓐ Ⓑ Ⓒ Ⓓ Ⓔ
5. Ⓐ Ⓑ ● Ⓓ Ⓔ	35. Ⓐ Ⓑ Ⓒ Ⓓ Ⓔ	65. Ⓐ Ⓑ Ⓒ Ⓓ Ⓔ
6. Ⓐ Ⓑ Ⓒ Ⓓ Ⓔ	36. Ⓐ Ⓑ ● Ⓓ Ⓔ	66. Ⓐ Ⓑ Ⓒ Ⓓ Ⓔ
7. Ⓐ Ⓑ Ⓒ Ⓓ ●	37. Ⓐ Ⓑ Ⓒ Ⓓ Ⓔ	67. Ⓐ Ⓑ Ⓒ Ⓓ Ⓔ
8. Ⓐ Ⓑ Ⓒ Ⓓ Ⓔ	38. Ⓐ Ⓑ ● Ⓓ Ⓔ	68. Ⓐ Ⓑ Ⓒ Ⓓ ●
9. Ⓐ Ⓑ Ⓒ Ⓓ Ⓔ	39. Ⓐ Ⓑ Ⓒ Ⓓ Ⓔ	69. Ⓐ Ⓑ Ⓒ ● Ⓔ
10. Ⓐ Ⓑ Ⓒ Ⓓ Ⓔ	40. Ⓐ Ⓑ Ⓒ Ⓓ Ⓔ	70. Ⓐ Ⓑ Ⓒ Ⓓ Ⓔ
11. Ⓐ Ⓑ Ⓒ Ⓓ Ⓔ	41. Ⓐ Ⓑ Ⓒ Ⓓ ●	71. Ⓐ Ⓑ ● Ⓓ Ⓔ
12. Ⓐ Ⓑ ● Ⓓ Ⓔ	42. Ⓐ Ⓑ Ⓒ Ⓓ Ⓔ	72. Ⓐ Ⓑ Ⓒ Ⓓ Ⓔ
13. Ⓐ Ⓑ Ⓒ Ⓓ Ⓔ	43. Ⓐ Ⓑ Ⓒ Ⓓ ●	73. Ⓐ Ⓑ Ⓒ Ⓓ Ⓔ
14. ● Ⓑ Ⓒ Ⓓ Ⓔ	44. Ⓐ Ⓑ Ⓒ Ⓓ Ⓔ	74. Ⓐ Ⓑ Ⓒ Ⓓ Ⓔ
15. Ⓐ Ⓑ Ⓒ Ⓓ Ⓔ	45. Ⓐ Ⓑ Ⓒ Ⓓ ●	75. Ⓐ Ⓑ Ⓒ Ⓓ Ⓔ
16. Ⓐ Ⓑ Ⓒ Ⓓ Ⓔ	46. Ⓐ Ⓑ Ⓒ Ⓓ Ⓔ	76. Ⓐ Ⓑ Ⓒ Ⓓ Ⓔ
17. Ⓐ Ⓑ Ⓒ Ⓓ Ⓔ	47. Ⓐ Ⓑ Ⓒ Ⓓ Ⓔ	77. Ⓐ Ⓑ ● Ⓓ Ⓔ
18. Ⓐ Ⓑ Ⓒ Ⓓ Ⓔ	48. Ⓐ Ⓑ Ⓒ Ⓓ Ⓔ	78. Ⓐ Ⓑ Ⓒ Ⓓ Ⓔ
19. Ⓐ Ⓑ Ⓒ ● Ⓔ	49. Ⓐ ● Ⓒ Ⓓ Ⓔ	79. Ⓐ Ⓑ Ⓒ Ⓓ Ⓔ
20. Ⓐ Ⓑ Ⓒ Ⓓ Ⓔ	50. Ⓐ Ⓑ Ⓒ Ⓓ Ⓔ	80. Ⓐ Ⓑ Ⓒ ● Ⓔ
21. Ⓐ Ⓑ Ⓒ Ⓓ Ⓔ	51. Ⓐ Ⓑ Ⓒ Ⓓ Ⓔ	81. Ⓐ Ⓑ Ⓒ Ⓓ Ⓔ
22. Ⓐ Ⓑ Ⓒ Ⓓ Ⓔ	52. Ⓐ Ⓑ Ⓒ Ⓓ Ⓔ	82. Ⓐ Ⓑ Ⓒ Ⓓ Ⓔ
23. Ⓐ Ⓑ Ⓒ Ⓓ Ⓔ	53. Ⓐ Ⓑ Ⓒ Ⓓ Ⓔ	83. Ⓐ Ⓑ Ⓒ Ⓓ ●
24. Ⓐ Ⓑ Ⓒ Ⓓ ●	54. Ⓐ Ⓑ Ⓒ ● Ⓔ	84. Ⓐ Ⓑ Ⓒ Ⓓ Ⓔ
25. Ⓐ Ⓑ Ⓒ Ⓓ Ⓔ	55. Ⓐ Ⓑ Ⓒ Ⓓ Ⓔ	85. Ⓐ Ⓑ Ⓒ Ⓓ Ⓔ
26. ● Ⓑ Ⓒ Ⓓ Ⓔ	56. Ⓐ Ⓑ Ⓒ Ⓓ Ⓔ	86. ● Ⓑ Ⓒ Ⓓ Ⓔ
27. Ⓐ Ⓑ Ⓒ Ⓓ Ⓔ	57. Ⓐ Ⓑ Ⓒ Ⓓ Ⓔ	87. Ⓐ Ⓑ Ⓒ Ⓓ Ⓔ
28. Ⓐ Ⓑ Ⓒ Ⓓ Ⓔ	58. Ⓐ Ⓑ Ⓒ Ⓓ Ⓔ	88. Ⓐ Ⓑ ● Ⓓ Ⓔ
29. Ⓐ Ⓑ Ⓒ Ⓓ Ⓔ	59. ● Ⓑ Ⓒ Ⓓ Ⓔ	89. Ⓐ Ⓑ Ⓒ Ⓓ Ⓔ
30. Ⓐ ● Ⓒ Ⓓ Ⓔ	60. Ⓐ Ⓑ Ⓒ Ⓓ Ⓔ	90. Ⓐ Ⓑ Ⓒ Ⓓ Ⓔ

THIRD MODEL EXAM ANSWER SHEET

ADDRESS CHECKING TEST

1. Ⓐ Ⓓ
2. Ⓐ Ⓓ
3. Ⓐ Ⓓ
4. Ⓐ Ⓓ
5. Ⓐ Ⓓ
6. Ⓐ Ⓓ
7. Ⓐ Ⓓ
8. Ⓐ Ⓓ
9. Ⓐ Ⓓ
10. Ⓐ Ⓓ
11. Ⓐ Ⓓ
12. Ⓐ Ⓓ
13. Ⓐ Ⓓ
14. Ⓐ Ⓓ
15. Ⓐ Ⓓ
16. Ⓐ Ⓓ

17. Ⓐ Ⓓ
18. Ⓐ Ⓓ
19. Ⓐ Ⓓ
20. Ⓐ Ⓓ
21. Ⓐ Ⓓ
22. Ⓐ Ⓓ
23. Ⓐ Ⓓ
24. Ⓐ Ⓓ
25. Ⓐ Ⓓ
26. Ⓐ Ⓓ
27. Ⓐ Ⓓ
28. Ⓐ Ⓓ
29. Ⓐ Ⓓ
30. Ⓐ Ⓓ
31. Ⓐ Ⓓ
32. Ⓐ Ⓓ

33. Ⓐ Ⓓ
34. Ⓐ Ⓓ
35. Ⓐ Ⓓ
36. Ⓐ Ⓓ
37. Ⓐ Ⓓ
38. Ⓐ Ⓓ
39. Ⓐ Ⓓ
40. Ⓐ Ⓓ
41. Ⓐ Ⓓ
42. Ⓐ Ⓓ
43. Ⓐ Ⓓ
44. Ⓐ Ⓓ
45. Ⓐ Ⓓ
46. Ⓐ Ⓓ
47. Ⓐ Ⓓ
48. Ⓐ Ⓓ

49. Ⓐ Ⓓ
50. Ⓐ Ⓓ
51. Ⓐ Ⓓ
52. Ⓐ Ⓓ
53. Ⓐ Ⓓ
54. Ⓐ Ⓓ
55. Ⓐ Ⓓ
56. Ⓐ Ⓓ
57. Ⓐ Ⓓ
58. Ⓐ Ⓓ
59. Ⓐ Ⓓ
60. Ⓐ Ⓓ
61. Ⓐ Ⓓ
62. Ⓐ Ⓓ
63. Ⓐ Ⓓ
64. Ⓐ Ⓓ

65. Ⓐ Ⓓ
66. Ⓐ Ⓓ
67. Ⓐ Ⓓ
68. Ⓐ Ⓓ
69. Ⓐ Ⓓ
70. Ⓐ Ⓓ
71. Ⓐ Ⓓ
72. Ⓐ Ⓓ
73. Ⓐ Ⓓ
74. Ⓐ Ⓓ
75. Ⓐ Ⓓ
76. Ⓐ Ⓓ
77. Ⓐ Ⓓ
78. Ⓐ Ⓓ
79. Ⓐ Ⓓ
80. Ⓐ Ⓓ

81. Ⓐ Ⓓ
82. Ⓐ Ⓓ
83. Ⓐ Ⓓ
84. Ⓐ Ⓓ
85. Ⓐ Ⓓ
86. Ⓐ Ⓓ
87. Ⓐ Ⓓ
88. Ⓐ Ⓓ
89. Ⓐ Ⓓ
90. Ⓐ Ⓓ
91. Ⓐ Ⓓ
92. Ⓐ Ⓓ
93. Ⓐ Ⓓ
94. Ⓐ Ⓓ
95. Ⓐ Ⓓ

MEANING OF WORDS TEST

1. Ⓐ Ⓑ Ⓒ Ⓓ Ⓔ
2. Ⓐ Ⓑ Ⓒ Ⓓ Ⓔ
3. Ⓐ Ⓑ Ⓒ Ⓓ Ⓔ
4. Ⓐ Ⓑ Ⓒ Ⓓ Ⓔ
5. Ⓐ Ⓑ Ⓒ Ⓓ Ⓔ
6. Ⓐ Ⓑ Ⓒ Ⓓ Ⓔ
7. Ⓐ Ⓑ Ⓒ Ⓓ Ⓔ

8. Ⓐ Ⓑ Ⓒ Ⓓ Ⓔ
9. Ⓐ Ⓑ Ⓒ Ⓓ Ⓔ
10. Ⓐ Ⓑ Ⓒ Ⓓ Ⓔ
11. Ⓐ Ⓑ Ⓒ Ⓓ Ⓔ
12. Ⓐ Ⓑ Ⓒ Ⓓ Ⓔ
13. Ⓐ Ⓑ Ⓒ Ⓓ Ⓔ
14. Ⓐ Ⓑ Ⓒ Ⓓ Ⓔ

15. Ⓐ Ⓑ Ⓒ Ⓓ Ⓔ
16. Ⓐ Ⓑ Ⓒ Ⓓ Ⓔ
17. Ⓐ Ⓑ Ⓒ Ⓓ Ⓔ
18. Ⓐ Ⓑ Ⓒ Ⓓ Ⓔ
19. Ⓐ Ⓑ Ⓒ Ⓓ Ⓔ
20. Ⓐ Ⓑ Ⓒ Ⓓ Ⓔ
21. Ⓐ Ⓑ Ⓒ Ⓓ Ⓔ

22. Ⓐ Ⓑ Ⓒ Ⓓ Ⓔ
23. Ⓐ Ⓑ Ⓒ Ⓓ Ⓔ
24. Ⓐ Ⓑ Ⓒ Ⓓ Ⓔ
25. Ⓐ Ⓑ Ⓒ Ⓓ Ⓔ
26. Ⓐ Ⓑ Ⓒ Ⓓ Ⓔ
27. Ⓐ Ⓑ Ⓒ Ⓓ Ⓔ

28. Ⓐ Ⓑ Ⓒ Ⓓ Ⓔ
29. Ⓐ Ⓑ Ⓒ Ⓓ Ⓔ
30. Ⓐ Ⓑ Ⓒ Ⓓ Ⓔ
31. Ⓐ Ⓑ Ⓒ Ⓓ Ⓔ
32. Ⓐ Ⓑ Ⓒ Ⓓ Ⓔ

FOLLOWING ORAL DIRECTIONS TEST

1. Ⓐ Ⓑ Ⓒ Ⓓ Ⓔ
2. Ⓐ Ⓑ Ⓒ Ⓓ Ⓔ
3. Ⓐ Ⓑ Ⓒ Ⓓ Ⓔ
4. Ⓐ Ⓑ Ⓒ Ⓓ Ⓔ
5. Ⓐ Ⓑ Ⓒ Ⓓ Ⓔ
6. Ⓐ Ⓑ Ⓒ Ⓓ Ⓔ
7. Ⓐ Ⓑ Ⓒ Ⓓ Ⓔ
8. Ⓐ Ⓑ Ⓒ Ⓓ Ⓔ
9. Ⓐ Ⓑ Ⓒ Ⓓ Ⓔ
10. Ⓐ Ⓑ Ⓒ Ⓓ Ⓔ
11. Ⓐ Ⓑ Ⓒ Ⓓ Ⓔ
12. Ⓐ Ⓑ Ⓒ Ⓓ Ⓔ
13. Ⓐ Ⓑ Ⓒ Ⓓ Ⓔ
14. Ⓐ Ⓑ Ⓒ Ⓓ Ⓔ
15. Ⓐ Ⓑ Ⓒ Ⓓ Ⓔ
16. Ⓐ Ⓑ Ⓒ Ⓓ Ⓔ
17. Ⓐ Ⓑ Ⓒ Ⓓ Ⓔ
18. Ⓐ Ⓑ Ⓒ Ⓓ Ⓔ

19. Ⓐ Ⓑ Ⓒ Ⓓ Ⓔ
20. Ⓐ Ⓑ Ⓒ Ⓓ Ⓔ
21. Ⓐ Ⓑ Ⓒ Ⓓ Ⓔ
22. Ⓐ Ⓑ Ⓒ Ⓓ Ⓔ
23. Ⓐ Ⓑ Ⓒ Ⓓ Ⓔ
24. Ⓐ Ⓑ Ⓒ Ⓓ Ⓔ
25. Ⓐ Ⓑ Ⓒ Ⓓ Ⓔ
26. Ⓐ Ⓑ Ⓒ Ⓓ Ⓔ
27. Ⓐ Ⓑ Ⓒ Ⓓ Ⓔ
28. Ⓐ Ⓑ Ⓒ Ⓓ Ⓔ
29. Ⓐ Ⓑ Ⓒ Ⓓ Ⓔ
30. Ⓐ Ⓑ Ⓒ Ⓓ Ⓔ
31. Ⓐ Ⓑ Ⓒ Ⓓ Ⓔ
32. Ⓐ Ⓑ Ⓒ Ⓓ Ⓔ
33. Ⓐ Ⓑ Ⓒ Ⓓ Ⓔ
34. Ⓐ Ⓑ Ⓒ Ⓓ Ⓔ
35. Ⓐ Ⓑ Ⓒ Ⓓ Ⓔ
36. Ⓐ Ⓑ Ⓒ Ⓓ Ⓔ

37. Ⓐ Ⓑ Ⓒ Ⓓ Ⓔ
38. Ⓐ Ⓑ Ⓒ Ⓓ Ⓔ
39. Ⓐ Ⓑ Ⓒ Ⓓ Ⓔ
40. Ⓒ Ⓑ Ⓒ Ⓓ Ⓔ
41. Ⓐ Ⓑ Ⓒ Ⓓ Ⓔ
42. Ⓐ Ⓑ Ⓒ Ⓓ Ⓔ
43. Ⓐ Ⓑ Ⓒ Ⓓ Ⓔ
44. Ⓐ Ⓑ Ⓒ Ⓓ Ⓔ
45. Ⓐ Ⓑ Ⓒ Ⓓ Ⓔ
46. Ⓐ Ⓑ Ⓒ Ⓓ Ⓔ
47. Ⓐ Ⓑ Ⓒ Ⓓ Ⓔ
48. Ⓐ Ⓑ Ⓒ Ⓓ Ⓔ
49. Ⓐ Ⓑ Ⓒ Ⓓ Ⓔ
50. Ⓐ Ⓑ Ⓒ Ⓓ Ⓔ
51. Ⓐ Ⓑ Ⓒ Ⓓ Ⓔ
52. Ⓐ Ⓑ Ⓒ Ⓓ Ⓔ
53. Ⓐ Ⓑ Ⓒ Ⓓ Ⓔ
54. Ⓐ Ⓑ Ⓒ Ⓓ Ⓔ

55. Ⓐ Ⓑ Ⓒ Ⓓ Ⓔ
56. Ⓐ Ⓑ Ⓒ Ⓓ Ⓔ
57. Ⓐ Ⓑ Ⓒ Ⓓ Ⓔ
58. Ⓐ Ⓑ Ⓒ Ⓓ Ⓔ
59. Ⓐ Ⓑ Ⓒ Ⓓ Ⓔ
60. Ⓐ Ⓑ Ⓒ Ⓓ Ⓔ
61. Ⓐ Ⓑ Ⓒ Ⓓ Ⓔ
62. Ⓐ Ⓑ Ⓒ Ⓓ Ⓔ
63. Ⓐ Ⓑ Ⓒ Ⓓ Ⓔ
64. Ⓐ Ⓑ Ⓒ Ⓓ Ⓔ
65. Ⓐ Ⓑ Ⓒ Ⓓ Ⓔ
66. Ⓐ Ⓑ Ⓒ Ⓓ Ⓔ
67. Ⓐ Ⓑ Ⓒ Ⓓ Ⓔ
68. Ⓐ Ⓑ Ⓒ Ⓓ Ⓔ
69. Ⓐ Ⓑ Ⓒ Ⓓ Ⓔ
70. Ⓐ Ⓑ Ⓒ Ⓓ Ⓔ
71. Ⓐ Ⓑ Ⓒ Ⓓ Ⓔ
72. Ⓐ Ⓑ Ⓒ Ⓓ Ⓔ

73. Ⓐ Ⓑ Ⓒ Ⓓ Ⓔ
74. Ⓐ Ⓑ Ⓒ Ⓓ Ⓔ
75. Ⓐ Ⓑ Ⓒ Ⓓ Ⓔ
76. Ⓐ Ⓑ Ⓒ Ⓓ Ⓔ
77. Ⓐ Ⓑ Ⓒ Ⓓ Ⓔ
78. Ⓐ Ⓑ Ⓒ Ⓓ Ⓔ
79. Ⓐ Ⓑ Ⓒ Ⓓ Ⓔ
80. Ⓐ Ⓑ Ⓒ Ⓓ Ⓔ
81. Ⓐ Ⓑ Ⓒ Ⓓ Ⓔ
82. Ⓐ Ⓑ Ⓒ Ⓓ Ⓔ
83. Ⓐ Ⓑ Ⓒ Ⓓ Ⓔ
84. Ⓐ Ⓑ Ⓒ Ⓓ Ⓔ
85. Ⓐ Ⓑ Ⓒ Ⓓ Ⓔ
86. Ⓐ Ⓑ Ⓒ Ⓓ Ⓔ
87. Ⓐ Ⓑ Ⓒ Ⓓ Ⓔ
88. Ⓐ Ⓑ Ⓒ Ⓓ Ⓔ
89. Ⓐ Ⓑ Ⓒ Ⓓ Ⓔ
90. Ⓐ Ⓑ Ⓒ Ⓓ Ⓔ

TEAR HERE

THIRD MODEL EXAM

SCORE SHEET

ADDRESS CHECKING TEST: Your score on the Address Checking Test is based upon the number of questions you answered correctly minus the number of questions you answered incorrectly. To determine your score, subtract the number of wrong answers from the number of correct answers.

Number Right   —   Number Wrong   =   Raw Score

_____   −   _____   =   _____

MEANING OF WORDS TEST: Your score on the Meaning of Words Test is based only upon the number of questions you answered correctly.

Number Right   =   Raw Score

_____   =   _____

FOLLOWING ORAL DIRECTIONS TEST: Your score on the Following Oral Directions Test is based only upon the number of questions you marked correctly on the answer sheet. The Worksheet is not scored, and wrong answers on the answer sheet do not count against you.

Number Right   =   Raw Score

_____   _____

TOTAL SCORE: To find your total raw score, add together the raw scores for each section of the exam.

Address Checking Score   _____
+
Meaning of Words Score   _____
+
Following Oral Directions Score   _____
=
Total Raw Score   _____

ADDRESS CHECKING

DIRECTIONS AND SAMPLE QUESTIONS

In the Address Checking Test you will have to decide whether two addresses are alike or different. Any difference at all makes the two addresses different. Look carefully at the address at the left and the address at the right. If the two addresses are *exactly alike in every way*, darken space Ⓐ for the question. If the two addresses are *different in any way*, darken space Ⓓ for the question. Mark your answers to these sample questions on the sample answer sheet on this page.

1. Essex CT 06426   Essex CT 06426
2. Lumberville PA   Lumberville PN
3. Stillwater OK 74704   Stillwater OK 47404
4. Orono ME 04473   Onoro ME 04473
5. Gainsville FL   Gainsville FL
6. Greenvale NY 11548   Greenvale NJ 11548

```
┌─────────────────────────┐
│   SAMPLE ANSWER         │
│     SHEET               │
│   1. Ⓐ Ⓓ               │
│   2. Ⓐ Ⓓ               │
│   3. Ⓐ Ⓓ               │
│   4. Ⓐ Ⓓ               │
│   5. Ⓐ Ⓓ               │
│   6. Ⓐ Ⓓ               │
└─────────────────────────┘
```

**CORRECT ANSWERS TO
SAMPLE QUESTIONS**

1. ●Ⓓ
2. Ⓐ●
3. Ⓐ●
4. Ⓐ●
5. ●Ⓓ
6. Ⓐ●

Explanations

Question 2 is marked Ⓓ because the state is abbreviated differently.
Question 3 is marked Ⓓ because numbers are reversed in the zip code.
Question 4 is marked Ⓓ because the city is spelled differently.
Question 6 is marked Ⓓ because there are two different states.

ADDRESS CHECKING TEST

95 Questions—6 Minutes

DIRECTIONS: This is a test of your speed and accuracy in comparing addresses. For each question in the test, blacken the correspondingly numbered answer space as follows:

- Blacken Ⓐ if the two addresses are exactly ALIKE.
- Blacken Ⓓ if the two addresses are DIFFERENT in **any** way.

Correct answers are on page 147.

1. Hutchinson KS 67501   Hutchinson KS 67501
2. Laie HI 96762   Laie HI 96726
3. Washington DC 20058   Washington DC 20058
4. South Holland IL   South Holland IN
5. Barbourville KY 40906   Barberville KY 40906
6. Bloomfield Hills MI   Bloomfield Hills MI
7. Poughkeepsie NY   Poughkeepsie NY
8. Monmouth OR 97361   Mammoth OR 97361
9. Aiken SC 29801   Aiken SC 28901
10. Winchester VA 22601   Winchester VA 26601
11. Johnstown NY 12095   Johnstown NM 12095
12. McCook NB 69001   MacCook NB 69001
13. Framingham MA   Framingham MA
14. Thibodaux LA   Thibodaux GA
15. River Forest IL   River Forest IL
16. Moorpark CA 93021   Moorpark CA 93021
17. Selma AL 36701   Selma AL 36710
18. Fairbanks AK 99701   Fairbanks AR 99701
19. Scottsdale AZ 85251   Scottsdale AZ 85251
20. North Little Rock AR   North Little Rock AR
21. Toccoa Falls GA   Tococoa Falls GA
22. DeKalb IL 60115   DeKalb IL 60115
23. St. Meinrad IN 47577   St. Meinrad IN 47557
24. Davenport IA 52803   Davenport LA 52803
25. Crookston MN   Crookstown MN
26. Durham NH 03824   Durham NH 03824
27. Cranford NJ 07016   Cranford NJ 07016
28. Cobleskill NY 12043   Cobbleskill NY 12043
29. Raleigh NC 27611   Raleigh NC 27611
30. St. Clairsville OH   St. Clairsville OH
31. Altus OK 73521   Altus OK 73521
32. Cambridge Springs PA   Cambridge Springs PA
33. Mayaguez PR 00708   Mayaguez PR 07008
34. Chattanooga TN   Chattannooga TN
35. Killeen TX 76541   Killeen TX 76541
36. Lyndonville VT   Lyndonville VA
37. Conception MO 64433   Concepcion MO 64433
38. Mankato MN 56001   Mankato MN 56001

39.	Campbellsville KY 42718	Cambellsville KY 42718
40.	Sioux City IA	Sioux City IA
41.	Panama City FL	Panama City PA
42.	La Jolla CA 92993	La Jolla CA 92993
43.	Durango CO 81301	Durango CO 81201
44.	Phoenix AZ 85061	Phoenix AR 85061
45.	Alexander City AL	Alexander City AL
46.	Sitka AK 99835	Sitka AK 99835
47.	Savannah GA 31406	Savannah GA 31406
48.	Grayslake IL 60030	Greyslake IL 60030
49.	Winona Lake IN	Winona Lake IN
50.	Bowling Green KY	Bowling Green WY
51.	Onamia MN 56359	Onamia MN 56359
52.	Manchester NH 03104	Manchester NY 30104
53.	Glens Falls NY	Glens Falls NY
54.	Rocky Mount NC 27801	Rocky Mount ND 27801
55.	Cedarville OH 45314	Cedarville OH 45314
56.	Muskogee OK	Muskogee OK
57.	Klamath Falls OR	Klamath Falls OR
58.	Shippensburg PA 17257	Shippensdale PA 17257
59.	Kingston RI 02881	Kingston RI 02881
60.	Spearfish SD	Spearfish SD
61.	Beaufort SC 29902	Beaufort SC 29202
62.	Pulaski TN	Pulaski TN
63.	Wichita Falls TX 76308	Wichita Falls KS 76308
64.	St. George UT	St. Georges UT
65.	Carson City NV 89701	Carson City NV 89701
66.	Omaha NB 68105	Omaha NB 68105
67.	Point Lookout MO	Pt. Lookout MO
68.	Grand Rapids MI 49509	Grand Rapids MI 48509
69.	Chestnut Hill MA	Chestnut Hill ME
70.	Cumberland MD 21502	Cumberland MD 21502
71.	New Orleans LA 70126	New Orleans LA 71026
72.	Berea KY 40404	Berea KY 40404
73.	Hawarden IA 51023	Hawarden HI 51023
74.	Naperville IL	Naperville IL
75.	Waleska GA 30183	Waleska GA 30183
76.	Middletown CT	Middleton CT
77.	Gunnison CO 81230	Gunnison CO 81230
78.	San Jacinto CA	San Jacinto CA
79.	Juneau AK 99803	Juneau AK 98803
80.	Phil Campbell AL	Phil Campbell AL
81.	Willimantic CT	Willimantic CT
82.	Newark DE 19711	Newark DE 17911
83.	Miami Shores FL	Miamis Shore FL
84.	Honolulu HI 96822	Honolulu HI 96822
85.	East Peoria IL 61635	East Peoria IL 61635
86.	Indianapolis IN	Indianapolis IN
87.	Keokuk IA 52632	Keokuk IA 52623
88.	Bar Harbor ME	Bar Harbour ME
89.	Chicopee MA 01013	Chicopee MA 01013
90.	Grand Rapids MI 49506	Grand Rapids WI 49506
91.	Minneapolis MN 55404	Minneapolis MN 55404
92.	Hattiesburg MS	Hattiesburg MS

93. Rolla MO 65401   Rolla MD 65401
94. Laconia NH 03246   Laconia NH 03246
95. Socorro NM   Socorro NM

END OF ADDRESS CHECKING TEST

Do not turn to the next page until you are told to do so.

MEANING OF WORDS TEST

DIRECTIONS AND SAMPLE QUESTIONS

The Meaning of Words Test asks you what a word or phrase means. In each question, a word or phrase is in *italics*. Five other words or phrases—lettered A, B, C, D, and E—are given as possible meanings. Choose the lettered word or phrase that means most nearly the same as the question and darken the space with the letter of the right answer. Mark your answers to these sample questions on the sample answer sheet below.

1. A rural carrier may have to *calculate* postage for parcels. *Calculate* means most nearly
   (A) charge
   (B) total
   (C) collect
   (D) refund
   (E) figure out

2. Below the rapids, there were *eddies* in the river. *Eddies* means most nearly
   (A) rocks
   (B) small fish
   (C) whirlpools
   (D) surface insects
   (F) tadpoles

3. The menacing dog has *shaggy* hair. *Shaggy* means most nearly
   (A) sleek and smooth
   (B) long and unkempt
   (C) long and silky
   (D) black and shiny
   (E) short and spotted

4. *Leaflets* are usually carried as bulk mail. *Leaflets* means most nearly
   (A) recycled paper products
   (B) literature about ecology
   (C) agricultural products
   (D) pamphlets
   (E) insecticides

```
SAMPLE ANSWER
   SHEET
1. Ⓐ Ⓑ Ⓒ Ⓓ Ⓔ
2. Ⓐ Ⓑ Ⓒ Ⓓ Ⓔ
3. Ⓐ Ⓑ Ⓒ Ⓓ Ⓔ
4. Ⓐ Ⓑ Ⓒ Ⓓ Ⓔ
```

**CORRECT ANSWERS TO
SAMPLE QUESTIONS**

1. Ⓐ Ⓑ Ⓒ Ⓓ ●
2. Ⓐ Ⓑ ● Ⓓ Ⓔ
3. Ⓐ ● Ⓒ Ⓓ Ⓔ
4. Ⓐ Ⓑ Ⓒ ● Ⓔ

Explanations

1. **(E)** To CALCULATE is to *count,* to *reckon* or to *figure out.*
2. **(C)** EDDIES are small *whirlpools* moving against the current.
3. **(B)** SHAGGY means *long, tangled* and *unkempt.*
4. **(D)** In the context of this sentence, LEAFLETS are *pamphlets.* In an entirely different context, a leaflet may be a young leaf or one of the divisions of a compound leaf.

MEANING OF WORDS TEST

32 Questions—25 Minutes

DIRECTIONS: In each of the sentences below, one word is in *italics*. Following each sentence are five lettered words or phrases. You are to choose the word or phrase with the same meaning as the *italicized* word and mark its letter on the answer sheet. Correct answers are on page 149.

1. The reporter gave an *objective* account of the rally. *Objective* means most nearly
   (A) strict
   (B) fair
   (C) courteous
   (D) personal
   (E) inflammatory

2. The ambulance is equipped with a *portable* oxygen supply. *Portable* means most nearly
   (A) drinkable
   (B) convenient
   (C) having wheels
   (D) borrowed
   (E) able to be carried

3. The *intrepid* climber reached the summit of the mountain. *Intrepid* means most nearly
   (A) fearless
   (B) cowardly
   (C) fanciful
   (D) foolish
   (E) cautious

4. A *petty* disagreement led to breakdown of the negotiations. *Petty* means most nearly
   (A) lengthy
   (B) private
   (C) minor
   (D) basic
   (E) total

5. Despite the icy roads, the driver *endeavored* to deliver the mail. *Endeavored* means most nearly
   (A) managed
   (B) attempted
   (C) expected
   (D) promised
   (E) refused

6. It is not enough to take notes; you must also *transcribe* them. *Transcribe* means most nearly
   (A) write a copy
   (B) type
   (C) invent
   (D) interpret
   (E) dictate

7. On the top of the stack of papers was the warehouse *inventory*. *Inventory* means most nearly
   (A) statement of purpose
   (B) back order list
   (C) catalog of possessions
   (D) patent application
   (E) suggestion sheet

8. The sixteen-inning ballgame was *prolonged*. *Prolonged* means most nearly
   (A) tiring
   (B) exciting
   (C) tied
   (D) refined
   (E) drawn out

9. The CIA is alert to possibilities of *subversive* activity. *Subversive* means most nearly
   (A) secret
   (B) foreign
   (C) evasive
   (D) destructive
   (E) riot-causing

10. The airline has a charge for *excess* baggage. *Excess* means most nearly
    (A) surplus
    (B) oversize
    (C) luxury
    (D) damaged
    (E) overweight

11. The club held its *annual* meeting at a nearby restaurant. *Annual* means most nearly
    (A) seasonal
    (B) occasional
    (C) yearly
    (D) infrequent
    (E) regular

12. Please *dispatch* a messenger as soon as you receive the documents. *Dispatch* means most nearly
    (A) omit mention of
    (B) kill
    (C) do without
    (D) hire
    (E) send out

13. She is likely to *construe* the instructions according to her own beliefs. *Construe* means most nearly
    (A) violate
    (B) interpret
    (C) question
    (D) contradict
    (E) judge

14. The starting date of my new job will *preclude* my taking a vacation. *Preclude* means most nearly
    (A) arise from
    (B) account for
    (C) define
    (D) prevent
    (E) require

15. All *relevant* facts must be included on the application. *Relevant* means most nearly
    (A) controversial
    (B) recent
    (C) impressive
    (D) applicable
    (E) verifiable

16. Many large corporations provide space for *recreation*. *Recreation* means most nearly
    (A) sports
    (B) auditoriums
    (C) escapades
    (D) quiet thought
    (E) diversion

17. The *quantity* of work will make it difficult for me to leave early today. *Quantity* means most nearly
    (A) amount
    (B) difficulty
    (C) variety
    (D) odd format
    (E) special requirement

18. The *coordinator* of the conference made the opening statement. *Coordinator* means most nearly
    (A) enumerator
    (B) organizer
    (C) spokesman
    (D) advertiser
    (E) sponsor

19. An *invoice* was attached to the outside of the package. *Invoice* means most nearly
    (A) speech
    (B) subpoena
    (C) supplement
    (D) bill
    (E) receipt

20. If the economy is growing, jobs should be *abundant*. *Abundant* means most nearly
    (A) plentiful
    (B) accessible
    (C) concentrated
    (D) scattered
    (E) high paying

21. He was an old man, but he had incredible *stamina*. *Stamina* means most nearly
    (A) intelligence
    (B) agility
    (C) posture
    (D) endurance
    (E) curiosity

22. There was a *minute* difference between the highest score on the exam and the second highest. *Minute* means most nearly
    (A) 60 seconds
    (B) short
    (C) significant
    (D) timed
    (E) tiny

23. First-class mail should be *expedited* to the address on the envelope. *Expedited* means most nearly
    (A) hand-carried
    (B) forwarded
    (C) rushed
    (D) returned
    (E) charged

24. If we refuse to *negotiate*, we will never have a new contract. *Negotiate* means most nearly
    (A) suffer
    (B) bargain
    (C) speak
    (D) think
    (E) meet

25. We expected the lecture to be interesting, but actually it was too *verbose*. *Verbose* means most nearly
    (A) vague
    (B) informative
    (C) brief
    (D) silly
    (E) wordy

26. The fireman made a *futile* effort to save the child. *Futile* means most nearly
    (A) heroic
    (B) successful
    (C) unfortunate
    (D) fruitless
    (E) half-hearted

27. The young offender was given *parole* after serving four months. *Parole* means most nearly
    (A) good behavior
    (B) special privileges
    (C) sentence
    (D) pardon
    (E) conditional release

28. The Postal Inspector watches for cases of mail *fraud*. *Fraud* means most nearly
    (A) cheating
    (B) explosives
    (C) pornography
    (D) pilfering
    (E) inefficiency

29. Our neighbors were *inhospitable* to door-to-door salesmen. *Inhospitable* means most nearly
    (A) sick
    (B) friendly
    (C) very large
    (D) unwelcoming
    (E) relaxed

30. When you finish proofreading, please *collate* the pages of the document. *Collate* means most nearly
    (A) destroy
    (B) separate
    (C) assemble
    (D) correct
    (E) copy

31. The owner of the chain of department stores is a man of great *affluence*. *Affluence* means most nearly
    (A) power
    (B) wealth
    (C) philanthropy
    (D) stinginess
    (E) persuasiveness

32. The *normal* attire of a mail handler consists of slacks, shirt and sturdy shoes. *Normal* means most nearly
    (A) required
    (B) comfortable
    (C) safe
    (D) necessary
    (E) usual

END OF MEANING OF WORDS TEST

> **If you finish before time is up, check over your work on this test only. Do not turn back to the Address Checking Test. Do not go on to the next page until you are told to do so.**

FOLLOWING ORAL DIRECTIONS TEST

DIRECTIONS AND SAMPLE QUESTIONS

LISTENING TO INSTRUCTIONS: When you are ready to try these sample questions, give the following instructions to a friend and have the friend read them aloud to you at 80 words per minute. Do not read them to yourself. Your friend will need a watch with a second hand. Listen carefully and do exactly what your friend tells you to do with the worksheet and answer sheet. Your friend will tell you some things to do with each item on the worksheet. After each set of instructions, your friend will give you time to mark your answer by darkening a circle on the sample answer sheet. Since B and D sound very much alike, your friend will say "B as in baker" when he or she means B and "D as in dog" when he or she means D.

Before proceeding further, tear out the worksheet on page 139. Then hand this book to your friend.

TO THE PERSON WHO IS TO READ THE DIRECTIONS: The directions are to be read at the rate of 80 words per minute. Do not read aloud the material which is in parentheses. Do not repeat any directions.

READ ALOUD TO THE CANDIDATE

Look at line 1 on your worksheet. (Pause slightly.) Write a C in the third box. (Pause 2 seconds.) Now, on your answer sheet, find the number in that box and darken space C for that number. (Pause 5 seconds.)

Look at line 2 on your worksheet. (Pause slightly.) The number in each circle is the number of employees in a post office. In the circle for the post office holding more than 10 employees, but less than 15, write the letter E next to the number. (Pause 5 seconds.) Now, on your answer sheet, darken the space for the number-letter combination that is in the circle you just wrote in. (Pause 5 seconds.)

Look at the circles on line 3 of your worksheet. (Pause slightly.) In the second circle, write the answer to this question: Which of the following numbers is smallest: 9, 21, 16, 17, 23? (Pause 5 seconds.) In the third circle, write the answer to this question: How many days are there in a week? (Pause 2 seconds.) Now, on your answer sheet, darken the number-letter combinations that are in the circles you wrote in. (Pause 10 seconds.)

Look at line 4 of your worksheet. (Pause slightly.) Count the number of "O's" in the line. (Pause 5 seconds.) Subtract 2 from the number which you have counted, and darken the space for the letter B as in baker on your answer sheet next to that number. (Pause 10 seconds.)

WORKSHEET

DIRECTIONS: Listening carefully to each set of instructions, mark each item on this worksheet as directed. Then complete each question by marking the sample answer sheet below as directed. For each answer you will darken the answer for a number-letter combination. Should you fall behind and miss an instruction, don't become excited. Let that one go and listen for the next one. If when you start to darken a space for a number, you find that you have already darkened another space for that number, either erase the first mark and darken the space for the new combination or let the first mark stay and do not darken a space for the new combination. Write with a pencil that has a clean eraser. When you finish, you should have no more than one space darkened for each number.

TEAR HERE

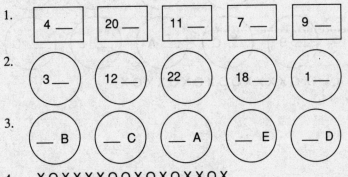

1. | 4 __ | 20 __ | 11 __ | 7 __ | 9 __ |

2. (3 __) (12 __) (22 __) (18 __) (1 __)

3. (__ B) (__ C) (__ A) (__ E) (__ D)

4. X O X X X X O O X O X O X X O X

```
┌─────────────────────────────────────────────┐
│            SAMPLE ANSWER SHEET                │
│  1. Ⓐ Ⓑ Ⓒ Ⓓ Ⓔ    6. Ⓐ Ⓑ Ⓒ Ⓓ Ⓔ   11. Ⓐ Ⓑ Ⓒ Ⓓ Ⓔ │
│  2. Ⓐ Ⓑ Ⓒ Ⓓ Ⓔ    7. Ⓐ Ⓑ Ⓒ Ⓓ Ⓔ   12. Ⓐ Ⓑ Ⓒ Ⓓ Ⓔ │
│  3. Ⓐ Ⓑ Ⓒ Ⓓ Ⓔ    8. Ⓐ Ⓑ Ⓒ Ⓓ Ⓔ   13. Ⓐ Ⓑ Ⓒ Ⓓ Ⓔ │
│  4. Ⓐ Ⓑ Ⓒ Ⓓ Ⓔ    9. Ⓐ Ⓑ Ⓒ Ⓓ Ⓔ   14. Ⓐ Ⓑ Ⓒ Ⓓ Ⓔ │
│  5. Ⓐ Ⓑ Ⓒ Ⓓ Ⓔ   10. Ⓐ Ⓑ Ⓒ Ⓓ Ⓔ   15. Ⓐ Ⓑ Ⓒ Ⓓ Ⓔ │
└─────────────────────────────────────────────┘
```

CORRECT ANSWERS TO SAMPLE QUESTIONS

1. Ⓐ Ⓑ Ⓒ Ⓓ Ⓔ	6. Ⓐ Ⓑ Ⓒ Ⓓ Ⓔ	11. Ⓐ Ⓑ ● Ⓓ Ⓔ
2. Ⓐ Ⓑ Ⓒ Ⓓ Ⓔ	7. ● Ⓑ Ⓒ Ⓓ Ⓔ	12. Ⓐ Ⓑ Ⓒ Ⓓ ●
3. Ⓐ Ⓑ Ⓒ Ⓓ Ⓔ	8. Ⓐ Ⓑ Ⓒ Ⓓ Ⓔ	13. Ⓐ Ⓑ Ⓒ Ⓓ Ⓔ
4. Ⓐ ● Ⓒ Ⓓ Ⓔ	9. Ⓐ Ⓑ ● Ⓓ Ⓔ	14. Ⓐ Ⓑ Ⓒ Ⓓ Ⓔ
5. Ⓐ Ⓑ Ⓒ Ⓓ Ⓔ	10. Ⓐ Ⓑ Ⓒ Ⓓ Ⓔ	15. Ⓐ Ⓑ Ⓒ Ⓓ Ⓔ

Correctly Filled Worksheet

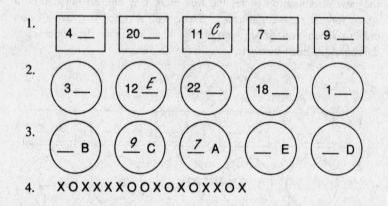

1. | 4 __ | 20 __ | 11 _C_ | 7 __ | 9 __ |

2. (3 __) (12 _E_) (22 __) (18 __) (1 __)

3. (__ B) (_9_ C) (_7_ A) (__ E) (__ D)

4. X O X X X X O O X O X O X X O X

FOLLOWING ORAL DIRECTIONS TEST

Total Time—25 Minutes

LISTENING TO DIRECTIONS

DIRECTIONS: When you are ready to try this test of the Model Exam, give the following instructions to a friend and have the friend read them aloud to you at 80 words per minute. Do NOT read them to yourself. Your friend will need a watch with a second hand. Listen carefully and do exactly what your friend tells you to do with the worksheet and with the answer sheet. Your friend will tell you some things to do with each item on the worksheet. After each set of instructions, your friend will give you time to mark your answer by darkening a circle on the answer sheet. Since B and D sound very much alike, your friend will say "B as in baker" when he or she means B and "D as in dog" when he or she means D.

Before proceeding further, tear out the worksheet on page 145. Then hand this book to your friend.

TO THE PERSON WHO IS TO READ THE DIRECTIONS: The directions are to be read at the rate of 80 words per minute. Do not read aloud the material which is in parentheses. Once you have begun the test itself, do not repeat any directions. The next three paragraphs consist of approximately 120 words. Read these three paragraphs aloud to the candidate in about one and one-half minutes. You may reread these paragraphs as often as necessary to establish an 80 words per minute reading speed.

READ ALOUD TO THE CANDIDATE

On the job you will have to listen to directions and then do what you have been told to do. In this test, I will read instructions to you. Try to understand them as I read them; I cannot repeat them. Once we begin, you may not ask any questions until the end of the test.

On the job you won't have to deal with pictures, numbers and letters like those in the test, but you will have to listen to instructions and follow them. We are using this test to see how well you can follow instructions.

You are to mark your test booklet according to the instructions that I'll read to you. After each set of instructions, I'll give you time to record your answers on the separate answer sheet.

The actual test begins now.

Look at line 1 on your worksheet. (Pause slightly.) Draw a line under the largest number in the line. (Pause 2 seconds.) Now on your answer sheet, find the number under which you just drew a line and darken box D as in dog for that number. (Pause 5 seconds.)

Look at line 1 on your worksheet again. (Pause slightly.) Draw two lines under the smallest number in the line. (Pause 2 seconds.) Now on your answer sheet, find the number under which you just drew two lines and darken box E. (Pause 5 seconds.)

Look at the circles in line 2 on your worksheet. (Pause slightly.) In the second circle, write the answer to this question: How much is 6 plus 4? (Pause 8 seconds.) In the third circle, write the answer to this question: Which of the following numbers is largest: 67, 48, 15, 73, 61? (Pause 5 seconds.) In the fourth circle, write the answer to this question: How many months are there in a year? (Pause 2 seconds.) Now, on your answer sheet, darken the number-letter combinations that are in the circles you wrote in. (Pause 10 seconds.)

Now look at line 3 on your worksheet. (Pause slightly.) Write the letter C on the blank next to the right-hand number. (Pause 2 seconds.) Now on your answer sheet, find the space for the number beside which you wrote and darken box C. (Pause 5 seconds.)

Now look at line 3 on your worksheet again. (Pause slightly.) Write the letter B as in baker on the blank next to the left-hand number. (Pause 2 seconds.) Now on your answer sheet, find the space for the number beside which you just wrote and darken box B as in baker. (Pause 5 seconds.)

Look at the boxes and words in line 4 on your worksheet. (Pause slightly.) Write the first letter of the second word in the third box. (Pause 2 seconds.) Write the last letter of the first word in the second box. (Pause 2 seconds.) Write the first letter of the third word in the first box. (Pause 2 seconds.) Now on your answer sheet, darken the space for the number-letter combinations that are in the three boxes you just wrote in. (Pause 10 seconds.)

Look at the letters on line 5 on your worksheet. (Pause slightly.) Draw a line under the fifth letter in the line. (Pause 2 seconds.) Now on your answer sheet, find the number 56 (pause 2 seconds) and darken the space for the letter under which you drew a line. (Pause 5 seconds.)

Look at the letters on line 5 on your worksheet again. (Pause slightly.) Draw two lines under the fourth letter in the line. (Pause 2 seconds.) Now on your answer sheet, find the number 66 (pause 2 seconds) and darken the space for the letter under which you drew two lines. (Pause 5 seconds.)

Look at the drawings on line 6 on your worksheet. (Pause slightly.) The four boxes indicate the number of buildings in four different carrier routes. In the box for the route with the fewest number of buildings, write an A. (Pause 2 seconds.) Now on your answer sheet, darken the space for the number-letter combination that is in the box you just wrote in. (Pause 5 seconds.)

Now look at line 7 on your worksheet. (Pause slightly.) If fall comes before summer, write the letter B as in baker on the line next to the middle number. (Pause slightly.) Otherwise, write an E on the blank next to the left-hand number. (Pause 5 seconds.) Now on your answer sheet, darken the space for the number-letter combination that you have just written. (Pause 5 seconds.)

Now look at line 8 on your worksheet. (Pause slightly.) Write a D as in dog in the circle with the lowest number. (Pause 2 seconds.) Now on your answer sheet, darken the space for the number-letter combination that is in the circle you just wrote in. (Pause 5 seconds.)

Look at the drawings in line 9 on your worksheet. The four boxes are planes for carrying mail. (Pause slightly.) The plane with the highest number is to be loaded first. Write an E in the box with the highest number. (Pause 2 seconds.) Now on your answer sheet, darken the space for the number-letter combination that is in the box you just wrote in. (Pause 5 seconds.)

Look at line 10 on your worksheet. (Pause slightly.) Draw a line under every number that is more than 35 but less than 55. (Pause 12 seconds.) Now on your answer sheet, for each number that you drew a line under darken box A. (Pause 25 seconds.)

Now look at line 10 on your worksheet again. (Pause slightly.) Draw two lines under every number that is more than 55 and less than 80. (Pause 12 seconds.) Now on your answer sheet for each number that you drew two lines under darken box C. (Pause 25 seconds.)

Look at line 11 on your worksheet. (Pause slightly.) Write an E in the last box. (Pause 2 seconds.) Now on your answer sheet, find the number in that box and darken box E for that number. (Pause 5 seconds.)

Look at line 12 on your worksheet. (Pause slightly.) Draw a line under every "X" in the line. (Pause 5 seconds.) Count the number of lines that you have drawn, add 3, and write that number at the end of the line. (Pause 5 seconds.) Now on your answer sheet, find that number and darken space E for that number. (Pause 5 seconds.)

Look at line 13 on your worksheet. (Pause slightly.) If the number in the right-hand box is larger than the number in the left-hand circle, add 4 to the number in the left-hand circle, and change the number in the circle to this number. (Pause 8 seconds.) Then write C next to the new number. (Pause slightly.) Otherwise, write A next to the number in the smaller box. (Pause 3 seconds.) Now on your answer sheet, darken the space for the number-letter combination that is in the box or circle you just wrote in. (Pause 5 seconds.)

Now look at line 14 on your worksheet. (Pause slightly.) Draw a line under the middle number in the line. (Pause 2 seconds.) Now on your answer sheet, find the number under which you just drew the line and darken box D as in dog for that number. (Pause 5 seconds.)

Now look at line 15 on your worksheet. (Pause slightly.) Write a B as in baker in the third circle. (Pause 2 seconds.) Now on your answer sheet, find the number in that circle and darken box B as in baker for that number. (Pause 5 seconds.)

Now look at line 15 again. (Pause slightly.) Write a C in the last circle. (Pause 2 seconds.) Now on your answer sheet, find the number in that circle and darken box C for that number. (Pause 5 seconds.)

Look at the drawings on line 16 on your worksheet. The number in each box is the number of employees in a post office. (Pause slightly.) In the box for the post office with the smallest number of employees, write on the line the last two figures of the number of employees. (Pause 5 seconds.) Now on your answer sheet, darken the space for the number-letter combination that is in the box you just wrote in. (Pause 5 seconds.)

Now look at line 17 on your worksheet. (Pause slightly.) Write an A on the line next to the right-hand number. (Pause 2 seconds.) Now on your answer sheet find the space for the number next to which you just wrote and darken box A. (Pause 5 seconds.)

Look at line 18 on your worksheet. (Pause slightly.) In the fourth box, write the answer to this question: How many feet are in a yard? (Pause 2 seconds.) Now on your answer sheet darken the space for the number-letter combination that is in the box you just wrote in. (Pause 5 seconds.)

Look at line 18 again. (Pause slightly.) In the second box, write the number 32. (Pause 2 seconds.) Now on your answer sheet, find the number-letter combination that is in the box you just wrote in. (Pause 5 seconds.)

FOLLOWING ORAL DIRECTIONS TEST

Total Time—25 Minutes

WORKSHEET

DIRECTIONS: Listening carefully to each set of instructions, mark each item on this worksheet as directed. Then complete each question by marking the answer sheet as directed. For each answer you will darken the answer for a number-letter combination. Should you fall behind and miss an instruction, don't get excited. Let that one go and listen for the next one. If when you go to darken a box for a number, you find that you have already darkened another box for that number, either erase the first mark and darken the box for the new combination; or let the first mark stay and do not darken a box for the new combination. Write with a pencil that has a clean eraser. When you finish, you should have no more than one box darkened for each number. Correct Answers are on page 151.

TEAR HERE

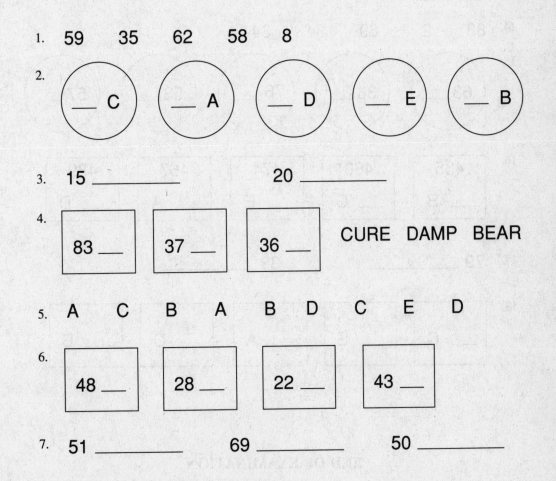

1. 59   35   62   58   8

2. __ C   __ A   __ D   __ E   __ B

3. 15 _____   20 _____

4. 83 __   37 __   36 __   CURE DAMP BEAR

5. A C B A B D C E D

6. 48 __   28 __   22 __   43 __

7. 51 _____   69 _____   50 _____

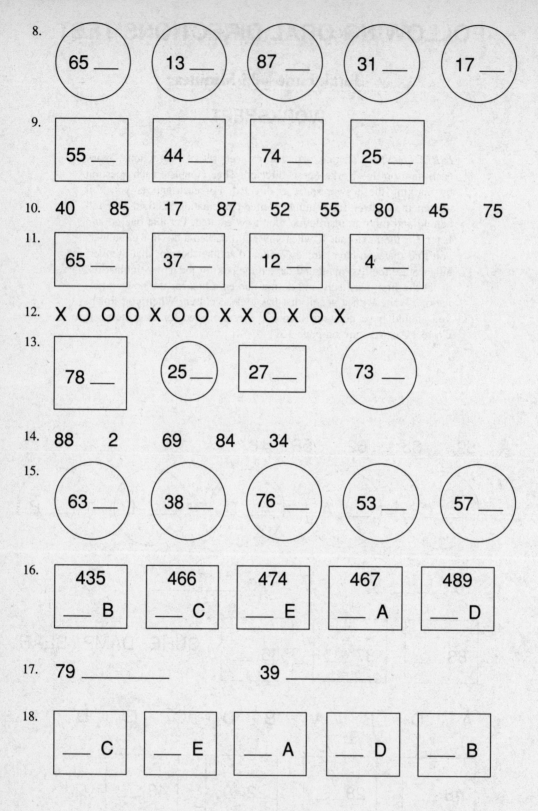

8. 65 ___   13 ___   87 ___   31 ___   17 ___

9. 55 ___   44 ___   74 ___   25 ___

10. 40   85   17   87   52   55   80   45   75

11. 65 ___   37 ___   12 ___   4 ___

12. X O O O X O O X X O X O X

13. 78 ___   25 ___   27 ___   73 ___

14. 88   2   69   84   34

15. 63 ___   38 ___   76 ___   53 ___   57 ___

16. 435 ___ B   466 ___ C   474 ___ E   467 ___ A   489 ___ D

17. 79 _____   39 _____

18. ___ C   ___ E   ___ A   ___ D   ___ B

END OF EXAMINATION

THIRD MODEL EXAM ANSWER KEY

ADDRESS CHECKING TEST

1. A	17. D	33. D	49. A	65. A	81. A
2. D	18. D	34. D	50. D	66. A	82. D
3. A	19. A	35. A	51. A	67. D	83. D
4. D	20. A	36. D	52. D	68. D	84. A
5. D	21. D	37. D	53. A	69. D	85. A
6. A	22. A	38. A	54. D	70. A	86. A
7. A	23. D	39. D	55. A	71. D	87. D
8. D	24. D	40. A	56. A	72. A	88. D
9. D	25. D	41. D	57. A	73. D	89. A
10. D	26. A	42. A	58. D	74. A	90. D
11. D	27. A	43. D	59. A	75. A	91. A
12. D	28. D	44. D	60. A	76. D	92. A
13. A	29. A	45. A	61. D	77. A	93. D
14. D	30. A	46. A	62. A	78. A	94. A
15. A	31. A	47. A	63. D	79. D	95. A
16. A	32. A	48. D	64. D	80. A	

ADDRESS CHECKING TEST

Explanations of Differences

2. number reversal
4. different states
5. spelling of city
8. different cities
9. number reversal
10. different numbers
11. different states
12. spelling of city
14. different states
17. number reversal
18. different states
21. different cities
23. different numbers
24. different states
25. different cities
28. spelling of city
33. number reversal
34. spelling of city
36. different states
37. spelling of city
39. spelling of city
41. different states
43. different numbers
44. different states
48. spelling of city
50. different states
52. number reversal
54. different states
58. different cities
61. different numbers

63. different states
64. different cities
67. spelling of city
68. different numbers
69. different states
71. number reversal
73. different states
76. different cities
79. different numbers
82. number reversal
83. spelling of city
87. number reversal
88. spelling of city
90. different states
93. different states

Analysis of Differences		
Fill in the column on the right with the total number of questions you answered incorrectly.		
City difference	16	
Number difference	14	
State difference	15	
Total addresses with differences	45	
Total addresses with no differences	50	

MEANING OF WORDS TEST

1. B	7. C	12. E	17. A	22. E	27. E
2. E	8. E	13. B	18. B	23. C	28. A
3. A	9. D	14. D	19. D	24. B	29. D
4. C	10. A	15. D	20. A	25. E	30. C
5. B	11. C	16. E	21. D	26. D	31. B
6. A					32. E

MEANING OF WORDS TEST

Explanatory Answers

1. **(B)** OBJECTIVE means expressing the facts without distortion by personal feelings or prejudices, in other words, *fair*. All the choices fit sensibly into the sentence, but if you see *object* in *objective* you might work out for yourself that *objective* would mean directly related to the *thing* or *fact*.

2. **(E)** PORTABLE means *able to be carried about*. The suffix *able* means *capable of*, and the stem *port* means *carry*.

3. **(A)** INTREPID means *brave* and *fearless*.

4. **(C)** PETTY means *of little importance* or *minor*. It is a minor alteration of the French word *petit*.

5. **(B)** To ENDEAVOR is to *make a serious, determined effort*, to *strive* or to *attempt*. This is another word which you really ought to know.

6. **(A)** To TRANSCRIBE is to *make a written copy*. The copy may be typewritten or handwritten. When one *transcribes* dictation, one must first interpret the shorthand notes, but the *transcribing* is the *writing out* of those notes.

7. **(C)** An INVENTORY is an *itemized list* or *catalog* of objects on hand.

8. **(E)** PROLONGED means *extended* or *drawn out*. Sometimes the most obvious answer is the correct one. Don't be afraid to choose an answer just because it looks too easy.

9. **(D)** SUBVERSIVE means *tending to overthrow, ruin* or *destroy*. The prefix *sub* means *under;* the stem *vers* (often *vert*) means *turn*. The type of activities that the CIA watches for are those that would tend to *turn under* or *destroy* our government.

10. **(A)** EXCESS means *too much, extra* or *surplus*. The airline may charge for excess size or for excess weight, but the word *excess* itself refers to the *extra* amount, not to the size or weight.

11. **(C)** ANNUAL means *once a year* or *yearly*. To be sure, an annual meeting occurs at regular intervals, but you are to choose a synonym, not a description.

12. **(E)** To DISPATCH is to *send out*. True, *to dispatch* is also *to kill*. Many words have more than one meaning. When you are given the word in a sentence, you must choose the most reasonable synonym for that sentence.

13. **(B)** To CONSTRUE is to *explain*, to *understand* or to *interpret*. Looking closely at the word, you may notice that *construe* appears to be related to *construct*.

14. **(D)** To PRECLUDE is to *prevent*. The prefix *pre*, meaning *before*, along with the stem *clud*, meaning *close*, leads us to *close before* or *prevent*.

15. **(D)** RELEVANT means *pertinent* or *applicable*. You should see *related* in *relevant*.

16. **(E)** RECREATION means *refreshment of strength and spirits* or *diversion*. *Sports* are a *form of recreation*. *Quiet thoughts* are *reflection* which might also be a *form* of spiritual renewal, but not really recreation.

17. **(A)** QUANTITY means *amount*.

18. **(B)** A COORDINATOR is one who brings people or groups into common action so that

they can work together in a smooth, concerted way, hence an *organizer*. The prefix *co* means *together*. If you combine *together* with *order*, you see that *ordering together* is *organizing*.

19. **(D)** An INVOICE is an *itemized bill*.

20. **(A)** ABUNDANT means *abounding* or *plentiful*. You should be able to answer this correctly from context alone.

21. **(D)** STAMINA is *staying power* or *endurance*. Neither the context nor etymology can help you here.

22. **(E)** MINUTE means *small* or *tiny*. The word is pronounced **my-NOOT**. Use the context of the sentence to choose the correct pronunciation of the word. Once you realize that any reference to time makes no sense, you narrow the choices to C and E. Without knowing the meaning of *minute,* this is the point at which you guess.

23. **(C)** To EXPEDITE is to *accelerate*, to *speed up* or to *rush*.

24. **(B)** To NEGOTIATE is to *confer*, to *compromise* and to *bargain*. In the absence of a true synonym, *speak* or even *meet* would not be totally incorrect. Both are vital aspects of *negotiate*. However, you must choose the **BEST** synonym.

25. **(E)** VERBOSE means containing more words than necessary, hence *wordy*. The suffix *ose* meaning *full of* with the stem *verb* meaning of *word* leads us to *full of words*.

26. **(D)** FUTILE means *vain, ineffective* or *fruitless*. If you don't know this word, learn it now.

27. **(F)** PAROLE means *conditional release* of a prisoner after serving a part of a sentence. The paroled prisoner must fulfill certain requirements during the time of parole. In effect, he or she is still guilty and is still a prisoner, though not behind bars. *Parole* is very different from *pardon*, which is *forgiveness*.

28. **(A)** FRAUD is *deceit, trickery* or *cheating*. The Postal Inspector also watches for the other four choices. Postal *fraud* is commited when one uses the mails to extort money, to convince people to send away for inferior or imaginary items, or to cheat by any means.

29. **(D)** INHOSPITABLE means *unfriendly* or *unwelcoming*. The negative prefix *in* meaning *not* in front of the word *hospitable* meaning *cordial to guests* gives the clue even though all the choices fit into the sentence.

30. **(C)** To COLLATE is to *assemble pages in proper order*. The prefix *col* meaning *together* should help you here.

31. **(B)** AFFLUENCE is an *abundant supply, profusion* or *wealth*. This is a word you should know.

32. **(E)** NORMAL means *regular, standard* or *usual*.

FOLLOWING ORAL DIRECTIONS TEST

Correctly Filled Worksheet

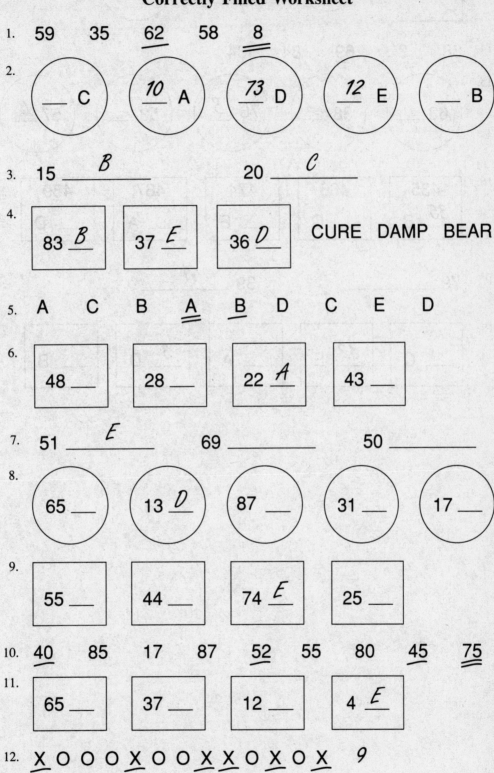

1. 59　35　<u>62</u>　58　<u>=</u>8

2. ⊙ __ C　⊙ <u>10</u> A　⊙ <u>73</u> D　⊙ <u>12</u> E　⊙ __ B

3. 15 ___*B*___　　20 ___*C*___

4. ☐ 83 <u>*B*</u>　☐ 37 <u>*E*</u>　☐ 36 <u>*D*</u>　CURE DAMP BEAR

5. A　C　B　<u>A</u>　<u>B</u>　D　C　E　D

6. ☐ 48 __　☐ 28 __　☐ 22 <u>*A*</u>　☐ 43 __

7. 51 ___*E*___　　69 ___　　50 ___

8. ⊙ 65 __　⊙ 13 <u>*D*</u>　⊙ 87 __　⊙ 31 __　⊙ 17 __

9. ☐ 55 __　☐ 44 __　☐ 74 <u>*E*</u>　☐ 25 __

10. <u>40</u>　85　17　87　<u>52</u>　55　80　<u>45</u>　<u>75</u>

11. ☐ 65 __　☐ 37 __　☐ 12 __　☐ 4 <u>*E*</u>

12. <u>X</u> O O O <u>X</u> O O <u>X</u> <u>X</u> O <u>X</u> O <u>X</u>　*9*

13.
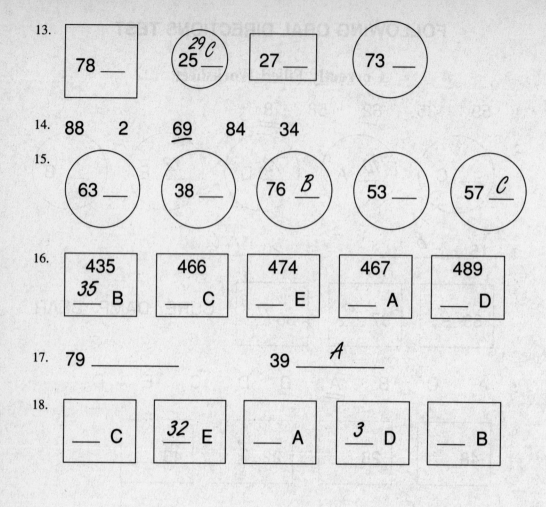

| 78 ___ | 25 *29 C* | 27 ___ | 73 ___ |

14. 88   2   69   84   34

15. 63 ___   38 ___   76 *B*   53 ___   57 *C*

16.
| 435 *35* B | 466 ___ C | 474 ___ E | 467 ___ A | 489 ___ D |

17. 79 _____   39 ____ *A* ____

18. ___ C   *32* E   ___ A   *3* D   ___ B

FOLLOWING ORAL DIRECTIONS TEST

Correctly Filled Answer Grid

#	Answer		#	Answer		#	Answer
1.	A B C D E		31.	A B C D E		61.	A B C D E
2.	A B C D E		32.	A B C D ●		62.	A B C ● E
3.	A B C ● E		33.	A B C D E		63.	A B C D E
4.	A B C D ●		34.	A B C D E		64.	A B C D E
5.	A B C D E		35.	A ● C D E		65.	A B C D E
6.	A B C D E		36.	A B C ● E		66.	● B C D E
7.	A B C D E		37.	A B C D ●		67.	A B C D E
8.	A B C D ●		38.	A B C D E		68.	A B C D E
9.	A B C D ●		39.	● B C D E		69.	A B C ● E
10.	● B C D E		40.	● B C D E		70.	A B C D E
11.	A B C D E		41.	A B C D E		71.	A B C D E
12.	A B C D ●		42.	A B C D E		72.	A B C D E
13.	A B C ● E		43.	A B C D E		73.	A B C ● E
14.	A B C D E		44.	A B C D E		74.	A B C D ●
15.	A ● C D E		45.	● B C D E		75.	A B C D E
16.	A B C D E		46.	A B C D E		76.	A ● C D E
17.	A B C D E		47.	A B C D E		77.	A B C D E
18.	A B C D E		48.	A B C D E		78.	A B C D E
19.	A B C D E		49.	A B C D E		79.	A B C D E
20.	A B ● D E		50.	A B C D E		80.	A B C D E
21.	A B C D E		51.	A B C D ●		81.	A B C D E
22.	● B C D E		52.	● B C D E		82.	A B C D E
23.	A B C D E		53.	A B C D E		83.	A ● C D E
24.	A B C D E		54.	A B C D E		84.	A B C D E
25.	A B C D E		55.	A B C D E		85.	A B C D E
26.	A B C D E		56.	A ● C D E		86.	A B C D E
27.	A B C D E		57.	A B ● D E		87.	A B C D E
28.	A B C D E		58.	A B C D E		88.	A B C D E
29.	A B ● D E		59.	A B C D E		89.	A B C D E
30.	A B C D E		60.	A B C D E			

FOURTH MODEL EXAM ANSWER SHEET

ADDRESS CHECKING TEST

1. ⒶⒹ	17. ⒶⒹ	33. ⒶⒹ	49. ⒶⒹ	65. ⒶⒹ	81. ⒶⒹ
2. ⒶⒹ	18. ⒶⒹ	34. ⒶⒹ	50. ⒶⒹ	66. ⒶⒹ	82. ⒶⒹ
3. ⒶⒹ	19. ⒶⒹ	35. ⒶⒹ	51. ⒶⒹ	67. ⒶⒹ	83. ⒶⒹ
4. ⒶⒹ	20. ⒶⒹ	36. ⒶⒹ	52. ⒶⒹ	68. ⒶⒹ	84. ⒶⒹ
5. ⒶⒹ	21. ⒶⒹ	37. ⒶⒹ	53. ⒶⒹ	69. ⒶⒹ	85. ⒶⒹ
6. ⒶⒹ	22. ⒶⒹ	38. ⒶⒹ	54. ⒶⒹ	70. ⒶⒹ	86. ⒶⒹ
7. ⒶⒹ	23. ⒶⒹ	39. ⒶⒹ	55. ⒶⒹ	71. ⒶⒹ	87. ⒶⒹ
8. ⒶⒹ	24. ⒶⒹ	40. ⒶⒹ	56. ⒶⒹ	72. ⒶⒹ	88. ⒶⒹ
9. ⒶⒹ	25. ⒶⒹ	41. ⒶⒹ	57. ⒶⒹ	73. ⒶⒹ	89. ⒶⒹ
10. ⒶⒹ	26. ⒶⒹ	42. ⒶⒹ	58. ⒶⒹ	74. ⒶⒹ	90. ⒶⒹ
11. ⒶⒹ	27. ⒶⒹ	43. ⒶⒹ	59. ⒶⒹ	75. ⒶⒹ	91. ⒶⒹ
12. ⒶⒹ	28. ⒶⒹ	44. ⒶⒹ	60. ⒶⒹ	76. ⒶⒹ	92. ⒶⒹ
13. ⒶⒹ	29. ⒶⒹ	45. ⒶⒹ	61. ⒶⒹ	77. ⒶⒹ	93. ⒶⒹ
14. ⒶⒹ	30. ⒶⒹ	46. ⒶⒹ	62. ⒶⒹ	78. ⒶⒹ	94. ⒶⒹ
15. ⒶⒹ	31. ⒶⒹ	47. ⒶⒹ	63. ⒶⒹ	79. ⒶⒹ	95. ⒶⒹ
16. ⒶⒹ	32. ⒶⒹ	48. ⒶⒹ	64. ⒶⒹ	80. ⒶⒹ	

MEANING OF WORDS TEST

1. ⒶⒷⒸⒹⒺ	8. ⒶⒷⒸⒹⒺ	15. ⒶⒷⒸⒹⒺ	22. ⒶⒷⒸⒹⒺ	29. ⒶⒷⒸⒹⒺ
2. ⒶⒷⒸⒹⒺ	9. ⒶⒷⒸⒹⒺ	16. ⒶⒷⒸⒹⒺ	23. ⒶⒷⒸⒹⒺ	30. ⒶⒷⒸⒹⒺ
3. ⒶⒷⒸⒹⒺ	10. ⒶⒷⒸⒹⒺ	17. ⒶⒷⒸⒹⒺ	24. ⒶⒷⒸⒹⒺ	31. ⒶⒷⒸⒹⒺ
4. ⒶⒷⒸⒹⒺ	11. ⒶⒷⒸⒹⒺ	18. ⒶⒷⒸⒹⒺ	25. ⒶⒷⒸⒹⒺ	32. ⒶⒷⒸⒹⒺ
5. ⒶⒷⒸⒹⒺ	12. ⒶⒷⒸⒹⒺ	19. ⒶⒷⒸⒹⒺ	26. ⒶⒷⒸⒹⒺ	
6. ⒶⒷⒸⒹⒺ	13. ⒶⒷⒸⒹⒺ	20. ⒶⒷⒸⒹⒺ	27. ⒶⒷⒸⒹⒺ	
7. ⒶⒷⒸⒹⒺ	14. ⒶⒷⒸⒹⒺ	21. ⒶⒷⒸⒹⒺ	28. ⒶⒷⒸⒹⒺ	

FOLLOWING ORAL DIRECTIONS TEST

1. ⒶⒷⒸⒹⒺ	19. ⒶⒷⒸⒹⒺ	37. ⒶⒷⒸⒹⒺ	55. ⒶⒷⒸⒹⒺ	73. ⒶⒷⒸⒹⒺ
2. ⒶⒷⒸⒹⒺ	20. ⒶⒷⒸⒹⒺ	38. ⒶⒷⒸⒹⒺ	56. ⒶⒷⒸⒹⒺ	74. ⒶⒷⒸⒹⒺ
3. ⒶⒷⒸⒹⒺ	21. ⒶⒷⒸⒹⒺ	39. ⒶⒷⒸⒹⒺ	57. ⒶⒷⒸⒹⒺ	75. ⒶⒷⒸⒹⒺ
4. ⒶⒷⒸⒹⒺ	22. ⒶⒷⒸⒹⒺ	40. ⒶⒷⒸⒹⒺ	58. ⒶⒷⒸⒹⒺ	76. ⒶⒷⒸⒹⒺ
5. ⒶⒷⒸⒹⒺ	23. ⒶⒷⒸⒹⒺ	41. ⒶⒷⒸⒹⒺ	59. ⒶⒷⒸⒹⒺ	77. ⒶⒷⒸⒹⒺ
6. ⒶⒷⒸⒹⒺ	24. ⒶⒷⒸⒹⒺ	42. ⒶⒷⒸⒹⒺ	60. ⒶⒷⒸⒹⒺ	78. ⒶⒷⒸⒹⒺ
7. ⒶⒷⒸⒹⒺ	25. ⒶⒷⒸⒹⒺ	43. ⒶⒷⒸⒹⒺ	61. ⒶⒷⒸⒹⒺ	79. ⒶⒷⒸⒹⒺ
8. ⒶⒷⒸⒹⒺ	26. ⒶⒷⒸⒹⒺ	44. ⒶⒷⒸⒹⒺ	62. ⒶⒷⒸⒹⒺ	80. ⒶⒷⒸⒹⒺ
9. ⒶⒷⒸⒹⒺ	27. ⒶⒷⒸⒹⒺ	45. ⒶⒷⒸⒹⒺ	63. ⒶⒷⒸⒹⒺ	81. ⒶⒷⒸⒹⒺ
10. ⒶⒷⒸⒹⒺ	28. ⒶⒷⒸⒹⒺ	46. ⒶⒷⒸⒹⒺ	64. ⒶⒷⒸⒹⒺ	82. ⒶⒷⒸⒹⒺ
11. ⒶⒷⒸⒹⒺ	29. ⒶⒷⒸⒹⒺ	47. ⒶⒷⒸⒹⒺ	65. ⒶⒷⒸⒹⒺ	83. ⒶⒷⒸⒹⒺ
12. ⒶⒷⒸⒹⒺ	30. ⒶⒷⒸⒹⒺ	48. ⒶⒷⒸⒹⒺ	66. ⒶⒷⒸⒹⒺ	84. ⒶⒷⒸⒹⒺ
13. ⒶⒷⒸⒹⒺ	31. ⒶⒷⒸⒹⒺ	49. ⒶⒷⒸⒹⒺ	67. ⒶⒷⒸⒹⒺ	85. ⒶⒷⒸⒹⒺ
14. ⒶⒷⒸⒹⒺ	32. ⒶⒷⒸⒹⒺ	50. ⒶⒷⒸⒹⒺ	68. ⒶⒷⒸⒹⒺ	86. ⒶⒷⒸⒹⒺ
15. ⒶⒷⒸⒹⒺ	33. ⒶⒷⒸⒹⒺ	51. ⒶⒷⒸⒹⒺ	69. ⒶⒷⒸⒹⒺ	87. ⒶⒷⒸⒹⒺ
16. ⒶⒷⒸⒹⒺ	34. ⒶⒷⒸⒹⒺ	52. ⒶⒷⒸⒹⒺ	70. ⒶⒷⒸⒹⒺ	88. ⒶⒷⒸⒹⒺ
17. ⒶⒷⒸⒹⒺ	35. ⒶⒷⒸⒹⒺ	53. ⒶⒷⒸⒹⒺ	71. ⒶⒷⒸⒹⒺ	89. ⒶⒷⒸⒹⒺ
18. ⒶⒷⒸⒹⒺ	36. ⒶⒷⒸⒹⒺ	54. ⒶⒷⒸⒹⒺ	72. ⒶⒷⒸⒹⒺ	90. ⒶⒷⒸⒹⒺ

FOURTH MODEL EXAM

SCORE SHEET

ADDRESS CHECKING TEST: Your score on the Address Checking Test is based upon the number of questions you answered correctly minus the number of questions you answered incorrectly. To determine your score, subtract the number of wrong answers from the number of correct answers.

Number Right   –   Number Wrong   =   Raw Score
_____   –   _____   =   _____

MEANING OF WORDS TEST: Your score on the Meaning of Words Test is based only upon the number of questions you answered correctly.

Number Right   =   Raw Score
_____   =   _____

FOLLOWING ORAL DIRECTIONS TEST: Your score on the Following Oral Directions Test is based only upon the number of questions you marked correctly on the answer sheet. The Worksheet is not scored, and wrong answers on the answer sheet do not count against you.

Number Right   =   Raw Score
_____   =   _____

TOTAL SCORE: To find your total raw score, add together the raw scores for each section of the exam.

Address Checking Score   _____
         +
Meaning of Words Score   _____
         +
Following Oral Directions Score   _____
         =
Total Raw Score   _____

ADDRESS CHECKING TEST

DIRECTIONS AND SAMPLE QUESTIONS

In the Address Checking Test you will have to decide whether two addresses are alike or different. Any difference at all makes the two addresses different. Look carefully at the address at the left and the address at the right. If the two addresses are *exactly alike in every way*, darken space Ⓐ for the question. If the two addresses are *different in any way*, darken space Ⓓ for the question. Mark your answers to these sample questions on the sample answer sheet on this page.

1. Hempstead NY 11550   Hempsted NY 11550
2. St. Paul MI 55105   St. Paul MN 55105
3. Missoula MT   Missoula MT
4. Rochester NY 14627   Rochester NY 14267
5. Lubbock TX   Lubbock TX
6. Sarasota FL 33580   Saratoga FL 33580

```
SAMPLE ANSWER
    SHEET
    1. Ⓐ Ⓓ
    2. Ⓐ Ⓓ
    3. Ⓐ Ⓓ
    4. Ⓐ Ⓓ
    5. Ⓐ Ⓓ
    6. Ⓐ Ⓓ
```

**CORRECT ANSWERS TO
SAMPLE QUESTIONS**
1. Ⓐ ●
2. Ⓐ ●
3. ● Ⓓ
4. Ⓐ ●
5. ● Ⓓ
6. Ⓐ ●

Explanations

Question 1 is marked Ⓓ because the city spelling is different.
Question 2 is marked Ⓓ because the state abbreviation is different.
Question 4 is marked Ⓓ because of a number reversal.
Question 6 is marked Ⓓ because the cities are different.

ADDRESS CHECKING TEST

95 Questions—6 Minutes

DIRECTIONS: This is a test of your speed and accuracy in comparing addresses. For each question in the test blacken the correspondingly-numbered answer space as follows:

- Blacken Ⓐ if the two addresses are exactly ALIKE.
- Blacken Ⓓ if the two addresses are DIFFERENT in any way.

Correct answers are on page 179.

1. Purdin Mo — Purdon Mo
2. Hobart Ind 46342 — Hobart Ind 46342
3. Kuna Idaho — Kuna Idaho
4. Janesville Calif 96114 — Janesville Calif 96119
5. Sioux Falls S Dak — Sioux Falls S Dak
6. Homewood Miss — Homewood Miss
7. Kaweah Calif — Kawaeh Calif
8. Unionport Ohio — Unionport Ohio
9. Meyersdale Pa — Meyersdale Va
10. Coquille Oreg 97423 — Coqville Oreg 97423
11. Milan Wis — Milam Wis
12. Prospect Ky — Prospect Ky
13. Cloversville N Y — Cloverville N Y
14. Locate Mont 59340 — Locate Mont 59340
15. Bozman Md — Bozeman Md
16. Orient Ill — Orient Ill
17. Yosemite Ky 42566 — Yosemite Ky 42566
18. Camden Miss 39045 — Camden Miss 39054
19. Bennington Vt — Bennington Vt
20. La Farge Wis — La Farge Wis
21. Fairfield N Y — Fairfield N C
22. Wynot Nebr — Wynot Nebr
23. Arona Pa — Aroda Pa
24. Thurman N C 28683 — Thurmond N C 28683
25. Zenda Kans — Zenba Kans
26. Pike N H — Pike N H
27. Gorst Wash 98337 — Gorst Wash 98837
28. Joiner Ark — Joiner Ark
29. Normangee Tex — Normangee Tex
30. Toccoa Ga — Tococa Ga
31. Small Point Maine 04567 — Small Point Maine 04567
32. Eagan Tenn — Eagar Tenn
33. Belfield N Dak — Belford N Dak
34. De Ridder La 70634 — De Ridder La 70634
35. Van Meter Iowa — Van Meter Iowa
36. Valparaiso Fla — Valparaiso Ind
37. Souris N Dak — Souris N Dak
38. Robbinston Maine — Robbinstown Maine

39. Dawes W Va 25054	Dawes W Va 25054
40. Goltry Okla	Goltrey Okla
41. Irmo S C	Irmo S C
42. East Barnet Vt	East Barnet Vt
43. Ellenburg Center N Y 12900	Ellenburg Depot N Y 12900
44. Helena Mo	Helena Mo
45. Grafton Wis	Granton Wis
46. Columbia N C	Columbus N C
47. Dumont Colo	Dupont Colo
48. McClusky N Dak	McClosky N Dak
49. Sheldon S C	Shelton S C
50. Fredericksburg Iowa	Fredericksburg Iowa
51. Holden Vt	Holton Vt
52. Karlsruhe N Dak	Karlsruhe N Dak
53. East Springfield Pa	West Springfield Pa
54. Villa Prades P R	Villa Prades P R
55. Cadmus Mich	Cadmus Mich
56. New London N H 03200	New London N H 03200
57. Anchorage Alaska 95501	Anchorage Alaska 99501
58. Garciasville Tex 78547	Garciasville Tex 78547
59. Edenton Ohio	Edenton Ohio
60. Vernal Utah	Vernon Utah
61. Tullahassee Okla	Tallahassee Okla
62. Carlton Wash	Carson Wash
63. Tucson Ariz 85721	Tucson Ariz 85751
64. Vermillion S Dak 57069	Vermillion S Dak 57069
65. Oxford N H	Orford N H
66. Evanston Wyo	Evanston Wyo
67. Gonzalez Fla 32560	Gonzalez Fla 32560
68. Clifton Tenn	Clinton Tenn
69. Lindsborg Kans	Lindsborg Kans
70. Greenbush Va	Greenbush Va
71. Paterson N J 07400	Paterson N J 07500
72. Monticello Minn	Monticello Minn
73. Haina Hawaii	Hana Hawaii
74. Barre Mass	Barre Mass
75. Beech Creek Ky 42300	Beech Grove Ky 42300
76. Biddeford Maine 04005	Biddeford Maine 04006
77. Richford N Y	Richland N Y
78. Shamko Oreg 97057	Shaneko Oreg 97057
79. Farmington N Mex	Framington N Mex
80. Goodwell Okla	Goodwell Okla
81. Saginaw Tex	Saginaw Tex
82. Jersey City N J 07323	Jersey City N J 07328
83. Fremont N C	Fremont N C
84. Ottumwa S Dak	Ottumwa S Dak
85. Alasha S Dak	Alaska S Dak
86. Oklahoma City Okla 73106	Oklahoma City Okla 73106
87. Slocum R I	Slocam R I
88. Leesburg Va	Leesburg Va
89. Wilmot Ark	Wilmor Ark
90. Seaford Del 19973	Seaford Del 19973
91. Aldan Pa	Alden Pa
92. Washington D C 20008	Washington D C 20018

93. Wilson Ark   Wilton Ark
94. Fresno Calif 93705   Fresno Calif 93705
95. Clearmont Wyo   Clearmont Wyo

END OF ADDRESS CHECKING TEST

Do not turn to the next page until the signal is given.

MEANING OF WORDS TEST

DIRECTIONS AND SAMPLE QUESTIONS

The Meaning of Words Test asks you what a word or phrase means. In each question, a word or phrase is in *italics*. Five other words or phrases—lettered A, B, C, D, and E—are given as possible meanings. Choose the lettered word or phrase that means most nearly the same as the word that is in *italics*. When you have chosen your answer, find the answer space numbered the same as the question and darken the space with the letter of the right answer. Mark your answers to these sample questions on the sample answer sheet below.

1. Earthquakes usually occur along a *fault* line. *Fault* means most nearly
   (A) excessive
   (B) responsible
   (C) weakness
   (D) disappointing
   (E) puzzled

2. The *eccentric* old man wore one boot and one sandal. *Eccentric* means most nearly
   (A) poor
   (B) odd
   (C) drunken
   (D) retarded
   (E) nasty

3. The gourmet was *catholic* in his tastes. *Catholic* means most nearly
   (A) religious
   (B) intolerant
   (C) discriminating
   (D) disciplined
   (E) comprehensive

4. When we brought the dog home from the kennel he was extremely *lethargic*. *Lethargic* means most nearly
   (A) sluggish
   (B) active
   (C) happy
   (D) angry
   (E) affectionate

SAMPLE ANSWER SHEET
1. Ⓐ Ⓑ Ⓒ Ⓓ Ⓔ
2. Ⓐ Ⓑ Ⓒ Ⓓ Ⓔ
3. Ⓐ Ⓑ Ⓒ Ⓓ Ⓔ
4. Ⓐ Ⓑ Ⓒ Ⓓ Ⓔ

```
┌─────────────────────────┐
│  CORRECT ANSWERS TO     │
│  SAMPLE QUESTIONS       │
│   1. Ⓐ Ⓑ ● Ⓓ Ⓔ          │
│   2. Ⓐ ● Ⓒ Ⓓ Ⓔ          │
│   3. Ⓐ Ⓑ Ⓒ Ⓓ ●          │
│   4. ● Ⓑ Ⓒ Ⓓ Ⓔ          │
└─────────────────────────┘
```

Explanations

1. **(C)** A FAULT line along which earthquakes occur is a *fracture*, an *imperfection* or a *weakness*. The context of the sentence should help you choose the correct answer.
2. **(B)** ECCENTRIC means *deviating from usual behavior, strange* or *odd*. The word derives from the prefix *e* meaning *out of* and the root *center*.
3. **(E)** CATHOLIC beginning with a small *c* means *broad in tastes and interests, universal* or *comprehensive*.
4. **(A)** LETHARGIC means *inert, apathetic* or *sluggish*.

MEANING OF WORDS TEST

32 Questions—25 Minutes

DIRECTIONS: In each of the sentences below, one word is in *italics*. Following each sentence are five lettered words or phrases. You are to choose the word or phrase with the same meaning as the *italicized* word and mark its letter on the answer sheet. Correct answers are on page 181.

1. From his testimony, we can *infer* that the accused is innocent. *Infer* means most nearly
   (A) guess
   (B) conclude
   (C) prove
   (D) deny
   (E) rebut

2. The evangelist gave a *logical* argument for his position. *Logical* means most nearly
   (A) calm
   (B) inflexible
   (C) reasoned
   (D) impassioned
   (E) far-fetched

3. My son now prepares his letters on the computer so they are *legible*. *Legible* means most nearly
   (A) printed
   (B) long
   (C) evenly spaced
   (D) permitted
   (E) readable

4. Let us *assemble* in front of town hall before the parade. *Assemble* means most nearly
   (A) put in order
   (B) march
   (C) practice
   (D) gather
   (E) pretend

5. The lecture was *slated* to begin right after lunch. *Slated* means most nearly
   (A) postponed
   (B) scheduled
   (C) ticketed
   (D) advertised
   (E) elected

6. He hides a spare housekey in a *secure* place. *Secure* means most nearly
   (A) convenient
   (B) nearby
   (C) secret
   (D) obvious
   (E) safe

7. The Supreme Court ruled that schools must be integrated with all *deliberate* speed. *Deliberate* means most nearly
   (A) clever
   (B) daring
   (C) headlong
   (D) considered
   (E) slow

8. The Senator was *privileged* to be seated at the head table. *Privileged* means most nearly
   (A) annoyed
   (B) required
   (C) angry
   (D) requested
   (E) honored

9. After many years on the job, she will now have the opportunity to *supervise* others. *Supervise* means most nearly
   (A) persecute
   (B) restrain
   (C) oversee
   (D) train
   (E) hire

10. You should *utilize* all the fringe benefits that go with your new job. *Utilize* means most nearly
    (A) employ
    (B) enjoy
    (C) ponder
    (D) share
    (E) ignore

11. When he reaches the age of eighteen, a young man is *compelled* to register for the draft. *Compelled* means most nearly
    (A) tempted
    (B) urged
    (C) forced
    (D) persuaded
    (E) permitted

12. He has an *irritating* habit of cracking his knuckles. *Irritating* means most nearly
    (A) interesting
    (B) unnerving
    (C) annoying
    (D) unbearable
    (E) nervous

13. Our union is *affiliated* with a national organization. *Affiliated* means most nearly
    (A) connected with
    (B) ruled by
    (C) separated from
    (D) independent of
    (E) dependent upon

14. The *uniformity* of law officers' clothing leads to easy recognition. *Uniformity* means most nearly
    (A) costume
    (B) boredom
    (C) similarity
    (D) drabness
    (E) custom

15. The broken track will *effect* train delays. *Effect* means most nearly
    (A) concern
    (B) influence
    (C) pretend
    (D) assume
    (E) bring about

16. So far, the *outcome* of the election is in doubt. *Outcome* means most nearly
    (A) aim
    (B) premise
    (C) statistics
    (D) result
    (E) amendment

17. The *dogmatic* officer insisted that orders be carried out in his way. *Dogmatic* means most nearly
    (A) unprincipled
    (B) canine
    (C) ugly
    (D) easygoing
    (E) dictatorial

18. On the workbench was a neat array of woodworking *utensils*. *Utensils* means most nearly
    (A) machines
    (B) tools
    (C) objects
    (D) knives
    (E) products

19. The witness to the accident held to her story with *tenacity*. *Tenacity* means most nearly
    (A) firmness
    (B) temerity
    (C) timidity
    (D) discouragement
    (E) good humor

20. The waiter was *courteous* but not too clever. *Courteous* means most nearly
    (A) fast
    (B) impersonal
    (C) royal
    (D) eager
    (E) polite

21. If you don't make a *request*, you cannot expect satisfaction. *Request* means most nearly
    (A) demand
    (B) complaint
    (C) statement
    (D) contract
    (E) will

22. *Insert* the top portion of the bill along with your check. *Insert* means most nearly
    (A) copy
    (B) fold up
    (C) mail
    (D) tear off
    (E) put in

23. She is a *dynamic* spokesperson for our cause. *Dynamic* means most nearly
    (A) noisy
    (B) magnetic
    (C) forceful
    (D) intelligent
    (E) softspoken

24. In his oath, the President swears to faithfully *execute* the duties of his office. *Execute* means most nearly
    (A) delegate
    (B) behead
    (C) resign
    (D) carry out
    (E) cancel

25. After three years on a waiting list, Aunt Sherry is about to move into a middle-income housing *complex*. *Complex* means most nearly
    (A) tower
    (B) group of buildings
    (C) neighborhood
    (D) corporation
    (E) maze

26. The amount by which he overestimated the weight of the package was *insignificant*. *Insignificant* means most nearly
    (A) unimportant
    (B) useless
    (C) unrewarding
    (D) low
    (E) high

27. Just *discard* the junk mail. *Discard* means most nearly
    (A) ignore
    (B) refuse
    (C) throw away
    (D) return
    (E) tear up

28. A copy of the *memorandum* was circulated to everyone in the office. *Memorandum* means most nearly
    (A) formal letter
    (B) command
    (C) minutes of a meeting
    (D) thank-you letter
    (E) note

29. The weather bureau will *monitor* the progress of the storm. *Monitor* means most nearly
    (A) warn
    (B) keep ahead of
    (C) keep track of
    (D) alter
    (E) chart

30. The sick old man sat in a chair with a *vacant* look on his face. *Vacant* means most nearly
    (A) empty
    (B) preoccupied
    (C) quiet
    (D) angry
    (E) happy

31. The soldier fell to the ground *mortally* wounded. *Mortally* means most nearly
    (A) seriously
    (B) slightly
    (C) spiritually
    (D) fatally
    (E) by a car

32. There is *sufficient* money for the soup kitchen to operate for another year. *Sufficient* means most nearly
    (A) excessive
    (B) donated
    (C) invested
    (D) enough
    (E) designated

END OF MEANING OF WORDS TEST

> **If you finish this test before time is up, check over your work on
> this test only. Do not turn back to the Address Checking Test. Do
> not turn to the next page until you are told to do so.**

FOLLOWING ORAL DIRECTIONS TEST

DIRECTIONS AND SAMPLE QUESTIONS

LISTENING TO INSTRUCTIONS: When you are ready to try these sample questions, give the following instructions to a friend and have the friend read them aloud to you at 80 words per minute. Do not read them to yourself. Your friend will need a watch with a second hand. Listen carefully and do exactly what your friend tells you to do with the worksheet and answer sheet. Your friend will tell you some things to do with each item on the worksheet. After each set of instructions, your friend will give you time to mark your answer by darkening a circle on the sample answer sheet. Since B and D sound very much alike, your friend will say "B as in baker" when he or she means B and "D as in dog" when he or she means D.

Before proceeding further, tear out the worksheet on page 171. Then hand this book to your friend.

TO THE PERSON WHO IS TO READ THE DIRECTIONS: The directions are to be read at the rate of 80 words per minute. Do not read aloud the material which is in parentheses. Do not repeat any directions.

READ ALOUD TO THE CANDIDATE

Look at line 1 on your worksheet. (Pause slightly.) Draw a line under the third letter in the line. (Pause 2 seconds.) Now, on your answer sheet, find the number that is 2 less than 17 and darken the space for the letter which you drew a line under. (Pause 10 seconds.)

Look at line 2 on your worksheet. (Pause slightly.) Locate the smallest number and draw a circle around it. (Pause 5 seconds.) Now, on your answer sheet, darken the space next to letter C for the number you have circled. (Pause 5 seconds.)

Look at line 3 on your worksheet. (Pause slightly.) There are 5 boxes. Each box has a number. In each box containing a number which can be found on a foot-long ruler, write the letter E. (Pause 10 seconds.) Now, on your answer sheet, darken the space for the number-letter combination that is in each box which you wrote in. (Pause 10 seconds.)

Look at line 4 on your worksheet. (Pause slightly.) If in a week Wednesday comes before Thursday, write D as in dog in the box with the largest number. (Pause 5 seconds.) If it does not, write E in the box of the second-to-largest number. (Pause 5 seconds.) Now, on your answer sheet, darken the space for the number-letter combination that is in the box you just wrote in. (Pause 5 seconds.)

WORKSHEET

DIRECTIONS: Listening carefully to each set of instructions, mark each item on this worksheet as directed. Then complete each question by marking the sample answer sheet below as directed. For each answer you will darken the answer for a number-letter combination. Should you fall behind and miss an instruction, don't become excited. Let that one go and listen for the next one. If when you start to darken a space for a number, you find that you have already darkened another space for that number, either erase the first mark and darken the space for the new combination or let the first mark stay and do not darken a space for the new combination. Write with a pencil that has a clean eraser. When you finish, you should have no more than one space darkened for each number.

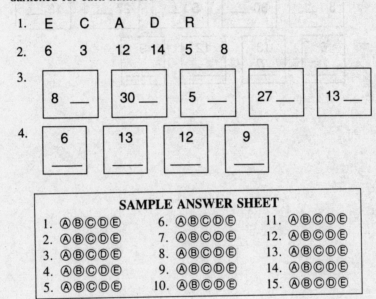

1. E C A D R

2. 6 3 12 14 5 8

3. | 8 __ | 30 __ | 5 __ | 27 __ | 13 __ |

4. | 6 ___ | 13 ___ | 12 ___ | 9 ___ |

SAMPLE ANSWER SHEET

1. Ⓐ Ⓑ Ⓒ Ⓓ Ⓔ 6. Ⓐ Ⓑ Ⓒ Ⓓ Ⓔ 11. Ⓐ Ⓑ Ⓒ Ⓓ Ⓔ
2. Ⓐ Ⓑ Ⓒ Ⓓ Ⓔ 7. Ⓐ Ⓑ Ⓒ Ⓓ Ⓔ 12. Ⓐ Ⓑ Ⓒ Ⓓ Ⓔ
3. Ⓐ Ⓑ Ⓒ Ⓓ Ⓔ 8. Ⓐ Ⓑ Ⓒ Ⓓ Ⓔ 13. Ⓐ Ⓑ Ⓒ Ⓓ Ⓔ
4. Ⓐ Ⓑ Ⓒ Ⓓ Ⓔ 9. Ⓐ Ⓑ Ⓒ Ⓓ Ⓔ 14. Ⓐ Ⓑ Ⓒ Ⓓ Ⓔ
5. Ⓐ Ⓑ Ⓒ Ⓓ Ⓔ 10. Ⓐ Ⓑ Ⓒ Ⓓ Ⓔ 15. Ⓐ Ⓑ Ⓒ Ⓓ Ⓔ

TEAR HERE

```
┌─────────────────────────────────────────────┐
│      CORRECT ANSWERS TO SAMPLE QUESTIONS      │
│  1. Ⓐ Ⓑ Ⓒ Ⓓ Ⓔ    6. Ⓐ Ⓑ Ⓒ Ⓓ Ⓔ   11. Ⓐ Ⓑ Ⓒ Ⓓ Ⓔ │
│  2. Ⓐ Ⓑ Ⓒ Ⓓ Ⓔ    7. Ⓐ Ⓑ Ⓒ Ⓓ Ⓔ   12. Ⓐ Ⓑ Ⓒ Ⓓ Ⓔ │
│  3. Ⓐ Ⓑ ● Ⓓ Ⓔ    8. Ⓐ Ⓑ Ⓒ Ⓓ ●   13. Ⓐ Ⓑ Ⓒ ● Ⓔ │
│  4. Ⓐ Ⓑ Ⓒ Ⓓ Ⓔ    9. Ⓐ Ⓑ Ⓒ Ⓓ Ⓔ   14. Ⓐ Ⓑ Ⓒ Ⓓ Ⓔ │
│  5. Ⓐ Ⓑ Ⓒ Ⓓ ●   10. Ⓐ Ⓑ Ⓒ Ⓓ Ⓔ   15. ● Ⓑ Ⓒ Ⓓ Ⓔ │
└─────────────────────────────────────────────┘
```

Correctly Filled Worksheet

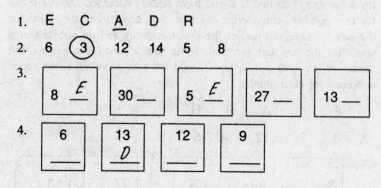

1.   E   C   <u>A</u>   D   R

2.   6   ③   12   14   5   8

3.

| 8 *E* | 30 __ | 5 *E* | 27 __ | 13 __ |

4.

| 6 __ | 13 *D* | 12 __ | 9 __ |

FOLLOWING ORAL DIRECTIONS TEST

Total Time—25 Minutes

LISTENING TO DIRECTIONS

DIRECTIONS: When you are ready to try this test of the Model Exam, give the following instructions to a friend and have the friend read them aloud to you at 80 words per minute. Do NOT read them to yourself. Your friend will need a watch with a second hand. Listen carefully and do exactly what your friend tells you to do with the worksheet and with the answer sheet. Your friend will tell you some things to do with each item on the worksheet. After each set of instructions, your friend will give you time to mark your answer by darkening a circle on the answer sheet. Since B and D sound very much alike, your friend will say "B as in baker" when he or she means B and "D as in dog" when he or she means D.

Before proceeding further, tear out the worksheet on page 177 of this test. Then hand this book to your friend.

TO THE PERSON WHO IS TO READ THE DIRECTIONS: The directions are to be read at the rate of 80 words per minute. Do not read aloud the material which is in parentheses. Once you have begun the test itself, do not repeat any directions. The next three paragraphs consist of approximately 120 words. Read these three paragraphs aloud to the candidate in about one and one-half minutes. You may reread these paragraphs as often as necessary to establish an 80 words per minute reading speed.

READ ALOUD TO THE CANDIDATE

On the job you will have to listen to directions and then do what you have been told to do. In this test, I will read instructions to you. Try to understand them as I read them; I cannot repeat them. Once we begin, you may not ask any questions until the end of the test.

On the job you won't have to deal with pictures, numbers and letters like those in the test, but you will have to listen to instructions and follow them. We are using this test to see how well you can follow instructions.

You are to mark your test booklet according to the instructions that I'll read to you. After each set of instructions, I'll give you time to record your answers on the separate answer sheet.

The actual test begins now.

Look at line 1 on your worksheet. (Pause slightly.) Underline the fifth number on line 1. (Pause 2 seconds.) Now, on your answer sheet, find the number you have underlined and mark D as in dog. (Pause 5 seconds.)

Now look at line 2 on your worksheet. (Pause slightly.) In each box that contains a vowel, write that vowel next to the number in the box. (Pause 5 seconds.) Now, on your answer sheet, blacken the spaces for the number-letter combinations in the box or boxes in which you just wrote. (Pause 10 seconds.)

Look at line 3 on your worksheet. (Pause slightly.) Find the smallest number on line 3 and multiply it by 2. Write the number at the end of line 3. (Pause 5 seconds.) Now, on your answer sheet, darken space C for that number. (Pause 5 seconds.)

Look at line 3 again. (Pause slightly.) Divide the third number by 10 and write that number at the end of the line. (Pause 2 seconds.) Now, on your answer sheet, darken space A for the number which you just wrote. (Pause 5 seconds.)

Now look at line 4 on your worksheet. (Pause slightly.) Mail for Detroit and Hartford is to be put in box 3. (Pause slightly.) Mail for Cleveland and St. Louis is to be put in box 26. (Pause slightly.) Write C in the box in which you put mail for St. Louis. (Pause 2 seconds.) Now, on your answer sheet, darken the space for the number-letter combination that is in the box you just wrote in. (Pause 5 seconds.)

Look at line 5 on your worksheet. (Pause slightly.) Write B as in baker on the line next to the highest number. (Pause 2 seconds.) Now, on your answer sheet, blacken the space for the number-letter combination in the circle in which you just wrote. (Pause 5 seconds.)

Look at line 5 again. (Pause slightly.) Write the letter C on the line next to the lowest number. (Pause 2 seconds.) Now, on your answer sheet, blacken the space for the number-letter combination in the circle in which you just wrote. (Pause 5 seconds.)

Look at the boxes and words on line 6 of your worksheet. (Pause 2 seconds.) In Box 1, write the first letter of the third word. (Pause 5 seconds.) In Box 2, write the last letter of the first word. (Pause 5 seconds.) In Box 3, write the last letter of the second word. (Pause 5 seconds.) Now, on your answer sheet, blacken spaces for the number-letter combinations in all three boxes. (Pause 15 seconds.)

Look at line 7 on your worksheet. (Pause slightly.) Write the number 33 next to the letter in the mid-size circle. (Pause 2 seconds.) Now, on your answer sheet, darken the space for number-letter combination in the circle in which you just wrote. (Pause 5 seconds.)

Look at line 8 on your worksheet. (Pause slightly.) If July comes before June, write D as in dog on the line after the second number; if not, write A on the line after the first number. (Pause 10 seconds.) Now, on your answer sheet, darken the space for the number-letter combination you just wrote. (Pause 5 seconds.)

Look at line 9 on your worksheet. (Pause slightly.) The number on each sack represents the number of pieces of mail in that sack. Next to the letter, write the last two figures of the sack containing the most pieces of mail. (Pause 2 seconds.) On your answer sheet, darken the space for the number-letter combination in the sack you just wrote in. (Pause 5 seconds.)

Look at line 9 again. (Pause slightly.) Now write next to the letter the first two figures in the sack containing the fewest pieces of mail. (Pause 2 seconds.) On your answer sheet, darken the space for the number-letter combination in the sack you just wrote in. (Pause 5 seconds.)

Look at line 10 on your worksheet. (Pause slightly.) Answer this question: What is the sum of 8 plus 13? (Pause 2 seconds.) If the answer is 25, write 25 in the second box; if not, write the correct answer in the fourth box. (Pause 2 seconds.) Now, on your answer sheet, blacken the number-letter combination in the box you just wrote in. (Pause 5 seconds.)

Look at line 10 again. (Pause slightly.) In the fifth box, write the number of ounces in a pound. (Pause 2 seconds.) Now, on your answer sheet, blacken the number-letter combination in the box you just wrote in. (Pause 5 seconds.)

Look at line 11 on your worksheet. (Pause slightly.) If the number in the circle is greater than the number in the star, write B as in baker in the triangle; if not, write E in the box. (Pause 5 seconds.) Now, on your answer sheet, darken the number-letter combination in the figure you just wrote in. (Pause 5 seconds.)

Look at line 12 on your worksheet. (Pause slightly.) Draw one line under each P in line 12. (Pause 5 seconds.) Draw two lines under each Q in line 12. (Pause 5 seconds.) Count the number of P's and the number of Q's. (Pause 5 seconds.) If there are more P's than Q's, blacken 71A on your answer sheet; if there are not more P's than Q's, blacken 71C on your answer sheet. (Pause 5 seconds.)

Look at line 13 on your worksheet. (Pause slightly.) Circle each odd number that falls between 65 and 85. (Pause 10 seconds.) Now, on your answer sheet, darken space D as in dog for each number that you circled. (Pause 10 seconds.)

Look at line 13 again. (Pause slightly.) Find the number that is divisible by 6 and underline it. (Pause 2 seconds.) Now, on your answer sheet, darken space A for that number. (Pause 5 seconds.)

Look at line 14 on your worksheet. (Pause slightly.) Each circled time represents a pickup time from a street letter box. Find the pickup time which is farthest from noon and write the last two figures of that time on the line in the circle. (Pause 2 seconds.) Now, on your answer sheet, darken the number-letter combination that is in the circle you just wrote in. (Pause 5 seconds.)

Look at line 14 again. (Pause slightly.) Find the pickup time that is closest to noon and write the last two figures of that time on the line in the circle. (Pause 2 seconds.) Now, on your answer sheet, darken the number-letter combination that is in the circle you just wrote in. (Pause 5 seconds.)

Look at line 15 on your worksheet. (Pause slightly.) Write the highest number in the small box. (Pause 2 seconds.) Write the lowest number in the large box. (Pause 2 seconds.) Now, on your answer sheet, darken the number-letter combinations in the boxes you just wrote in. (Pause 10 seconds.)

Look at line 16 on your worksheet. (Pause slightly.) If, in the alphabet, the fourth letter on line 16 comes before the first letter on line 16, draw a line under the fourth letter (Pause 2 seconds); if not, draw a line under the first letter on line 16. (Pause 2 seconds.) Now, on your answer sheet, find number 39 and blacken the space for the letter you underlined. (Pause 5 seconds.)

Look at line 17 on your worksheet. (Pause slightly.) Find the number that does not belong on line 17 and circle that number. (Pause 2 seconds.) Now, on your answer sheet, darken D as in dog for the number you just circled. (Pause 5 seconds.)

Look at line 17 again. (Pause slightly.) Find the number that answers this question: 60 minus 20 equals . . . and draw two lines under that number. (Pause 2 seconds.) Now, on your answer sheet, darken space C for the number under which you just drew two lines. (Pause 5 seconds.)

Look at line 18 on your worksheet. (Pause slightly.) If 3 is less than 7 and 4 is more than 6, write the number 12 in the first box (Pause 5 seconds); if not, write the number 90 in the third box. (Pause 5 seconds.) Now, on your answer sheet, darken the space for the number-letter combination in the box you just wrote in. (Pause 5 seconds.)

FOLLOWING ORAL DIRECTIONS TEST

Total Time—25 Minutes

WORKSHEET

DIRECTIONS: Listening carefully to each set of instructions, mark each item on this worksheet as directed. Then complete each question by marking the answer sheet as directed. For each answer you will darken the answer for a number-letter combination. Should you fall behind and miss an instruction, don't become excited. Let that one go and listen for the next one. If when you start to darken a space for a number, you find that you have already darkened another space for that number, either erase the first mark and darken the space for the new combination or let the first mark stay and do not darken a space for the new combination. Write with a pencil that has a clean eraser. When you finish, you should have no more than one space darkened for each number. Correct answers are on page 183.

TEAR HERE

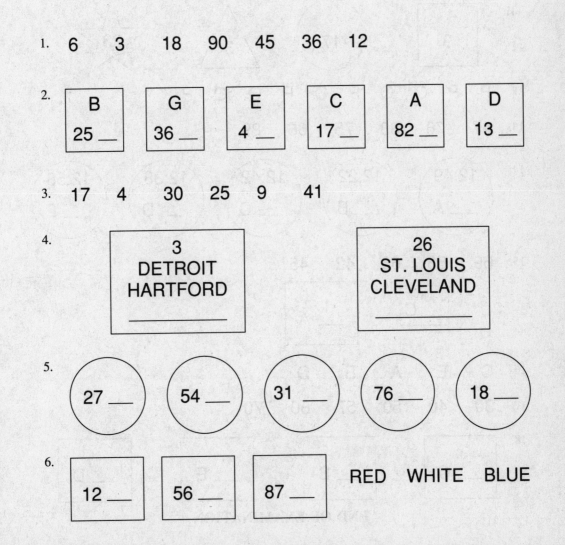

1.   6   3   18   90   45   36   12

2.

B	G	E	C	A	D
25 __	36 __	4 __	17 __	82 __	13 __

3.   17   4   30   25   9   41

4.

3 DETROIT HARTFORD _____	26 ST. LOUIS CLEVELAND _____

5.   27 __   54 __   31 __   76 __   18 __

6.   12 __   56 __   87 __   RED   WHITE   BLUE

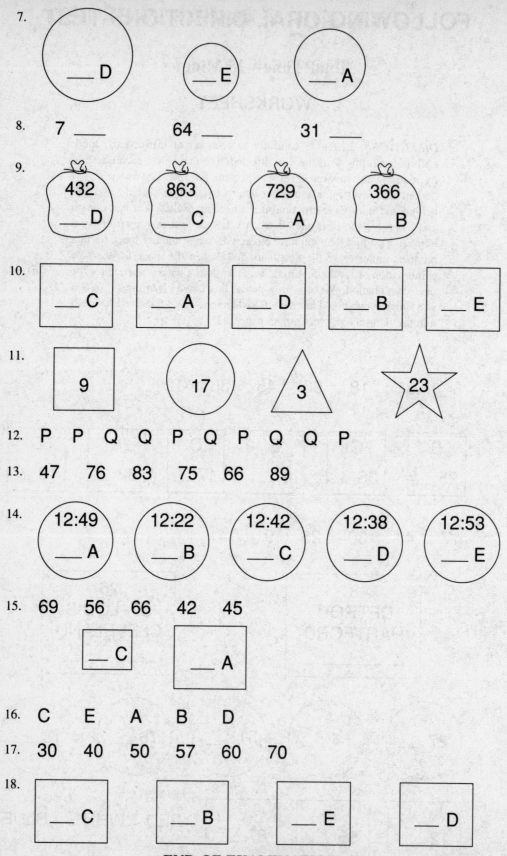

7. ___D   ___E   ___A

8. 7 ___   64 ___   31 ___

9. 432 ___D   863 ___C   729 ___A   366 ___B

10. ___C   ___A   ___D   ___B   ___E

11. 9   17   3   23

12. P P Q Q P Q P Q Q P

13. 47   76   83   75   66   89

14. 12:49 ___A   12:22 ___B   12:42 ___C   12:38 ___D   12:53 ___E

15. 69   56   66   42   45

___C   ___A

16. C   E   A   B   D

17. 30   40   50   57   60   70

18. ___C   ___B   ___E   ___D

END OF EXAMINATION

FOURTH MODEL EXAM ANSWER KEY

ADDRESS CHECKING TEST

1. D	17. A	33. D	49. D	65. D	81. A
2. A	18. D	34. A	50. A	66. A	82. D
3. A	19. A	35. A	51. D	67. A	83. A
4. D	20. A	36. D	52. A	68. D	84. A
5. A	21. D	37. A	53. D	69. A	85. D
6. A	22. A	38. D	54. A	70. A	86. A
7. D	23. D	39. A	55. A	71. D	87. D
8. A	24. D	40. D	56. A	72. A	88. A
9. D	25. D	41. A	57. D	73. D	89. D
10. D	26. A	42. A	58. A	74. A	90. A
11. D	27. D	43. D	59. A	75. D	91. D
12. A	28. A	44. A	60. D	76. D	92. D
13. D	29. A	45. D	61. D	77. D	93. D
14. A	30. D	46. D	62. D	78. D	94. A
15. D	31. A	47. D	63. D	79. D	95. A
16. A	32. D	48. D	64. A	80. A	

ADDRESS CHECKING TEST

Explanations of Differences

1. spelling of city
4. different numbers
7. spelling of city
9. different states
10. different cities
11. spelling of city
13. different cities
15. spelling of city
18. number reversal
21. different states
23. different cities
24. different cities
25. spelling of city
27. different numbers
30. spelling of city
32. different cities
33. different cities
36. different states
38. spelling of city
40. spelling of city
43. different cities
45. different cities
46. different cities
47. different cities
48. different cities
49. different cities
51. different cities
53. different cities

57. different numbers
60. different cities
61. spelling of city
62. different cities
63. different numbers
65. spelling of city
68. different cities
71. different numbers
73. spelling of city
75. different cities
76. different numbers
77. different cities
78. different cities
79. different cities
82. different numbers
85. different cities
87. spelling of city
89. different cities
91. spelling of city
92. different numbers
93. different cities

Analysis of Differences

Fill in the column on the right with the total number of questions you answered incorrectly.

City difference	37	
Number difference	9	
State difference	3	
Total addresses with differences	49	
Total addresses with no differences	46	

MEANING OF WORDS TEST

1. A	7. D	12. C	17. E	22. E	27. C
2. C	8. E	13. A	18. B	23. C	28. E
3. E	9. C	14. C	19. A	24. D	29. C
4. D	10. A	15. E	20. E	25. B	30. A
5. B	11. C	16. D	21. A	26. A	31. D
6. E					32. D

MEANING OF WORDS TEST

Explanatory Answers

1. **(A)** To INFER is to *derive a conclusion* from facts, to *surmise* or to *guess*.
2. **(C)** LOGICAL means *orderly* or *reasoned*. The suffix *al*, meaning *pertaining to*, added to *logic*, which you probably know to mean *reason* or *common sense*, should make it easy for you to answer this question correctly.
3. **(E)** LEGIBLE means *plain* or *readable*. The Latin root, *leg*, means *read*, so etymologically the word means *able to be read*.
4. **(D)** To ASSEMBLE is to *meet together*, to *convene* or to *gather*. The entirely different word that means *pretend* is *dissemble*.
5. **(B)** That which is SLATED is *registered* or *scheduled*.
6. **(E)** SECURE means *free from risk of loss*, *dependable* or *safe*. Of course, a secret hiding place is secure, but you must choose the closest synonym to the italicized word.
7. **(D)** DELIBERATE means *thought out* or characterized by *careful* and thorough *consideration*. Deliberate speed may well be slow, but that is not its meaning. Choices B and C offer antonyms (opposites). Choice A makes no sense.
8. **(E)** PRIVILEGED means *granted a special favor or honor*, hence *honored*.
9. **(C)** To SUPERVISE is to *direct*, to *superintend* or to *oversee*. A supervisor may also hire and train others, but that is his or her hiring and training function not the supervising function.
10. **(A)** To UTILIZE is to *use* or to *employ*.
11. **(C)** COMPELLED means *forced*. If you know the facts, you know the answer without knowing the word.
12. **(C)** IRRITATING means causing displeasure or *annoying*. *Unnerving* and *unbearable* are both stronger words than *irritating*, but in the absence of a true synonym like *annoying*, either might have been acceptable as *nearly* the same. When you notice more than one possible synonym, you must choose the **BEST**.
13. **(A)** AFFILIATED with means *closely associated* with or *connected* with.
14. **(C)** UNIFORMITY means *sameness*, *conformity* or *similarity*. A *uniform* is the dress of a distinctive design worn by members of a particular group which makes them all the same.
15. **(E)** To EFFECT is to *cause*, to *accomplish* or to *bring about*. It is pronounced ee-FECT. The word meaning *influence* or *concern* is *affect* (accent on the second syllable, uh-*fect*). The word meaning *pretend* is *affect* (accent on the first syllable, *af*-ect).
16. **(D)** The OUTCOME is the way something turns out, the *consequence* or the *result*. If you thought carefully about the structure of this word, you should have answered this question correctly.
17. **(E)** DOGMATIC means *doctrinaire* or *dictatorial*. One who is dogmatic insists upon unswervingly following a set of statements based upon faith and specifying certain behaviors and acts based upon that set of statements.
18. **(B)** UTENSILS are *implements* or *tools*. The word comes from the same root as *utility*; both imply *usefulness*.

19. **(A)** TENACITY is *persistence* or *firmness*. *Timidity* is the opposite and *discouragement* a near opposite. *Temerity* is *brashness* or *nerve*, not really the same meaning. *Good humor* is just plain wrong.

20. **(E)** COURTEOUS means *good mannered, civil* or *polite*. The word stems from the fine manners once used in a royal court.

21. **(A)** A REQUEST is a *demand*. The noun is somewhat stronger than the verb TO RE-QUEST which means *to ask*. However, if you know that the verb means to *ask*, the only possible meaning of the noun (from among the choices) is *demand*.

22. **(E)** To INSERT is to *put in*. The stem *sert* means *place*, and the prefix *in* means *into*. Even if you only know the prefix, you should have been able to figure this one out.

23. **(C)** DYNAMIC means marked by energy or *forceful*. Can you see *dynamo* in this word?

24. **(D)** To EXECUTE in this context means to *administer* or to *carry out*. Part of executing one's duties may involve delegating, but that is a part of, not the meaning of *execute*. Obviously, the alternative meaning of execute, to *kill*, makes no sense in this sentence.

25. **(B)** A COMPLEX is a *group of buildings* related as to their purpose. Other complexes may be a university complex or an office complex. The prefix *com* implies that there be some togetherness.

26. **(A)** INSIGNIFICANT means *not worth considering* or *unimportant*.

27. **(C)** To DISCARD is to *cast off* or to *throw away*. The prefix *dis* means *away*.

28. **(E)** A MEMORANDUM (memo for short) is a reminder *note* to oneself or an informative internal communication.

29. **(C)** To MONITOR is to *watch*, to *observe*, to *check* and to *keep track of*. Monitoring may then lead to *charting* and *warning*, but not *altering*.

30. **(A)** VACANT means *expressionless* or *empty*.

31. **(D)** MORTALLY means in a *deadly* or *fatal* manner. The suffix *al* means *pertaining to;* the root *mort* means *death*.

32. **(D)** SUFFICIENT means *adequate* or *enough*.

FOLLOWING ORAL DIRECTIONS TEST

Correctly Filled Worksheet

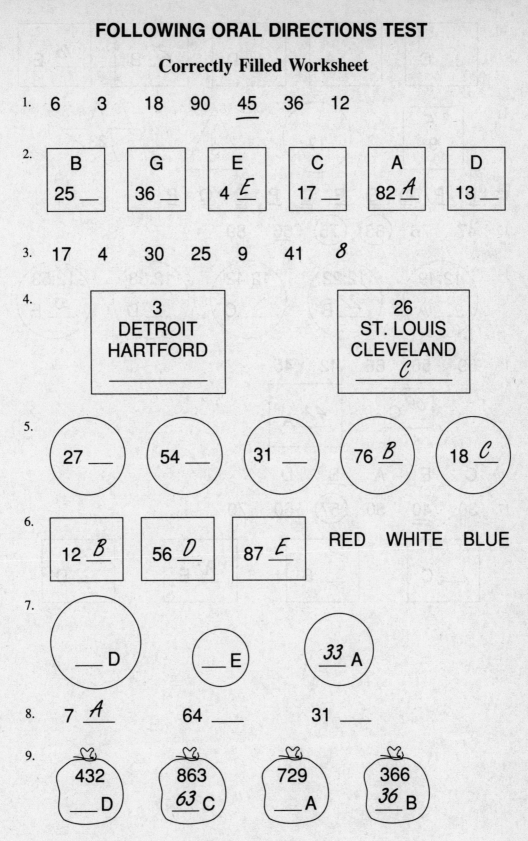

1. 6   3   18   90   <u>45</u>   36   12

2.
B	G	E	C	A	D
25 __	36 __	4 *E*	17 __	82 *A*	13 __

3. 17   4   30   25   9   41   *8*

4.
    3
    DETROIT
    HARTFORD
    _____

    26
    ST. LOUIS
    CLEVELAND
    __*C*__

5. 27 __   54 __   31 __   76 *B*   18 *C*

6. 12 *B*   56 *D*   87 *E*   RED   WHITE   BLUE

7. __ D   __ E   *33* A

8. 7 *A*   64 __   31 __

9. 432 __ D   863 *63* C   729 __ A   366 *36* B

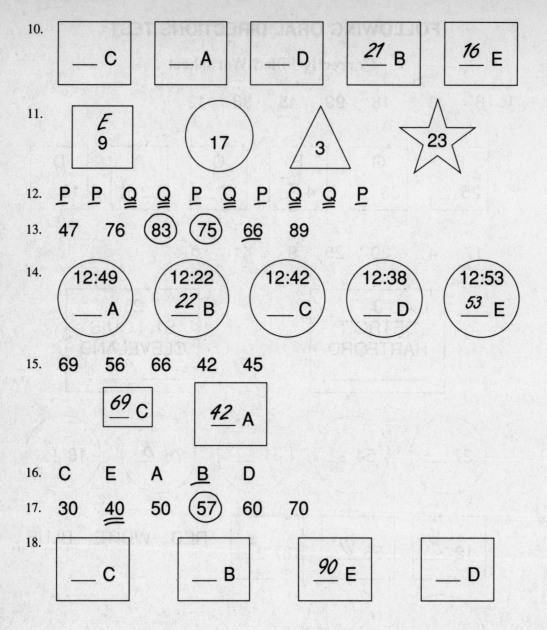

10.

| $\underline{\quad}$ C | $\underline{\quad}$ A | $\underline{\quad}$ D | $\underline{21}$ B | $\underline{16}$ E |

11.

$\boxed{\begin{array}{c}E \\ 9\end{array}}$ $\bigcirc 17$ $\triangle 3$ $\star 23$

12. $\underline{P}$ $\underline{P}$ $\underline{\underline{Q}}$ $\underline{\underline{Q}}$ $\underline{P}$ $\underline{\underline{Q}}$ $\underline{P}$ $\underline{\underline{Q}}$ $\underline{\underline{Q}}$ $\underline{P}$

13. 47   76   ⑧③   ⑦⑤ $\underline{66}$ 89

14. $\begin{array}{c}12:49 \\ \underline{\quad} A\end{array}$ $\begin{array}{c}12:22 \\ \underline{22} B\end{array}$ $\begin{array}{c}12:42 \\ \underline{\quad} C\end{array}$ $\begin{array}{c}12:38 \\ \underline{\quad} D\end{array}$ $\begin{array}{c}12:53 \\ \underline{53} E\end{array}$

15. 69   56   66   42   45

$\boxed{\underline{69} \text{ C}}$ $\boxed{\underline{42} \text{ A}}$

16. C   E   A $\underline{B}$ D

17. 30 $\underline{\underline{40}}$ 50   ⑤⑦   60   70

18.

| $\underline{\quad}$ C | $\underline{\quad}$ B | $\underline{90}$ E | $\underline{\quad}$ D |

FOLLOWING ORAL DIRECTIONS TEST

Correctly Filled Answer Grid

#		#		#	
1.	Ⓐ Ⓑ Ⓒ Ⓓ Ⓔ	31.	Ⓐ Ⓑ Ⓒ Ⓓ Ⓔ	61.	Ⓐ Ⓑ Ⓒ Ⓓ Ⓔ
2.	Ⓐ Ⓑ Ⓒ Ⓓ Ⓔ	32.	Ⓐ Ⓑ Ⓒ Ⓓ Ⓔ	62.	Ⓐ Ⓑ Ⓒ Ⓓ Ⓔ
3.	● Ⓑ Ⓒ Ⓓ Ⓔ	33.	● Ⓑ Ⓒ Ⓓ Ⓔ	63.	Ⓐ Ⓑ ● Ⓓ Ⓔ
4.	Ⓐ Ⓑ Ⓒ Ⓓ ●	34.	Ⓐ Ⓑ Ⓒ Ⓓ Ⓔ	64.	Ⓐ Ⓑ Ⓒ Ⓓ Ⓔ
5.	Ⓐ Ⓑ Ⓒ Ⓓ Ⓔ	35.	Ⓐ Ⓑ Ⓒ Ⓓ Ⓔ	65.	Ⓐ Ⓑ Ⓒ Ⓓ Ⓔ
6.	Ⓐ Ⓑ Ⓒ Ⓓ Ⓔ	36.	Ⓐ ● Ⓒ Ⓓ Ⓔ	66.	● Ⓑ Ⓒ Ⓓ Ⓔ
7.	● Ⓑ Ⓒ Ⓓ Ⓔ	37.	Ⓐ Ⓑ Ⓒ Ⓓ Ⓔ	67.	Ⓐ Ⓑ Ⓒ Ⓓ Ⓔ
8.	Ⓐ Ⓑ ● Ⓓ Ⓔ	38.	Ⓐ Ⓑ Ⓒ Ⓓ Ⓔ	68.	Ⓐ Ⓑ Ⓒ Ⓓ Ⓔ
9.	Ⓐ Ⓑ Ⓒ Ⓓ ●	39.	Ⓐ ● Ⓒ Ⓓ Ⓔ	69.	Ⓑ Ⓒ ● Ⓓ Ⓔ
10.	Ⓐ Ⓑ Ⓒ Ⓓ Ⓔ	40.	Ⓐ Ⓑ ● Ⓓ Ⓔ	70.	Ⓐ Ⓑ Ⓒ Ⓓ Ⓔ
11.	Ⓐ Ⓑ Ⓒ Ⓓ Ⓔ	41.	Ⓐ Ⓑ Ⓒ Ⓓ Ⓔ	71.	Ⓐ Ⓑ ● Ⓓ Ⓔ
12.	Ⓐ ● Ⓒ Ⓓ Ⓔ	42.	● Ⓑ Ⓒ Ⓓ Ⓔ	72.	Ⓐ Ⓑ Ⓒ Ⓓ Ⓔ
13.	Ⓐ Ⓑ Ⓒ Ⓓ Ⓔ	43.	Ⓐ Ⓑ Ⓒ Ⓓ Ⓔ	73.	Ⓐ Ⓑ Ⓒ Ⓓ Ⓔ
14.	Ⓐ Ⓑ Ⓒ Ⓓ Ⓔ	44.	Ⓐ Ⓑ Ⓒ Ⓓ Ⓔ	74.	Ⓐ Ⓑ Ⓒ Ⓓ Ⓔ
15.	Ⓐ Ⓑ Ⓒ Ⓓ Ⓔ	45.	Ⓐ Ⓑ Ⓒ ● Ⓔ	75.	Ⓐ Ⓑ Ⓒ ● Ⓔ
16.	Ⓐ Ⓑ Ⓒ Ⓓ ●	46.	Ⓐ Ⓑ Ⓒ Ⓓ Ⓔ	76.	Ⓐ ● Ⓒ Ⓓ Ⓔ
17.	Ⓐ Ⓑ Ⓒ Ⓓ Ⓔ	47.	Ⓐ Ⓑ Ⓒ Ⓓ Ⓔ	77.	Ⓐ Ⓑ Ⓒ Ⓓ Ⓔ
18.	Ⓐ Ⓑ ● Ⓓ Ⓔ	48.	Ⓐ Ⓑ Ⓒ Ⓓ Ⓔ	78.	Ⓐ Ⓑ Ⓒ Ⓓ Ⓔ
19.	Ⓐ Ⓑ Ⓒ Ⓓ Ⓔ	49.	Ⓐ Ⓑ Ⓒ Ⓓ Ⓔ	79.	Ⓐ Ⓑ Ⓒ Ⓓ Ⓔ
20.	Ⓐ Ⓑ Ⓒ Ⓓ Ⓔ	50.	Ⓐ Ⓑ Ⓒ Ⓓ Ⓔ	80.	Ⓐ Ⓑ Ⓒ Ⓓ Ⓔ
21.	Ⓐ ● Ⓒ Ⓓ Ⓔ	51.	Ⓐ Ⓑ Ⓒ Ⓓ Ⓔ	81.	Ⓐ Ⓑ Ⓒ Ⓓ Ⓔ
22.	Ⓐ ● Ⓒ Ⓓ Ⓔ	52.	Ⓐ Ⓑ Ⓒ Ⓓ Ⓔ	82.	● Ⓑ Ⓒ Ⓓ Ⓔ
23.	Ⓐ Ⓑ Ⓒ Ⓓ Ⓔ	53.	Ⓐ Ⓑ Ⓒ Ⓓ ●	83.	Ⓐ Ⓑ Ⓒ ● Ⓔ
24.	Ⓐ Ⓑ Ⓒ Ⓓ Ⓔ	54.	Ⓐ Ⓑ Ⓒ Ⓓ Ⓔ	84.	Ⓐ Ⓑ Ⓒ Ⓓ Ⓔ
25.	Ⓐ Ⓑ Ⓒ Ⓓ Ⓔ	55.	Ⓐ Ⓑ Ⓒ Ⓓ Ⓔ	85.	Ⓐ Ⓑ Ⓒ Ⓓ Ⓔ
26.	Ⓐ Ⓑ ● Ⓓ Ⓔ	56.	Ⓐ Ⓑ Ⓒ ● Ⓔ	86.	Ⓐ Ⓑ Ⓒ Ⓓ Ⓔ
27.	Ⓐ Ⓑ Ⓒ Ⓓ Ⓔ	57.	Ⓐ Ⓑ Ⓒ ● Ⓔ	87.	Ⓐ Ⓑ Ⓒ Ⓓ ●
28.	Ⓐ Ⓑ Ⓒ Ⓓ Ⓔ	58.	Ⓐ Ⓑ Ⓒ Ⓓ Ⓔ	88.	Ⓐ Ⓑ Ⓒ Ⓓ Ⓔ
29.	Ⓐ Ⓑ Ⓒ Ⓓ Ⓔ	59.	Ⓐ Ⓑ Ⓒ Ⓓ Ⓔ	89.	Ⓐ Ⓑ Ⓒ Ⓓ Ⓔ
30.	Ⓐ Ⓑ Ⓒ Ⓓ Ⓔ	60.	Ⓐ Ⓑ Ⓒ Ⓓ Ⓔ	90.	Ⓐ Ⓑ Ⓒ Ⓓ ●

FIFTH MODEL EXAM ANSWER SHEET

Address Checking Test

1. Ⓐ Ⓓ	17. Ⓐ Ⓓ	33. Ⓐ Ⓓ	49. Ⓐ Ⓓ	65. Ⓐ Ⓓ	81. Ⓐ Ⓓ
2. Ⓐ Ⓓ	18. Ⓐ Ⓓ	34. Ⓐ Ⓓ	50. Ⓐ Ⓓ	66. Ⓐ Ⓓ	82. Ⓐ Ⓓ
3. Ⓐ Ⓓ	19. Ⓐ Ⓓ	35. Ⓐ Ⓓ	51. Ⓐ Ⓓ	67. Ⓐ Ⓓ	83. Ⓐ Ⓓ
4. Ⓐ Ⓓ	20. Ⓐ Ⓓ	36. Ⓐ Ⓓ	52. Ⓐ Ⓓ	68. Ⓐ Ⓓ	84. Ⓐ Ⓓ
5. Ⓐ Ⓓ	21. Ⓐ Ⓓ	37. Ⓐ Ⓓ	53. Ⓐ Ⓓ	69. Ⓐ Ⓓ	85. Ⓐ Ⓓ
6. Ⓐ Ⓓ	22. Ⓐ Ⓓ	38. Ⓐ Ⓓ	54. Ⓐ Ⓓ	70. Ⓐ Ⓓ	86. Ⓐ Ⓓ
7. Ⓐ Ⓓ	23. Ⓐ Ⓓ	39. Ⓐ Ⓓ	55. Ⓐ Ⓓ	71. Ⓐ Ⓓ	87. Ⓐ Ⓓ
8. Ⓐ Ⓓ	24. Ⓐ Ⓓ	40. Ⓐ Ⓓ	56. Ⓐ Ⓓ	72. Ⓐ Ⓓ	88. Ⓐ Ⓓ
9. Ⓐ Ⓓ	25. Ⓐ Ⓓ	41. Ⓐ Ⓓ	57. Ⓐ Ⓓ	73. Ⓐ Ⓓ	89. Ⓐ Ⓓ
10. Ⓐ Ⓓ	26. Ⓐ Ⓓ	42. Ⓐ Ⓓ	58. Ⓐ Ⓓ	74. Ⓐ Ⓓ	90. Ⓐ Ⓓ
11. Ⓐ Ⓓ	27. Ⓐ Ⓓ	43. Ⓐ Ⓓ	59. Ⓐ Ⓓ	75. Ⓐ Ⓓ	91. Ⓐ Ⓓ
12. Ⓐ Ⓓ	28. Ⓐ Ⓓ	44. Ⓐ Ⓓ	60. Ⓐ Ⓓ	76. Ⓐ Ⓓ	92. Ⓐ Ⓓ
13. Ⓐ Ⓓ	29. Ⓐ Ⓓ	45. Ⓐ Ⓓ	61. Ⓐ Ⓓ	77. Ⓐ Ⓓ	93. Ⓐ Ⓓ
14. Ⓐ Ⓓ	30. Ⓐ Ⓓ	46. Ⓐ Ⓓ	62. Ⓐ Ⓓ	78. Ⓐ Ⓓ	94. Ⓐ Ⓓ
15. Ⓐ Ⓓ	31. Ⓐ Ⓓ	47. Ⓐ Ⓓ	63. Ⓐ Ⓓ	79. Ⓐ Ⓓ	95. Ⓐ Ⓓ
16. Ⓐ Ⓓ	32. Ⓐ Ⓓ	48. Ⓐ Ⓓ	64. Ⓐ Ⓓ	80. Ⓐ Ⓓ	

MEANING OF WORDS TEST

1. Ⓐ Ⓑ Ⓒ Ⓓ Ⓔ	8. Ⓐ Ⓑ Ⓒ Ⓓ Ⓔ	15. Ⓐ Ⓑ Ⓒ Ⓓ Ⓔ	22. Ⓐ Ⓑ Ⓒ Ⓓ Ⓔ	29. Ⓐ Ⓑ Ⓒ Ⓓ Ⓔ
2. Ⓐ Ⓑ Ⓒ Ⓓ Ⓔ	9. Ⓐ Ⓑ Ⓒ Ⓓ Ⓔ	16. Ⓐ Ⓑ Ⓒ Ⓓ Ⓔ	23. Ⓐ Ⓑ Ⓒ Ⓓ Ⓔ	30. Ⓐ Ⓑ Ⓒ Ⓓ Ⓔ
3. Ⓐ Ⓑ Ⓒ Ⓓ Ⓔ	10. Ⓐ Ⓑ Ⓒ Ⓓ Ⓔ	17. Ⓐ Ⓑ Ⓒ Ⓓ Ⓔ	24. Ⓐ Ⓑ Ⓒ Ⓓ Ⓔ	31. Ⓐ Ⓑ Ⓒ Ⓓ Ⓔ
4. Ⓐ Ⓑ Ⓒ Ⓓ Ⓔ	11. Ⓐ Ⓑ Ⓒ Ⓓ Ⓔ	18. Ⓐ Ⓑ Ⓒ Ⓓ Ⓔ	25. Ⓐ Ⓑ Ⓒ Ⓓ Ⓔ	32. Ⓐ Ⓑ Ⓒ Ⓓ Ⓔ
5. Ⓐ Ⓑ Ⓒ Ⓓ Ⓔ	12. Ⓐ Ⓑ Ⓒ Ⓓ Ⓔ	19. Ⓐ Ⓑ Ⓒ Ⓓ Ⓔ	26. Ⓐ Ⓑ Ⓒ Ⓓ Ⓔ	
6. Ⓐ Ⓑ Ⓒ Ⓓ Ⓔ	13. Ⓐ Ⓑ Ⓒ Ⓓ Ⓔ	20. Ⓐ Ⓑ Ⓒ Ⓓ Ⓔ	27. Ⓐ Ⓑ Ⓒ Ⓓ Ⓔ	
7. Ⓐ Ⓑ Ⓒ Ⓓ Ⓔ	14. Ⓐ Ⓑ Ⓒ Ⓓ Ⓔ	21. Ⓐ Ⓑ Ⓒ Ⓓ Ⓔ	28. Ⓐ Ⓑ Ⓒ Ⓓ Ⓔ	

FOLLOWING ORAL DIRECTIONS TEST

1. Ⓐ Ⓑ Ⓒ Ⓓ Ⓔ	19. Ⓐ Ⓑ Ⓒ Ⓓ Ⓔ	37. Ⓐ Ⓑ Ⓒ Ⓓ Ⓔ	55. Ⓐ Ⓑ Ⓒ Ⓓ Ⓔ	73. Ⓐ Ⓑ Ⓒ Ⓓ Ⓔ
2. Ⓐ Ⓑ Ⓒ Ⓓ Ⓔ	20. Ⓐ Ⓑ Ⓒ Ⓓ Ⓔ	38. Ⓐ Ⓑ Ⓒ Ⓓ Ⓔ	56. Ⓐ Ⓑ Ⓒ Ⓓ Ⓔ	74. Ⓐ Ⓑ Ⓒ Ⓓ Ⓔ
3. Ⓐ Ⓑ Ⓒ Ⓓ Ⓔ	21. Ⓐ Ⓑ Ⓒ Ⓓ Ⓔ	39. Ⓐ Ⓑ Ⓒ Ⓓ Ⓔ	57. Ⓐ Ⓑ Ⓒ Ⓓ Ⓔ	75. Ⓐ Ⓑ Ⓒ Ⓓ Ⓔ
4. Ⓐ Ⓑ Ⓒ Ⓓ Ⓔ	22. Ⓐ Ⓑ Ⓒ Ⓓ Ⓔ	40. Ⓐ Ⓑ Ⓒ Ⓓ Ⓔ	58. Ⓐ Ⓑ Ⓒ Ⓓ Ⓔ	76. Ⓐ Ⓑ Ⓒ Ⓓ Ⓔ
5. Ⓐ Ⓑ Ⓒ Ⓓ Ⓔ	23. Ⓐ Ⓑ Ⓒ Ⓓ Ⓔ	41. Ⓐ Ⓑ Ⓒ Ⓓ Ⓔ	59. Ⓐ Ⓑ Ⓒ Ⓓ Ⓔ	77. Ⓐ Ⓑ Ⓒ Ⓓ Ⓔ
6. Ⓐ Ⓑ Ⓒ Ⓓ Ⓔ	24. Ⓐ Ⓑ Ⓒ Ⓓ Ⓔ	42. Ⓐ Ⓑ Ⓒ Ⓓ Ⓔ	60. Ⓐ Ⓑ Ⓒ Ⓓ Ⓔ	78. Ⓐ Ⓑ Ⓒ Ⓓ Ⓔ
7. Ⓐ Ⓑ Ⓒ Ⓓ Ⓔ	25. Ⓐ Ⓑ Ⓒ Ⓓ Ⓔ	43. Ⓐ Ⓑ Ⓒ Ⓓ Ⓔ	61. Ⓐ Ⓑ Ⓒ Ⓓ Ⓔ	79. Ⓐ Ⓑ Ⓒ Ⓓ Ⓔ
8. Ⓐ Ⓑ Ⓒ Ⓓ Ⓔ	26. Ⓐ Ⓑ Ⓒ Ⓓ Ⓔ	44. Ⓐ Ⓑ Ⓒ Ⓓ Ⓔ	62. Ⓐ Ⓑ Ⓒ Ⓓ Ⓔ	80. Ⓐ Ⓑ Ⓒ Ⓓ Ⓔ
9. Ⓐ Ⓑ Ⓒ Ⓓ Ⓔ	27. Ⓐ Ⓑ Ⓒ Ⓓ Ⓔ	45. Ⓐ Ⓑ Ⓒ Ⓓ Ⓔ	63. Ⓐ Ⓑ Ⓒ Ⓓ Ⓔ	81. Ⓐ Ⓑ Ⓒ Ⓓ Ⓔ
10. Ⓐ Ⓑ Ⓒ Ⓓ Ⓔ	28. Ⓐ Ⓑ Ⓒ Ⓓ Ⓔ	46. Ⓐ Ⓑ Ⓒ Ⓓ Ⓔ	64. Ⓐ Ⓑ Ⓒ Ⓓ Ⓔ	82. Ⓐ Ⓑ Ⓒ Ⓓ Ⓔ
11. Ⓐ Ⓑ Ⓒ Ⓓ Ⓔ	29. Ⓐ Ⓑ Ⓒ Ⓓ Ⓔ	47. Ⓐ Ⓑ Ⓒ Ⓓ Ⓔ	65. Ⓐ Ⓑ Ⓒ Ⓓ Ⓔ	83. Ⓐ Ⓑ Ⓒ Ⓓ Ⓔ
12. Ⓐ Ⓑ Ⓒ Ⓓ Ⓔ	30. Ⓐ Ⓑ Ⓒ Ⓓ Ⓔ	48. Ⓐ Ⓑ Ⓒ Ⓓ Ⓔ	66. Ⓐ Ⓑ Ⓒ Ⓓ Ⓔ	84. Ⓐ Ⓑ Ⓒ Ⓓ Ⓔ
13. Ⓐ Ⓑ Ⓒ Ⓓ Ⓔ	31. Ⓐ Ⓑ Ⓒ Ⓓ Ⓔ	49. Ⓐ Ⓑ Ⓒ Ⓓ Ⓔ	67. Ⓐ Ⓑ Ⓒ Ⓓ Ⓔ	85. Ⓐ Ⓑ Ⓒ Ⓓ Ⓔ
14. Ⓐ Ⓑ Ⓒ Ⓓ Ⓔ	32. Ⓐ Ⓑ Ⓒ Ⓓ Ⓔ	50. Ⓐ Ⓑ Ⓒ Ⓓ Ⓔ	68. Ⓐ Ⓑ Ⓒ Ⓓ Ⓔ	86. Ⓐ Ⓑ Ⓒ Ⓓ Ⓔ
15. Ⓐ Ⓑ Ⓒ Ⓓ Ⓔ	33. Ⓐ Ⓑ Ⓒ Ⓓ Ⓔ	51. Ⓐ Ⓑ Ⓒ Ⓓ Ⓔ	69. Ⓐ Ⓑ Ⓒ Ⓓ Ⓔ	87. Ⓐ Ⓑ Ⓒ Ⓓ Ⓔ
16. Ⓐ Ⓑ Ⓒ Ⓓ Ⓔ	34. Ⓐ Ⓑ Ⓒ Ⓓ Ⓔ	52. Ⓐ Ⓑ Ⓒ Ⓓ Ⓔ	70. Ⓐ Ⓑ Ⓒ Ⓓ Ⓔ	88. Ⓐ Ⓑ Ⓒ Ⓓ Ⓔ
17. Ⓐ Ⓑ Ⓒ Ⓓ Ⓔ	35. Ⓐ Ⓑ Ⓒ Ⓓ Ⓔ	53. Ⓐ Ⓑ Ⓒ Ⓓ Ⓔ	71. Ⓐ Ⓑ Ⓒ Ⓓ Ⓔ	89. Ⓐ Ⓑ Ⓒ Ⓓ Ⓔ
18. Ⓐ Ⓑ Ⓒ Ⓓ Ⓔ	36. Ⓐ Ⓑ Ⓒ Ⓓ Ⓔ	54. Ⓐ Ⓑ Ⓒ Ⓓ Ⓔ	72. Ⓐ Ⓑ Ⓒ Ⓓ Ⓔ	90. Ⓐ Ⓑ Ⓒ Ⓓ Ⓔ

TEAR HERE

FIFTH MODEL EXAM

SCORE SHEET

ADDRESS CHECKING TEST: Your score on the Address Checking Test is based upon the number of questions you answered correctly minus the number of questions you answered incorrectly. To determine your score, subtract the number of wrong answers from the number of correct answers.

Number Right   −   Number Wrong   =   Raw Score

_____   −   _____   =   _____

MEANING OF WORDS TEST: Your score on the Meaning of Words Test is based only upon the number of questions you answered correctly.

Number Right   =   Raw Score

_____   =   _____

FOLLOWING ORAL DIRECTIONS TEST: Your score on the Following Oral Directions Test is based only upon the number of questions you marked correctly on the answer sheet. The Worksheet is not scored, and wrong answers on the answer sheet do not count against you.

Number Right   =   Raw Score

_____   =   _____

TOTAL SCORE: To find your total raw score, add together the raw scores for each section of the exam.

Address Checking Score   _____
+
Meaning of Words Score   _____
+
Following Oral Directions Score   _____
=
Total Raw Score   _____

ADDRESS CHECKING TEST

DIRECTIONS AND SAMPLE QUESTIONS

In the Address Checking Test you will have to decide whether two addresses are alike or different. Any difference at all makes the two addresses different. Look carefully at the address at the left and the address at the right. If the two addresses are *exactly alike in every way*, darken space Ⓐ for the question. If the two addresses are *different in any way*, darken space Ⓓ for the question. Mark your answers to these sample questions on the sample answer sheet on this page.

1. St. Louis MO   St. Louis MO
2. New York NY 10033   New York NY 10003
3. Atlanta GA 30303   Atlanta GA 30303
4. Granville OH 43023   Granville OH 43023
5. Denver CO   Denver CA
6. Manhattan KS 66506   Manhattan KY 66506

**SAMPLE ANSWER
SHEET**
1. Ⓐ Ⓓ
2. Ⓐ Ⓓ
3. Ⓐ Ⓓ
4. Ⓐ Ⓓ
5. Ⓐ Ⓓ
6. Ⓐ Ⓓ

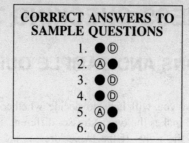

CORRECT ANSWERS TO SAMPLE QUESTIONS

1. ●Ⓓ
2. Ⓐ●
3. ●Ⓓ
4. ●Ⓓ
5. Ⓐ●
6. Ⓐ●

Explanations

Question 2 is marked Ⓓ because of a difference in zip code.
Question 5 is marked Ⓓ because of a difference in state.
Question 6 is marked Ⓓ because of a difference in state.

ADDRESS CHECKING TEST

95 Questions—6 Minutes

DIRECTIONS: This is a test of your speed and accuracy in comparing addresses. For each question in the test, blacken the correspondingly numbered answer space as follows:

- Blacken Ⓐ if the two addresses are exactly ALIKE.
- Blacken Ⓓ if the two addresses are DIFFERENT in **any** way.

Correct answers are on page 211.

1. Daytona Beach FL   Daytona Beach FL
2. Palantine IL 60067   Palatine IL 60067
3. Presque Isle ME 04769   Presque Isle ME 04769
4. Medford MA 02155   Medford MA 02155
5. Muskegon MI 49442   Muskegon MN 49442
6. St. Louis MO   St. Louis MO
7. Rutherford NJ 07070   Rutherford ND 07070
8. Cazenovia NY   Cazenovia NY
9. Murfreesboro NC   Murfeesboro NC
10. Wooster OH 43055   Wooster OH 43055
11. Center Valley PA   Centre Valley PA
12. Cayey PR 00633   Cayey PR 00633
13. Brookings SD 57006   Brookings SD 57706
14. Abilene TX 79601   Abilene KS 79601
15. Ephraim UT   Ephriam UT
16. Ferrum VA 24088   Ferrum VA 24008
17. Olympia WA 98503   Olympic WA 98503
18. Keyser WV 26726   Geyser WV 26726
19. Cleveland WI   Cleveland WI
20. Torrington WY   Torrington WY
21. Martin TN 38238   Martin TN 38283
22. Hartsville SC   Hartesville SC
23. Villanova PA 19085   Villanova PA 19085
24. Weatherford OK   Weatherford OK
25. Pepper Pike OH 44124   Pepper Pike OH 44124
26. Greenville NC   Greenville NC
27. Stony Brook NY 11794   Stonybrook NY 11794
28. Essex Fells NJ   Essex Falls NJ
29. Neosho MO 64850   Neosho MD 64850
30. Duluth MN 55911   Duluth MN 55911
31. Sault Ste. Marie MI   Sault Ste. Marie MI
32. Worcester MA   Worcester MA
33. Biddeford ME 04005   Biddeford ME 04055
34. Winchester KY 30491   Winchester KY 30491
35. Fayette IA 52142   Fayette LA 52142
36. Bloomington IN   Bloomington IN
37. Edwardsville IL 62026   Edwardsville IL 62026
38. Kahului HI 96732   Kahului HI 96732

39.	Pensacola FL 32504	Pensacola FL 35204
40.	Storrs CT 06268	Stores CT 06268
41.	Fort Morgan CO	Fort Morgan CO
42.	Reedley CA 93654	Reedley CA 96354
43.	Fayetteville AR	Fayetteville AR
44.	Thatcher AZ	Thatcher AZ
45.	Monroeville AL	Monroesville AL
46.	Wilmington DE 19803	Wilmington DL 19803
47.	Oglesby IL 61348	Oglesby IN 61348
48.	Orange City IA 51401	Orange City IA 51401
49.	North Manchester IN	No. Manchester IN
50.	Urbana IL 61801	Urbana IL 61810
51.	Franklin Springs GA	Franklin Springs GA
52.	Stanton DE 19702	Stanton DE 19702
53.	Tallahassee FL	Tallahassee FLA
54.	Cromwell CT 06415	Cornwall CT 06415
55.	Leadville CO 80461	Leadville CA 80461
56.	Oxnard CA 93030	Oxnard CA 93030
57.	Monticello AR	Monticello AR
58.	Tsaile AZ 86556	Tsaile AZ 86556
59.	Ketchikan AK	Ketchikan AK
60.	St. Bernard AL 35138	St. Bernard AL 35128
61.	Renssellaer IN	Renssellaer IN
62.	Bowling Green KY	Bowling Green WY
63.	Leicester MA 01534	Leicester MA 01534
64.	Dearborn MI 48126	Dearborne MI 48126
65.	Mississippi State MS	Mississippi State MS
66.	Lee's Summit MO	Lees Summit MO
67.	Seward NB 68434	Seward NB 68343
68.	Hooksett NH 03106	Hooksett NM 03106
69.	Williamston NC	Williamstown NC
70.	Yellow Springs OH	Yellow Springs OH
71.	Pittsburgh PA	Pittsfield PA
72.	Providence RI 02918	Providence RI 02918
73.	Yankton SD 57078	Yankton SD 57078
74.	Knoxville TN	Knoxville TN
75.	Kilgore TX 75662	Kilgore TX 75562
76.	Bennington VT	Bennington VA
77.	Buckhannon WV	Buckhannon WV
78.	Green Bay WI 54303	Green Bay WI 54303
79.	Agana Guam 96910	Agana Guam 96910
80.	Wytheville VA	Wyethville VA
81.	Edinburg TX 78539	Edinburgh TX 78539
82.	Sewanee TN 37375	Sewanee TN 37575
83.	Nanticoke PA 18634	Nanticoke PA 18634
84.	Wilberforce OH 45384	Wilburforce OH 45384
85.	Ahoskie NC 27910	Ahoskie NC 27910
86.	Fredonia NY	Fredonia NY
87.	Hattiesburg MS	Hattiesburg MS
88.	Fergus Falls MN 56537	Ferbus Falls MN 56565
89.	Port Huron MI	Port Huron MI
90.	Westminister MD	Westminster MD
91.	Lawrence KS 66045	Lawrance KS 66045
92.	Marshalltown IA	Marshalltown IA

93. Pearl City HI 96782   Pearl City HI 98762
94. Beloit WI 53511   Beloit WI 53511
95. Cheraw SC 29520   Cheraw SC 29520

END OF ADDRESS CHECKING TEST

Do not turn the page until you are told to do so.

MEANING OF WORDS TEST

DIRECTIONS AND SAMPLE QUESTIONS

The Meaning of Words Test asks you what a word or phrase means. In each question, a word or phrase is in *italics*. Five other words or phrases—lettered A, B, C, D, and E—are given as possible meanings. Choose the lettered word or phrase that means most nearly the same as the question and darken the space with the letter of the right answer. Mark your answers to these sample questions on the sample answer sheet below.

1. The new tax law will *abolish* a number of deductions. *Abolish* means most nearly
   (A) add on
   (B) weaken
   (C) do away with
   (D) include
   (E) explain

2. Years after the war, the former Marine went *berserk*. *Berserk* means most nearly
   (A) religious
   (B) crazy
   (C) back to war
   (D) weak
   (E) into business

3. The *facade* of the building was covered with carvings. *Facade* means most nearly
   (A) floor
   (B) ceiling
   (C) staircase
   (D) steeple
   (E) front

4. The artist stood at his *easel* and painted the hills. *Easel* means most nearly
   (A) canvass
   (B) paint box
   (C) palette
   (D) stand
   (E) leisure

SAMPLE ANSWER SHEET
1. Ⓐ Ⓑ Ⓒ Ⓓ Ⓔ
2. Ⓐ Ⓑ Ⓒ Ⓓ Ⓔ
3. Ⓐ Ⓑ Ⓒ Ⓓ Ⓔ
4. Ⓐ Ⓑ Ⓒ Ⓓ Ⓔ

**CORRECT ANSWERS TO
SAMPLE QUESTIONS**
1. Ⓐ Ⓑ ● Ⓓ Ⓔ
2. Ⓐ ● Ⓒ Ⓓ Ⓔ
3. Ⓐ Ⓑ Ⓒ Ⓓ ●
4. Ⓐ Ⓑ Ⓒ ● Ⓔ

Explanations

1. **(C)** To ABOLISH is to *destroy* or to *do away with completely*.
2. **(B)** BERSERK means *frenzied* or *crazy*.
3. **(E)** The FACADE is the *front* or *face*.
4. **(D)** An EASEL is a *frame* or *stand* for supporting something such as an artist's canvass.

MEANING OF WORDS TEST

32 Questions—25 Minutes

DIRECTIONS: In each of the sentences below, one word is in *italics*. Following each sentence, are five lettered words or phrases. You are to choose the word or phrase with the same meaning as the *italicized* word and mark its letter on the answer sheet. Correct answers are on page 213.

1. *Simple* clothing should be worn to work. *Simple* means most nearly
   (A) plain
   (B) inexpensive
   (C) nice
   (D) comfortable
   (E) old

2. Take your *finished* work to that area of the work floor. *Finished* means most nearly
   (A) inspected
   (B) assigned
   (C) outgoing
   (D) completed
   (E) rejected

3. The mail handler was a *rapid* worker. *Rapid* means most nearly
   (A) trained
   (B) rash
   (C) fast
   (D) regular
   (E) strong

4. There is an *abundant* supply of envelopes for our use. *Abundant* means most nearly
   (A) accessible
   (B) plentiful
   (C) concentrated
   (D) divided
   (E) scattered

5. The department is working on *experiments* in that area. *Experiments* means most nearly
   (A) tests
   (B) refinements
   (C) statements
   (D) plans
   (E) patents

6. We did not mean to *alarm* the children. *Alarm* means most nearly
   (A) endanger
   (B) insult
   (C) accuse
   (D) frighten
   (E) confuse

7. The kind of car he bought was *costly*. *Costly* means most nearly
   - (A) custom made
   - (B) desirable
   - (C) cheap
   - (D) scarce
   - (E) expensive ✓

8. The material used to make mail sacks is *durable*. *Durable* means most nearly
   - (A) thick
   - (B) waterproof
   - (C) lasting ✓
   - (D) elastic
   - (E) light

9. The worker was affected by his *fatigue*. *Fatigue* means most nearly
   - (A) problem
   - (B) relaxation
   - (C) sickness
   - (D) worry
   - (E) weariness ✓

10. Each office was asked to *restrict* the number of forms it used. *Restrict* means most nearly
    - (A) watch
    - (B) record
    - (C) limit ✓
    - (D) replace
    - (E) provide

11. The supervisor *demonstrated* the sorting procedure. *Demonstrated* means most nearly
    - (A) changed
    - (B) controlled
    - (C) determined
    - (D) showed ✓
    - (E) described

12. The retired postal worker led an *inactive* life. *Inactive* means most nearly
    - (A) restful
    - (B) idle ✓
    - (C) peaceful
    - (D) ordinary
    - (E) weary

13. Tapping on the desk can be an *irritating* habit. *Irritating* means most nearly
    - (A) nervous
    - (B) annoying ✓
    - (C) noisy
    - (D) startling
    - (E) unsuitable

14. The postal service is *essential* in this country. *Essential* means most nearly
    - (A) inevitable
    - (B) needless
    - (C) economical
    - (D) indispensable ✓
    - (E) established

15. Each carrier must recognize his *obligation*. *Obligation* means most nearly
    (A) importance
    (B) need
    (C) kindness
    (D) honor
    (E) duty

16. Each person expects *compensation* for his work. *Compensation* means most nearly
    (A) fulfillment
    (B) remuneration
    (C) appreciation
    (D) approval
    (E) recommendation

17. He sent the *irate* employee to the personnel manager. *Irate* means most nearly
    (A) angry
    (B) irresponsible
    (C) insubordinate
    (D) untidy
    (E) strong

18. The letter sorter reported that he found his work to be *tedious*. *Tedious* means most nearly
    (A) technical
    (B) interesting
    (C) tiresome
    (D) confidential
    (E) important

19. He was a good clerk because he was *alert*. *Alert* means most nearly
    (A) watchful
    (B) busy
    (C) honest
    (D) helpful
    (E) faithful

20. The machine was *revolving* rapidly. *Revolving* means most nearly
    (A) working
    (B) inclining
    (C) vibrating
    (D) producing
    (E) turning

21. The men were *commended* for their actions during the emergency. *Commended* means most nearly
    (A) blamed
    (B) reprimanded
    (C) promoted
    (D) encouraged
    (E) praised

22. All the employees *vied* for that award. *Vied* means most nearly
    (A) contended
    (B) cooperated
    (C) petitioned
    (D) persevered
    (E) prepared

23. The collector described the *blemish* on the new stamp. *Blemish* means most nearly
    (A) color
    (B) flaw
    (C) design
    (D) imprint
    (E) figure

24. The employee was given *distinct* instructions. *Distinct* means most nearly
    (A) clear
    (B) short
    (C) new
    (D) regular
    (E) loud

25. Some of the statements made at the meeting were *absurd*. *Absurd* means most nearly
    (A) clever
    (B) original
    (C) careless
    (D) foolish
    (E) serious

26. The supervisor *implied* that the schedule would be changed. *Implied* means most nearly
    (A) acknowledged
    (B) imagined
    (C) suggested
    (D) predicted
    (E) insisted

27. The new post office building is *huge*. *Huge* means most nearly
    (A) ugly
    (B) tall
    (C) sturdy
    (D) narrow
    (E) immense

28. The machine was *designed* for stamping envelopes. *Designed* means most nearly
    (A) fine
    (B) used
    (C) essential
    (D) approved
    (E) intended

29. Employees with previous training *assisted* the others. *Assisted* means most nearly
    (A) instructed
    (B) warned
    (C) stimulated
    (D) praised
    (E) aided

30. The traffic signs were *observable* to everyone. *Observable* means most nearly
    (A) noticeable
    (B) understandable
    (C) acceptable
    (D) agreeable
    (E) available

31. The *mended* mail sacks will be delivered tomorrow. *Mended* means most nearly
    (A) repaired
    (B) torn
    (C) clean
    (D) labelled
    (E) tied

32. Attendance at safety lectures is *obligatory*. *Obligatory* means most nearly
    (A) optional
    (B) important
    (C) inconvenient
    (D) compulsory
    (E) advisable

END OF MEANING OF WORDS TEST

If you finish your work on this test before time is up, check over your work on this test only. Do not go back to the Address Checking Test. Do not turn the page until you are told to do so.

FOLLOWING ORAL DIRECTIONS TEST

DIRECTIONS AND SAMPLE QUESTIONS

LISTENING TO INSTRUCTIONS: When you are ready to try these sample questions, give the following instructions to a friend and have the friend read them aloud to you at 80 words per minute. Do not read them to yourself. Your friend will need a watch with a second hand. Listen carefully and do exactly what your friend tells you to do with the worksheet and answer sheet. Your friend will tell you some things to do with each item on the worksheet. After each set of instructions, your friend will give you time to mark your answer by darkening a circle on the sample answer sheet. Since B and D sound very much alike, your friend will say ''B as in baker'' when he or she means B and ''D as in dog'' when he or she means D.

Before proceeding further, tear out the worksheet on page 203.

TO THE PERSON WHO IS TO READ THE DIRECTIONS: The directions are to be read at the rate of 80 words per minute. Do not read aloud the material which is in parentheses. Do not repeat any directions.

READ ALOUD TO THE CANDIDATE

Look at line 1 on your worksheet. (Pause slightly.) Draw a line under all the odd numbers between 5 and 14 which cannot be divided by 3. (Pause 10 seconds.) Now, on your answer sheet, darken the space for the letter D as in dog next to the number or numbers which you have underlined. (Pause 10 seconds.)

Look at line 2 on your worksheet. (Pause slightly.) In each circle there is a time when the mail must leave. In the circle for the earliest time, write on the line the last two figures of the time. (Pause 5 seconds.) Now, on your answer sheet, darken the space for the number-letter combination that is in the circle you just wrote in. (Pause 5 seconds.)

Look at line 2 again. (Pause slightly.) Find the circle with the latest time and write on the line the last two figures of the time. (Pause 5 seconds.) Now, on your answer sheet, darken the space for the number-letter combination that is in the circle you just wrote in. (Pause 5 seconds.)

Look at line 3 on your worksheet. (Pause slightly.) Draw two lines under every number between 7 and 15 that is odd. (Pause 10 seconds.) Now, on your answer sheet, for every number that you drew two lines under, darken space B as in baker. (Pause 10 seconds.)

WORKSHEET

DIRECTIONS: Listening carefully to each set of instructions, mark each item on this worksheet as directed. Then complete each question by marking the sample answer sheet below as directed. For each answer you will darken the answer for a number-letter combination. Should you fall behind and miss an instruction, don't become excited. Let that one go and listen for the next one. If when you start to darken a space for a number, you find that you have already darkened another space for that number, either erase the first mark and darken the space for the new combination or let the first mark stay and do not darken a space for the new combination. Write with a pencil that has a clean eraser. When you finish, you should have no more than one space darkened for each number.

1. 8   10   6   5   3   9   7   14

2. (9:03 __A)   (9:12 __B)   (9:02 __C)   (9:07 __D)   (9:10 __E)

3. 9   12   15   5   13   8   7   14

SAMPLE ANSWER SHEET		
1. Ⓐ Ⓑ Ⓒ Ⓓ Ⓔ	6. Ⓐ Ⓑ Ⓒ Ⓓ Ⓔ	11. Ⓐ Ⓑ Ⓒ Ⓓ Ⓔ
2. Ⓐ Ⓑ Ⓒ Ⓓ Ⓔ	7. Ⓐ Ⓑ Ⓒ Ⓓ Ⓔ	12. Ⓐ Ⓑ Ⓒ Ⓓ Ⓔ
3. Ⓐ Ⓑ Ⓒ Ⓓ Ⓔ	8. Ⓐ Ⓑ Ⓒ Ⓓ Ⓔ	13. Ⓐ Ⓑ Ⓒ Ⓓ Ⓔ
4. Ⓐ Ⓑ Ⓒ Ⓓ Ⓔ	9. Ⓐ Ⓑ Ⓒ Ⓓ Ⓔ	14. Ⓐ Ⓑ Ⓒ Ⓓ Ⓔ
5. Ⓐ Ⓑ Ⓒ Ⓓ Ⓔ	10. Ⓐ Ⓑ Ⓒ Ⓓ Ⓔ	15. Ⓐ Ⓑ Ⓒ Ⓓ Ⓔ

```
┌─────────────────────────────────────────────────────┐
│         CORRECT ANSWERS TO SAMPLE QUESTIONS           │
│   1. Ⓐ Ⓑ Ⓒ Ⓓ Ⓔ    6. Ⓐ Ⓑ Ⓒ Ⓓ Ⓔ   11. Ⓐ Ⓑ Ⓒ Ⓓ Ⓔ  │
│   2. Ⓐ Ⓑ ● Ⓓ Ⓔ     7. Ⓐ Ⓑ Ⓒ ● Ⓔ   12. Ⓐ ● Ⓒ Ⓓ Ⓔ   │
│   3. Ⓐ Ⓑ Ⓒ Ⓓ Ⓔ     8. Ⓐ Ⓑ Ⓒ Ⓓ Ⓔ   13. Ⓐ ● Ⓒ Ⓓ Ⓔ   │
│   4. Ⓐ Ⓑ Ⓒ Ⓓ Ⓔ     9. Ⓐ ● Ⓒ Ⓓ Ⓔ   14. Ⓐ Ⓑ Ⓒ Ⓓ Ⓔ   │
│   5. Ⓐ Ⓑ Ⓒ Ⓓ Ⓔ    10. Ⓐ Ⓑ Ⓒ Ⓓ Ⓔ   15. Ⓐ Ⓑ Ⓒ Ⓓ Ⓔ   │
└─────────────────────────────────────────────────────┘
```

Correctly Filled Worksheet

1.   8   10   6   5   3   9   <u>7</u>   14

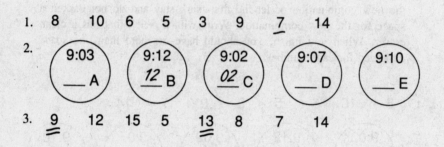

2.

3.   <u>9</u>   12   15   5   <u>13</u>   8   7   14

FOLLOWING ORAL DIRECTIONS TEST

Total Time—25 Minutes

LISTENING TO DIRECTIONS

DIRECTIONS: When you are ready to try this test of the Model Exam, give the following instructions to a friend and have the friend read them aloud to you at 80 words per minute. Do NOT read them to yourself. Your friend will need a watch with a second hand. Listen carefully and do exactly what your friend tells you to do with the worksheet and with the answer sheet. Your friend will tell you some things to do with each item on the worksheet. After each set of instructions, your friend will give you time to mark your answer by darkening a circle on the answer sheet. Since B and D sound very much alike, your friend will say "B as in baker" when he or she means B and "D as in dog" when he or she means D.

Before proceeding further, tear out the worksheet on page 209 of this test. Then hand this book to your friend.

TO THE PERSON WHO IS TO READ THE DIRECTIONS: The directions are to be read at the rate of 80 words per minute. Do not read aloud the material which is in parentheses. Once you have begun the test itself, do not repeat any directions. The next three paragraphs consist of approximately 120 words. Read these three paragraphs aloud to the candidate in about one and one-half minutes. You may reread these paragraphs as often as necessary to establish an 80 words per minute reading speed.

READ ALOUD TO THE CANDIDATE

On the job you will have to listen to directions and then do what you have been told to do. In this test, I will read instructions to you. Try to understand them as I read them; I cannot repeat them. Once we begin, you may not ask any questions until the end of the test.

On the job you won't have to deal with pictures, numbers and letters like those in the test, but you will have to listen to instructions and follow them. We are using this test to see how well you can follow instructions.

You are to mark your test booklet according to the instructions that I'll read to you. After each set of instructions, I'll give you time to record your answers on the separate answer sheet.

The actual test begins now.

Look at line 1 on your worksheet. (Pause slightly.) Draw a line under the sixth number in line 1. (Pause 2 seconds.) Now, on your answer sheet, darken space E for the number under which you just drew a line. (Pause 5 seconds.)

Look at line 1 again. (Pause slightly.) Draw two lines under the third number on the line. (Pause 2 seconds.) Now, on your answer sheet, darken space B as in baker for the number under which you drew two lines. (Pause 5 seconds.)

Look at line 2 on your worksheet. (Pause slightly.) Find the letter that is fifth in the alphabet and circle it (pause 2 seconds). Now darken that letter for number 77 on your answer sheet. (Pause 5 seconds.)

Look at line 3 on your worksheet. (Pause slightly.) Write the number 17 in the third box. (Pause 2 seconds.) Now, on your answer sheet, darken the number-letter combination that is in the box you just wrote in. (Pause 5 seconds.)

Look at line 3 again. (Pause slightly.) In the fourth box, write the number of hours in a day. (Pause 2 seconds.) Now, on your answer sheet, darken the number-letter combination that is in the box you just wrote in. (Pause 5 seconds.)

Look at line 4 on your worksheet. (Pause slightly.) Write D as in dog in the circle right next to the second lowest number. (Pause 5 seconds.) Now, on your answer sheet, darken the space for the number-letter combination in the circle you just wrote in. (Pause 5 seconds.)

Look at line 4 again. (Pause slightly.) Write the letter C on the line in the middle circle. (Pause 2 seconds.) Now, on your answer sheet, darken the space for the number-letter combination in the circle you just wrote in. (Pause 5 seconds.)

Look at line 5 on your worksheet. Each box represents a letter carrier and the amount of money that he or she collected on the route in one day. (Pause slightly.) Find the carrier who collected the smallest amount of money that day and circle his or her letter (pause 2 seconds). On your answer sheet, darken the number-letter combination in the box in which you circled a letter. (Pause 5 seconds.)

Look at line 6 on your worksheet. (Pause slightly.) Write the first letter of the third means of transportation on the second line. (Pause 8 seconds.) Write the last letter of the first means of transportation on the first line. (Pause 8 seconds.) Write the middle letter of the middle means of transportation on the last line. (Pause 8 seconds.) Now, on your answer sheet, darken the number-letter combinations on the three lines. (Pause 15 seconds.)

Look at line 7 on your worksheet. (Pause slightly.) Reading right to left, find the first number that is higher than the number 39 and draw a box around the number. (Pause 5 seconds.) Now, on your answer sheet, darken D as in dog for the number around which you just drew a box. (Pause 5 seconds.)

Look at line 8 on your worksheet. (Pause slightly.) Find, on line 8, the letter which appears first in the alphabet and underline that letter. (Pause 5 seconds.) Now, on your answer sheet, darken that letter for space number 1. (Pause 5 seconds.)

Look at line 9 on your worksheet. (Pause slightly.) In the figure with the least number of points, write the letter A. (Pause 2 seconds.) In the figure with the greatest number of points, write the letter E. (Pause 2 seconds.) Now, on your answer sheet, darken the number-letter combinations in the two figures you just wrote in. (Pause 10 seconds.)

Look at line 10 on your worksheet. (Pause slightly.) If the third number in line 10 should, in normal counting, appear before the fourth number in line 10, write the letter B above the third number; if not, write the letter A above the fourth number. (Pause 5 seconds.) Now, on your answer sheet, darken the number-letter combination of the number you just wrote above. (Pause 5 seconds.)

Look at line 11 on your worksheet. (Pause slightly.) Write the letter A in the second box. (Pause 2 seconds.) Now, on your answer sheet, darken the number-letter combination in the box you just wrote in. (Pause 5 seconds.)

Look at line 11 again. (Pause slightly.) If the number in the smallest box is greater than the number in the first box, write the letter C in the largest box (pause 5 seconds); if not, write the letter D as in dog in the largest box. (Pause 2 seconds.) Now, on your answer sheet, darken the number-letter combination in the box you just wrote in. (Pause 5 seconds.)

Look at line 12 on your worksheet. (Pause slightly.) Draw one line under each number that falls between 75 and 90 and is even. (Pause 8 seconds.) Now, on your answer sheet, blacken space D as in dog for each number that you drew one line under. (Pause 10 seconds.)

Look at line 12 again. (Pause slightly.) Draw two lines under each number that falls between 75 and 90 and is odd. (Pause 8 seconds.) Now, on your answer sheet, darken space E for each number under which you drew two lines. (Pause 5 seconds.)

Look at line 13 on your worksheet. (Pause slightly.) Write the letter A in the left-hand circle. (Pause 2 seconds.) Now, on your answer sheet, darken the space for the number-letter combination in the figure you just wrote in. (Pause 5 seconds.)

Look at line 13 again. (Pause slightly.) Write the letter B as in baker in the right-hand square. (Pause 2 seconds.) Now, on your answer sheet, darken the space for the number-letter combination in the figure in which you just wrote. (Pause 5 seconds.)

Look at line 14 on your worksheet. (Pause slightly.) Write the answer to this question at the end of line 14: $22 \times 2 =$ . . . . (Pause 2 seconds.) Find the answer that you wrote among the numbers on line 14 (pause 2 seconds) and darken that number-letter combination on your answer sheet. (Pause 5 seconds.)

Look at line 15 on your worksheet. (Pause slightly.) If 3 is less than 5 and more than 7, write the letter E next to number 89 (pause 5 seconds); if not, write the letter E next to number 61. (Pause 2 seconds.) Now, on your answer sheet, darken the number-letter combination of the line you just wrote on. (Pause 5 seconds.)

Look at line 16 on your worksheet. (Pause slightly.) Count the number of V's on line 16 and write the number at the end of the line. (Pause 2 seconds.) Now, add 11 to that number and, on your answer sheet, darken space D as in dog for the number of V's plus 11. (Pause 10 seconds.)

Look at line 17 on your worksheet. (Pause slightly.) Each time represents the scheduled arrival time of a mail truck. Write the letter A on the line beside the earliest scheduled time. (Pause 2 seconds.) Write the letter C next to the latest scheduled time. (Pause 2 seconds.) Now, on your answer sheet, darken the number-letter combinations the last two digits of the times beside which you wrote letters. (Pause 10 seconds.)

Look at line 18 on your worksheet. (Pause slightly.) If in one day there are more hours before noon than after noon, write the number 47 in the second circle; (pause 2 seconds) if not, write the number 38 in the first circle. (Pause 2 seconds.) Now, on your answer sheet, blacken the space for the number-letter combination in the circle in which you just wrote. (Pause 5 seconds.)

Look at line 18 again. (Pause slightly.) Write the number 69 in the second circle from the right. (Pause 2 seconds.) Now, on your answer sheet, darken the space for the number-letter combination in the circle in which you just wrote. (Pause 5 seconds.)

FOLLOWING ORAL DIRECTIONS TEST

Total Time—25 Minutes

WORKSHEET

DIRECTIONS: Listening carefully to each set of instructions, mark each item on this worksheet as directed. Then complete each question by marking the answer sheet as directed. For each answer you will darken the answer for a number-letter combination. Should you fall behind and miss an instruction, don't become excited. Let that one go and listen for the next one. If when you start to darken a space for a number, you find that you have already darkened another space for that number, either erase the first mark and darken the space for the new combination or let the first mark stay and do not darken a space for the new combination. Write with a pencil that has a clean eraser. When you finish, you should have no more than one space darkened for each number. Correct answers are on page 215.

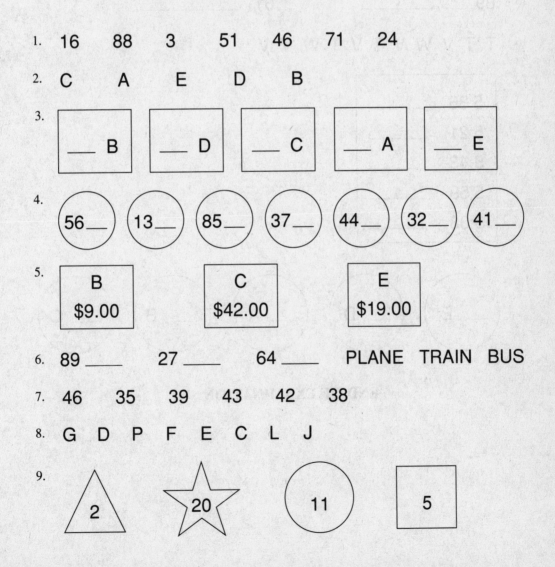

1.   16   88   3   51   46   71   24

2.   C   A   E   D   B

3.   __ B   __ D   __ C   __ A   __ E

4.   56__   13__   85__   37__   44__   32__   41__

5.   B $9.00   C $42.00   E $19.00

6.   89 ____   27 ____   64 ____   PLANE TRAIN BUS

7.   46   35   39   43   42   38

8.   G D P F E C L J

9.   2   20   11   5

TEAR HERE

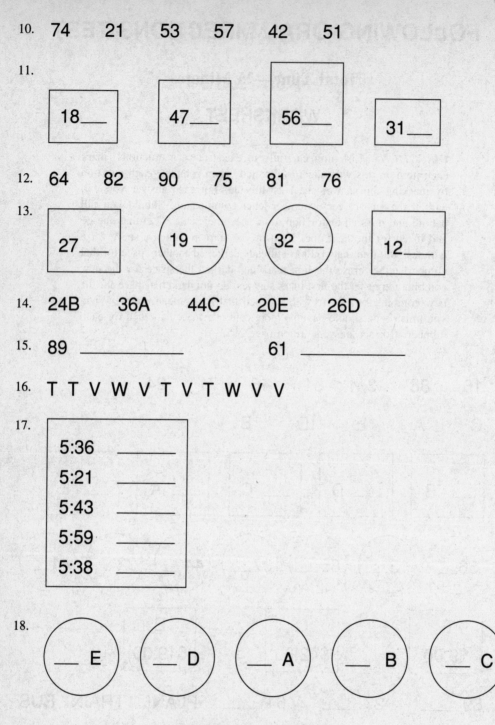

10. 74   21   53   57   42   51

11. 18___   47___   56___   31___

12. 64   82   90   75   81   76

13. 27___   19___   32___   12___

14. 24B   36A   44C   20E   26D

15. 89 _____   61 _____

16. T T V W V T V T W V V

17.
5:36 _____
5:21 _____
5:43 _____
5:59 _____
5:38 _____

18. ___E   ___D   ___A   ___B   ___C

END OF EXAMINATION

FIFTH MODEL EXAM ANSWER KEY

ADDRESS CHECKING TEST

1. A	17. D	33. D	49. D	65. A	81. D
2. D	18. D	34. A	50. D	66. D	82. D
3. A	19. A	35. D	51. A	67. D	83. A
4. A	20. A	36. A	52. A	68. D	84. D
5. D	21. D	37. A	53. D	69. D	85. A
6. A	22. D	38. A	54. D	70. A	86. A
7. D	23. A	39. D	55. D	71. D	87. A
8. A	24. A	40. D	56. A	72. A	88. D
9. D	25. A	41. A	57. A	73. A	89. A
10. A	26. A	42. D	58. A	74. A	90. D
11. D	27. D	43. A	59. A	75. D	91. D
12. A	28. D	44. A	60. D	76. D	92. A
13. D	29. D	45. D	61. A	77. A	93. D
14. D	30. A	46. D	62. D	78. A	94. A
15. D	31. A	47. D	63. A	79. A	95. A
16. D	32. A	48. A	64. D	80. D	

ADDRESS CHECKING TEST

Explanations of Differences

2. different cities
5. different states
7. different states
9. different cities
11. spelling of city
13. different numbers
14. different states
15. spelling of city
16. different numbers
17. different cities
18. different cities
21. reversal of numbers
22. spelling of city
27. spelling of city
28. different cities
29. different states
33. different numbers
35. different states
39. number reversal
40. spelling of city
42. number reversal
45. different cities
46. state abbreviation
47. different states
49. spelling of city
50. number reversal

53. state abbreviation
54. different cities
55. different states
60. different numbers
62. different states
64. spelling of city
66. spelling of city
67. different numbers
68. different states
69. different cities
71. different cities
75. different numbers
76. different states
80. spelling of city
81. spelling of city
82. different numbers
84. spelling of city
88. spelling of city
90. spelling of city
91. spelling of city
93. number reversal

Analysis of Differences

Fill in the column on the right with the total number of questions you answered incorrectly.

City difference	23	
Number difference	12	
State difference	12	
Total addresses with differences	47	
Total addresses with no differences.	48	

MEANING OF WORDS TEST

1. A	7. E	12. B	17. A	22. A	27. E
2. D	8. C	13. B	18. C	23. B	28. E
3. C	9. E	14. D	19. A	24. A	29. E
4. B	10. C	15. E	20. E	25. D	30. A
5. A	11. D	16. B	21. E	26. C	31. A
6. D					32. D

MEANING OF WORDS TEST

Explanatory Answers

1. **(A)** SIMPLE means *uncomplicated, modest* or *plain*.
2. **(D)** FINISHED means *terminated, done* or *completed*.
3. **(C)** RAPID means *fast*.
4. **(B)** ABUNDANT means *ample, abounding,* or *plentiful*. *Abundance* implies a comfortable feeling of ''more than enough.''
5. **(A)** EXPERIMENTS are controlled *trials* or *tests*. *Experiments* lead to inventions and *patents* or to *refinements*, but the *experiments* themselves are carefully watched *tests*.
6. **(D)** To ALARM is to *disturb*, to *excite* or to *frighten*. An *alarm* serves to *alert* or to *frighten* into action so as to avoid danger.
7. **(E)** COSTLY means *dear* or *expensive*. Since *cost* means *price* and there is no prefix or suffix to indicate ''low cost,'' you must assume *costly* to refer to *high price*. *Custom, desireable* and *scarce* may all contribute to the high price.
8. **(C)** DURABLE means *long-lasting*. The material that makes mail sacks wear well is most likely *thick* and *waterproof*, but the *durability* itself is the *long-lasting* quality.
9. **(E)** FATIGUE means *exhaustion* or *weariness*. *Fatigue* may be caused by overwork, *problems, sickness* or *worry*, but the *fatigue* itself is *weariness*.
10. **(C)** To RESTRICT is to *restrain*, to *confine* or to *limit*.
11. **(D)** To DEMONSTRATE is to *illustrate* or to *show*.
12. **(B)** INACTIVE means *not active, sluggish* or *idle*. The prefix *in* before the word *active* means *not*.
13. **(B)** IRRITATING means *annoying*. The habit may be a *nervous* one and surely tapping is *noisy*. The *irritation* is the *annoyance*.
14. **(D)** ESSENTIAL means *necessary, vital* or *indispensable*.
15. **(E)** OBLIGATION means *commitment* or *duty*.
16. **(B)** COMPENSATION means *payment* or *remuneration*. Actually, *fulfillment, appreciation* and *approval* are all forms of payment, but *money payment* or *remuneration* is most vital for the worker. You must pick the best synonym in the context of the sentence.
17. **(A)** IRATE means *incensed* or *angry*.
18. **(C)** TEDIOUS means *dull, boring* or *tiresome*.
19. **(A)** ALERT means *watchful*.
20. **(E)** To REVOLVE is to *rotate* or to *turn* or *roll around*. The machine may well have been *operating, vibrating* and *producing*, but its *revolving* was its *turning*.
21. **(E)** To COMMEND is to *compliment* or to *praise*. A *commendation* is very positive. *Blame* and *reprimand* are direct opposites. *Commendation* may eventually lead to *promotion*.
22. **(A)** To VIE is to *strive*, to *compete* or to *contend*.
23. **(B)** BLEMISH means *imperfection, defect* or *flaw*. Postal printing office quality control is strict, so *blemished* stamps are rare.

24. **(A)** DISTINCT means *unmistakeable* and *clear*.
25. **(D)** ABSURD means *ridiculous, meaningless* or *foolish*.
26. **(C)** To IMPLY is to *express indirectly* or to *suggest*. It would be better for a supervisor to keep silent until he or she was certain of the schedule change and then to make a direct announcement, but supervisors are human and sometimes *drop hints*.
27. **(E)** HUGE means *enormous, vast* or *immense*.
28. **(E)** To DESIGN is to *plan*, to *construct* or to *intend*.
29. **(E)** To ASSIST is to *help* or to *aid*. There is, of course, an element of *instruction* in *assistance,* but the *assistance* is the *aid* and the *instruction* a fringe benefit or side-effect.
30. **(A)** OBSERVABLE means *discernible* or *noticeable*. Take the word apart. *Observable* = Able to be observed = able to be noticed = noticeable.
31. **(A)** MENDED means *fixed, patched,* or *repaired*.
32. **(D)** OBLIGATORY means *mandatory, required* or *compulsory*. An *obligation* is a *debt* or a *duty*. If you are *obliged* to do something, you have to do it. *Obligatory* stems from the same root and means *compulsory*.

FOLLOWING ORAL DIRECTIONS TEST

Correctly Filled Worksheet

1. 16   88   <u>3</u>   51   46   <u>71</u>   24

2. C   A   Ⓔ   D   B

3.
__ B	__ D	*17* C	*24* A	__ E

4. (56 __) (13 __) (85 __) (37 *C*) (44 __) (32 *D*) (41 __)

5.
Ⓑ $9.00	C $42.00	E $19.00

6. 89 *E*   27 *B*   64 *A*   PLANE   TRAIN   BUS

7. 46   35   39   43   ⬜42   38

8. G   D   P   F   E   <u>C</u>   L   J

9.
△ 2   ☆ *E* 20   ◯ *A* 11   ⬜ 5

B

10. 74   21   53   57   42   51

11.
18 __	47 *A*	56 *C*	31 __

12. 64   <u>82</u>   90   75   <u>81</u>   <u>76</u>

13.

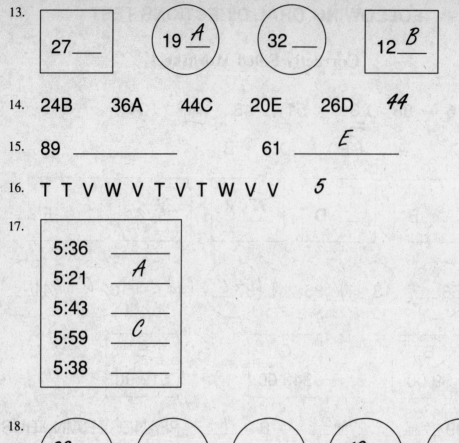

27 ___   19 *A*   32 ___   12 *B*

14.   24B   36A   44C   20E   26D   *44*

15.   89 _____   61 _____*E*_____

16.   T T V W V T V T W V V   *5*

17.

5:36 _____
5:21 __*A*__
5:43 _____
5:59 __*C*__
5:38 _____

18.

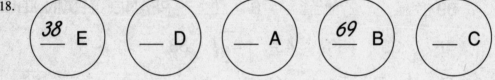

38 E   ___ D   ___ A   *69* B   ___ C

FOLLOWING ORAL DIRECTIONS TEST

Correctly Filled Answer Grid

1. Ⓐ Ⓑ ● Ⓓ Ⓔ
2. Ⓐ Ⓑ Ⓒ Ⓓ Ⓔ
3. Ⓐ ● Ⓒ Ⓓ Ⓔ
4. Ⓐ Ⓑ Ⓒ Ⓓ Ⓔ
5. Ⓐ Ⓑ Ⓒ Ⓓ Ⓔ
6. Ⓐ Ⓑ Ⓒ Ⓓ Ⓔ
7. Ⓐ Ⓑ Ⓒ Ⓓ Ⓔ
8. Ⓐ Ⓑ Ⓒ Ⓓ Ⓔ
9. Ⓐ ● Ⓒ Ⓓ Ⓔ
10. Ⓐ Ⓑ Ⓒ Ⓓ Ⓔ
11. ● Ⓑ Ⓒ Ⓓ Ⓔ
12. Ⓐ ● Ⓒ Ⓓ Ⓔ
13. Ⓐ Ⓑ Ⓒ Ⓓ Ⓔ
14. Ⓐ Ⓑ Ⓒ Ⓓ Ⓔ
15. Ⓐ Ⓑ Ⓒ Ⓓ Ⓔ
16. Ⓐ Ⓑ Ⓒ ● Ⓔ
17. Ⓐ Ⓑ ● Ⓓ Ⓔ
18. Ⓐ Ⓑ Ⓒ Ⓓ Ⓔ
19. ● Ⓑ Ⓒ Ⓓ Ⓔ
20. Ⓐ Ⓑ Ⓒ Ⓓ ●
21. ● Ⓑ Ⓒ Ⓓ Ⓔ
22. Ⓐ Ⓑ Ⓒ Ⓓ Ⓔ
23. Ⓐ Ⓑ Ⓒ Ⓓ Ⓔ
24. ● Ⓑ Ⓒ Ⓓ Ⓔ
25. Ⓐ Ⓑ Ⓒ Ⓓ Ⓔ
26. Ⓐ Ⓑ Ⓒ Ⓓ Ⓔ
27. Ⓐ ● Ⓒ Ⓓ Ⓔ
28. Ⓐ Ⓑ Ⓒ Ⓓ Ⓔ
29. Ⓐ Ⓑ Ⓒ Ⓓ Ⓔ
30. Ⓐ Ⓑ Ⓒ Ⓓ Ⓔ

31. Ⓐ Ⓑ Ⓒ Ⓓ Ⓔ
32. Ⓐ Ⓑ Ⓒ ● Ⓔ
33. Ⓐ Ⓑ Ⓒ Ⓓ Ⓔ
34. Ⓐ Ⓑ Ⓒ Ⓓ Ⓔ
35. Ⓐ Ⓑ Ⓒ Ⓓ Ⓔ
36. Ⓐ Ⓑ Ⓒ Ⓓ Ⓔ
37. Ⓐ Ⓑ ● Ⓓ Ⓔ
38. Ⓐ Ⓑ Ⓒ Ⓓ ●
39. Ⓐ Ⓑ Ⓒ Ⓓ Ⓔ
40. Ⓐ Ⓑ Ⓒ Ⓓ Ⓔ
41. Ⓐ Ⓑ Ⓒ Ⓓ Ⓔ
42. Ⓐ Ⓑ Ⓒ ● Ⓔ
43. Ⓐ Ⓑ Ⓒ Ⓓ Ⓔ
44. Ⓐ Ⓑ ● Ⓓ Ⓔ
45. Ⓐ Ⓑ Ⓒ Ⓓ Ⓔ
46. Ⓐ Ⓑ Ⓒ Ⓓ Ⓔ
47. ● Ⓑ Ⓒ Ⓓ Ⓔ
48. Ⓐ Ⓑ Ⓒ Ⓓ Ⓔ
49. Ⓐ Ⓑ Ⓒ Ⓓ Ⓔ
50. Ⓐ Ⓑ Ⓒ Ⓓ Ⓔ
51. Ⓐ Ⓑ Ⓒ Ⓓ Ⓔ
52. Ⓐ Ⓑ Ⓒ Ⓓ Ⓔ
53. Ⓐ ● Ⓒ Ⓓ Ⓔ
54. Ⓐ Ⓑ Ⓒ Ⓓ Ⓔ
55. Ⓐ Ⓑ Ⓒ Ⓓ Ⓔ
56. Ⓐ Ⓑ ● Ⓓ Ⓔ
57. Ⓐ Ⓑ Ⓒ Ⓓ Ⓔ
58. Ⓐ Ⓑ Ⓒ Ⓓ Ⓔ
59. Ⓐ Ⓑ ● Ⓓ Ⓔ
60. Ⓐ Ⓑ Ⓒ Ⓓ Ⓔ

61. Ⓐ Ⓑ Ⓒ Ⓓ ●
62. Ⓐ Ⓑ Ⓒ Ⓓ Ⓔ
63. Ⓐ Ⓑ Ⓒ Ⓓ Ⓔ
64. ● Ⓑ Ⓒ Ⓓ Ⓔ
65. Ⓐ Ⓑ Ⓒ Ⓓ Ⓔ
66. Ⓐ Ⓑ Ⓒ Ⓓ Ⓔ
67. Ⓐ Ⓑ Ⓒ Ⓓ Ⓔ
68. Ⓐ Ⓑ Ⓒ Ⓓ Ⓔ
69. Ⓐ ● Ⓒ Ⓓ Ⓔ
70. Ⓐ Ⓑ Ⓒ Ⓓ Ⓔ
71. Ⓐ Ⓑ Ⓒ Ⓓ ●
72. Ⓐ Ⓑ Ⓒ Ⓓ Ⓔ
73. Ⓐ Ⓑ Ⓒ Ⓓ Ⓔ
74. Ⓐ Ⓑ Ⓒ Ⓓ Ⓔ
75. Ⓐ Ⓑ Ⓒ Ⓓ Ⓔ
76. Ⓐ Ⓑ Ⓒ ● Ⓔ
77. Ⓐ Ⓑ Ⓒ Ⓓ ●
78. Ⓐ Ⓑ Ⓒ Ⓓ Ⓔ
79. Ⓐ Ⓑ Ⓒ Ⓓ Ⓔ
80. Ⓐ Ⓑ Ⓒ Ⓓ Ⓔ
81. Ⓐ Ⓑ Ⓒ Ⓓ ●
82. Ⓐ Ⓑ Ⓒ ● Ⓔ
83. Ⓐ Ⓑ Ⓒ Ⓓ Ⓔ
84. Ⓐ Ⓑ Ⓒ Ⓓ Ⓔ
85. Ⓐ Ⓑ Ⓒ Ⓓ Ⓔ
86. Ⓐ Ⓑ Ⓒ Ⓓ Ⓔ
87. Ⓐ Ⓑ Ⓒ Ⓓ Ⓔ
88. Ⓐ Ⓑ Ⓒ Ⓓ Ⓔ
89. Ⓐ Ⓑ Ⓒ Ⓓ ●
90. Ⓐ Ⓑ Ⓒ Ⓓ Ⓔ

FINAL MODEL EXAM ANSWER SHEET

ADDRESS CHECKING TEST

1. Ⓐ Ⓓ
2. Ⓐ Ⓓ
3. Ⓐ Ⓓ
4. Ⓐ Ⓓ
5. Ⓐ Ⓓ
6. Ⓐ Ⓓ
7. Ⓐ Ⓓ
8. Ⓐ Ⓓ
9. Ⓐ Ⓓ
10. Ⓐ Ⓓ
11. Ⓐ Ⓓ
12. Ⓐ Ⓓ
13. Ⓐ Ⓓ
14. Ⓐ Ⓓ
15. Ⓐ Ⓓ
16. Ⓐ Ⓓ

17. Ⓐ Ⓓ
18. Ⓐ Ⓓ
19. Ⓐ Ⓓ
20. Ⓐ Ⓓ
21. Ⓐ Ⓓ
22. Ⓐ Ⓓ
23. Ⓐ Ⓓ
24. Ⓐ Ⓓ
25. Ⓐ Ⓓ
26. Ⓐ Ⓓ
27. Ⓐ Ⓓ
28. Ⓐ Ⓓ
29. Ⓐ Ⓓ
30. Ⓐ Ⓓ
31. Ⓐ Ⓓ
32. Ⓐ Ⓓ

33. Ⓐ Ⓓ
34. Ⓐ Ⓓ
35. Ⓐ Ⓓ
36. Ⓐ Ⓓ
37. Ⓐ Ⓓ
38. Ⓐ Ⓓ
39. Ⓐ Ⓓ
40. Ⓐ Ⓓ
41. Ⓐ Ⓓ
42. Ⓐ Ⓓ
43. Ⓐ Ⓓ
44. Ⓐ Ⓓ
45. Ⓐ Ⓓ
46. Ⓐ Ⓓ
47. Ⓐ Ⓓ
48. Ⓐ Ⓓ

49. Ⓐ Ⓓ
50. Ⓐ Ⓓ
51. Ⓐ Ⓓ
52. Ⓐ Ⓓ
53. Ⓐ Ⓓ
54. Ⓐ Ⓓ
55. Ⓐ Ⓓ
56. Ⓐ Ⓓ
57. Ⓐ Ⓓ
58. Ⓐ Ⓓ
59. Ⓐ Ⓓ
60. Ⓐ Ⓓ
61. Ⓐ Ⓓ
62. Ⓐ Ⓓ
63. Ⓐ Ⓓ
64. Ⓐ Ⓓ

65. Ⓐ Ⓓ
66. Ⓐ Ⓓ
67. Ⓐ Ⓓ
68. Ⓐ Ⓓ
69. Ⓐ Ⓓ
70. Ⓐ Ⓓ
71. Ⓐ Ⓓ
72. Ⓐ Ⓓ
73. Ⓐ Ⓓ
74. Ⓐ Ⓓ
75. Ⓐ Ⓓ
76. Ⓐ Ⓓ
77. Ⓐ Ⓓ
78. Ⓐ Ⓓ
79. Ⓐ Ⓓ
80. Ⓐ Ⓓ

81. Ⓐ Ⓓ
82. Ⓐ Ⓓ
83. Ⓐ Ⓓ
84. Ⓐ Ⓓ
85. Ⓐ Ⓓ
86. Ⓐ Ⓓ
87. Ⓐ Ⓓ
88. Ⓐ Ⓓ
89. Ⓐ Ⓓ
90. Ⓐ Ⓓ
91. Ⓐ Ⓓ
92. Ⓐ Ⓓ
93. Ⓐ Ⓓ
94. Ⓐ Ⓓ
95. Ⓐ Ⓓ

MEANING OF WORDS TEST

1. Ⓐ Ⓑ Ⓒ Ⓓ Ⓔ
2. Ⓐ Ⓑ Ⓒ Ⓓ Ⓔ
3. Ⓐ Ⓑ Ⓒ Ⓓ Ⓔ
4. Ⓐ Ⓑ Ⓒ Ⓓ Ⓔ
5. Ⓐ Ⓑ Ⓒ Ⓓ Ⓔ
6. Ⓐ Ⓑ Ⓒ Ⓓ Ⓔ
7. Ⓐ Ⓑ Ⓒ Ⓓ Ⓔ

8. Ⓐ Ⓑ Ⓒ Ⓓ Ⓔ
9. Ⓐ Ⓑ Ⓒ Ⓓ Ⓔ
10. Ⓐ Ⓑ Ⓒ Ⓓ Ⓔ
11. Ⓐ Ⓑ Ⓒ Ⓓ Ⓔ
12. Ⓐ Ⓑ Ⓒ Ⓓ Ⓔ
13. Ⓐ Ⓑ Ⓒ Ⓓ Ⓔ
14. Ⓐ Ⓑ Ⓒ Ⓓ Ⓔ

15. Ⓐ Ⓑ Ⓒ Ⓓ Ⓔ
16. Ⓐ Ⓑ Ⓒ Ⓓ Ⓔ
17. Ⓐ Ⓑ Ⓒ Ⓓ Ⓔ
18. Ⓐ Ⓑ Ⓒ Ⓓ Ⓔ
19. Ⓐ Ⓑ Ⓒ Ⓓ Ⓔ
20. Ⓐ Ⓑ Ⓒ Ⓓ Ⓔ
21. Ⓐ Ⓑ Ⓒ Ⓓ Ⓔ

22. Ⓐ Ⓑ Ⓒ Ⓓ Ⓔ
23. Ⓐ Ⓑ Ⓒ Ⓓ Ⓔ
24. Ⓐ Ⓑ Ⓒ Ⓓ Ⓔ
25. Ⓐ Ⓑ Ⓒ Ⓓ Ⓔ
26. Ⓐ Ⓑ Ⓒ Ⓓ Ⓔ
27. Ⓐ Ⓑ Ⓒ Ⓓ Ⓔ
28. Ⓐ Ⓑ Ⓒ Ⓓ Ⓔ

29. Ⓐ Ⓑ Ⓒ Ⓓ Ⓔ
30. Ⓐ Ⓑ Ⓒ Ⓓ Ⓔ
31. Ⓐ Ⓑ Ⓒ Ⓓ Ⓔ
32. Ⓐ Ⓑ Ⓒ Ⓓ Ⓔ

FOLLOWING ORAL DIRECTIONS TEST

1. Ⓐ Ⓑ Ⓒ Ⓓ Ⓔ
2. Ⓐ Ⓑ Ⓒ Ⓓ Ⓔ
3. Ⓐ Ⓑ Ⓒ Ⓓ Ⓔ
4. Ⓐ Ⓑ Ⓒ Ⓓ Ⓔ
5. Ⓐ Ⓑ Ⓒ Ⓓ Ⓔ
6. Ⓐ Ⓑ Ⓒ Ⓓ Ⓔ
7. Ⓐ Ⓑ Ⓒ Ⓓ Ⓔ
8. Ⓐ Ⓑ Ⓒ Ⓓ Ⓔ
9. Ⓐ Ⓑ Ⓒ Ⓓ Ⓔ
10. Ⓐ Ⓑ Ⓒ Ⓓ Ⓔ
11. Ⓐ Ⓑ Ⓒ Ⓓ Ⓔ
12. Ⓐ Ⓑ Ⓒ Ⓓ Ⓔ
13. Ⓐ Ⓑ Ⓒ Ⓓ Ⓔ
14. Ⓐ Ⓑ Ⓒ Ⓓ Ⓔ
15. Ⓐ Ⓑ Ⓒ Ⓓ Ⓔ
16. Ⓐ Ⓑ Ⓒ Ⓓ Ⓔ
17. Ⓐ Ⓑ Ⓒ Ⓓ Ⓔ
18. Ⓐ Ⓑ Ⓒ Ⓓ Ⓔ

19. Ⓐ Ⓑ Ⓒ Ⓓ Ⓔ
20. Ⓐ Ⓑ Ⓒ Ⓓ Ⓔ
21. Ⓐ Ⓑ Ⓒ Ⓓ Ⓔ
22. Ⓐ Ⓑ Ⓒ Ⓓ Ⓔ
23. Ⓐ Ⓑ Ⓒ Ⓓ Ⓔ
24. Ⓐ Ⓑ Ⓒ Ⓓ Ⓔ
25. Ⓐ Ⓑ Ⓒ Ⓓ Ⓔ
26. Ⓐ Ⓑ Ⓒ Ⓓ Ⓔ
27. Ⓐ Ⓑ Ⓒ Ⓓ Ⓔ
28. Ⓐ Ⓑ Ⓒ Ⓓ Ⓔ
29. Ⓐ Ⓑ Ⓒ Ⓓ Ⓔ
30. Ⓐ Ⓑ Ⓒ Ⓓ Ⓔ
31. Ⓐ Ⓑ Ⓒ Ⓓ Ⓔ
32. Ⓐ Ⓑ Ⓒ Ⓓ Ⓔ
33. Ⓐ Ⓑ Ⓒ Ⓓ Ⓔ
34. Ⓐ Ⓑ Ⓒ Ⓓ Ⓔ
35. Ⓐ Ⓑ Ⓒ Ⓓ Ⓔ
36. Ⓐ Ⓑ Ⓒ Ⓓ Ⓔ

37. Ⓐ Ⓑ Ⓒ Ⓓ Ⓔ
38. Ⓐ Ⓑ Ⓒ Ⓓ Ⓔ
39. Ⓐ Ⓑ Ⓒ Ⓓ Ⓔ
40. Ⓐ Ⓑ Ⓒ Ⓓ Ⓔ
41. Ⓐ Ⓑ Ⓒ Ⓓ Ⓔ
42. Ⓐ Ⓑ Ⓒ Ⓓ Ⓔ
43. Ⓐ Ⓑ Ⓒ Ⓓ Ⓔ
44. Ⓐ Ⓑ Ⓒ Ⓓ Ⓔ
45. Ⓐ Ⓑ Ⓒ Ⓓ Ⓔ
46. Ⓐ Ⓑ Ⓒ Ⓓ Ⓔ
47. Ⓐ Ⓑ Ⓒ Ⓓ Ⓔ
48. Ⓐ Ⓑ Ⓒ Ⓓ Ⓔ
49. Ⓐ Ⓑ Ⓒ Ⓓ Ⓔ
50. Ⓐ Ⓑ Ⓒ Ⓓ Ⓔ
51. Ⓐ Ⓑ Ⓒ Ⓓ Ⓔ
52. Ⓐ Ⓑ Ⓒ Ⓓ Ⓔ
53. Ⓐ Ⓑ Ⓒ Ⓓ Ⓔ
54. Ⓐ Ⓑ Ⓒ Ⓓ Ⓔ

55. Ⓐ Ⓑ Ⓒ Ⓓ Ⓔ
56. Ⓐ Ⓑ Ⓒ Ⓓ Ⓔ
57. Ⓐ Ⓑ Ⓒ Ⓓ Ⓔ
58. Ⓐ Ⓑ Ⓒ Ⓓ Ⓔ
59. Ⓐ Ⓑ Ⓒ Ⓓ Ⓔ
60. Ⓐ Ⓑ Ⓒ Ⓓ Ⓔ
61. Ⓐ Ⓑ Ⓒ Ⓓ Ⓔ
62. Ⓐ Ⓑ Ⓒ Ⓓ Ⓔ
63. Ⓐ Ⓑ Ⓒ Ⓓ Ⓔ
64. Ⓐ Ⓑ Ⓒ Ⓓ Ⓔ
65. Ⓐ Ⓑ Ⓒ Ⓓ Ⓔ
66. Ⓐ Ⓑ Ⓒ Ⓓ Ⓔ
67. Ⓐ Ⓑ Ⓒ Ⓓ Ⓔ
68. Ⓐ Ⓑ Ⓒ Ⓓ Ⓔ
69. Ⓐ Ⓑ Ⓒ Ⓓ Ⓔ
70. Ⓐ Ⓑ Ⓒ Ⓓ Ⓔ
71. Ⓐ Ⓑ Ⓒ Ⓓ Ⓔ
72. Ⓐ Ⓑ Ⓒ Ⓓ Ⓔ

73. Ⓐ Ⓑ Ⓒ Ⓓ Ⓔ
74. Ⓐ Ⓑ Ⓒ Ⓓ Ⓔ
75. Ⓐ Ⓑ Ⓒ Ⓓ Ⓔ
76. Ⓐ Ⓑ Ⓒ Ⓓ Ⓔ
77. Ⓐ Ⓑ Ⓒ Ⓓ Ⓔ
78. Ⓐ Ⓑ Ⓒ Ⓓ Ⓔ
79. Ⓐ Ⓑ Ⓒ Ⓓ Ⓔ
80. Ⓐ Ⓑ Ⓒ Ⓓ Ⓔ
81. Ⓐ Ⓑ Ⓒ Ⓓ Ⓔ
82. Ⓐ Ⓑ Ⓒ Ⓓ Ⓔ
83. Ⓐ Ⓑ Ⓒ Ⓓ Ⓔ
84. Ⓐ Ⓑ Ⓒ Ⓓ Ⓔ
85. Ⓐ Ⓑ Ⓒ Ⓓ Ⓔ
86. Ⓐ Ⓑ Ⓒ Ⓓ Ⓔ
87. Ⓐ Ⓑ Ⓒ Ⓓ Ⓔ
88. Ⓐ Ⓑ Ⓒ Ⓓ Ⓔ
89. Ⓐ Ⓑ Ⓒ Ⓓ Ⓔ
90. Ⓐ Ⓑ Ⓒ Ⓓ Ⓔ

TEAR HERE

FINAL MODEL EXAM

SCORE SHEET

ADDRESS CHECKING TEST: Your score on the Address Checking Test is based upon the number of questions you answered correctly minus the number of questions you answered incorrectly. To determine your score, subtract the number of wrong answers from the number of correct answers.

Number Right   −   Number Wrong   =   Raw Score

_____ − _____ = _____

MEANING OF WORDS TEST: Your score on the Meaning of Words Test is based only upon the number of questions you answered correctly.

Number Right   =   Raw Score

_____ = _____

FOLLOWING ORAL DIRECTIONS TEST: Your score on the Following Oral Directions Test is based only upon the number of questions you marked correctly on the answer sheet. The Worksheet is not scored, and wrong answers on the answer sheet do not count against you.

Number Right   =   Raw Score

_____ = _____

TOTAL SCORE: To find your total raw score, add together the raw scores for each section of the exam.

Address Checking Score   _____
+
Meaning of Words Score   _____
+
Following Oral Directions Score   _____
=
Total Raw Score   _____

ADDRESS CHECKING TEST

DIRECTIONS AND SAMPLE QUESTIONS

In the Address Checking Test you will have to decide whether two addresses are alike or different. Any difference at all makes the two addresses different. Look carefully at the address at the left and the address at the right. If the two addresses are *exactly alike in every way*, darken space Ⓐ for the question. If the two addresses are *different in any way*, darken space Ⓓ for the question. Mark your answers to these sample questions on the sample answer sheet on this page.

1.	Montreal QU	Montreal QC
2.	Galesburg IL 61401	Galesberg IL 61401
3.	Bethlehem PA 18015	Bethlehem PA 18015
4.	Baton Rouge LA	Baton Rouge LA
5.	Omaha NE 68178	Omaha NE 68187
6.	Worcester MA 01610	Worcester MA 01610

SAMPLE ANSWER SHEET
1. Ⓐ Ⓓ
2. Ⓐ Ⓓ
3. Ⓐ Ⓓ
4. Ⓐ Ⓓ
5. Ⓐ Ⓓ
6. Ⓐ Ⓓ

CORRECT ANSWERS TO SAMPLE QUESTIONS

1. Ⓐ ●
2. Ⓐ ●
3. ● Ⓓ
4. ● Ⓓ
5. Ⓐ ●
6. ● Ⓓ

Explanations

Question 1 is marked Ⓓ because of a difference in province abbreviation.

Question 2 is marked Ⓓ because of a city spelling difference.

Question 5 is marked Ⓓ because of a zip code reversal.

ADDRESS CHECKING TEST

95 Questions—6 Minutes

DIRECTIONS: This is a test of your speed and accuracy in comparing addresses. For each question in the test, blacken the correspondingly numbered answer space as follows:

- Blacken Ⓐ if the two addresses are exactly ALIKE.
- Blacken Ⓓ if the two addresses are DIFFERENT in **any** way.

Correct answers are on page 243.

1. North Dartmouth MA — North Dartmouth NH
2. Scottville MI 49454 — Scottsville MI 49454
3. Inver Grove Heights MN — Inver Grove Heights MN
4. Hannibal MO 63401 — Hannibal MO 64301
5. Scottsbluff NB — Scottsbluff NB
6. Scotch Plains NJ 07076 — Scotts Plains NJ 07076
7. Keuka Park NY 14478 — Keuka Park NY 14478
8. Montreal NC 28757 — Montreat NC 28757
9. Ashtabula OH 44004 — Ashtabula OR 44004
10. East Stroudsburg PA — East Stroudsburg PA
11. Pawtucket RI 02929 — Pawtucket RI 02929
12. Yankton SD 57078 — Yankton SC 57078
13. Brenham TX 77833 — Brenham TX 78833
14. Brattleboro VT — Brattleboro VT
15. Hampden-Sydney VA — Hampden-Sydney VA
16. Moses Lake WA 98837 — Moses Lake WA 98387
17. Shepherdstown WV — Shephardstown WV
18. La Crosse WI 54601 — LaCrosse WI 54601
19. Cheyenne WY 82001 — Cheyenne KY 82001
20. Tigerville SC 29688 — Tigertown SC 29688
21. St. Georges N. DE — St. Georges S. DE
22. Hibbing MN 55746 — Hibbing Minn 55746
23. Cicero Ill 60650 — Cicero Ill 60650
24. New Haven CT 06520 — New Haven CT 05620
25. Santa Monica CA — Santa Monica CA
26. Brockport NY 14420 — Brockton NY 14420
27. Wilkesboro NC — Wilkesbarre NC
28. Marylhurst OR 97046 — Marylhurst OR 97046
29. Gettysburg PA 17325 — Gettysburg Penn 17325
30. Madisonville Tenn — Madisonville Tenn
31. Lake Jackson TX 77566 — Lake Jackson TX 77566
32. Montpelier VT — Montplier VT
33. Buena Vista VA 24416 — Buena Vista VA 24116
34. Centralia WA 98531 — Centralia WA 98531
35. Philippi WV 26416 — Phillippi WV 26416
36. Sheboygan Wisc — Sheboygan Wisc
37. Rock Springs WY — Rock Springs WG
38. Pago Pago American Samoa — Pago Pago American Samoa

39.	Oil City Penn	Oil City Penna
40.	Point Lookout MO	Point Lookout MO
41.	St. Peter MN 56082	St. Peter MN 56802
42.	Framingham Mass	Farmingham Mass
43.	Hagerstown MD 21740	Hagerstown MO 21740
44.	Washington DC 20057.	Washington DC 20057
45.	Milledgeville GA	Milledgeville GA
46.	Rexburg ID 83440	Rexburg IA 83440
47.	West Lafayette IN	West Lafayette IN
48.	Emporia KS 66801	Emporium KS 66801
49.	Shreveport LA 71107	Shreveport LA 71707
50.	Haverhill Mass 01830	Haverhill Mass 01830
51.	Petoskey MI 49770	Petoskey MI 49770
52.	Mathiston Miss	Mathiston Miss
53.	Socorro NM 87801	Sorocco NM 87801
54.	Paul Smith's NY	Paul Smith's NY
55.	Hickory NC 28601	Hickory NC 28601
56.	Steubenville OH 43952	Steubenville Ohio 43952
57.	Astoria OR 97103	Astoria OR 97103
58.	Cresson PA 16630	Cresson PA 16620
59.	Due West SC 29639	Due West SC 29936
60.	Aberdeen SD 57401	Aberdeen S Dak 57401
61.	Harrogate TN	Harrowgate TN
62.	Schenectady NY	Schenectady NY
63.	Bozeman MT 59715	Boozeman MT 59715
64.	Lake Charles LA 70609	Lake Charles LA 70906
65.	North Manchester IN	No. Manchester IN
66.	Mesa Verde Colo	Mesa Verda Colo
67.	Azusa CA 91702	Asuza CA 91702
68.	Gunnison CO 81230	Gunnison CO 81320
69.	Babson Park FL 33827	Babson Park FL 33827
70.	Glen Ellyn IL 60137	Glen Ellyn IL 60137
71.	West Baden IN 47469	West Baden TN 47469
72.	Storm Lake Iowa	Storm Lake Iowa
73.	Manhattan KS 66502	Manhattan KS 66502
74.	Emmitsburg MD	Emmetsburg MD
75.	Perkinston Miss 39573	Perkinton Miss 39573
76.	Fremont NB 68025	Fremont NB 68035
77.	West New York NJ	West New York NY
78.	Albemarle NC 28001	Albemarle NC 28001
79.	Tishomingo OK 73460	Tishomingo OK 76430
80.	Gwynedd Valley Penna	Gwynedd Valley Penna
81.	Hartsville SC 29550	Hartsville SD 29550
82.	Harrogate TN 37752	Harrigate TN 37752
83.	Lubbock TX 79407	Lubbock TX 79407
84.	Winooski VT 05404	Winsooki VT 05404
85.	Elkins West VA	Elkins WVA
86.	Fond du Lac Wisc	Fond Du Lac Wisc
87.	Montreal Quebec	Montreal Quebec
88.	Laramie WY 82071	Laramie WY 82071
89.	Blacksburg VA 24061	Blacksburg VA 24061
90.	Barrington RI 02806	Barrington RI 02806
91.	Niagara Falls NY	Niagra Falls NY
92.	Hanover NH 03775	Hangover NH 03775

93. Dubuque IA 52001   Dubuque IA 52001
94. Fort Morgan CO 80701   Fort Morgan MO 80701
95. Front Royal NC   Front Royal NC

END OF ADDRESS CHECKING TEST

Do not turn the page until you are told to do so.

MEANING OF WORDS TEST

DIRECTIONS AND SAMPLE QUESTIONS

The Meaning of Words Test asks you what a word or phrase means. In each question, a word or phrase is in *italics*. Five other words or phrases—lettered A, B, C, D, and E—are given as possible meanings. Choose the lettered word or phrase that means most nearly the same as the word that is in *italics*. When you have chosen your answer find the answer space numbered the same as the question and darken the space with the letter of the right answer. Mark your answers to these sample questions on the sample answer sheet below.

1. The *merchants* prospered during the Gold Rush. *Merchants* means most nearly
   (A) producers
   (B) gold diggers
   (C) advertisers
   (D) storekeepers
   (E) entertainers

2. The judge finally announced the *verdict*. *Verdict* means most nearly
   (A) approval
   (B) decision
   (C) sentence
   (D) penalty
   (E) arrival

3. If you want to keep your job, you had better be *punctual*. *Punctual* means most nearly
   (A) polite
   (B) thoughtful
   (C) proper
   (D) neat
   (E) prompt

4. Each morning the soldiers pledge *allegiance* to the flag. *Allegiance* means most nearly
   (A) freedom
   (B) homeland
   (C) loyalty
   (D) protection
   (E) defense

SAMPLE ANSWER SHEET
1. Ⓐ Ⓑ Ⓒ Ⓓ Ⓔ
2. Ⓐ Ⓑ Ⓒ Ⓓ Ⓔ
3. Ⓐ Ⓑ Ⓒ Ⓓ Ⓔ
4. Ⓐ Ⓑ Ⓒ Ⓓ Ⓔ

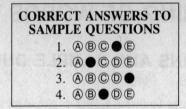

Explanations

1. **(D)** A MERCHANT is a *trader, seller* or *storekeeper*.
2. **(B)** The VERDICT is the *opinion, judgment* or *decision*.
3. **(E)** PUNCTUAL means *on time* or *prompt*.
4. **(C)** ALLEGIANCE means *devotion* or *loyalty*.

MEANING OF WORDS TEST

32 Questions—25 Minutes

DIRECTIONS: In each of the sentences below, one word is in *italics*. Following each sentence, are five lettered words or phrases. You are to choose the word or phrase with the same meaning as the *italicized* word and mark its letter on the answer sheet. Correct answers are on page 245.

1. The veteran employee will *instruct* the newcomers in office procedures. *Instruct* means most nearly
   (A) teach
   (B) demonstrate
   (C) accompany
   (D) learn
   (E) correct

2. The mechanic will have to *determine* why the truck keeps stalling. *Determine* means most nearly
   (A) find fault with
   (B) regulate
   (C) find out
   (D) arbitrate
   (E) convince

3. Before you begin work, you must have an *extensive* physical examination. *Extensive* means most nearly
   (A) superficial
   (B) leisurely
   (C) costly
   (D) thorough
   (E) strenuous

4. I cannot hire him because he has a reputation for being *unreliable*. *Unreliable* means most nearly
   (A) late
   (B) dishonest
   (C) temporary
   (D) undependable
   (E) independent

5. The minister is a *common* guest at our table. *Common* means most nearly
   (A) occasional
   (B) frequent
   (C) rare
   (D) vulgar
   (E) welcome

6. I would *employ* a light household oil to stop the squeaking door. *Employ* means most nearly
   (A) hire
   (B) use up
   (C) squeeze
   (D) use
   (E) spread

7. The clerk who insulted the customer received a *reprimand*. *Reprimand* means most nearly
   (A) engraved invitation
   (B) investigation
   (C) formal rebuke
   (D) revocation of privileges
   (E) suspension

8. When morale is high, black and white co-workers *mingle* with one another. *Mingle* means most nearly
   (A) visit
   (B) dance
   (C) sing
   (D) study
   (E) mix

9. The young man felt an *urgent* need to visit his dying mother. *Urgent* means most nearly
   (A) desirous
   (B) sudden
   (C) startling
   (D) pressing
   (E) foolish

10. One of his jobs in the Army was to *procure* rations for field maneuvers. *Procure* means most nearly
    (A) serve
    (B) obtain
    (C) possess
    (D) legalize
    (E) prepare

11. The new farmhand was *neglectful* of his duties. *Neglectful* means most nearly
    (A) unworthy
    (B) unfit
    (C) inattentive
    (D) abandoned
    (E) conscientious

12. The *origin* of the Connecticut River is in New Hampshire. *Origin* means most nearly
    (A) direction
    (B) end
    (C) model
    (D) beginning
    (E) double

13. The sculptor would like to *exhibit* her work. *Exhibit* means most nearly
    (A) suppress
    (B) display
    (C) promote
    (D) publicize
    (E) sell

14. The sideshow act is meant to *deceive* the public. *Deceive* means most nearly
    (A) trick
    (B) undermine
    (C) infuriate
    (D) thrill
    (E) inspire

15. Our aim is to *rehabilitate* the child who was handicapped by the accident. *Rehabilitate* means most nearly
    (A) cure
    (B) discharge
    (C) restore to function
    (D) parole
    (E) compensate for damages

16. If we do not limit our use of oil, we may *deplete* our supplies. *Deplete* means most nearly
    (A) omit
    (B) replenish
    (C) substitute
    (D) deposit
    (E) exhaust

17. Despite her screams for aid, the frightened woman *denied* entry to the policemen. *Denied* means most nearly
    (A) injured
    (B) hindered
    (C) blockaded
    (D) refused
    (E) lied about

18. The *legislature* granted pay raises to federal employees. *Legislature* means most nearly
    (A) court of appeals
    (B) high officer
    (C) lawmaking body
    (D) session
    (E) superintendent's office

19. I have read the *complete* document. *Complete* means most nearly
    (A) entire
    (B) retired
    (C) mediocre
    (D) fancy
    (E) boring

20. Both parties signed a *contract* to sell the house. *Contract* means most nearly
    (A) license
    (B) formal agreement
    (C) death warrant
    (D) commission
    (E) letter

21. Articles in the *Reader's Digest* are usually *abridged*. *Abridged* means most nearly
    (A) alphabetized
    (B) shortened
    (C) expanded
    (D) linked
    (E) inspirational

22. His version of the story was *partially* correct. *Partially* means most nearly
    (A) seemingly
    (B) particularly
    (C) not entirely
    (D) probably
    (E) in no way

23. The man on the operating table was the *recipient* of a pint of blood. *Recipient* means most nearly
    (A) receiver
    (B) borrower
    (C) donor
    (D) carrier
    (E) spiller

24. In the hospital incubators, you can see *premature* babies. *Premature* means most nearly
    (A) too small
    (B) too late
    (C) too easy
    (D) too yellow
    (E) too early

25. The *probability* is that the corrupt official will resign before he is convicted. *Probability* means most nearly
    (A) guess
    (B) theory
    (C) preference
    (D) likelihood
    (E) fact

26. The prisoner's alibi is completely *absurd*. *Absurd* means most nearly
    (A) careless
    (B) regrettable
    (C) ridiculous
    (D) frightening
    (E) plausible

27. The *increase* in the cost of living requires that we get a raise in wages. *Increase* means most nearly
    (A) decline
    (B) plenty
    (C) quantity
    (D) instability
    (E) growth

28. The *anticipated* appearance by the rock star created a near riot at the train station. *Anticipated* means most nearly
    (A) required
    (B) expected
    (C) revised
    (D) extraordinary
    (E) dreaded

29. If you live near a highway, you hear the *constant* sound of flowing traffic. *Constant* means most nearly
    (A) unchanging
    (B) tiring
    (C) annoying
    (D) soothing
    (E) loud

30. The airplane flew at an *altitude* of 30,000 feet. *Altitude* means most nearly
    (A) outlook
    (B) speed
    (C) height
    (D) depth
    (E) distance

31. You will have much more fun at the square dance if you *participate*. *Participate* means most nearly
    (A) supervise
    (B) break it up
    (C) relax
    (D) join in
    (E) plan to

32. The *rapidity* of Japanese trains is amazing to Americans. *Rapidity* means most nearly
    (A) efficiency
    (B) cleanliness
    (C) politeness
    (D) delays
    (E) speed

END OF MEANING OF WORDS TEST

> **If you finish this test before time is up, check over your work on this test only. Do not turn back to the Address Checking Test. Do not turn to the next page until you are told to do so.**

FOLLOWING ORAL DIRECTIONS TEST

DIRECTIONS AND SAMPLE QUESTIONS

LISTENING TO INSTRUCTIONS: When you are ready to try these sample questions, give the following instructions to a friend and have the friend read them aloud to you at 80 words per minute. Do not read them to yourself. Your friend will need a watch with a second hand. Listen carefully and do exactly what your friend tells you to do with the worksheet and answer sheet. Your friend will tell you some things to do with each item on the worksheet. After each set of instructions, your friend will give you time to mark your answer by darkening a circle on the sample answer sheet. Since B and D sound very much alike, your friend will say "B as in baker" when he or she means B and "D as in dog" when he or she means D.

Before proceeding further, tear out the worksheet on page 235. Then hand this book to your friend.

TO THE PERSON WHO IS TO READ THE DIRECTIONS: The directions are to be read at the rate of 80 words per minute. Do not read aloud the material which is in parentheses. Do not repeat any directions.

READ ALOUD TO THE CANDIDATE

Look at line 1 on your worksheet. (Pause slightly.) In the fourth box, write the letter A. (Pause 2 seconds.) Now, on your answer sheet, darken the space for the number-letter combination for the box you just wrote in. (Pause 5 seconds.)

Look at line 2 on your worksheet. (Pause slightly.) Circle the only letter that is in the line which is not in the word BEARD. (Pause 5 seconds.) On your answer sheet, find the answer to 9 ÷ 3. (Pause 5 seconds.) Darken the space for the letter you have circled next to the number you have found. (Pause 10 seconds.)

Look at line 3 on your worksheet. (Pause slightly.) Write the first letter of the last word in the third box. (Pause 5 seconds.) Write the last letter of the second word in the first box. (Pause 5 seconds.) Now, on your answer sheet, darken the spaces for the number-letter combinations in the two boxes you just wrote in. (Pause 10 seconds.)

Look at line 4 on your worksheet. (Pause slightly.) Draw a line under every number that is under 12 and even. (Pause 5 seconds.) Now, on your answer sheet, for each number that you drew a line under, darken space A. (Pause 5 seconds.)

WORKSHEET

DIRECTIONS: Listening carefully to each set of instructions, mark each item on this worksheet as directed. Then complete each question by marking the sample answer sheet below as directed. For each answer you will darken the answer for a number-letter combination. Should you fall behind and miss an instruction, don't become excited. Let that one go and listen for the next one. If when you start to darken a space for a number, you find that you have already darkened another space for that number, either erase the first mark and darken the space for the new combination or let the first mark stay and do not darken a space for the new combination. Write with a pencil that has a clean eraser. When you finish, you should have no more than one space darkened for each number.

TEAR HERE

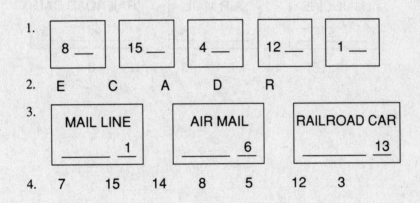

1. | 8 __ | 15 __ | 4 __ | 12 __ | 1 __ |

2. E   C   A   D   R

3. | MAIL LINE _____ 1 | | AIR MAIL _____ 6 | | RAILROAD CAR _____ 13 |

4. 7   15   14   8   5   12   3

```
              SAMPLE ANSWER SHEET
 1. Ⓐ Ⓑ Ⓒ Ⓓ Ⓔ     6. Ⓐ Ⓑ Ⓒ Ⓓ Ⓔ    11. Ⓐ Ⓑ Ⓒ Ⓓ Ⓔ
 2. Ⓐ Ⓑ Ⓒ Ⓓ Ⓔ     7. Ⓐ Ⓑ Ⓒ Ⓓ Ⓔ    12. Ⓐ Ⓑ Ⓒ Ⓓ Ⓔ
 3. Ⓐ Ⓑ Ⓒ Ⓓ Ⓔ     8. Ⓐ Ⓑ Ⓒ Ⓓ Ⓔ    13. Ⓐ Ⓑ Ⓒ Ⓓ Ⓔ
 4. Ⓐ Ⓑ Ⓒ Ⓓ Ⓔ     9. Ⓐ Ⓑ Ⓒ Ⓓ Ⓔ    14. Ⓐ Ⓑ Ⓒ Ⓓ Ⓔ
 5. Ⓐ Ⓑ Ⓒ Ⓓ Ⓔ    10. Ⓐ Ⓑ Ⓒ Ⓓ Ⓔ    15. Ⓐ Ⓑ Ⓒ Ⓓ Ⓔ
```

CORRECT ANSWERS TO SAMPLE QUESTIONS

1. Ⓐ Ⓑ Ⓒ Ⓓ ●	6. Ⓐ Ⓑ Ⓒ Ⓓ Ⓔ	11. Ⓐ Ⓑ Ⓒ Ⓓ Ⓔ
2. Ⓐ Ⓑ Ⓒ Ⓓ Ⓔ	7. Ⓐ Ⓑ Ⓒ Ⓓ Ⓔ	12. ● Ⓑ Ⓒ Ⓓ Ⓔ
3. Ⓐ Ⓑ ● Ⓓ Ⓔ	8. ● Ⓑ Ⓒ Ⓓ Ⓔ	13. Ⓐ Ⓑ ● Ⓓ Ⓔ
4. Ⓐ Ⓑ Ⓒ Ⓓ Ⓔ	9. Ⓐ Ⓑ Ⓒ Ⓓ Ⓔ	14. Ⓐ Ⓑ Ⓒ Ⓓ Ⓔ
5. Ⓐ Ⓑ Ⓒ Ⓓ Ⓔ	10. Ⓐ Ⓑ Ⓒ Ⓓ Ⓔ	15. Ⓐ Ⓑ Ⓒ Ⓓ Ⓔ

CORRECTLY FILLED WORKSHEET

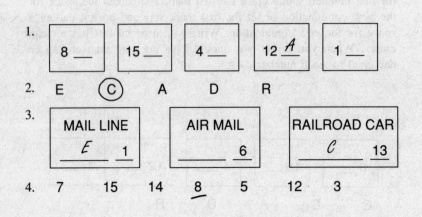

FOLLOWING ORAL DIRECTIONS TEST

Total Time—25 Minutes

LISTENING TO DIRECTIONS

DIRECTIONS: When you are ready to try this test of the Model Exam, give the following instructions to a friend and have the friend read them aloud to you at 80 words per minute. Do NOT read them to yourself. Your friend will need a watch with a second hand. Listen carefully and do exactly what your friend tells you to do with the worksheet and with the answer sheet. Your friend will tell you some things to do with each item on the worksheet. After each set of instructions, your friend will give you time to mark your answer by darkening a circle on the answer sheet. Since B and D sound very much alike, your friend will say ''B as in baker'' when he or she means B and ''D as in dog'' when he or she means D.

Before proceeding further, tear out the worksheet on page 241 of this test. Then hand this book to your friend.

TO THE PERSON WHO IS TO READ THE DIRECTIONS: The directions are to be read at the rate of 80 words per minute. Do not read aloud the material which is in parentheses. Once you have begun the test itself, do not repeat any directions. The next three paragraphs consist of approximately 120 words. Read these three paragraphs aloud to the candidate in about one and one-half minutes. You may reread these paragraphs as often as necessary to establish an 80 words per minute reading speed.

READ ALOUD TO THE CANDIDATE

On the job you will have to listen to directions and then do what you have been told to do. In this test, I will read instructions to you. Try to understand them as I read them; I cannot repeat them. Once we begin, you may not ask any questions until the end of the of the test.

On the job you won't have to deal with pictures, numbers and letters like those in the test, but you will have to listen to instructions and follow them. We are using this test to see how well you can follow instructions.

You are to mark your test booklet according to the instructions that I'll read to you. After each set of instructions, I'll give you time to record your answers on the separate answer sheet.

The actual test begins now.

Look at line 1 on your worksheet. (Pause slightly.) Circle the seventh letter on line 1. (Pause 5 seconds.) Now, on your answer sheet, find number 83 and for number 83 darken the space for the letter you just circled. (Pause 5 seconds.)

Look at line 2 on your worksheet. (Pause slightly.) Draw a line under all the odd numbers between 12 and 20. (Pause 5 seconds.) Now, on your answer sheet, darken space B as in baker for all the numbers under which you drew a line. (Pause 5 seconds.)

Look at line 2 again. (Pause slightly.) Find the number that is two times another number on line 2 and circle it. (Pause 5 seconds.) Now, on your answer sheet, darken space A for the number you just circled. (Pause 5 seconds.)

Look at line 3 on your worksheet. (Pause slightly.) Write the letter C in the middle box. (Pause 2 seconds.) Now, on your answer sheet, darken the space for the number-letter combination in the figure you just wrote in. (Pause 5 seconds.)

Look at line 3 again. (Pause slightly.) Write the letter D as in dog in the left-hand circle. (Pause 2 seconds.) Now, on your answer sheet, darken the space for the number-letter combination in the figure you just wrote in. (Pause 5 seconds.)

Look at line 4 on your worksheet. (Pause slightly.) If first class mail costs more than bulk rate mail, write the number 22 on the third line; if not, write the number 19 on the fourth line. (Pause 5 seconds.) Now, on your answer sheet, darken the space for the number-letter combination on the line you just wrote on. (Pause 5 seconds.)

Look at line 4 again. (Pause slightly.) Write the number 31 on the second line from the left. (Pause 2 seconds.) Now, on your answer sheet, darken the space for the number-letter combination on the line on which you just wrote. (Pause 5 seconds.)

Look at line 5 on your worksheet. (Pause slightly.) Find the highest number on line 5 and draw a line under the number. (Pause 2 seconds.) Now, on your answer sheet, find the number under which you just drew a line and darken space E for that number. (Pause 5 seconds.)

Look at line 5 again. (Pause slightly.) Find the lowest number on line 5 and draw two lines under the number. (Pause 2 seconds.) Now, on your answer sheet, find the number under which you just drew two lines and darken space A for that number. (Pause 5 seconds.)

Look at line 6 on your worksheet. (Pause slightly.) Write the number 57 in the figure which does not belong on line 6. (Pause 2 seconds.) Now, on your answer sheet, darken the number-letter combination that is in the figure in which you just wrote. (Pause 5 seconds.)

Look at line 7 on your worksheet. (Pause slightly.) Write the second letter of the second word in the first box. (Pause 5 seconds.) Write the fifth letter of the first word in the third box. (Pause 5 seconds.) Write the fourth letter of the second word in the second box. (Pause 5 seconds.) Now, on your answer sheet, darken the number-letter combinations in all three boxes. (Pause 15 seconds.)

Look at line 8 on your worksheet. (Pause slightly.) Count the number of G's on line 8 and divide the number of G's by 2. Write that number at the end of the line. (Pause 5 seconds.) Now, on your answer sheet, darken space D as in dog for the number you wrote at the end of line 8. (Pause 5 seconds.)

Look at line 9 on your worksheet. (Pause slightly.) Write the letter B as in baker in the middle-sized circle. (Pause 2 seconds.) Now, on your answer sheet, darken the space for the number-letter combination in the circle in which you just wrote. (Pause 5 seconds.)

Look at line 10 on your worksheet. (Pause slightly.) The time in each circle represents the last scheduled pickup of the day from a street letter box. Find the circle with the earliest pickup time and write the last two figures of that time on the line in the circle. (Pause 10 seconds.) Now, on your answer sheet, darken the space for the number-letter combination in the circle you just wrote in. (Pause 5 seconds.)

Look at line 10 again. (Pause slightly.) Find the circle with the latest pickup time and write the last two figures of that time on the line in the circle. (Pause 10 seconds.) Now, on your answer sheet, darken the space for the number-letter combination in the circle in which you just wrote. (Pause 5 seconds.)

Look at line 11 on your worksheet. (Pause slightly.) Mail directed for San Francisco and Los Angeles is to be placed in box 37; mail for Milwaukee and Green Bay in box 84; mail for Springfield and Chicago in box 65. Find the box for mail being sent to Green Bay and write the letter A in the box. (Pause 2 seconds.) Now, on your answer sheet, darken the number-letter combination for the box you just wrote in. (Pause 5 seconds.)

Look at line 11 again. (Pause slightly.) Mr. Green lives in Springfield. Find the box in which to put Mr. Green's mail and write E on the line. (Pause 2 seconds.) Now, on your answer sheet, darken the space for the number-letter combination in the box in which you just wrote. (Pause 5 seconds.)

Look at line 12 on your worksheet. (Pause slightly.) Find the letter on line 12 that is not in the word CREAM and draw a line under the letter. (Pause 2 seconds.) Now, on your answer sheet, find number 38 and darken the space for the letter under which you just drew a line. (Pause 5 seconds.)

Look at line 13 on your worksheet. (Pause slightly.) Write the smallest number in the largest circle. (Pause 2 seconds.) Write the largest number in the left-hand circle. (Pause 2 seconds.) Now, on your answer sheet, darken the number-letter combinations that are in the circles in which you just wrote. (Pause 10 seconds.)

Look at line 14 on your worksheet. (Pause slightly.) If there are 36 inches in a foot, write B as in baker in the first box; is not, write D as in dog in the third box. (Pause 5 seconds.) Now, on your answer sheet, darken the number-letter combination that is in the box in which you just wrote. (Pause 5 seconds.)

Look at line 14 again. (Pause slightly.) Find the box which contains a number in the teens and write B as in baker in that box. (Pause 2 seconds.) Now, on your answer sheet, darken the number-letter combination that is in the box in which you just wrote. (Pause 5 seconds.)

Look at line 15 on your worksheet. (Pause slightly.) Circle the only number on line 15 that is not divisible by 2. (Pause 2 seconds.) Now, on your answer sheet, darken space A for the number you circled. (Pause 5 seconds.)

Look at line 16 on your worksheet. (Pause slightly.) If the number in the circle is greater than the number in the box, write the letter E in the box; if not, write the letter E in the circle. (Pause 5 seconds.) Now, on your answer sheet, darken the number-letter combination that is in the figure in which you just wrote. (Pause 5 seconds.)

Look at line 16 again. (Pause slightly.) If the number in the triangle is smaller than the number in the figure directly to its left, write the letter A in the triangle; if not, write the letter C in the triangle. (Pause 5 seconds.) Now, on your answer sheet, darken the number-letter combination that is in the figure you just wrote in. (Pause 5 seconds.)

Look at line 17 on your worksheet. (Pause slightly.) Count the number of J's on line 17, multiply the number of J's by 5 and write that number at the end of the line. (Pause 5 seconds.) Now, on your answer sheet, find the number you just wrote at the end of the line and darken space C for that number. (Pause 5 seconds.)

Look at line 18 on your worksheet. (Pause slightly.) Draw one line under the number that is at the middle of line 18. (Pause 5 seconds.) Now, on your answer sheet, darken space B as in baker for the number under which you just drew a line. (Pause 5 seconds.)

Look at line 18 again. (Pause slightly.) Draw two lines under each odd number that falls between 35 and 45. (Pause 10 seconds.) Now, on your answer sheet, darken space D as in dog for each number under which you drew two lines. (Pause 5 seconds.)

FOLLOWING ORAL DIRECTIONS TEST

Total Time—25 Minutes

WORKSHEET

DIRECTIONS: Listening carefully to each set of instructions, mark each item on this worksheet as directed. Then complete each question by marking the answer for a number-letter combination. Should you fall behind and miss an instruction, don't become excited. Let that one go and listen for the next one. If when you start to darken a space for a number, you find that you have already darkened another space for that number, either erase the first mark and darken the space for the new combination or let the first mark stay and do not darken a space for the new combination. Write with a pencil that has a clean eraser. When you finish, you should have no more than one space darkened for each number. Correct answers are on page 247.

TEAR HERE

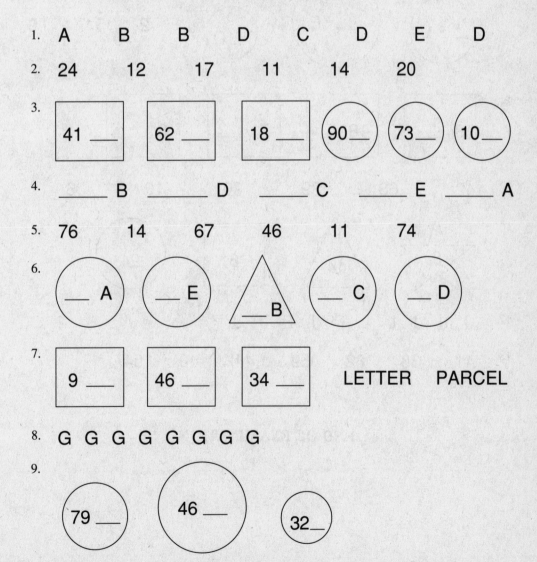

1. A   B   B   D   C   D   E   D

2. 24   12   17   11   14   20

3. 41 ___   62 ___   18 ___   90 ___   73 ___   10 ___

4. ___ B   ___ D   ___ C   ___ E   ___ A

5. 76   14   67   46   11   74

6. ___ A   ___ E   ___ B   ___ C   ___ D

7. 9 ___   46 ___   34 ___   LETTER   PARCEL

8. G G G G G G G

9. 79 ___   46 ___   32 ___

10.

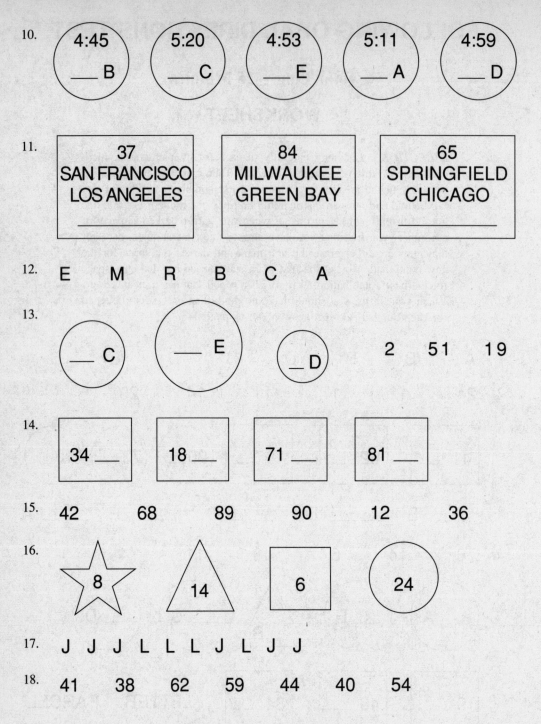

11.

| 37 SAN FRANCISCO LOS ANGELES | 84 MILWAUKEE GREEN BAY | 65 SPRINGFIELD CHICAGO |

12. E M R B C A

13.

14.

15. 42   68   89   90   12   36

16.

17. J J J L L L J L J J

18. 41   38   62   59   44   40   54

END OF EXAMINATION

FINAL MODEL EXAM ANSWER KEY

ADDRESS CHECKING TEST

1. D	17. D	33. D	49. D	65. D	81. D
2. D	18. D	34. A	50. A	66. D	82. D
3. A	19. D	35. D	51. A	67. D	83. A
4. D	20. D	36. A	52. A	68. D	84. D
5. A	21. D	37. D	53. D	69. A	85. D
6. D	22. D	38. A	54. A	70. A	86. D
7. A	23. A	39. D	55. A	71. D	87. A
8. D	24. D	40. A	56. D	72. A	88. A
9. D	25. A	41. D	57. A	73. A	89. A
10. A	26. D	42. D	58. D	74. D	90. A
11. A	27. D	43. D	59. D	75. D	91. D
12. D	28. A	44. A	60. D	76. D	92. D
13. D	29. D	45. A	61. D	77. D	93. A
14. A	30. A	46. D	62. A	78. A	94. D
15. A	31. A	47. A	63. D	79. D	95. A
16. D	32. D	48. D	64. D	80. A	

ADDRESS CHECKING TEST

Explanations of Differences

1. different states
2. spelling of city
4. number reversal
6. different cities
8. different cities
9. different states
12. different states
13. different numbers
16. number reversal
17. spelling of city
18. spelling of city
19. different states
20. different cities
21. different cities
22. spelling of state
24. number reversal
26. different cities
27. different cities
29. spelling of state
32. spelling of city
33. different numbers
35. spelling of city
37. spelling of state
39. spelling of state
41. number reversal
42. different cities
43. different states
46. different states
48. different cities
49. different numbers
53. spelling of city
56. spelling of state
58. different numbers
59. different numbers
60. spelling of state
61. spelling of city

63. spelling of city
64. number reversal
65. spelling of city
66. spelling of city
67. spelling of city
68. number reversal
71. different states
74. spelling of city
75. different cities
76. different numbers
77. different states
79. number reversal
81. different states
82. spelling of city
84. different cities
85. spelling of state
86. spelling of city
91. spelling of city
92. spelling of city
94. different states

Analysis of Differences

Fill in the column on the right with the total number of questions you answered incorrectly.

City difference	26	
Number difference	13	
State difference	17	
Total addresses with differences	56	
Total addresses with no differences	39	

MEANING OF WORDS TEST

1. A	7. C	12. D	17. D	22. C	27. E
2. C	8. E	13. B	18. C	23. A	28. B
3. D	9. D	14. A	19. A	24. E	29. A
4. D	10. B	15. C	20. B	25. D	30. C
5. B	11. C	16. E	21. B	26. C	31. D
6. D					32. E

MEANING OF WORDS
Explanatory Answers

1. **(A)** To INSTRUCT is to *impart knowledge* or to *teach*. The instruction may include correction and demonstration, but the aim is teaching.

2. **(C)** To DETERMINE is to *resolve*, to *decide*, to *discover* or to *find out*. The context of the sentence should immediately narrow your choices to B and C. A little more concentration should then lead you to the only possible answer. Once the mechanic *determines* what the problem is, he can *regulate* the part that is malfunctioning, but he cannot regulate why.

3. **(D)** EXTENSIVE means *long and drawn out* or *thorough*. You may see *extend* in *extensive* and figure out the meaning. An extensive physical examination is likely to be expensive or costly, but that is not the meaning of extensive.

4. **(D)** UNRELIABLE means *not to be relied upon* or *undependable*. The person upon whom one cannot depend may be late, dishonest or just too independent, but the word *unreliable* is more inclusive than any one of these.

5. **(B)** COMMON means *familiar* or *frequent*. *Vulgar* is also a meaning of *common*, but it clearly is not the meaning in this context.

6. **(D)** To EMPLOY is to *make use of* or to *use*. Squeezing and spreading are ways to employ the oil in stopping the squeak. *To hire* is specifically *to employ* or *to use a person*.

7. **(C)** A REPRIMAND is a *formal reproof* or *rebuke*. A *reprimand* is a sharp criticism by someone in authority but not a punishment of any sort.

8. **(E)** To MINGLE is to *mix*. People who mingle can do any number of things together while they mingle.

9. **(D)** URGENT means *insistent* or *pressing*. You can easily see *urge* in *urgent*, but that in itself cannot help you to choose the best synonym. This is a difficult question. The person who is not certain of the precise meaing of *urgent* must guess between *sudden* and *pressing*.

10. **(B)** To PROCURE is to *get* or to *obtain*.

11. **(C)** NEGLECTFUL means *heedless*, *negligent* or *inattentive*. This question is not difficult. The farmhand was *full of neglect* of his duties.

12. **(D)** The ORIGIN is the *source*, the *starting point* or the *beginning*. You may see *origin* as part of *original* which means *new, inventive* or *creative*.

13. **(B)** To EXHIBIT is to *show publicly* or to *display*. Of course, the sculptor would also like to promote, publicize and sell so the context does not give you much help. *Exhibit* is a word you should know.

14. **(A)** To DECEIVE is to *mislead* or to *trick*.

15. **(C)** To REHABILITATE is to *restore to a condition of useful or constructive activity*. *Rehabilitation* of the disabled means training them to live the most independent lives possible within the limitations of their handicaps. *Rehabilitation* of decayed housing means reconstruction to make the housing livable again. The prefix *re* meaning *again* gives you a clue.

16. **(E)** To DEPLETE is to *drain,* to *use up* or to *exhaust.* In the context of this sentence, this is the only choice that makes sense.

17. **(D)** DENIED in the context of this sentence means *refused.* To DENY is to say "no." The woman said, "No you can't come in" to the policeman even though she screamed for aid. Another meaning of *to deny* is *to declare something to be untrue.*

18. **(C)** A LEGISLATURE is a *lawmaking body.*

19. **(A)** COMPLETE means *total* or *entire.* The prefix *com* means *together,* implying the *whole thing. To complete* means *to finish.* The adjective *complete* and the verb *to complete* convey very similar meanings.

20. **(B)** A CONTRACT is a *binding agreement* between two parties to do something. In real estate a *contract* is always a *formal written agreement.* The prefix *con* meaning *together* should lead you to the choice which seems to require more than one party.

21. **(B)** ABRIDGED means *condensed, digested* or *shortened.* If you are familiar with the *Reader's Digest,* you know that articles are digested for you and are shortened for easy reading.

22. **(C)** PARTIALLY means *partly,* which in turn means *not entirely,* but *somewhat.*

23. **(A)** RECIPIENT means *receiver.* In the context of the sentence, this is the most sensible synonym.

24. **(E)** PREMATURE means happening *too early. Premature* babies tend to be too small, but that is a function of their being born too soon. The prefix *pre* means *before;* the word *mature* means *ripe.*

25. **(D)** PROBABILITY means *likelihood.* Something that is *probable* is *likely* to happen.

26. **(C)** ABSURD means *meaningless* or *ridiculous.*

27. **(E)** INCREASE means *enlargement* or *growth.* This is a common word which is probably already a part of your vocabulary. If not, the context of the sentence should confirm the choice.

28. **(B)** ANTICIPATED means *looked forward to, awaited* or *expected.* Security personnel may have *dreaded* the arrival of the rock star and the riot that the rock star's arrival would create, but they too *anticipated* or *expected* it.

29. **(A)** CONSTANT means *continuous, regular* and *unchanging.* The context of this sentence will not help you here, but the word is not uncommon.

30. **(C)** ALTITUDE means *vertical distance* or *height.* If you carefully substitute the other choices into this sentence, you will see that this is the only choice that fits.

31. **(D)** To PARTICIPATE is to *share,* to *take part* or to *join in.* The suffix *ate* means *an action of.* Thus, *participating* is *an action of taking part.*

32. **(E)** RAPIDITY is *speed.* The suffix *ty* means *the condition of being* and the word *rapid* means *fast.*

FOLLOWING ORAL DIRECTIONS TEST

Correctly Filled Worksheet

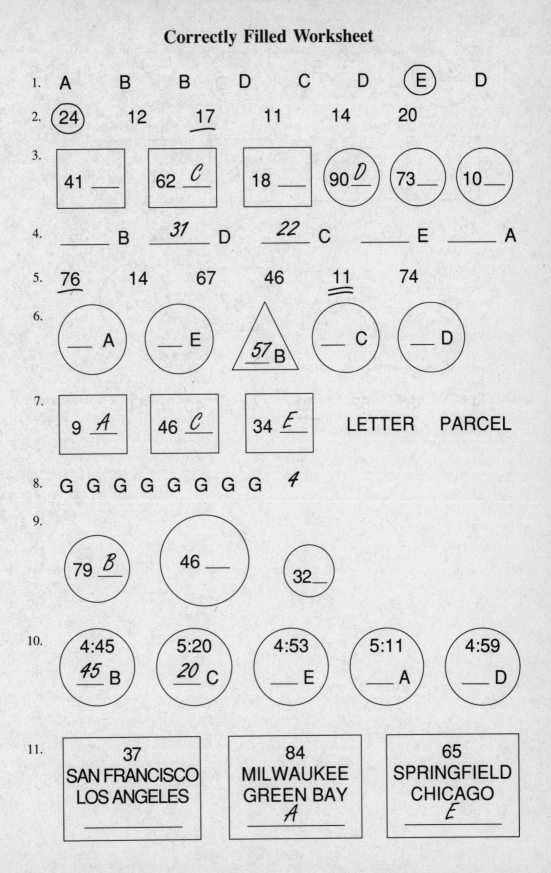

1. A   B   B   D   C   D   (E)   D

2. (24)   12   17   11   14   20

3. 41 ___   62 *C*   18 ___   90 *D*   73 ___   10 ___

4. ___ B   *31* D   *22* C   ___ E   ___ A

5. 76   14   67   46   11   74

6. ___ A   ___ E   *57* B   ___ C   ___ D

7. 9 *A*   46 *C*   34 *E*   LETTER   PARCEL

8. G G G G G G G G   *4*

9. 79 *B*   46 ___   32 ___

10. 4:45 *45* B   5:20 *20* C   4:53 ___ E   5:11 ___ A   4:59 ___ D

11.

| 37 SAN FRANCISCO LOS ANGELES ___ | 84 MILWAUKEE GREEN BAY *A* | 65 SPRINGFIELD CHICAGO *E* |

12. E   M   R   <u>B</u>   C   A

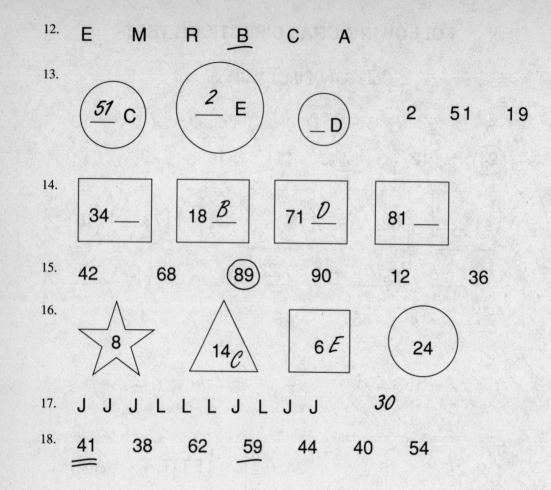

13.

<u>51</u> C   <u>2</u> E   _ D   2   51   19

14. 34 __   18 <u>B</u>   71 <u>D</u>   81 __

15. 42   68   (89)   90   12   36

16. 8   14 C   6 E   24

17. J J J L L L J L J J   *30*

18. <u>41</u>   38   62   <u>59</u>   44   40   54

FOLLOWING ORAL DIRECTIONS TEST

Correctly Filled Answer Grid

1. Ⓐ Ⓑ Ⓒ Ⓓ Ⓔ
2. Ⓐ Ⓑ Ⓒ Ⓓ ●
3. Ⓐ Ⓑ Ⓒ Ⓓ Ⓔ
4. Ⓐ Ⓑ Ⓒ ● Ⓔ
5. Ⓐ Ⓑ Ⓒ Ⓓ Ⓔ
6. Ⓐ Ⓑ Ⓒ Ⓓ ●
7. Ⓐ Ⓑ Ⓒ Ⓓ Ⓔ
8. Ⓐ Ⓑ Ⓒ Ⓓ Ⓔ
9. ● Ⓑ Ⓒ Ⓓ Ⓔ
10. Ⓐ Ⓑ Ⓒ Ⓓ Ⓔ
11. ● Ⓑ Ⓒ Ⓓ Ⓔ
12. Ⓐ Ⓑ Ⓒ Ⓓ Ⓔ
13. Ⓐ Ⓑ Ⓒ Ⓓ Ⓔ
14. Ⓐ Ⓑ ● Ⓓ Ⓔ
15. Ⓐ Ⓑ Ⓒ Ⓓ Ⓔ
16. Ⓐ Ⓑ Ⓒ Ⓓ Ⓔ
17. Ⓐ ● Ⓒ Ⓓ Ⓔ
18. Ⓐ ● Ⓒ Ⓓ Ⓔ
19. Ⓐ Ⓑ Ⓒ Ⓓ Ⓔ
20. Ⓐ Ⓑ ● Ⓓ Ⓔ
21. Ⓐ Ⓑ Ⓒ Ⓓ Ⓔ
22. Ⓐ Ⓑ ● Ⓓ Ⓔ
23. Ⓐ Ⓑ Ⓒ Ⓓ Ⓔ
24. ● Ⓑ Ⓒ Ⓓ Ⓔ
25. Ⓐ Ⓑ Ⓒ Ⓓ Ⓔ
26. Ⓐ Ⓑ Ⓒ Ⓓ Ⓔ
27. Ⓐ Ⓑ Ⓒ Ⓓ Ⓔ
28. Ⓐ Ⓑ Ⓒ Ⓓ Ⓔ
29. Ⓐ Ⓑ Ⓒ Ⓓ Ⓔ
30. Ⓐ Ⓑ ● Ⓓ Ⓔ

31. Ⓐ Ⓑ Ⓒ ● Ⓔ
32. Ⓐ Ⓑ Ⓒ Ⓓ Ⓔ
33. Ⓐ Ⓑ Ⓒ Ⓓ Ⓔ
34. Ⓐ Ⓑ Ⓒ Ⓓ ●
35. Ⓐ Ⓑ Ⓒ Ⓓ Ⓔ
36. Ⓐ Ⓑ Ⓒ Ⓓ Ⓔ
37. Ⓐ Ⓑ Ⓒ Ⓓ Ⓔ
38. Ⓐ ● Ⓒ Ⓓ Ⓔ
39. Ⓐ Ⓑ Ⓒ Ⓓ Ⓔ
40. Ⓐ Ⓑ Ⓒ Ⓓ Ⓔ
41. Ⓐ Ⓑ Ⓒ ● Ⓔ
42. Ⓐ Ⓑ Ⓒ Ⓓ Ⓔ
43. Ⓐ Ⓑ Ⓒ Ⓓ Ⓔ
44. Ⓐ Ⓑ Ⓒ Ⓓ Ⓔ
45. Ⓐ ● Ⓒ Ⓓ Ⓔ
46. Ⓐ Ⓑ ● Ⓓ Ⓔ
47. Ⓐ Ⓑ Ⓒ Ⓓ Ⓔ
48. Ⓐ Ⓑ Ⓒ Ⓓ Ⓔ
49. Ⓐ Ⓑ Ⓒ Ⓓ Ⓔ
50. Ⓐ Ⓑ Ⓒ Ⓓ Ⓔ
51. Ⓐ Ⓑ ● Ⓓ Ⓔ
52. Ⓐ Ⓑ Ⓒ Ⓓ Ⓔ
53. Ⓐ Ⓑ Ⓒ Ⓓ Ⓔ
54. Ⓐ Ⓑ Ⓒ Ⓓ Ⓔ
55. Ⓐ Ⓑ Ⓒ Ⓓ Ⓔ
56. Ⓐ Ⓑ Ⓒ Ⓓ Ⓔ
57. Ⓐ ● Ⓒ Ⓓ Ⓔ
58. Ⓐ Ⓑ Ⓒ Ⓓ Ⓔ
59. Ⓐ ● Ⓒ Ⓓ Ⓔ
60. Ⓐ Ⓑ Ⓒ Ⓓ Ⓔ

61. Ⓐ Ⓑ Ⓒ Ⓓ Ⓔ
62. Ⓐ Ⓑ ● Ⓓ Ⓔ
63. Ⓐ Ⓑ Ⓒ Ⓓ Ⓔ
64. Ⓐ Ⓑ Ⓒ Ⓓ Ⓔ
65. Ⓐ Ⓑ Ⓒ Ⓓ ●
66. Ⓐ Ⓑ Ⓒ Ⓓ Ⓔ
67. Ⓐ Ⓑ Ⓒ Ⓓ Ⓔ
68. Ⓐ Ⓑ Ⓒ Ⓓ Ⓔ
69. Ⓐ Ⓑ Ⓒ Ⓓ Ⓔ
70. Ⓐ Ⓑ Ⓒ Ⓓ Ⓔ
71. Ⓐ Ⓑ Ⓒ ● Ⓔ
72. Ⓐ Ⓑ Ⓒ Ⓓ Ⓔ
73. Ⓐ Ⓑ Ⓒ Ⓓ Ⓔ
74. Ⓐ Ⓑ Ⓒ Ⓓ Ⓔ
75. Ⓐ Ⓑ Ⓒ Ⓓ Ⓔ
76. Ⓐ Ⓑ Ⓒ Ⓓ ●
77. Ⓐ Ⓑ Ⓒ Ⓓ Ⓔ
78. Ⓐ Ⓑ Ⓒ Ⓓ Ⓔ
79. Ⓐ ● Ⓒ Ⓓ Ⓔ
80. Ⓐ Ⓑ Ⓒ Ⓓ Ⓔ
81. Ⓐ Ⓑ Ⓒ Ⓓ Ⓔ
82. Ⓐ Ⓑ Ⓒ Ⓓ Ⓔ
83. Ⓐ Ⓑ Ⓒ Ⓓ ●
84. ● Ⓑ Ⓒ Ⓓ Ⓔ
85. Ⓐ Ⓑ Ⓒ Ⓓ Ⓔ
86. Ⓐ Ⓑ Ⓒ Ⓓ Ⓔ
87. Ⓐ Ⓑ Ⓒ Ⓓ Ⓔ
88. Ⓐ Ⓑ Ⓒ Ⓓ Ⓔ
89. ● Ⓑ Ⓒ Ⓓ Ⓔ
90. Ⓐ Ⓑ Ⓒ ● Ⓔ

PROGRESS CHARTS

Darken the column up to your score for each test of the exam.

FOLLOWING ORAL DIRECTIONS

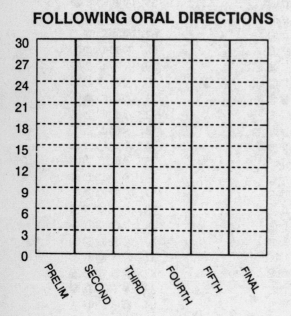

ADDRESS CHECKING

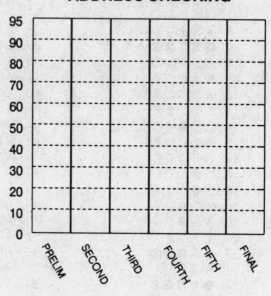

MEANING OF WORDS

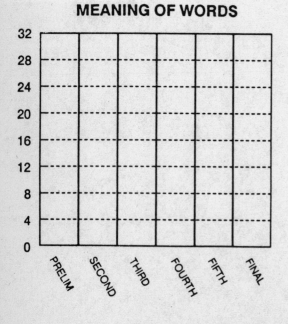

TOTAL SCORE

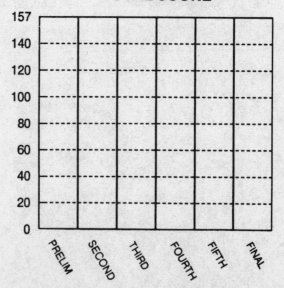

DISTRIBUTION CLERK, MACHINE
(LETTER-SORTING MACHINE OPERATOR)

Duties of the Job

Distribution clerks work indoors. Often clerks must handle sacks of mail weighing as much as seventy pounds. They sort mail and distribute it by using a complicated scheme that must be memorized. Machine distribution clerks must learn computer codes for the automatic routing of mail. Clerks may be on their feet all day. They also have to stretch, reach, and throw mail. The work of the distribution clerk is more routine than that of other postal clerks; however, the starting salary is higher. Distribution clerks begin at postal pay level six while other clerks and carriers begin at level five. Increasing automation within the postal service has made the job of the distribution clerk quite secure.

Although the amount of mail post offices handle is expected to grow as both the population and the number of businesses grow, modernization of post offices and installation of new equipment will increase the amount of mail each clerk can handle. For example, machines that semiautomatically mark destination codes on envelopes are now being tested. These codes can be read by computer-controlled letter-sorting machines, which automatically drop each letter into the proper slot for its destination. With this system, clerks read addresses only once, at the time they are coded, instead of several times, as they now do. Eventually this equipment will be installed in all large post offices.

Qualification Requirements

No experience is required. All applicants are required to take a written examination designed to test aptitude for learning and performing the duties of the position. The test consists of four parts: (A) Number Series, (B) Address Coding, (C) Address Code Memory, (D) Address Checking. The test and completion of the forms requires approximately two and a half hours.

Applicants must be physically able to perform the duties described. Any physical condition that causes the applicant to be a hazard to him/herself or to others will be a disqualification for appointment.

The distant vision for clerk positions must test at least 20/30 (Snellen) in one eye (glasses are permitted). Some distribution clerk positions may be filled by the deaf.

A physical examination is required before appointment.

DISTRIBUTION CLERK, MACHINE
MODEL EXAM ANSWER SHEET

PART A—NUMBER SERIES

1. Ⓐ Ⓑ Ⓒ Ⓓ Ⓔ
2. Ⓐ Ⓑ Ⓒ Ⓓ Ⓔ
3. Ⓐ Ⓑ Ⓒ Ⓓ Ⓔ
4. Ⓐ Ⓑ Ⓒ Ⓓ Ⓔ
5. Ⓐ Ⓑ Ⓒ Ⓓ Ⓔ

6. Ⓐ Ⓑ Ⓒ Ⓓ Ⓔ
7. Ⓐ Ⓑ Ⓒ Ⓓ Ⓔ
8. Ⓐ Ⓑ Ⓒ Ⓓ Ⓔ
9. Ⓐ Ⓑ Ⓒ Ⓓ Ⓔ
10. Ⓐ Ⓑ Ⓒ Ⓓ Ⓔ

11. Ⓐ Ⓑ Ⓒ Ⓓ Ⓔ
12. Ⓐ Ⓑ Ⓒ Ⓓ Ⓔ
13. Ⓐ Ⓑ Ⓒ Ⓓ Ⓔ
14. Ⓐ Ⓑ Ⓒ Ⓓ Ⓔ
15. Ⓐ Ⓑ Ⓒ Ⓓ Ⓔ

16. Ⓐ Ⓑ Ⓒ Ⓓ Ⓔ
17. Ⓐ Ⓑ Ⓒ Ⓓ Ⓔ
18. Ⓐ Ⓑ Ⓒ Ⓓ Ⓔ
19. Ⓐ Ⓑ Ⓒ Ⓓ Ⓔ
20. Ⓐ Ⓑ Ⓒ Ⓓ Ⓔ

21. Ⓐ Ⓑ Ⓒ Ⓓ Ⓔ
22. Ⓐ Ⓑ Ⓒ Ⓓ Ⓔ
23. Ⓐ Ⓑ Ⓒ Ⓓ Ⓔ
24. Ⓐ Ⓑ Ⓒ Ⓓ Ⓔ

PART B—ADDRESS CODING

1. Ⓐ Ⓑ Ⓒ Ⓓ Ⓔ
2. Ⓐ Ⓑ Ⓒ Ⓓ Ⓔ
3. Ⓐ Ⓑ Ⓒ Ⓓ Ⓔ
4. Ⓐ Ⓑ Ⓒ Ⓓ Ⓔ
5. Ⓐ Ⓑ Ⓒ Ⓓ Ⓔ
6. Ⓐ Ⓑ Ⓒ Ⓓ Ⓔ
7. Ⓐ Ⓑ Ⓒ Ⓓ Ⓔ
8. Ⓐ Ⓑ Ⓒ Ⓓ Ⓔ
9. Ⓐ Ⓑ Ⓒ Ⓓ Ⓔ
10. Ⓐ Ⓑ Ⓒ Ⓓ Ⓔ
11. Ⓐ Ⓑ Ⓒ Ⓓ Ⓔ
12. Ⓐ Ⓑ Ⓒ Ⓓ Ⓔ
13. Ⓐ Ⓑ Ⓒ Ⓓ Ⓔ
14. Ⓐ Ⓑ Ⓒ Ⓓ Ⓔ
15. Ⓐ Ⓑ Ⓒ Ⓓ Ⓔ
16. Ⓐ Ⓑ Ⓒ Ⓓ Ⓔ
17. Ⓐ Ⓑ Ⓒ Ⓓ Ⓔ
18. Ⓐ Ⓑ Ⓒ Ⓓ Ⓔ

19. Ⓐ Ⓑ Ⓒ Ⓓ Ⓔ
20. Ⓐ Ⓑ Ⓒ Ⓓ Ⓔ
21. Ⓐ Ⓑ Ⓒ Ⓓ Ⓔ
22. Ⓐ Ⓑ Ⓒ Ⓓ Ⓔ
23. Ⓐ Ⓑ Ⓒ Ⓓ Ⓔ
24. Ⓐ Ⓑ Ⓒ Ⓓ Ⓔ
25. Ⓐ Ⓑ Ⓒ Ⓓ Ⓔ
26. Ⓐ Ⓑ Ⓒ Ⓓ Ⓔ
27. Ⓐ Ⓑ Ⓒ Ⓓ Ⓔ
28. Ⓐ Ⓑ Ⓒ Ⓓ Ⓔ
29. Ⓐ Ⓑ Ⓒ Ⓓ Ⓔ
30. Ⓐ Ⓑ Ⓒ Ⓓ Ⓔ
31. Ⓐ Ⓑ Ⓒ Ⓓ Ⓔ
32. Ⓐ Ⓑ Ⓒ Ⓓ Ⓔ
33. Ⓐ Ⓑ Ⓒ Ⓓ Ⓔ
34. Ⓐ Ⓑ Ⓒ Ⓓ Ⓔ
35. Ⓐ Ⓑ Ⓒ Ⓓ Ⓔ
36. Ⓐ Ⓑ Ⓒ Ⓓ Ⓔ

37. Ⓐ Ⓑ Ⓒ Ⓓ Ⓔ
38. Ⓐ Ⓑ Ⓒ Ⓓ Ⓔ
39. Ⓐ Ⓑ Ⓒ Ⓓ Ⓔ
40. Ⓐ Ⓑ Ⓒ Ⓓ Ⓔ
41. Ⓐ Ⓑ Ⓒ Ⓓ Ⓔ
42. Ⓐ Ⓑ Ⓒ Ⓓ Ⓔ
43. Ⓐ Ⓑ Ⓒ Ⓓ Ⓔ
44. Ⓐ Ⓑ Ⓒ Ⓓ Ⓔ
45. Ⓐ Ⓑ Ⓒ Ⓓ Ⓔ
46. Ⓐ Ⓑ Ⓒ Ⓓ Ⓔ
47. Ⓐ Ⓑ Ⓒ Ⓓ Ⓔ
48. Ⓐ Ⓑ Ⓒ Ⓓ Ⓔ
49. Ⓐ Ⓑ Ⓒ Ⓓ Ⓔ
50. Ⓐ Ⓑ Ⓒ Ⓓ Ⓔ
51. Ⓐ Ⓑ Ⓒ Ⓓ Ⓔ
52. Ⓐ Ⓑ Ⓒ Ⓓ Ⓔ
53. Ⓐ Ⓑ Ⓒ Ⓓ Ⓔ
54. Ⓐ Ⓑ Ⓒ Ⓓ Ⓔ

55. Ⓐ Ⓑ Ⓒ Ⓓ Ⓔ
56. Ⓐ Ⓑ Ⓒ Ⓓ Ⓔ
57. Ⓐ Ⓑ Ⓒ Ⓓ Ⓔ
58. Ⓐ Ⓑ Ⓒ Ⓓ Ⓔ
59. Ⓐ Ⓑ Ⓒ Ⓓ Ⓔ
60. Ⓐ Ⓑ Ⓒ Ⓓ Ⓔ
61. Ⓐ Ⓑ Ⓒ Ⓓ Ⓔ
62. Ⓐ Ⓑ Ⓒ Ⓓ Ⓔ
63. Ⓐ Ⓑ Ⓒ Ⓓ Ⓔ
64. Ⓐ Ⓑ Ⓒ Ⓓ Ⓔ
65. Ⓐ Ⓑ Ⓒ Ⓓ Ⓔ
66. Ⓐ Ⓜ Ⓒ Ⓓ Ⓔ
67. Ⓐ Ⓑ Ⓒ Ⓓ Ⓔ
68. Ⓐ Ⓑ Ⓒ Ⓓ Ⓔ
69. Ⓐ Ⓑ Ⓒ Ⓓ Ⓔ
70. Ⓐ Ⓑ Ⓒ Ⓓ Ⓔ
71. Ⓐ Ⓑ Ⓒ Ⓓ Ⓔ
72. Ⓐ Ⓑ Ⓒ Ⓓ Ⓔ

73. Ⓐ Ⓑ Ⓒ Ⓓ Ⓔ
74. Ⓐ Ⓑ Ⓒ Ⓓ Ⓔ
75. Ⓐ Ⓑ Ⓒ Ⓓ Ⓔ
76. Ⓐ Ⓑ Ⓒ Ⓓ Ⓔ
77. Ⓐ Ⓑ Ⓒ Ⓓ Ⓔ
78. Ⓐ Ⓑ Ⓒ Ⓓ Ⓔ
79. Ⓐ Ⓑ Ⓒ Ⓓ Ⓔ
80. Ⓐ Ⓑ Ⓒ Ⓓ Ⓔ
81. Ⓐ Ⓑ Ⓒ Ⓓ Ⓔ
82. Ⓐ Ⓑ Ⓒ Ⓓ Ⓔ
83. Ⓐ Ⓑ Ⓒ Ⓓ Ⓔ
84. Ⓐ Ⓑ Ⓒ Ⓓ Ⓔ
85. Ⓐ Ⓑ Ⓒ Ⓓ Ⓔ
86. Ⓐ Ⓑ Ⓒ Ⓓ Ⓔ
87. Ⓐ Ⓑ Ⓒ Ⓓ Ⓔ
88. Ⓐ Ⓑ Ⓒ Ⓓ Ⓔ

Tear here

PART C—ADDRESS CODE MEMORY

1. Ⓐ Ⓑ Ⓒ Ⓓ Ⓔ
2. Ⓐ Ⓑ Ⓒ Ⓓ Ⓔ
3. Ⓐ Ⓑ Ⓒ Ⓓ Ⓔ
4. Ⓐ Ⓑ Ⓒ Ⓓ Ⓔ
5. Ⓐ Ⓑ Ⓒ Ⓓ Ⓔ
6. Ⓐ Ⓑ Ⓒ Ⓓ Ⓔ
7. Ⓐ Ⓑ Ⓒ Ⓓ Ⓔ
8. Ⓐ Ⓑ Ⓒ Ⓓ Ⓔ
9. Ⓐ Ⓑ Ⓒ Ⓓ Ⓔ
10. Ⓐ Ⓑ Ⓒ Ⓓ Ⓔ
11. Ⓐ Ⓑ Ⓒ Ⓓ Ⓔ
12. Ⓐ Ⓑ Ⓒ Ⓓ Ⓔ
13. Ⓐ Ⓑ Ⓒ Ⓓ Ⓔ
14. Ⓐ Ⓑ Ⓒ Ⓓ Ⓔ
15. Ⓐ Ⓑ Ⓒ Ⓓ Ⓔ
16. Ⓐ Ⓑ Ⓒ Ⓓ Ⓔ
17. Ⓐ Ⓑ Ⓒ Ⓓ Ⓔ
18. Ⓐ Ⓑ Ⓒ Ⓓ Ⓔ

19. Ⓐ Ⓑ Ⓒ Ⓓ Ⓔ
20. Ⓐ Ⓑ Ⓒ Ⓓ Ⓔ
21. Ⓐ Ⓑ Ⓒ Ⓓ Ⓔ
22. Ⓐ Ⓑ Ⓒ Ⓓ Ⓔ
23. Ⓐ Ⓑ Ⓒ Ⓓ Ⓔ
24. Ⓐ Ⓑ Ⓒ Ⓓ Ⓔ
25. Ⓐ Ⓑ Ⓒ Ⓓ Ⓔ
26. Ⓐ Ⓑ Ⓒ Ⓓ Ⓔ
27. Ⓐ Ⓑ Ⓒ Ⓓ Ⓔ
28. Ⓐ Ⓑ Ⓒ Ⓓ Ⓔ
29. Ⓐ Ⓑ Ⓒ Ⓓ Ⓔ
30. Ⓐ Ⓑ Ⓒ Ⓓ Ⓔ
31. Ⓐ Ⓑ Ⓒ Ⓓ Ⓔ
32. Ⓐ Ⓑ Ⓒ Ⓓ Ⓔ
33. Ⓐ Ⓑ Ⓒ Ⓓ Ⓔ
34. Ⓐ Ⓑ Ⓒ Ⓓ Ⓔ
35. Ⓐ Ⓑ Ⓒ Ⓓ Ⓔ
36. Ⓐ Ⓑ Ⓒ Ⓓ Ⓔ

37. Ⓐ Ⓑ Ⓒ Ⓓ Ⓔ
38. Ⓐ Ⓑ Ⓒ Ⓓ Ⓔ
39. Ⓐ Ⓑ Ⓒ Ⓓ Ⓔ
40. Ⓐ Ⓑ Ⓒ Ⓓ Ⓔ
41. Ⓐ Ⓑ Ⓒ Ⓓ Ⓔ
42. Ⓐ Ⓑ Ⓒ Ⓓ Ⓔ
43. Ⓐ Ⓑ Ⓒ Ⓓ Ⓔ
44. Ⓐ Ⓑ Ⓒ Ⓓ Ⓔ
45. Ⓐ Ⓑ Ⓒ Ⓓ Ⓔ
46. Ⓐ Ⓑ Ⓒ Ⓓ Ⓔ
47. Ⓐ Ⓑ Ⓒ Ⓓ Ⓔ
48. Ⓐ Ⓑ Ⓒ Ⓓ Ⓔ
49. Ⓐ Ⓑ Ⓒ Ⓓ Ⓔ
50. Ⓐ Ⓑ Ⓒ Ⓓ Ⓔ
51. Ⓐ Ⓑ Ⓒ Ⓓ Ⓔ
52. Ⓐ Ⓑ Ⓒ Ⓓ Ⓔ
53. Ⓐ Ⓑ Ⓒ Ⓓ Ⓔ
54. Ⓐ Ⓑ Ⓒ Ⓓ Ⓔ

55. Ⓐ Ⓑ Ⓒ Ⓓ Ⓔ
56. Ⓐ Ⓑ Ⓒ Ⓓ Ⓔ
57. Ⓐ Ⓑ Ⓒ Ⓓ Ⓔ
58. Ⓐ Ⓑ Ⓒ Ⓓ Ⓔ
59. Ⓐ Ⓑ Ⓒ Ⓓ Ⓔ
60. Ⓐ Ⓑ Ⓒ Ⓓ Ⓔ
61. Ⓐ Ⓑ Ⓒ Ⓓ Ⓔ
62. Ⓐ Ⓑ Ⓒ Ⓓ Ⓔ
63. Ⓐ Ⓑ Ⓒ Ⓓ Ⓔ
64. Ⓐ Ⓑ Ⓒ Ⓓ Ⓔ
65. Ⓐ Ⓑ Ⓒ Ⓓ Ⓔ
66. Ⓐ Ⓑ Ⓒ Ⓓ Ⓔ
67. Ⓐ Ⓑ Ⓒ Ⓓ Ⓔ
68. Ⓐ Ⓑ Ⓒ Ⓓ Ⓔ
69. Ⓐ Ⓑ Ⓒ Ⓓ Ⓔ
70. Ⓐ Ⓑ Ⓒ Ⓓ Ⓔ
71. Ⓐ Ⓑ Ⓒ Ⓓ Ⓔ
72. Ⓐ Ⓑ Ⓒ Ⓓ Ⓔ

73. Ⓐ Ⓑ Ⓒ Ⓓ Ⓔ
74. Ⓐ Ⓑ Ⓒ Ⓓ Ⓔ
75. Ⓐ Ⓑ Ⓒ Ⓓ Ⓔ
76. Ⓐ Ⓑ Ⓒ Ⓓ Ⓔ
77. Ⓐ Ⓑ Ⓒ Ⓓ Ⓔ
78. Ⓐ Ⓑ Ⓒ Ⓓ Ⓔ
79. Ⓐ Ⓑ Ⓒ Ⓓ Ⓔ
80. Ⓐ Ⓑ Ⓒ Ⓓ Ⓔ
81. Ⓐ Ⓑ Ⓒ Ⓓ Ⓔ
82. Ⓐ Ⓑ Ⓒ Ⓓ Ⓔ
83. Ⓐ Ⓑ Ⓒ Ⓓ Ⓔ
84. Ⓐ Ⓑ Ⓒ Ⓓ Ⓔ
85. Ⓐ Ⓑ Ⓒ Ⓓ Ⓔ
86. Ⓐ Ⓑ Ⓒ Ⓓ Ⓔ
87. Ⓐ Ⓑ Ⓒ Ⓓ Ⓔ
88. Ⓐ Ⓑ Ⓒ Ⓓ Ⓔ

Tear here

PART D—ADDRESS CHECKING

1. Ⓐⓓ
2. Ⓐⓓ
3. Ⓐⓓ
4. Ⓐⓓ
5. Ⓐⓓ
6. Ⓐⓓ
7. Ⓐⓓ
8. Ⓐⓓ
9. Ⓐⓓ
10. Ⓐⓓ
11. Ⓐⓓ
12. Ⓐⓓ
13. Ⓐⓓ
14. Ⓐⓓ
15. Ⓐⓓ
16. Ⓐⓓ
17. Ⓐⓓ
18. Ⓐⓓ
19. Ⓐⓓ

20. Ⓐⓓ
21. Ⓐⓓ
22. Ⓐⓓ
23. Ⓐⓓ
24. Ⓐⓓ
25. Ⓐⓓ
26. Ⓐⓓ
27. Ⓐⓓ
28. Ⓐⓓ
29. Ⓐⓓ
30. Ⓐⓓ
31. Ⓐⓓ
32. Ⓐⓓ
33. Ⓐⓓ
34. Ⓐⓓ
35. Ⓐⓓ
36. Ⓐⓓ
37. Ⓐⓓ
38. Ⓐⓓ

39. Ⓐⓓ
40. Ⓐⓓ
41. Ⓐⓓ
42. Ⓐⓓ
43. Ⓐⓓ
44. Ⓐⓓ
45. Ⓐⓓ
46. Ⓐⓓ
47. Ⓐⓓ
48. Ⓐⓓ
49. Ⓐⓓ
50. Ⓐⓓ
51. Ⓐⓓ
52. Ⓐⓓ
53. Ⓐⓓ
54. Ⓐⓓ
55. Ⓐⓓ
56. Ⓐⓓ
57. Ⓐⓓ

58. Ⓐⓓ
59. Ⓐⓓ
60. Ⓐⓓ
61. Ⓐⓓ
62. Ⓐⓓ
63. Ⓐⓓ
64. Ⓐⓓ
65. Ⓐⓓ
66. Ⓐⓓ
67. Ⓐⓓ
68. Ⓐⓓ
69. Ⓐⓓ
70. Ⓐⓓ
71. Ⓐⓓ
72. Ⓐⓓ
73. Ⓐⓓ
74. Ⓐⓓ
75. Ⓐⓓ
76. Ⓐⓓ

77. Ⓐⓓ
78. Ⓐⓓ
79. Ⓐⓓ
80. Ⓐⓓ
81. Ⓐⓓ
82. Ⓐⓓ
83. Ⓐⓓ
84. Ⓐⓓ
85. Ⓐⓓ
86. Ⓐⓓ
87. Ⓐⓓ
88. Ⓐⓓ
89. Ⓐⓓ
90. Ⓐⓓ
91. Ⓐⓓ
92. Ⓐⓓ
93. Ⓐⓓ
94. Ⓐⓓ
95. Ⓐⓓ

Tear here

DISTRIBUTION CLERK, MACHINE MODEL EXAM

SCORE SHEET

PART A—NUMBER SERIES

Number Right equals Score

_____ = _____

PART B—ADDRESS CODING

Number Right minus (Number Wrong ÷ 4) equals Score

_____ − _____ = _____

PART C—ADDRESS CODE MEMORY

Number Right minus (Number Wrong ÷ 4) equals Score

_____ − _____ = _____

PART D—ADDRESS CHECKING

Number Right minus Number Wrong equals Score

_____ − _____ = _____

SELF-EVALUATION CHART

Part	Excellent	Good	Average	Fair	Poor
Number Series	21–24	18–20	14–17	11–13	1–10
Address Coding	75–88	63–74	52–62	40–51	1–39
Address Code Memory	75–88	60–74	45–59	30–44	1–29
Address Checking	80–95	65–79	50–64	35–49	1–34

DISTRIBUTION CLERK, MACHINE MODEL EXAM

PART A—NUMBER SERIES

The following sample questions show you the type of question that will be used in Part A. Since this type of question may be new and unfamiliar to you, the examiner will work through the first five questions with you. Once you understand the task, you will have five minutes to answer sample questions 6 to 14 on your own. Correct answers and explanations follow.

Directions: Each number series question consists of a series of numbers which follows some definite order. The numbers progress from left to right according to some rule. One pair of numbers to the right of the series comprises the next two numbers in the series. Study each series to figure out the rule which governs the progression. Choose the answer pair which continues the series according to the pattern established and mark its letter on your answer sheet.

1. 17 20 20 23 23 26 26 ..... (A) 26 26 (B) 26 27 (C) 26 29 (D) 29 29 (E) 29 32

   In this series, the pattern is: $+3$, repeat the number, $+3$, repeat the number, $+3$, repeat the number. Since 26 has been repeated, the next number in the series should be 29, which should then be repeated. (D) is the correct answer.

2. 76 75 73 70 66 61 55 ..... (A) 50 41 (B) 54 51 (C) 46 40 (D) 45 35 (E) 48 40

   The pattern here is: $-1, -2, -3, -4, -5, -6, -7, -8 \ldots$ Continuing the series we see that $55 - 7 = 48 - 8 = 40$, so (E) is the correct answer.

3. 22 26 31 35 40 44 49 ..... (A) 53 58 (B) 54 58 (C) 54 59 (D) 53 57 (E) 55 61

   Here the pattern is $+4, +5, +4, +5; +4, +5 \ldots$ (A) is the correct answer because $49 + 4 = 53 + 5 = 58$.

4. 12 36 14 33 16 30 18 ..... (A) 20 27 (B) 27 20 (C) 20 22 (D) 28 26 (E) 16 14

   This series is actually two alternating series. The first series begins with 12 and ascends at the rate of $+2$. This series reads: 12 14 16 18 20. The alternating series begins with 36 and descends at the rate of -3. This series reads: 36 33 30 27. The correct answer is (B) because the next number in the total series must be the next number in the descending series, which is 27, followed by the text number in the ascending series, 20.

5. 4 12 8 12 12 12 16 12 20 . (A) 16 16 (B) 20 20 (C) 20 24 (D) 24 28 (E) 12 24

   This is a difficult series which has been extended to give you more opportunity to spot the pattern. Actually the basic series is a simple $+4$; 4 8 12 16 20 24. After each number in the basic series, you find the number 12. The problem would be easy if it were not for the coincidence of the number 12 appearing in the series itself. Once you understand the series, you can easily see that (E) is the answer. You will now have five minutes to complete the remaining sample number series questions.

6. 14 14 14 17 17 17 20 ...... (A) 17 14 (B) 17 20 (C) 20 20 (D) 20 23 (E) 20 21

7. 97 87 78 70 63 57 52 ..... (A) 48 45 (B) 50 48 (C) 51 50 (D) 48 46 (E) 47 42

8. 34 36 39 43 45 48 52 ..... (A) 54 56 (B) 54 57 (C) 55 57 (D) 55 58 (E) 56 59

9. 3 6 12 12 24 48 48 .... (A) 48 96 (B) 96 96 (C) 144 144 (D) 96 144 (E) 96 192

10. 10 68 20 63 30 58 40 ..... (A) 50 53 (B) 48 55 (C) 45 55 (D) 50 56 (E) 53 50

11. 38 32 32 38 38 32 32 ..... (A) 32 38 (B) 38 32 (C) 32 32 (D) 38 38 (E) 34 34

12. 15 28 14 30 13 32 12 ...... (A) 10 35 (B) 11 34 (C) 34 11 (D) 10 34 (E) 34 10

13. 11 13 16 20 25 31 38 ..... (A) 45 51 (B) 48 58 (C) 46 56 (D) 46 55 (E) 46 57

14. 54 52 17 50 48 17 46 ..... (A) 44 42 (B) 17 44 (C) 44 17 (D) 43 17 (E) 17 43

SAMPLE ANSWER SHEET		CORRECT ANSWERS	
1. ⒶⒷⒸⒹⒺ	8. ⒶⒷⒸⒹⒺ	1. D	8. B
2. ⒶⒷⒸⒹⒺ	9. ⒶⒷⒸⒹⒺ	2. E	9. E
3. ⒶⒷⒸⒹⒺ	10. ⒶⒷⒸⒹⒺ	3. A	10. E
4. ⒶⒷⒸⒹⒺ	11. ⒶⒷⒸⒹⒺ	4. B	11. D
5. ⒶⒷⒸⒹⒺ	12. ⒶⒷⒸⒹⒺ	5. E	12. C
6. ⒶⒷⒸⒹⒺ	13. ⒶⒷⒸⒹⒺ	6. C	13. D
7. ⒶⒷⒸⒹⒺ	14. ⒶⒷⒸⒹⒺ	7. A	14. C

Explanations

6. **(C)** The pattern is: Repeat the number three times, $+3$; repeat the number three times, $+3$ . . . The number 20 must be repeated two more times as in choice **(C)**. If the series were to be extended, the next number would be 23.

7. **(A)** This series follows the descending pattern: -10, -9, -8, -7, -6, -5. Continuing the pattern: $52 - 4 = 48 - 3 = 45$.

8. **(B)** The pattern is: $+2$, $+3$, $+4$; $+2$, $+3$, $+4$ . . . Then, $52 + 2 = 54 + 3 = 57$.

9. **(E)** The pattern is: $\times 2$, $\times 2$, repeat the number; $\times 2$, $\times 2$, repeat the number . . . . Having just repeated the number, the series continues: $48 \times 2 = 96 \times 2 = 192$.

10. **(E)** There are two alternating series. The first series ascends by $+10$. The alternating series descends by -5. Thus, the two series are: 10 20 30 40 50 and 68 63 58 53.

11. **(D)** The series consists of a repetition of the sequence: 38 32 32 38; 38 32 32 38; 38 . . .

12. **(C)** There are two alternating series. The first series, 15 14 13 12 11, descends at the rate of -1. The alternating series, 28 30 32 34, ascends at the rate of $+2$.

13. **(D)** The series ascends: $+2$, $+3$, $+4$, $+5$, $+6$, $+7$. Then, $38 + 8 = 46 + 9 = 55$.

14. **(C)** This is a -2 series with the number 17 intervening after each two numbers in the series. Continuing the series: $46 - 2 = 44$, then 17 and, if the series were to continue still further, $44 - 2 = 42$.

PART A—NUMBER SERIES

24 Questions—20 Minutes

Directions: *Each number series question consists of a series of numbers which follows some definite order. The numbers progress from left to right according to some rule. One lettered pair of numbers comprises the next two numbers in the series. Study each series to try to find a pattern to the series and to figure the rule which governs the progression. Choose the answer pair which continues the series according to the pattern established and mark its letter on your answer sheet. Correct answers are on page 270.*

1. 10 11 12 10 12 12 10 ...... (A) 10 11 (B) 12 10 (C) 11 10 (D) 11 12 (E) 10 12

2. 4 6 7 4 6 7 4 .... (A) 6 7 (B) 4 7 (C) 7 6 (D) 7 4 (E) 6 8

3. 10 10 9 11 11 10 12 .... (A) 13 14 (B) 12 11 (C) 13 13 (D) 12 12 (E) 12 13

4. 3 4 10 5 6 10 7 .... (A) 10 8 (B) 9 8 (C) 8 14 (D) 8 9 (E) 8 10

5. 6 6 7 7 8 8 9 .... (A) 10 11 (B) 10 10 (C) 9 10 (D) 9 9 (E) 10 9

6. 3 8 9 4 9 10 5 .... (A) 6 10 (B) 10 11 (C) 9 10 (D) 11 6 (E) 10 6

7. 2 4 3 6 4 8 5 .... (A) 6 10 (B) 10 7 (C) 10 6 (D) 9 6 (E) 6 7

8. 11 5 9 7 7 9 5 .... (A) 11 3 (B) 7 9 (C) 7 11 (D) 9 7 (E) 3 7

9. 7 16 9 15 11 14 13 .... (A) 12 14 (B) 13 15 (C) 17 15 (D) 15 12 (E) 13 12

10. 40 42 39 44 38 46 37 ..... (A) 48 36 (B) 37 46 (C) 36 48 (D) 43 39 (E) 46 40

11. 1 3 6 10 15 21 28 36 .... (A) 40 48 (B) 36 45 (C) 38 52 (D) 45 56 (E) 45 55

12. 1 2 3 3 4 7 5 6 11 7 .. (A) 8 12 (B) 9 15 (C) 8 15 (D) 6 12 (E) 8 7

13. 3 18 4 24 5 30 6 .... (A) 7 40 (B) 7 42 (C) 42 7 (D) 36 7 (E) 40 7

14. 3 3 4 8 10 30 33 132 .... (A) 152 158 (B) 136 680 (C) 165 500 (D) 143 560 (E) 300 900

15. 18 20 22 20 18 20 22 ..... (A) 18 20 (B) 20 18 (C) 22 20 (D) 24 20 (E) 18 22

16. 4 8 8 16 16 32 32 .... (A) 32 64 (B) 36 40 (C) 64 64 (D) 64 128 (E) 64 82

17. 1 2 12 3 4 34 5 .... (A) 6 65 (B) 7 12 (C) 5 6 (D) 6 60 (E) 6 56

18. 8 16 24 32 40 48 56 .... (A) 64 72 (B) 60 64 (C) 70 78 (D) 62 70 (E) 64 68

19. 5 15 18 54 57 171 174 ..... (A) 176 528(B) 522 821(C) 177 531(D) 522 525(E) 525 528

20. 25 20 24 21 23 22 22 ..... (A) 24 20 (B) 23 21 (C) 23 24 (D) 24 21 (E) 22 23

21. 99 88 77 66 55 44 33 ..... (A) 22 11 (B) 33 22 (C) 44 55 (D) 32 22 (E) 30 20

22. 7 5 9 7 11 9 13 .... (A) 9 11 (B) 11 9 (C) 7 11 (D) 9 15 (E) 11 15

23. 47 44 41 38 35 32 29 ..... (A) 28 27 (B) 27 24 (C) 26 23 (D) 25 21 (E) 26 22

24. 99 99 99 33 33 33 11 ..... (A) 9 7 (B) 22 33 (C) 11 0 (D) 11 33 (E) 11 11

END OF PART A

If you complete your work before time is up, check over your answers on this test only. Do not turn the page until you are told to do so.

PART B—ADDRESS CODING

SAMPLE QUESTIONS

The seven sample questions for this part are based upon the addresses in the five boxes below. Your task is to mark on your answer sheet the letter of the box in which each address belongs. The instructions for Part B permit you to look at the boxes if you cannot remember in which box an address belongs. You may look at the boxes while answering these Part B sample questions. The questions in Part C of the exam will be based upon the same boxes as the questions in Part B, but in answering Part C you may NOT look at the boxes. There will be no sample questions before Part C.

A	B	C	D	E
8300-8499 Oak Hillburn 4300-5199 Secor Abbey 1200-1899 Gilmore	8000-8299 Oak Brambach 5700-6099 Secor Winslow 2700-3199 Gilmore	6200-7599 Oak Woods 3100-4199 Secor Dobbs 3200-3899 Gilmore	7600-7999 Oak Burgess 5200-5699 Secor Plains 1900-2699 Gilmore	4900-6199 Oak Mercer 4200-4299 Secor Clayton 1100-1199 Gilmore

1. 3200-3899 Gilmore
2. Mercer
3. Abbey
4. 8000-8299 Oak

5. 5200-5699 Secor
6. 4300-5199 Secor
7. Dobbs

SAMPLE ANSWER SHEET	
1. Ⓐ Ⓑ Ⓒ Ⓓ Ⓔ	5. Ⓐ Ⓑ Ⓒ Ⓓ Ⓔ
2. Ⓐ Ⓑ Ⓒ Ⓓ Ⓔ	6. Ⓐ Ⓑ Ⓒ Ⓓ Ⓔ
3. Ⓐ Ⓑ Ⓒ Ⓓ Ⓔ	7. Ⓐ Ⓑ Ⓒ Ⓓ Ⓔ
4. Ⓐ Ⓑ Ⓒ Ⓓ Ⓔ	

CORRECT ANSWERS	
1. C	5. D
2. E	6. A
3. A	7. C
4. B	

PART B—ADDRESS CODING

Directions: *There are five boxes labeled A, B, C, D, and E. In each box are five addresses, three of which include a number span and a name, and two of which are names alone. You will have five (5) minutes to memorize the locations of all twenty-five addresses. Then you will have three (3) minutes to mark your answer sheet with the letter of the box in which each address in the question list belongs. For Part B you may refer to the boxes while answering, though you will lose speed by doing so. For Part C you may NOT look at the boxes, so do your best to memorize in the five minutes allowed you now. Correct answers are on page 271.*

Memorizing Time: 5 Minutes.

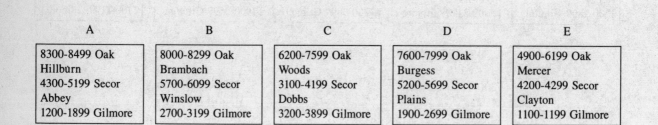

A	B	C	D	E
8300-8499 Oak	8000-8299 Oak	6200-7599 Oak	7600-7999 Oak	4900-6199 Oak
Hillburn	Brambach	Woods	Burgess	Mercer
4300-5199 Secor	5700-6099 Secor	3100-4199 Secor	5200-5699 Secor	4200-4299 Secor
Abbey	Winslow	Dobbs	Plains	Clayton
1200-1899 Gilmore	2700-3199 Gilmore	3200-3899 Gilmore	1900-2699 Gilmore	1100-1199 Gilmore

Answering Time: 3 Minutes—88 Questions

1. 3200-3899 Gilmore
2. 5200-5699 Secor
3. 4900-6199 Oak
4. Hillburn
5. 8300-8499 Oak
6. 2700-3199 Gilmore
7. Mercer
8. 1900-2699 Gilmore
9. 4200-4299 Secor
10. 5700-6099 Secor
11. Dobbs
12. Clayton
13. 7600-7999 Oak
14. 3100-4199 Secor
15. 8000-8299 Oak
16. 1200-1899 Gilmore
17. Brambach
18. Burgess
19. Woods
20. 6200-7599 Oak
21. 4300-5199 Secor
22. Abbey
23. Winslow
24. 1100-1199 Gilmore
25. Plains
26. 5200-5699 Secor
27. Brambach
28. 8000-8299 Oak

29. 4300-5199 Secor
30. 1900-2699 Gilmore
31. Hillburn
32. Dobbs
33. 4900-6199 Oak
34. 4300-5199 Secor
35. 3200-3899 Gilmore
36. Mercer
37. 7600-7999 Oak
38. 8300-8499 Oak
39. Brambach
40. Clayton
41. Abbey
42. 5700-6099 Secor
43. 4200-4299 Secor
44. 1200-1899 Gilmore
45. Winslow
46. Dobbs
47. 6200-7599 Oak
48. Plains
49. 3100-4199 Secor
50. 1100-1199 Gilmore
51. 2700-3199 Gilmore
52. 5200-5699 Secor
53. Hillburn
54. Woods
55. 5700-6099 Secor
56. 6200-7599 Oak
57. 1200-1899 Gilmore
58. 4900-6199 Oak

59. 1900-2699 Gilmore
60. Winslow
61. Dobbs
62. 1100-1199 Gilmore
63. 8300-8499 Oak
64. Clayton
65. Mercer
66. 3100-4199 Secor
67. Brambach
68. 2700-3199 Gilmore
69. 5200-5699 Secor
70. 7600-7999 Oak
71. Burgess
72. Woods
73. 4200-4299 Secor
74. Plains
75. 1900-2699 Gilmore
76. 3200-3899 Gilmore
77. 4200-4299 Secor
78. Abbey
79. Winslow
80. 1200-1899 Gilmore
81. 8000-8299 Oak
82. 7600-7999 Oak
83. Hillburn
84. Clayton
85. 8300-8499 Oak
86. 4300-5199 Secor
87. 5200-5699 Secor
88. Woods

END OF PART B

If you finish before time is up, use the remaining seconds to continue memorizing the locations of the addresses. Do not turn the page until you are told to do so.

PART C—ADDRESS CODE MEMORY

88 Questions—5 Minutes

Directions: Relying entirely upon your memory, mark your answer sheet with the letter of the box in which each address belongs. Correct answers are on page 271.

1. 1900-2699 Gilmore
2. 4900-6199 Oak
3. Dobbs
4. Abbey
5. 4300-5199 Secor
6. 4200-4299 Secor
7. 8300-8499 Oak
8. 3200-3899 Gilmore
9. Brambach
10. Mercer
11. Burgess
12. 1200-1899 Gilmore
13. 5700-6099 Secor
14. 8000-8299 Oak
15. Woods
16. 3100-4199 Secor
17. 7600-7999 Oak
18. 1100-1199 Gilmore
19. Clayton
20. Hillburn
21. 2700-3199 Gilmore
22. 6200-7599 Oak
23. Winslow
24. 5200-5699 Secor
25. Plains
26. 4300-5199 Secor
27. 7600-7999 Oak
28. Hillburn
29. 1100-1199 Gilmore
30. Clayton
31. 8300-8499 Oak
32. 3100-4199 Secor
33. 1900-2699 Gilmore
34. Mercer
35. Abbey
36. Woods
37. 1200-1899 Gilmore
38. 4900-6199 Oak
39. 6200-7599 Oak
40. 8000-8299 Oak
41. 5700-6099 Secor
42. Dobbs
43. Clayton
44. Burgess
45. 2700-3199 Gilmore
46. Plains
47. 4200-4299 Secor
48. 8000-8299 Oak
49. 3100-4199 Secor
50. 1900-2699 Gilmore
51. Hillburn
52. Brambach
53. 3200-3899 Gilmore
54. 4900-6199 Oak
55. 5200-5699 Secor
56. 8300-8499 Oak
57. Winslow
58. Clayton
59. Mercer
60. 1100-1199 Gilmore
61. 8000-8299 Oak
62. 4900-6199 Oak
63. 4300-5199 Secor
64. 3200-3899 Gilmore
65. 4200-4299 Secor
66. Burgess
67. Woods
68. Winslow
69. 7600-7999 Oak
70. 3100-4199 Secor

71. 2700-3199 Gilmore
72. 1900-2699 Gilmore
73. Abbey
74. Winslow
75. 5700-6099 Secor
76. 3200-3899 Gilmore
77. 8300-8499 Oak
78. Dobbs
79. 4200-4299 Secor

80. 4900-6199 Oak
81. Clayton
82. 1200-1899 Gilmore
83. 8000-8299 Oak
84. 5200-5699 Secor
85. Mercer
86. 1100-1199 Gilmore
87. 4300-5199 Secor
88. 6200-7599 Oak

END OF PART C

> **If you finish before time is up, check your answers on this part only.
> Do not turn the page until you are told to do so.**

PART D—ADDRESS CHECKING TEST

SAMPLE QUESTIONS

You will be allowed three minutes to read the directions and answer the five sample questions which follow. On the actual test, however, you will have only six minutes to answer 95 questions, so see how quickly you can compare addresses and still get the correct answer.

Directions: *Each question consists of two addresses. If the two addresses are* alike in EVERY *way, mark Ⓐ on your answer sheet. If the two addresses are* different in ANY *way, mark Ⓓ on your answer sheet.*

1 . . .	3969 Ardsley Rd	3696 Ardsley Rd
2 . . .	Bryn Mawr PA 19010	Bryn Mawr PA 19010
3 . . .	1684 Beechwood Rd	1684 Beachwood Rd
4 . . .	1885 Black Birch La	1885 Black Birch La
5 . . .	Indianapolis IN 46208	Indianapollis IN 46208

SAMPLE ANSWER SHEET	
1. ⒶⒹ	4. ⒶⒹ
2. ⒶⒹ	5. ⒶⒹ
3. ⒶⒹ	

CORRECT ANSWERS	
1. D	4. A
2. A	5. D
3. D	

PART D—ADDRESS CHECKING

95 Questions—6 Minutes

Directions: *For each question, compare the address in the left column with the address in the right column. If the addresses are alike in* EVERY *way, blacken space Ⓐ on your answer sheet. If the two addresses are different in* ANY *way, blacken space Ⓓ on your answer sheet. Correct answers for this test are on page 272.*

1.	9411 41st Rd	9411 41st St
2.	2843 Noe St	2834 Noe St
3.	E Williston NY 11596	E Williston NH 11596
4.	1151 Girard St	1151 Girard St
5.	841 St Francis Rd W	841 St Frances Rd W
6.	8001 E Broadway	8001 E Broadway
7.	Lake Worth FL 33463	Lake Worth FL 33463
8.	1161 Lefferts Blvd	1161 Lefferts Rd
9.	444 W 66th St	444 E 66th St
10.	1626 Butler Rd	1626 Butler Rd
11.	154 Woodside Ave	154 Woodland Ave
12.	Mountain Lakes NJ 07046	Mountain Lakes NJ 07064
13.	329 B Cranstoun Ct	329 B Cranstown Ct
14.	Medford MA 02155	Medford MA 02155
15.	148 Meritoria Dr	148 Meritorious Dr
16.	6032 Cannon Hill Rd	6032 Canon Hill Rd
17.	561 S Atlantic Ave	561 S Atlantic Ave
18.	5009 Stuyvesant Oval	5009 Stuyvesant Oval
19.	Wilmington DE 19808	Wilmington DE 19888
20.	2387 Bayview Ave	2378 Bayview Ave
21.	636 Briarcliff Rd	6363 Briarcliff Rd
22.	Santa Monica CA 90402	Santa Monica CA 90402
23.	5986 Echo Dr	5896 Echo Dr
24.	Brooklyn NY 11235	Brooklyn NY 12135
25.	132 E 35th St	132 E 35th St
26.	1786 W 79th St	1786 W 79th St
27.	1155 Central Park W	1155 Central Park S
28.	Ft. Washington PA 19034	Ft Washington PN 19034
29.	1736 Chatterton Ave	1736 Chaterton Ave
30.	666 N Bedford Rd	666 N Bedford Rd
31.	7591 Selleck St	7951 Selleck St
32.	120 Old Lake Dr	120 Old Lake Dr

33. Scarsdale NY 10583	Scarsdale NY 10585
34. 2907 Columbus Ave	2709 Columbus Ave
35. 693 S Moger Ave	693 S Moger Ave
36. 7557 N Greeley Ave	7557 N Greely Ave
37. 219 Park Ave S	291 Park Ave S
38. New York NY 10003	New York NY 10003
39. 1974 Commerce St	1974 Commerce St
40. 174 Grand St	174 Grand Pl
41. Mahopac Falls NY 10542	Maohpac Falls NY 10542
42. 1320 Stoneybrook Ave	1320 Stoney Brook Ave
43. 160 W 166th St	166 W 166th St
44. 2257 Saw Mill River Rd	257 Saw Mill River Rd
45. 4717 Sherwood Ave	4717 Sherwood Ave
46. Newton Lower Falls MA 02162	Newton Lower Falls MO 02162
47. 5300 Ocean Blvd	5300 Oceana Blvd
48. 1042 Barbary Rd	1024 Barbary Rd
49. 113 Crossways Park Dr	133 Crossways Park Dr
50. Maple Plain MN 55348	Maple Plain NM 55348
51. 790 Bronx River Rd	970 Bronx River Rd
52. 6587 Forest Ave	6587 Forrest Ave
53. Tuckahoe NY 10707	Tuckahoe NY 70707
54. 155 Riverside Dr	155 Riverside Dr
55. Princeton NJ 08541	Princeton NJ 08541
56. 222 Lake Ave	2222 Lake Ave
57. 1127 Hardscrabble Rd	1127 Hardscrable Rd
58. 1776 E 157th St	1776 E 157th St
59. 466 Union Ave	466 Union Ave
60. 4211 Hugunot Ave	4211 Huguenot Ave
61. 3435 DeKalb Ave	3435 Dekalb Ave
62. 4986 Spencer Pl	4986 Spenser Pl
63. Sarasota FL 33581	Saratoga FL 33581
64. 345 Belmore Pk	345 Belmore Pk
65. 1793 Purdy Ave	1973 Purdy Ave
66. 2764 Gaylor Rd	2764 Gaylord Rd
67. 2082 W 83rd Rd	2082 W 83rd Rd
68. 908 Adison Rd	908 Edison Rd
69. Cincinnati OH 45202	Cincinatti OH 45202
70. Alamo TX 78516	Alamo TX 78516
71. 3030 Garth Rd	3030 Garth Rd
72. 9806 NW Main St	9806 NE Main St
73. 615 C North Ave	615C North Ave
74. 5555 N Bedford Rd	5555 Bedford Rd
75. Framingham MA 01701	Farmingham MA 01701
76. 1415 Fiske Pl	1415 Fiske Way
77. 3354 N MacQuesten Pkwy	3354 N McQuesten Pkwy
78. 521 English Pl	521 English Pl
79. 3624 Reeder Ave	3624 Reader Ave
80. New Brunswick NJ 08903	New Brunswick NJ 08903
81. 3763 Kings Hwy E	3763 E Kings Hwy
82. 4573 White Plains Rd	4537 White Plains Rd
83. Miami Beach FL 33139	Miami Beach FL 33139

84.	5978 Putnam Ave	5978 Putnam Ave
85.	2754 Madison Rd	2754 Medison Rd
86.	128½ 4th Ave	128¼ 4th Ave
87.	132 E 35th St	132 E 35th St
88.	705 Kingsland Ave	507 Kingsland Ave
89.	Cleveland OH 44106	Cleveland OH 44601
90.	1626 E 115th St	1662 E 115th St
91.	Iowa City IA 52243	Iowa City IA 52443
92.	561 S Atlantic Ave	561 S Atlantic Ave
93.	8080 Knightsbridge Rd	8080 Kingsbridge Rd
94.	3292 Rugby Rd	2392 Rugby Rd
95.	Mesa AZ 85208	Mesa AR 85208

END OF PART D

If you finish Part D before time is up, check your answers on this part only. Do not return to any previous part.

DISTRIBUTION CLERK, MACHINE MODEL EXAM ANSWER KEY

PART A—NUMBER SERIES

1. D	4. E	7. C	10. A	13. D	16. C	19. D	22. E
2. A	5. C	8. A	11. E	14. B	17. E	20. B	23. C
3. B	6. B	9. B	12. C	15. B	18. A	21. A	24. E

Explanations—Number Series

1. **(D)** The sequence, 10 11 12, repeats itself.

2. **(A)** Another repeating sequence; this one is 4 6 7.

3. **(B)** Two sequences alternate. The first repeats itself, then advances by +1 and repeats again. The alternating sequence proceeds forward one number at a time.

4. **(E)** The sequence consists of numbers proceeding upward from 3, with the number 10 intervening between each set of two numbers in the sequence.

5. **(C)** The numbers proceed upward from 6 by +1, with each number repeating itself.

6. **(B)** One series starts at 3 and proceeds upward by +1. The alternating series consists of two numbers which ascend according to the following rule: +1, repeat; +1, repeat.

7. **(C)** One series proceeds upward by +1. The alternating series proceeds up by +2.

8. **(A)** The first series begins with 11 and descends by −2. The alternating series begins with 5 and ascends by +2.

9. **(B)** There are two alternating series, the first ascending by +2, the other descending one number at a time.

10. **(A)** The first series descends one number at a time while the alternating series ascends at the rate of +2.

11. **(E)** The rule is +2, +3, +4, +5, +6, +7, +8, +9.

12. **(C)** Basically the series ascends 1 2 3 4 5 6 7 8, but there is a twist to this problem. The number which intervenes after each two numbers of the series is the sum of those two numbers. Thus, the series may be read: 1 + 2 = 3; 3 + 4 = 7; 5 + 6 = 11; 7 + 8 = 15.

13. **(D)** Look carefully. This is a × 6 series. 3 × 6 = 18; 4 × 6 = 24; 5 × 6 = 30; 6 × 6 = 36, 7 . . . .

14. **(B)** This one is not easy, but if you wrote out the steps between numbers, you should have come up with: ×1, +1; ×2, +2; ×3, +3; ×4, +4; ×5 . . . .

15. **(B)** This series is deceptively simple. The sequence 18 20 22 20 is repeated over and over again.

16. **(C)** The series picks up with the second member of a repeat. The pattern is ×2 and repeat, ×2 and repeat . . . .

17. **(E)** There is no mathematical formula for this series. By inspection you may see that two successive numbers are brought together to form a larger number. Thus 1 2 12; 3 4 34; 5 6 56 . . . .

18. **(A)** Straightforward +8.

19. **(D)** The pattern is ×3, +3; ×3, +3 . . . .

20. **(B)** There are two alternating series. The first begins with <u>25</u> and descends, one number at a time. The alternating series begins with <u>20</u> and ascends one number at a time.

21. **(A)** A simple descending series of −11.

22. **(E)** You may see this as two alternating series, both ascending in steps of +2. You might also interpret the series as reading −2, +4; −2, +4 . . . With either solution you should reach the correct answer.

23. **(C)** The series is a simple −3 series which begins with an unusual number.

24. **(E)** Repeat, repeat, ÷3, repeat, repeat, ÷ 3 repeat, repeat, ÷ 3.

PART B—ADDRESS CODING

1. C	12. E	23. B	34. A	45. B	56. C	67. B	78. A
2. D	13. D	24. E	35. C	46. C	57. A	68. B	79. B
3. E	14. C	25. D	36. E	47. C	58. E	69. D	80. A
4. A	15. B	26. D	37. D	48. D	59. D	70. D	81. B
5. A	16. A	27. B	38. A	49. C	60. B	71. D	82. D
6. B	17. B	28. B	39. B	50. E	61. C	72. C	83. A
7. E	18. D	29. A	40. E	51. B	62. E	73. E	84. E
8. D	19. C	30. D	41. A	52. D	63. A	74. D	85. A
9. E	20. C	31. A	42. B	53. A	64. E	75. D	86. A
10. B	21. A	32. C	43. E	54. C	65. E	76. C	87. D
11. C	22. A	33. E	44. A	55. B	66. C	77. E	88. C

PART C—ADDRESS CODE MEMORY

1. D	12. A	23. B	34. E	45. B	56. A	67. C	78. C
2. E	13. B	24. D	35. A	46. D	57. B	68. B	79. E
3. C	14. B	25. D	36. C	47. E	58. E	69. D	80. E
4. A	15. C	26. A	37. A	48. B	59. E	70. C	81. E
5. A	16. C	27. D	38. E	49. C	60. E	71. B	82. A
6. E	17. D	28. A	39. C	50. D	61. B	72. D	83. B
7. A	18. E	29. E	40. B	51. A	62. E	73. A	84. D
8. C	19. E	30. E	41. B	52. B	63. A	74. B	85. E
9. B	20. A	31. A	42. C	53. C	64. C	75. B	86. E
10. E	21. B	32. C	43. E	54. E	65. E	76. C	87. A
11. D	22. C	33. D	44. D	55. D	66. D	77. A	88. C

PART D—ADDRESS CHECKING

1. D	13. D	25. A	37. D	49. D	61. D	73. D	85. D
2. D	14. A	26. A	38. A	50. D	62. D	74. D	86. D
3. D	15. D	27. D	39. A	51. D	63. D	75. D	87. A
4. A	16. D	28. D	40. D	52. D	64. D	76. D	88. D
5. D	17. A	29. D	41. D	53. D	65. D	77. D	89. D
6. A	18. A	30. A	42. D	54. A	66. D	78. A	90. D
7. A	19. D	31. D	43. D	55. A	67. A	79. D	91. D
8. D	20. D	32. A	44. D	56. D	68. D	80. A	92. A
9. D	21. D	33. D	45. A	57. D	69. D	81. D	93. D
10. A	22. A	34. D	46. D	58. A	70. A	82. D	94. D
11. D	23. D	35. A	47. D	59. A	71. A	83. A	95. D
12. D	24. D	36. D	48. D	60. D	72. D	84. A	

Address Checking Error Analysis Chart

Type of Difference	Question Numbers	Number of Questions You Missed
Difference in NUMBERS	2, 12, 19, 20, 21, 23, 24, 31, 33, 34, 37, 43, 44, 48, 49, 51, 53, 56, 65, 73, 82, 86, 88, 89, 90, 91, 94	
Difference in ABBREVIATIONS	1, 3, 8, 9, 27, 28, 40, 46, 50, 72, 74, 76, 81, 95	
Difference in NAMES	5, 11, 13, 15, 16, 29, 36, 41, 42, 47, 52, 57, 60, 61, 62, 63, 64, 66, 68, 69, 75, 77, 79, 85, 93	
No Difference	4, 6, 7, 10, 14, 17, 18, 22, 25, 26, 30, 32, 35, 38, 39, 45, 54, 55, 58, 59, 67, 70, 71, 78, 80, 83, 84, 87, 92	